Conserving Bird Biodiversity
General principles and their application

The Earth's biodiversity currently faces an extinction crisis that is unprecedented. Conservationists attempt to intervene in the extinction process either locally by protecting or restoring important species and habitats, or at national and international levels by influencing key policies and promoting debate. Reliable information is the foundation upon which these efforts are based, which places research at the heart of biodiversity conservation. The role of research in such conservation is diverse. It includes understanding why biodiversity is important, defining 'units' of biodiversity, priority-setting for species and sites, managing endangered and declining populations, understanding large-scale processes, making predictions about the future and interfacing with training, education, public awareness and policy initiatives. Using examples from a wide range of bird conservation work worldwide, researchers consider the principles underlying these issues, and illustrate how these principles have been applied to address actual conservation problems for students, practitioners and researchers in conservation biology.

KEN NORRIS is a lecturer in ecology and conservation at the University of Reading. His research interests include exploring the links between animal decision-making and the population dynamic consequences of those decisions, and avian conservation. He works on projects with a wide variety of endemic or threatened species including the Seychelles magpie robin, and St Helena wirebirds. He is joint editor of the *Journal of Animal Ecology*, and an editorial board member *of Bird Study*.

DEBORAH J. PAIN is Head of International Research at the Royal Society for the Protection of Birds, based in Sandy, Bedfordshire, where she is developing the Society's international research programme and managing the international research team who work in over 20 countries worldwide. She is also co-editor of *Farming and Birds in Europe*.

Conservation Biology

Conservation biology is a flourishing field, but there is still enormous potential for making further use of the science that underpins it. This new series aims to present internationally significant contributions from leading researchers in particularly active areas of conservation biology. It will focus on topics where basic theory is strong and where there are pressing problems for practical conservation. The series will include both single-authored and edited volumes and will adopt a direct and accessible style targeted at interested undergraduates, postgraduates, researchers and university teachers. Books and chapters will be rounded, authoritative accounts of particular areas with the emphasis on review rather than original data papers. The series is the result of a collaboration between the Zoological Society of London and Cambridge University Press. The series editors are Professor Morris Gosling, Professor of Animal Behaviour at the University of Newcastle upon Tyne, Professor John Gittleman, Professor of Biology at the University of Virginia, Charlottesville, Dr Rosie Woodroffe of the University of California, Davis and Dr Guy Cowlishaw of the Institute of Zoology, Zoological Society of London. The series ethos is that there are unexploited areas of basic science that can help define conservation biology and bring a radical new agenda to the solution of pressing conservation problems.

Published Titles

1. *Conservation in a Changing World*, edited by Georgina Mace, Andrew Balmford and Joshua Ginsberg 0 521 63270 6 (hardcover), 0 521 63445 8 (paperback)
2. *Behaviour and Conservation*, edited by Morris Gosling and William Sutherland 0 521 66230 3 (hardcover), 0 521 66539 6 (paperback)
3. *Priorities for the Conservation of Mammalian Diversity*, edited by Abigail Entwistle and Nigel Dunstone 0 521 77279 6 (hardcover), 0 521 77536 1 (paperback)
4. *Genetics, Demography and Viability of Fragmented Populations*, edited by Andrew G. Young and Geoffrey M. Clarke 0 521 782074 (hardcover), 0 521 794218 (paperback)
5. *Carnivore Conservation*, edited by John L. Gittleman, Stephan M. Funk, David Macdonald and Robert K. Wayne, 0 521 66232 X (hardcover), 0 521 66537 X (paperback)
6. *Conservation of Exploited Species*, edited by John D. Reynolds, Georgina M. Mace, Kent H. Redford, and John G. Robinson, 0 521 78216 3 (hardcover), 0 521 78733 5 (paperback)

Conserving Bird Biodiversity
General principles and their application

Edited by

KEN NORRIS
University of Reading

and

DEBORAH J. PAIN
RSPB

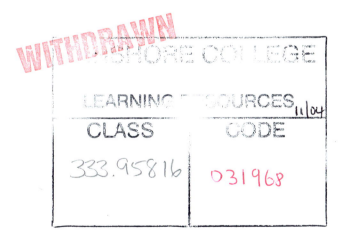

CAMBRIDGE
UNIVERSITY PRESS

PUBLISHED BY THE PRESS SYNDICATE OF THE UNIVERSITY OF CAMBRIDGE
The Pitt Building, Trumpington Street, Cambridge, United Kingdom

CAMBRIDGE UNIVERSITY PRESS
The Edinburgh Building, Cambridge CB2 2RU, UK
40 West 20th Street, New York, NY 10011-4211, USA
477 Williamstown Road, Port Melbourne, VIC 3207, Australia
Ruiz de Alarcón 13, 28014 Madrid, Spain
Dock House, The Waterfront, Cape Town 8001, South Africa

http://www.cambridge.org

First published 2002

Printed in the United Kingdom at the University Press, Cambridge

Typeface FF Scala 9.75/13 pt.   *System* LATEX 2$_\varepsilon$ [TB]

A catalogue record for this book is available from the British Library

Library of Congress Cataloguing in Publication data
Conserving bird biodiversity: general principles and their application / edited by Ken Norris and
Deborah J. Pain.
    p.   cm.
Includes bibliographical references (p.).
ISBN 0 521 78340 2 (hb)
ISBN 0 521 78949 4 (pbk.)
1. Birds, Protection of.   2. Biological diversity.   I. Norris, Ken, 1963–   II. Pain, Deborah J.
QL676.5 .C54   2002   333.95′816-dc21   2001043701

ISBN 0 521 78340 2 hardback
ISBN 0 521 78949 4 paperback

Contents

Contributors

ANDREW BALMFORD
Conservation Biology Group
Department of Zoology
University of Cambridge
Downing Street
Cambridge CB2 3EJ
UK

BEN D. BELL
School of Biological Sciences
Victoria University of Wellington
PO Box 600
Wellington
New Zealand

LEON BENNUN
Ornithology Department
National Museums of Kenya
PO Box 40658
Nairobi
Kenya

COLIN BIBBY
BirdLife International
Wellbrook Court
Girton Road
Cambridge CB3 0NA
UK

GERARD C. BOERE
Ministry of Agriculture, Nature
    Management and Fisheries
International Nature Management
PO Box 204 01
2500 EK, The Hague
The Netherlands

MICHAEL W. BRUFORD
School of Biosciences
Cardiff University
PO Box 915
Cathays Park
Cardiff CF10 3TL
UK

NIGEL J. COLLAR
Birdlife International
Wellbrook Court
Girton Road
Cambridge CB3 0NA
UK

PAUL F. DONALD
RSPB
The Lodge
Sandy
Bedfordshire SG19 2DL
UK

DAVID GIBBONS
Conservation Science Department
RSPB
The Lodge
Sandy
Bedfordshire SG19 2DL
UK

RHYS E. GREEN
Conservation Biology Group
Department of Zoology
University of Cambridge
Downing Street
Cambridge CB2 3EJ
UK

GEORGINA M. MACE
Institute of Zoology
Regent's Park
London NW1 4RY
UK

DON V. MERTON
National Kakapo Team
Biodiversity Recovery Unit
Department of Conservation
PO Box 10 420
Wellington
New Zealand

KEN NORRIS
School of Animal & Microbial Sciences
University of Reading
Whiteknights
PO Box 228
Reading RG6 6AJ
UK

PAUL OPDAM
ALTERRA
Wageningen University
   and Research Centre
Department of Landscape
Ecology
PO Box 47
6700 AA Wageningen
The Netherlands

DEBORAH J. PAIN
International Research Section,
   Conservation Science Department
RSPB
The Lodge
Sandy
Bedfordshire SG19 2DL
UK

CLAYTON D. A. RUBEC
Habitat Conservation Division
Canadian Wildlife Service
Ottawa
Ontario K1A OH3
Canada

RICHARD STILLMAN
Centre for Ecology & Hydrology
   (CEH) Dorset
Winfrith Technology Centre
Dorchester DT2 8ZH
UK

LES UNDERHILL
Avian Demography Unit
Department of Statistical Services
University of Cape Town
Rondebosch 7700
South Africa

JOHN A. WIENS
Department of Biology and Graduate
   Degree Program in Ecology
Colorado State University
Fort Collins
CO 80523
USA

Preface

The death of a pigeon called Martha in Cincinnati Zoo on 1st September 1914 was a significant event. She was the last passenger pigeon (*Ectopistes migratorius*) in existence. In 1878 the total population of passenger pigeons was estimated at 50 million birds, roaming the forests of the eastern United States. By March 1900, the last individual was killed in the wild (see Wilcove 1999). Although the dodo (*Raphus cucullatus*) of Mauritius has become a symbol of extinction and the efforts of conservationists to save endangered species, the story of the passenger pigeon is probably a starker example of the capacity of human activities to threaten the Earth's biodiversity.

Sadly, the passenger pigeon is not an isolated example. In its latest assessment, BirdLife International describes 1,186 species of bird that are currently threatened with extinction worldwide. A total of 128 species are believed to have become extinct in the last 500 years, 103 of these since 1800 (BirdLife International 2000). The rate at which bird species are being lost is currently much more rapid than at any time in the evolutionary history of this group (F.D.M. Smith *et al.* 1993; Pimm *et al.* 1995). The loss of biodiversity is not just the random deletion of species – certain families are more at risk than others. This bias in the extinction process means we are not just losing individual bird species, but significant parts of the Earth's evolutionary history (e.g. Purvis *et al.* 2000).

The scale of conservation efforts needed to save threatened birds is immense. Nevertheless, conservationists can intervene in the extinction process. Action can be local, at individual species or site levels, or can be national, influencing policies to protect the integrity of habitats or regions. Finally, conservationists can act to influence processes that contribute to biodiversity loss globally, such as climate change, through a range of international conventions and intergovernmental agreements.

One of several recent examples shows that individual species can be brought back from the verge of extinction. The Chatham Island black robin (*Petroica traversi*) was reduced to six birds with a single breeding female called 'Old Blue' in 1980. Intensive management efforts resulted in the population increasing to *c.* 300 individuals by 2001 (Butler & Merton 1992; see also Chapter 6).

The uneven distribution of threatened birds is highlighted by the fact that less than 5% of the Earth's land surface holds almost 75% of the world's threatened bird species (BirdLife International 2000). Conservationists have taken significant steps in identifying and advocating the protection of key sites and regions at national and continental scales through the identification of the most important sites for bird conservation, Important Bird Areas and Endemic Bird Areas (Stattersfield *et al.* 1998; Heath & Evans 2000). Influencing policies and processes that act globally to reduce biodiversity, such as world trade and climate change, is one of the greatest challenges facing conservationists.

Practical steps to conserve the world's birds are hampered by the fact that most threatened species occur in the tropics and subtropics (e.g. Stattersfield *et al.* 1998). Unfortunately, countries in these areas often lack the resources, be they monetary, infrastructural or technical, to undertake conservation projects. Conservation efforts in any country cannot hope to succeed without a sound information base on which to build initiatives for training, education, public awareness, conservation policy and practical action. This places research and monitoring at the heart of conservation efforts for biodiversity, including birds. The important question then becomes: what sort of research and monitoring skills are needed, and how can these be transferred to the people who need them?

In our view, the most important skill is in good project design and management that delivers effective conservation action. Technical skills, infrastructure and resources then support project implementation. As scientists, we need to teach people how to ask the 'right' question and how to design a project capable of answering that question. This need is global, but is urgent particularly in those countries 'rich' in biodiversity conservation problems yet 'poor' in terms of the resources necessary for dealing with these.

This was our primary motivation for producing this book. Currently, there are a number of excellent textbooks available that discuss the general principles of Conservation Biology, and a steadily increasing number on practical techniques used by conservationists, such as census techniques, habitat management, tracking techniques, etc. The main aim of our book is to bridge the gap between these areas. We aim to show, by means of detailed practical examples, how ecological principles can be applied to particular problems. We also hope to illustrate how practical techniques can be integrated into well-designed research that can promote effective action.

The book itself is organised into a series of chapters each dealing with a particular conservation problem or issue. Chapters are written by specialists, and include practical examples of actual projects plus an extensive review of the scientific literature. We hope that this is a good formula for transferring project-design skills and making different subject areas accessible to readers. The chapters are designed to be challenging and sometimes provocative to stimulate readers to think about unresolved problems.

Conservation science does not operate in a vacuum, and we felt it important to include areas that may be regarded by researchers as rather peripheral to the research or monitoring project itself, but which are important components of project-based conservation. These include Chapter 2 by Bibby on why we should conserve bird biodiversity, an important topic given the increasing role that economics plays in ecology and conservation (e.g. Edwards-Jones *et al.* 2000), and the different values societies and sectors within a society place on biodiversity conservation. Researchers should not be remote from this debate. Bennun discusses in Chapter 11 how research can interface directly with training and education. Research projects offer an excellent way of providing people with practical experience in project design and implementation, but they may also act as a catalyst for education and public awareness initiatives that can outlive the project. Finally, in Chapter 12, Boere and Rubec outline policy mechanisms involving birds. It is important to understand the needs of decision-makers when planning research, and existing policy instruments often require research and monitoring support for effective implementation.

Although we consider these areas important, the main body of the book concerns specific conservation problems and the science underpinning their resolution. In 'Biodiversity – evolution, species, genes', Bruford (Chapter 1) discusses the current debate about 'units' of biodiversity and their definition. Defining 'units' and identifying those that are most threatened is important because it influences many other decisions (research, training, education, public awareness, policy, action) contingent on threat assessment. Underhill and Gibbons (Chapter 3) go on to discuss how we describe the distribution and abundance of bird biodiversity. Typically, this takes a species approach to biodiversity, i.e. individual species are the 'unit' of biodiversity. Mace and Collar (Chapter 4) describe how we identify threatened species and prioritise which components of bird biodiversity are in urgent need of conservation efforts; Balmford (Chapter 5) recognises that saving each bird species individually is not likely to be practical, so discusses the growing body of experience and literature on methods for selecting priority sites for conservation. Chapter 6 and 7 describe areas that may be

more generally recognised as traditional components of conservation biology. Bell and Merton describe the management of critically endangered
species. What can conservationists do when faced with a population reduced
to only a small number of individuals? Green also deals with declining populations, but those in which abundance is still sufficiently high to enable
causes of the decline to be investigated, and actions designed to halt or reverse the decline before the population reaches critically endangered status.
Pain and Donald (Chapter 8) discuss large-scale processes threatening birds,
because effective action at this scale cannot depend on small-scale efforts for
specific populations. Norris and Stillman (Chapter 9) look into the future,
and ask how conservationists can predict how populations might respond
to future environmental change. This is an increasingly important area, and
one in which ecological modelling is assuming a potent role. Opdam and
Wiens (Chapter 10) examine what is arguably the greatest single threat to
all biodiversity – habitat loss and fragmentation in a landscape context.

Who should read this book? We have attempted to make this book interesting to a broad readership. First, we hope the text will prove valuable
for final year undergraduate and postgraduate students in applied ecology,
conservation biology or wildlife management. Second, it provides an up-
to-date review of conservation research of use to researchers at all levels
that are actively involved in conservation work. Third, the book is designed
with conservation policy-makers and practitioners in mind. In producing
a book with problem-based chapters, we hope that practitioners will recognise 'their' problem, and will then be able to get some ideas about the best
ways to tackle it.

Our discussion of biodiversity conservation up to this point has entirely
centred on birds. Since the general issues relate to any taxa, why produce a
book with such a narrow focus? There are a number of reasons for this. First,
we wanted to produce a book that dealt with actual conservation problems
both in principle and in practice. This is difficult to do without a narrow
taxonomic focus because there is a trade-off between breadth and depth.
Secondly, birds are perhaps the best known and most thoroughly studied
component of the Earth's biodiversity, thus considerable scientific information exists with which to illustrate how particular conservation problems are
tackled. However, the principles and the way they have been applied offer
general insights that are relevant to biodiversity conservation in all taxa. As
such, this book is about biodiversity conservation illustrated with examples
from birds, rather than a book about bird conservation *per se*. Thirdly, bird
conservation captures the imagination of the public. This means that birds

(together with mammals) have an important role as flagships for wider conservation efforts.

In putting this book together and reading the final product we have learned a considerable amount about biodiversity conservation – we hope you do too.

We would like to thank Neil Burgess and several other anonymous referees who made very valuable comments on our initial book proposal that helped shape the final book. We thank all the chapter authors for finding time in their hectic lives to contribute to the book, our families, friends and colleagues for their continued tolerance and support, and Tracey Sanderson and the other editorial staff at Cambridge University Press for keeping us on track and producing the final book. KN would like to thank NERC, The Darwin Initiative, The European Union, The Wellcome Trust, RSPB and WWF(UK) for financial support and Claire Hall for secretarial support. Thanks to the following who contributed to individual chapters: Luis Baptista, Paul Bell, Thomas Brooks, Paul Buckley, Graeme Elliott, David Gibbons, Rhys Green, Kelly Hare, Rachel McClellan, Duncan McNiven, Martin Jenkins, Joslin Moore, John O'Sullivan, Polly Phillpott, Hugh Robertson, Ali Stattersfield, Kirsty Swinnerton, Shaun O'Connor, Rosie Trevelyan and Jeremy Wilson. Finally, thanks to Don Merton for providing such a superb photograph of a kakapo for the book's cover.

Ken Norris
University of Reading

Debbie Pain
RSPB

July 2001

Biodiversity – evolution, species, genes

MICHAEL W. BRUFORD

INTRODUCTION

In many respects biodiversity, both present and past, is better understood for birds than for any other major group of organisms. This is because birds probably inspire more extreme interest in humans than all other animals (and most plants): they are often spectacular, are relatively easily observed and are usually neither too specious nor too cryptic to identify or study. Ironically, by being desirable to the collector and enigmatic and tractable to both the hobbyist and scientist, birds have helped us to document the effects of anthropogenic interference on the Earth's biodiversity during the last few hundred years in the most extraordinary detail. In birds, we benefit from an extremely rich history of scientific study, from much research of high quality in the modern era and from an enviable, though chequered, track record in conservation management. It is, however, abundantly clear that our ability to synthesise and utilise this level of knowledge will be sorely tested in the near future as we attempt to guide many avian populations through the profound environmental and biological changes that are taking place now and that will intensify in the future.

In this chapter, I will attempt to describe avian biological diversity not in the details of individual species, their distributions, status and ecological requirements, but in the context of the evolutionary history that has led to the roughly 9,000 species we have today and the broad patterns of avian diversity that we currently observe, from communities to individuals. I intend to concentrate slightly more on the role that molecular systematics and population genetics can play in this endeavour, primarily because this is not covered in detail elsewhere in the book. It will become apparent (I hope) that although we know a great deal about the history of modern birds, their taxonomy and distribution, we still lack much of the crucial information we may need for conservation management, especially below the species level, and we urgently need to draw lessons from ongoing research in avian biodiversity and its conservation so that we may apply this knowledge to other species and contexts.

LEVELS OF BIODIVERSITY

Biodiversity (shorthand for biological diversity) is simply a term to describe the diversity of biological entities on Earth, although it has been and continues to be applied in a huge variety of contexts and at many different levels (see Gaston 1996a). It can describe genetic diversity, morphological diversity, physiological diversity, behavioural diversity, and indeed any character that is used to mark out an individual, population or species as different from another. It is increasingly described at a variety of levels in an attempt to simplify what might at first seem an overwhelmingly complex system. A top-down hierarchy from communities to species to genes is often used (as I have done below) fully in the knowledge that it is an inadequate way to describe the way each component of biodiversity influences and interacts with the others.

Community/ecosystem

At its broadest scale, we can attempt to characterise and understand biodiversity at the community or ecosystem level. Disentangling the relationships within and among assemblages of broad classes of species which are often unconnected by recent evolutionary history, but which may perform common or integrated functions within an ecosystem, has proved to be extremely challenging. This bewildering level of complexity remains a 'black box' for the most part, and understanding and predicting the effects of interactions on community structure in nature remains a Herculean task for ecosystem-level researchers. Nonetheless, avian community structure is relatively well understood in comparison with many groups, and the effects of anthropogenic change on community interactions have led to some interesting case studies coming to light. Avian species, although comprising only a small element of any given ecosystem, have been shown to interact in crucial ways with other species to maintain ecosystem health. As major seed dispersers and pollinators, bird species can, for example, play a vital role in maintaining plant community structure and diversity (e.g. Whitney & Smith 1998) and where species are no longer represented in such ecosystems (e.g. Cooper et al. 1993) major ecological changes (e.g. Smith et al. 1995) and chains of extinction can result. Birds play important roles as predators, form major prey bases and engage in a wide range of apparently mutualistic (e.g. Weeks 2000) and host–parasite interactions. While it is quite clearly impossible to examine these roles in all but a small number of cases, we already know that loss of avian biodiversity, though tragic in its own right, can have much wider ramifications.

Species

Compared with other animal and plant groups, our knowledge of avian diversity at the species level is nothing short of immense, and one might almost conclude that it is as near to complete as is necessary at the present time. New species are still occasionally being discovered, sometimes in quite spectacular fashion (Smith *et al.* 1991). However, it is generally accepted that within the near future it is possible that we will have a complete picture of extant avian species diversity. In addition, our knowledge of the geographical distribution of many species and how this has changed in the last 100–200 years is also relatively good, thanks largely to the many hobbyist birdwatchers and ornithologists throughout the world who are continually augmenting and refining this knowledge, and thanks also to the considerable number of vast and well-curated museum collections found mainly in countries with a history of ornithology and/or colonialism. This wealth of information has allowed us to document and analyse geographical patterns of diversity in birds and has enabled conservationists to estimate species diversity (*species richness*: Gaston 1996b) and to examine patterns among geographically restricted species (*endemism*: Myers *et al.* 2000). This level of information has permitted the use of birds as model species to investigate the location of biodiversity '*hotspots*' of species-richness and endemism and potentially the establishment of a network of globally-based conservation priority areas recently refined by BirdLife International into 'Endemic Bird Areas' (e.g. Bibby *et al.* 1992; Stattersfield *et al.* 1998; see also Box 5.1 and Fig. 5.3).

Perhaps the most contentious problem facing species-level conservation today concerns the ongoing debate on which units of biological diversity should form the basis of conservation planning, and whereas biological species have traditionally occupied this role, increasing evidence points to the fact that this approach may poorly estimate the amount of diversity necessary for the conservation of biological units with future evolutionary potential. The rise of phylogenetic and mate recognition species concepts (see Patterson 1981; Vogler & DeSalle 1994; Kraaijeveld 2000), and even proposals to abandon species concepts in their entirety, raise serious questions about the universality of the species and its meaning in conservation

(Moritz 1994a, b; Avise & Walker 2000; Crandall *et al.* 2000; Hendry *et al.* 2000). Further, once a biological unit for conservation has been identified, the question of prioritisation arises, and here the debate continues. The relative importance of preserving distinctive species (e.g. phenotypically, behaviourally, genetically) – also known as *taxic diversity* (e.g. Vane-Wright *et al.* 1991), as opposed to evolutionarily active lineages which demonstrate evidence of ongoing diversification – also known as *evolutionary fronts* (e.g. Erwin 1991), is another factor for consideration in assigning conservation priorities. At its most extreme, an advocate might argue that prioritising taxic diversity conserves as much of our evolutionary heritage as is possible, whereas a counter-argument is that prioritising evolutionary fronts at least ensures that extant diversity has the potential for future adaptation in a rapidly changing world. It is unfortunately the case, therefore, that even when conservation biologists think they are on safe ground, philosophical and practical scientific problems abound (see below).

Genes

Understanding the patterns and processes that generate diversity below the species level is almost as difficult as understanding interactions among species at the community level, and as a consequence it has sometimes been regarded as less important in conservation. Genetic differentiation among populations or geographic regions may manifest itself in a number of ways and taxonomists have traditionally dealt with this diversity by describing the intraspecific units of the subspecies or race. However, given the current species concept debate, defining what constitutes a subspecies or race is fraught with inconsistency and some have argued for its abandonment (e.g. Hendry *et al.* 2000). However, we are still left with the requirement to identify, protect and legislate for diversity below the species and, as a consequence, conservationists are increasingly turning to phylogenetic definitions (Ryder 1986; Moritz 1994a, b; Vogler & DeSalle 1994; Pennock & Dimmick 1997; Waples 1998), the merits of which will be discussed below.

Genetic variation, together with its determinants within populations, is also a major issue in conservation, since natural levels of gene-flow in many continental bird species have been shown to be relatively high and should therefore be maintained where possible (e.g. Merila *et al.* 1997; Smith *et al.* 1997; Fry & Zink 1998). Since variation using neutral genetic markers is expected to correlate with recent demographic changes, small and/or isolated populations can lose genetic diversity rapidly, potentially compromising their future adaptive potential (Keller *et al.* 1994, 2001; Groombridge *et al.* 2000). Management of such populations through the maintenance of genetic diversity is a focus of much of today's 'hands-on' population management (see below).

CURRENT PATTERNS OF AVIAN DIVERSITY

As stated previously, our knowledge of today's avian diversity is as near to being complete as it is with any group of organisms. We know, for instance, that there are between 8,600 and about 10,000 bird species on Earth (depending on whose taxonomy one follows and allowing for further discoveries). It has been guessed that since the first birds appeared 130 million years ago between 150,000 and 1,500,000 species of bird have existed (the consensus seems to be about half a million), reaching a maximum of perhaps 11,500 at any one time, possibly during the Pleistocene, 250,000 years ago (Fuller 1987; Mountfort 1988). We also have a reasonable knowledge of how present-day species are distributed across the globe, where the greatest numbers of species are found, and where they are absent (see Chapter 5). Crucially, we also know pretty accurately how many species have gone extinct in the recent past (just over 100 in the last 400 years), where those extinctions took place and often why. We also know that at least 1,000 species are presently under threat of extinction, and this number needs to be constantly revised upwards (BirdLife International 2000).

Unfortunately, our knowledge of the basic biology and life history of bird species is much sketchier than of their distribution and taxonomy, a fact that is often thrown into sharp relief when urgent conservation measures need to be taken which rely, both for management and modelling, on basic information such as clutch size, generation time, mortality rates, etc. Some information can often be found at least within the family level, and studies have taken advantage of this information to use birds as a model to study the evolution of avian life history traits and their importance in conservation and other areas (e.g. Owens *et al.* 1999; Owens & Bennett 2000a). Such analyses would, however, not be possible were it not that a reasonably robust large-scale avian phylogeny exists, mainly through the efforts of Sibley and Ahlquist in the 1970s and 1980s, culminating in their book, *Phylogeny and Classification of Birds*, published in 1990. Their phylogeny, based on DNA–DNA hybridisation data (generated by experiments on the hybridisation properties of single-copy DNA strands from different species), has proved very useful and is generally regarded as plausible for many groups. These studies have also generated a number

of interesting ideas that have subsequently been tested using what are regarded as higher resolution approaches, such as analysis of mitochondrial
gene sequences. For example, Sibley *et al.* (1988) suggested that perching
birds (passerines) were divisible into two genealogical groups, the Corvida
(crow-like) including all crows and the Passerida, which includes nearly all
Old World and North American songbirds, and seemingly supported an established idea that passerines should be subdivided into the oscines (songbirds, possessing a voice box that can learn song) and the suboscines –
the mainly Neotropical group lacking these traits. Subsequent mitochondrial cytochrome *b* sequence analysis has supported these ideas (Edwards
et al. 1991), and indeed for broad- and fine-scale phylogenetic questions mitochondrial DNA is now being used routinely to map many parts of the
avian phylogeny. Recent studies involving relatively slowly evolving mitochondrial DNA sequences (especially the ribosomal RNA genes) are now
being used effectively to ask some fairly fundamental questions in avian
phylogenetics, whereas more rapidly evolving DNA sequences (such as the
cytochrome *b* gene) have been used to resolve relationships within families
(e.g. Sheldon *et al.* 1999; van Tuinen *et al.* 2000).

THE EVOLUTION OF AVIAN DIVERSITY

It is now accepted that birds evolved from and are recognised as members of the theropod dinosaurs, and that the earliest members of class Aves
appeared some 150 MYBP (i.e. Million Years Before Present – Padian &
Chiappe 1998). The first fossil member, discovered from the late Jurassic
(some 145 MYBP), is the well-known *Archaeopteryx*, now represented by
seven skeletons. Many of the 'avian' features in early birds are in fact shared
with their terrestrial carnivore ancestors, the dromaeosaurs, and probably
evolved for reasons other than flight. However, subsequent to *Archaeopteryx*,
direct flight apparatus evolved relatively rapidly as late Jurassic and early
Cretaceous birds exploited their arboreal habitat and started flying to greater
degrees, and a relatively diverse group of birds appeared in the Mesozoic,
possibly coincident with the break-up of the continental landmasses (Hedges
et al. 1996; Cooper *et al.* 2001).

Although nearly all of these groups have no record in the Tertiary, molecular evidence dates the origin of at least 22 avian orders prior to the
Cretaceous–Tertiary (K/T) boundary (Cooper & Penny 1997 – Box 1.1). This
casts doubt on the dogma of a mass extinction event at that time, and argues for a rapid diversification in the ensuing 5–10 million years in the
Palaeocene.

Box 1.1. Extant avian orders and lineages within them where sequence data estimates an origin pre-dating the K/T boundary (adapted from Cooper & Penny 1997).

Order	Number of lineages
Ratites	3
Tinamiformes	1
Galliformes	2
Anseriformes	1
Psittaciformes	3
Pelecaniformes	2
Charadriiformes	1
Passeriformes	1
Strigiformes	1
Falconiformes	1
Threskiorniformes	1
Gruiformes	1
Gaviiformes	1
Podicipediformes	1
Procellariiformes	2

Recent evidence from mitochondrial ribosomal RNA sequences (Van Tuinen *et al.* 2000) has re-contextualised the evolution of the major lineages within modern birds (Neornithes) (see Fig. 1.1), reaffirming the position of the ratites and tinamous (Palaeognathae) as the most basal lineage, followed by the ducks and Galliformes (Galloanserae) and with the Passeriformes (perching birds) as a monophyletic, derived group. This suggests that the ancestral neornithe was a large-bodied terrestrial species – a group sparsely represented in the fossil record, and divides modern birds into three major evolutionary groups. Debate remains, however, and evidence from the work of Mindell *et al.* (1999) and Härlid *et al.* (1999) even suggests that the Passeriformes may have preceded both other groups.

The arrival of convenient molecular approaches for the semi-automated analysis of long lengths of highly informative DNA sequences in extant and sometimes extinct birds (e.g. Sheldon *et al.* 1999; Omland *et al.* 2000; Cooper *et al.* 2001) has enabled a growing avian molecular phylogeny to accumulate, as current issues of journals such as *Molecular Phylogenetics and Evolution, Auk* and *Ibis* will testify. Unfortunately, and despite the well-documented sampling problems of inferring evolutionary events from

Fig. 1.1. Phylogenetic tree of modern birds based on nuclear and mitochondrial ribosomal genes. (From Van Tuinen *et al.* 2000.)

single genes, most phylogenies are based on a single gene (the mitochondrial cytochrome *b* gene) and often on fragments of that gene. The result is a rapidly expanding sequence database (Mindell 1997) with currently over 3,500 avian accessions accessible in *Genbank*, the global sequence database. This potentially allows comparisons among data sets and the construction of even larger phylogenies. However, more effort on sequencing alternative, independent, informative sequences is potentially crucial if phylogenetic hypotheses resulting from cytochrome *b* sequences are to be tested further.

It is, however, beyond question that the most pervasive influence on avian diversity in recent times has been anthropogenic (Temple 1986; Mountfort 1988; Caughley & Gunn 1996). A large proportion of birds that either have gone extinct since 1600 or are on the verge of extinction now are found on oceanic islands where they are endemic, and both the proximate and ultimate reasons for this are well documented (Temple 1986): nearly all involve the introduction of alien species, habitat loss or over-harvesting, or a combination of these factors. The continuing pressures on avian populations across the globe mean that reduction in avian diversity is likely to continue apace, and the proportion of threatened species living on islands may decline as a result, since islands contain relatively few species that can become extinct in comparison with those in continental regions.

SPECIES CONCEPTS, MOLECULES AND CONSERVATION

Geographical correlates of avian species diversity are becoming increasingly well understood and have led directly to a number of proposals regarding the establishment of a network of protected areas, as described in Chapter 5. These ideas have provoked much discussion (e.g. T.B. Smith *et al.* 1993) and the merits of conserving present-day patterns of species diversity, and the incorporation of a more detailed understanding of their evolutionary and ecological determinants, lie at the heart of this debate (e.g. Crandall *et al.* 2000). Incorporating intraspecific diversity into protected area conservation is an issue which is only now beginning to be addressed (see below); however, the role of species and other taxonomic definitions in conservation planning is also contentious, especially the concept of the Evolutionarily Significant Unit, which is increasingly replacing the species and subspecies as the fundamental unit for conservation management and prioritisation (e.g. Tarr & Fleischer 1999; Zink *et al.* 2000; see above).

The definition of Evolutionarily Significant Units (ESU) for conservation, introduced by Ryder (1986), has sparked much discussion on the merits and practical approaches of identifying them (e.g. Pennock & Dimmick 1997; Waples 1998). A variety of methods have been proposed based on ecology, biogeography, and phenotypic data (Waples 1991; Dizon *et al.* 1992; Vogler & DeSalle 1994; Legge *et al.* 1996), and although divergences in such characters are recognised as important parameters to define ESUs, it has also been suggested that the period of evolutionary time that populations have been isolated should be considered, and that their identification should be at least partially based on molecular genetic data (Avise & Ball 1990; Moritz 1994a).

The phylogenetic 'diagnosis' of separate ESUs currently advocates an operational definition which incorporates *reciprocal monophyly* of mitochondrial DNA (mtDNA) alleles, and *significant differences* in allele frequencies at nuclear loci. Using this approach, studies on the genetic structure of natural populations have been used to recognise or question ESUs for conservation in many taxa, such as marsupials (Moritz *et al.* 1996), fur seals (Lento *et al.* 1997), fish (e.g. Riddle *et al.* 1998) and birds (e.g. Lovette *et al.* 1999; Tarr & Fleischer 1999; Zink *et al.* 2000).

However, reciprocal monophyly can in principle be due to the sharing of a single substitution (e.g. Hammond *et al.* 2001) and, in birds, sequence divergence between ESUs has so far been shown to vary between 1% and 8% (Avise & Walker 1998; Zink *et al.* 2000). Furthermore, using genetic distances has been shown to be suspect when comparing among populations, because there are indistinct boundaries between the levels of divergence observed within and among different taxonomic units in many groups. The use of single diagnosable characters to define ESUs (Vogler & DeSalle 1994) has been questioned because it then becomes essentially a typological method, which ignores evolutionary processes; such patterns can potentially become established very rapidly in genetically diverse populations due to fragmentation, genetic bottlenecks and drift. This can result in an extremely conservative interpretation, and the over-diagnosis of units for conservation. While conservative approaches to species conservation are potentially very valuable, in practice conservation managers may need to be given information that will assist in prioritisation of effort in future management scenarios, and over-diagnosis could therefore be regarded as counter-productive.

Importantly, however, there are also several examples where nuclear markers with high levels of polymorphism, such as microsatellites or MHC loci, have provided an alternative picture of population divergence from that offered by mtDNA (e.g. Pope *et al.* 1996; Hedrick & Parker 1998; Kirchman *et al.* 2000). ESUs have also been defined on the basis of reciprocal monophyly assessed solely from differences at microsatellite allele frequencies (Small *et al.* 1998; Parker *et al.* 1999). Recent studies on ESU designation in endangered species using mtDNA have advocated the use of microsatellites to corroborate results and establish precise management guidelines (Moritz 1994b; Waits *et al.* 1998; Manceau *et al.* 1999), and it is in this direction that avian studies need to go since they have been predominantly mitochondrial in the approach taken until now.

CONSERVING DIVERSITY BELOW THE SPECIES LEVEL

Population level management

Traditionally, genetic diversity below the species level has been described in taxonomic terms using mainly morphological characters, sometimes taking into account geographic isolation, and has mainly used the concepts of the subspecies and/or race (they are often used interchangeably) and ecotype for the products of natural evolution, and landrace, breed or variety for the products of artificial selection. However, the definition of some of these descriptors varies greatly in the literature and there are many 'grey areas' where they overlap. The implicit assumption is that they encompass some cohesive and ultimately identifiable component of the genetic diversity found within a species. It is now becoming increasingly clear that we need to understand what these descriptors mean and what relevance they have for conservation, because the judicious management of these and other elements of intraspecific genetic diversity will become a key element of future conservation programmes in order to maintain evolutionary adaptability for the future. One problem with the taxonomy of subspecies, races and ecotypes, which have a variety of morphological and ecological definitions, is that although they may be operationally effective for taxonomists in the field or museum, they mostly lack any component which incorporates the evolutionary history of populations, whether they diverged in sympatry or allopatry, and how often they exchange genes now or did so in the past. For these reasons (and the more subjective argument that many modern subspecies were originally described more for arbitrary, geopolitical reasons rather than using sound taxonomic logic), their use has been called into question and molecular methods advocated (Ryder 1986).

The relationships between phylogenetic definitions of units for conservation such as the ESU (Ryder 1986) and the management unit (MU; Moritz 1994b) and traditional taxonomic descriptors such as the subspecies, race and ecotype are far from obvious. It is clear that many authors have in the past, and continue to, equate the ESU level with that of subspecies (e.g. Ball & Avise 1992; Zink *et al.* 2000) and indeed this was partly the original motivation for the ESU idea (Ryder 1986). However, ESUs, by many definitions, are automatically regarded as phylogenetic species and yet in some cases this division could, in principle, be applied from very recently derived subpopulations of the same species (e.g. in the Mariana crow; Tarr & Fleischer 1999). The concept of the management unit (MU) is now commonly in use to diagnose subdivided populations where divergence time has not been sufficient to accumulate evolutionarily distinct characters, or some other factor such as limited gene-flow has kept the populations genetically non-independent (Moritz 1994b).

Anthropogenic isolation

A common problem facing practising conservation biologists centres on the management of recent and often anthropogenically isolated populations, which may not, in many cases, be appropriately classed as ESUs (Tarr & Fleischer 1999). Such populations are often demographically inviable and may possess low amounts of genetic variation. In these cases, identification of the management unit may often be a more applicable approach (e.g. Britten *et al.* 1997; Baker *et al.* 1998; O'Ryan *et al.* 1998). Many of these studies are being carried out with the aim of identifying management units for translocating individuals to augment potentially demographically inviable populations (Moritz 1999). A major criterion identified by Moritz (1994b) for defining separate management units is the possession of significant haplotype frequency differences in mitochondrial DNA (although not necessarily at nuclear loci) regardless of the phylogenetic distinctiveness of the mitochondrial alleles.

Populations which have undergone rapid and radical changes in their habitat quality and quantity, which have a degree of isolation from other populations, and which are small, pose special problems when interpreting genetic data. Thus assignment of MU status needs to be carried out with caution. For example, the extreme demographic fluctuations which may be relatively common in small isolated populations are likely to result in genetic drift and/or inbreeding, thereby accentuating differences in allele frequency and resulting in the further loss of alleles (e.g. Saccheri *et al.* 1998, 1999). This may potentially result in the fixation of alleles that could be locally unique. It is common for isolated populations to possess no more than a few mitochondrial alleles, and many such populations may have suffered serious decline during the last 200 years. Genetic sampling of these populations may further lead to apparent differentiation among populations (e.g. Sjögren & Wyöni 1994). The genetic patterns often observed in endangered populations result from recent demographic events as opposed to longer-term divergence, potentially complicating translocation plans.

As an example, Barratt *et al.* (1999) found a large number of mitochondrial haplotypes, some of which were highly divergent, in small, isolated populations of the red squirrel in the United Kingdom. The frequencies of these alleles were also extremely different, with many populations only containing alleles unique to the data set. Phylogenetic analysis of the sequences revealed no geographically consistent pattern of diversity among haplotypes in different populations, either in the UK or in western Europe. However, the red squirrel is known to have been extremely common, widespread and continuously distributed across western Europe before deforestation for agriculture in the middle ages, and has been decimated following the introduction of the American grey squirrel in the nineteenth century. As a consequence many southern UK populations that are today extremely small and isolated have only been threatened for a few hundred years and may indeed have exchanged genes with neighbouring mainland European populations prior to the flooding of the English Channel, *c.* 9000 BP.

Under the criterion of diagnosability (Vogler & DeSalle 1994) the red squirrel has many diagnosable ESUs (indeed, one might argue, many phylogenetic 'species') in the mitochondrial data set, and certainly each population would be considered a separate management unit under standard criteria. However in the absence of phylogenetic structure in the populations analysed, and with the strong possibility of a purely demographic explanation of the data, one might consider whether any of the populations even represent separate management units. For populations with large numbers of alleles, such alleles may be found due to long-term population stability, rapid generation time and/or large effective population sizes (Bromham *et al.* 1996; Li *et al.* 1996; Good *et al.* 1997). In these cases, population fragmentation and the subsampling of a diverse mitochondrial gene pool could rapidly produce significant allele frequency differences among populations (e.g. Cornuet & Luikart 1996), a pattern that carries no evolutionary signal.

Therefore, under the circumstances described above for small subpopulations that are essentially remnants of once large, continuous and diverse populations, significant allele frequency differences or even fixation of different alleles in mtDNA can, in principle, accumulate in relatively few generations. This may be a general problem in endangered birds and island populations (e.g. Mundy *et al.* 1997) and also when managing isolated populations of sedentary species formerly possessing large amounts of genetic variation. The genetic trends often observed suggest that where possible (and certainly in birds, with their elevated capacity for gene-flow) a conservative management strategy involves the use of larger, geographically neighbouring populations for augmentation of small, isolated populations. Further, because of the small amounts of time since the fragmentation of many populations, such augmentation would be expected to be unlikely to result in genetic incompatibility. This does not preclude the possibility that locally adapted phenotypic characters may have become fixed within smaller isolated populations, a potential problem that may sometimes be tested (Crandall *et al.* 2000). The role of demography as a complicating factor in designating genetic management units is potentially important (and, for example, it predominates in domesticated species), and its incorporation into criteria setting on a case-by-case basis is a necessity.

Small populations/endangered species
Although the small population/*ex situ* conservation paradigm which dominated conservation biology in the 1980s and early 1990s was extremely

important in reviving conservation biology as a science (Frankel & Soulé 1981; Soulé 1986) it has often been justifiably criticised subsequently for (in general terms) under-emphasising the need to maintain viable habitats in the wild, failing to incorporate the importance of the causes of decline in larger populations and because many biologists believe that captive breeding, with its inevitable concentration on single species, has a relatively minor role to play in conservation. This has concomitantly led many biologists to question the role that small population processes play in species viability and how much effort it is worth expending to mitigate against them. The role of demographic and environmental stochasticity in population dynamics and persistence has been intensively studied by population ecologists since the 1960s, and has thus gained much credence. Demographic management of critically endangered populations either *in situ* or *ex situ* is known to be of fundamental importance for their survival (see Chapter 6). More controversial, however, is the role that genetic variation and its loss through drift and inbreeding have in population persistence, since although this issue has received much attention over the last 20 years, documented examples of the importance of drift and inbreeding to population survival are sparse. However, the recent study of Saccheri *et al.* (1998) linking heterozygosity with probability of subpopulation extinction in a metapopulation of Glanville fritillary (*Melitaea cinxia*) butterflies, followed closely by a study demonstrating that augmenting genetic variation in a threatened snake population reversed a long-term decline (Madsen *et al.* 1999), have revitalised the debate.

A long hiatus in studies of inbreeding and fitness at the level of the individual followed the first studies of avian inbreeding (in the great tit, *Parus major*) of Greenwood *et al.* in 1978 and van Noordwijk & Scharloo in 1981. However, the last ten years have seen the publication of several extremely important studies of inbreeding (and inbreeding depression) in birds, for both wild and captive populations. Many of these studies have explicitly applied molecular approaches to measure genetic diversity at the individual level (quantified, for example, by heterozygosity), within pedigrees or within small populations. Unsurprisingly, many studies have concerned island endemic species, a group which has suffered disproportionately from the effects of human intervention, and a group which is also expected to be least resilient in the face of environmental, demographic and genetic fluctuations (Frankham 1997).

In perhaps one of the most striking examples within a captive population, Brock & White (1992) convincingly demonstrated a causal relationship between genetic similarity of parents and inbreeding depression in offspring in the critically endangered Puerto Rican parrot (*Amazona vittata*), a species that went through a bottleneck of 13 individuals, by correlating parental DNA fingerprint band-sharing coefficients with offspring inbreeding depression measured by reproductive output. Interestingly, unrelated Puerto Rican parrots had band-sharing coefficients similar to those of second-degree relatives of the closely related Hispaniolan parrot (*Amazona ventralis*), which did not go through such a severe bottleneck, and where inbreeding depression was not found to be as severe.

One of the most celebrated examples of a conservation success involving *ex situ* management in a bird is the Mauritius kestrel (*Falco punctatus*), which has recovered from a single wild breeding pair in 1974 to a wild population consisting of over 200 breeding pairs by 1990 (Fig. 1.2a). Groombridge *et al.* (2000) measured the loss of genetic variation resulting from the bottleneck using microsatellite markers typed for modern birds and museum skins up to 170 years old. Although extant individuals showed predicted low levels of diversity, variability in the museum skins was remarkably high (see Fig. 1.2b) and, when compared with the genetic diversity expected for continental kestrel species, was found to be of a similar magnitude for a species of its range (Fig. 1.2c). Interestingly, therefore, the Mauritius kestrel did not survive because of unsuspected additional genes in the wild population or because of a reduction of its genetic load due to a history of small population size, inbreeding and drift. In fact allelic diversity fell by 55% and heterozygosity by 57% during the bottleneck although allelic diversity probably fell by a much higher percentage since these estimates are much more sensitive to the limited sample available through museum specimens. The fact that this species recovered without augmentation suggests that it was only weakly affected by this bottleneck. The generality of this observation is, however, difficult to assess in the absence of temporal or spatial replicates. Its significance, especially given the fact that many island endemics remain in real threat of extinction, is that there may be no 'special case' for managing diversity in island endemics, and that although this population patently survived, many others may not without genetic management.

The genetic trajectories of natural bottlenecks in bird or other populations have rarely been documented, and in the absence of museum specimens, researchers are sometimes left with the signatures of such bottlenecks in the genes of present-day populations (Cornuet & Luikart 1996), but how often? The importance of the study of Mandarte Island song sparrows (*Melospiza melodia*) by Keller *et al.* (1994) is that the population

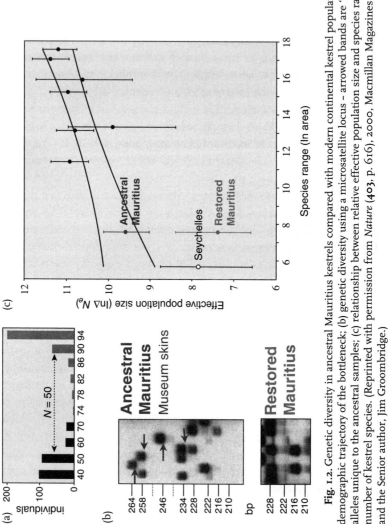

Fig. 1.2. Genetic diversity in ancestral Mauritius kestrels compared with modern continental kestrel populations; (a) demographic trajectory of the bottleneck; (b) genetic diversity using a microsatellite locus – arrowed bands are 'ghost' alleles unique to the ancestral samples; (c) relationship between relative effective population size and species range for a number of kestrel species. (Reprinted with permission from *Nature* (**403**, p. 616), 2000, Macmillan Magazines Limited, and the Senior author, Jim Groombridge.)

was followed through two bottlenecks in real time, so that real demographic data could be collected and, with the aid of a comprehensive pedigree of the island's small population, studbook estimates of inbreeding coefficients could be made. The consequence of this is that the genetic effects of the severe 1989 overwinter population crash, in which 95% of the population was killed, could be assessed. Inbred individuals were shown to have survived the crash with a much lower probability than non-inbred birds, and consequently this example has become one of the few convincing demonstrations of inbreeding depression in any wild population.

Subsequent analysis of the genetic trajectory of this bottleneck using molecular markers (Keller *et al.* 2001) has shown some striking results. Although, during the bottleneck, heterozygosity and allelic diversity were reduced similar to neutral theory expectation, these measures regained pre-bottleneck levels within two years of the crash, much faster than expected, so that a sample taken three years after the crash would show no evidence of the bottleneck having occurred, although average inbreeding did increase rapidly over this period. Low-level immigration (female arrived immediately after the storm) and genetic drift account for this recovery. Figure 1.3 shows the effect of immigration on expected heterozygosity. The descendents of crash survivors showed values reduced from 0.78 immediately before the crash to 0.64 five years after.

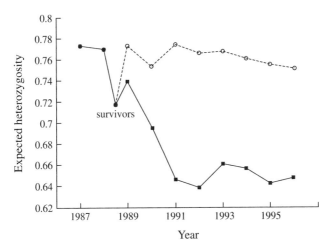

Fig. 1.3. The trajectory of average expected heterozygosity before, during and after the crash for all samples (open circles) and the subset excluding all immigrant lineages (closed squares). (From Keller *et al.* 2001.)

The role of inbreeding and drift in population and individual viability has been explored in as much, or perhaps more, detail in birds than in other vertebrates. However, as these examples and others show, much is still to be learned. More lessons need to be drawn from the many long-term studies of avian populations, for both endangered and stable species, and molecular studies on such populations are bound to be invaluable in highlighting new information.

PERSPECTIVE

The quantification, characterisation and prioritisation for conservation of avian biodiversity at all levels will be key to how many species and populations survive the next 100 years, and in what condition. There is no doubt that to best conserve both present-day diversity and future evolutionary processes, the first priority must be to conserve as much habitat of as many different types as is politically possible, and the avian communities within them may then be able to play their role in ecosystem maintenance as they have done for over 100 million years. The decisions over precisely which regions are afforded protection are likely to be crucial in many cases, and presence or absence of certain avian taxa is likely to play a significant role in these choices, although whether they could or should dominate the conservation agenda over other taxa is questionable.

The continuing and seemingly insolvable debate regarding operational species concepts for conservation continues to hamper policy decisions and is in danger of creating a logjam for both legislation and practical management. Such problems have been most keenly felt in the United States where the interaction between the Endangered Species Act, ESU designation and subspecies-level conservation in particular, is giving rise to much debate (e.g. Zink *et al.* 2000). Such problems should serve to inform other countries and regions when considering the setting up of legislative apparatus for conservation of biodiversity.

Although seen as a somewhat esoteric exercise by those scientists concerned with protecting as much biodiversity as rapidly as possible, incorporating variation below the species into management programmes could in fact hold the key to effective conservation in the future. The preservation of adaptive processes and evolutionary potential needs to focus on populations and individuals since these are the currency of natural selection and hold the key to the future viability of all taxa. Management of subpopulations using genetic criteria, while desirable, is potentially fraught with inconsistencies, problems of interpretation and the tendency to over-diagnose units for conservation or to follow guidelines too rigidly and without due regard to recent population demography. A pragmatic approach to interpreting and integrating genetic data in conservation, which takes into account both evolutionary 'signal' and demographic 'noise', but which is explicitly conservative when data are difficult to interpret (which they often are), may be needed in many cases. It is becoming clear that few, if any, 'hard and fast' rules can be used which are applicable to all situations and perhaps this is not surprising, given the myriad of evolutionary processes which can contribute the status of any given species, population or individual.

2

Why conserve bird diversity?

COLIN BIBBY

REASONS FOR CONSERVATION

To the reader of this chapter it probably seems self-evident why we should conserve birds. Birds are part of biodiversity and their widespread declines indicate a fundamental malaise in the way that humans treat the Earth. It may not be obvious in the daily lives of many city dwellers, but we are and remain part of biodiversity ourselves. We eat it, we make and trade goods from it and we depend on its services in many inescapable ways. There are strong utilitarian arguments for conservation. If we do not act to stem the current crisis now, we will pay later, and we may have to pay very heavily. Our unique cultural and technical development has tended to separate us from some obvious truths. We have altered a huge part of our natural life support system. With our vast numbers, we appropriate a large and growing fraction of finite natural resources. Modern transport and communications have enlarged the distance over which every one of us has impact. As a result, the social and environmental impacts of our resource use and abuse are remote from the daily lives of most of us, especially the more affluent. It appears easy and attractive to believe that there will be technical solutions to these ills. Meanwhile we can afford to continue business as usual.

In addition to utilitarian arguments, there are ethical reasons for conservation. Environmental ethics is a relatively new subject; the environment is barely treated in most of the main streams of philosophical tradition and thought. Consider a particular environmental decision, such as whether to develop a new mine in a wilderness area. Harm might be done to natural beauty or to particular species. There might be damage from clearance of vegetation or pollution of watercourses. All these things could be studied and facts agreed. How big an area of what vegetation is damaged; are any of the species involved globally threatened? There would be facts, too, on the benefits. How many jobs created, how much profit earned? Even if all the facts are known and agreed, the decision as to whether to proceed with the mine is not simple. Different people will weigh the facts with differing ethical perspectives and reach different conclusions.

A utilitarian viewpoint values the natural world purely from the perspective of its instrumental utility to humans. Others believe that natural things have an intrinsic value in their own right. This distinction is central to an environmental ethic. B.L. Taylor (1995) describes a contrast between strong and weak valuation. Weak valuation derives solely from use to the valuer while strong valuation is not contingent on a need or desire. Thus there is a fundamental difference in the way that we might value a car and a rainforest. Economic cost–benefit analyses are based on utilitarian valuation. The values are those deriving from the needs or desires of a set of people. The unfortunate implication of this is that if people do not value environmental goods or services then they have no value.

In a humanistic ethic, we would treat others as we would be prepared to have them treat us. Our responsibilities spread to various parties prejudiced by our behaviour but not well able to argue their cases. Billions of poor people currently on Earth are often the first to suffer some of the direct impacts of biodiversity loss but are disenfranchised by their poverty. Future generations obviously cannot speak for themselves but perhaps we owe them options at least as good as those that we ourselves inherited. Some people believe that we also carry an ethical responsibility for other creatures. The fact that they should be given moral consideration does not imply that they should be weighted equally with human interests. It is possible to develop such arguments further to include all living things or even the whole biosphere. Broadening the ethical scope in this direction raises questions about the basis on which we determine moral considerability.

All these arguments are well rehearsed and well familiar to a converted minority. However, judging from the behaviour of humanity, they clearly have rather little impact. Perhaps questions about the value of the conservation of birds and biodiversity are inadequate. Maybe we need to be more interested in why apparently truths self-evident to many have so little influence, why ethical considerations are so poorly enshrined in law and practice when it comes to environmental decision-making. Meanwhile, since everyday decisions about environmental use are so frequently made in a framework of utilitarian economics it would be as well to explore what opportunities there might be for the promotion of conservation (Diamond & Filion 1987).

SUSTAINABILITY AND EQUITABILITY

Conservation is about resolving the conflict between the material needs and aspirations of a fast-growing human population and the adverse effects of increasing demands for natural resources. The idea of sustainable development has emerged in the last 30 years. *Our Common Future* (WCED 1987) defined sustainable development as that which meets the needs of the present without compromising the ability of future generations to meet their own needs. Everyone knows roughly what this means but turning it into operational reality has proved much more difficult and contentious.

The World Conservation Strategy (IUCN/UNEP/WWF 1980) and particularly its successor, *Caring for the Earth* (IUCN/UNEP/WWF 1991) set out extensive agendas of action required to achieve sustainability. Formal political endorsement has been secured through Agenda 21 though there remain huge obstacles between these ideals and real-world practice (Holdgate 1996).

Sustainability can be seen as balancing three kinds of capital value – social, material and natural. Natural capital includes biodiversity at all its levels. Material capital consists of money, and built and manufactured objects. Social capital is invested in health, education and social organisation. Three major branches of science inform our understanding of these issues: ecology, economics and politics. Much of the challenge in sustainable development demands the reformation of relationships between the three. The natural environment is frequently ignored or undervalued in much economic and political analysis. Particular decisions might be supported by cost–benefit analysis but future costs arising from damage to natural capital are often ignored. Political systems frequently favour such flawed decision-making because it offers seemingly good value to the beneficiaries. Environmental degradation generally occurs because a powerful lobby is getting something for nothing (Cairncross 1995).

VALUES OF BIODIVERSITY AND ECOSYSTEMS

Ecosystem services
Human life depends on products derived from nature, which we use for food, fuel, housing and clothing, and as inputs to many manufactured products. Additionally we rely on processes, at least partly biotic, for decomposition of waste, cycling of key elements, maintenance of atmospheric quality and climate, and defence from flooding. Such processes and more, such as soil formation or pollination, are in turn essential for the continued growth

of the products we extract from nature. The absolute value of all these products and processes, or ecosystem services, is infinite in the sense that human life would not exist without them. Many of them would be very difficult to substitute with engineered alternatives.

Ecosystem services are not easy to describe in a clearly separated way because so many are interdependent, but the broad classes are fairly consistently acknowledged (Daily 1997) and include at least the following.

Climate regulation: Temperature and weather patterns are influenced by carbon dioxide and other greenhouse gases whose concentrations are regulated by biological and chemical processes. Emissions are increased by human activities especially the burning of fossil fuels. Climate change has the potential to incur costs from increased extremes such as droughts, storms and floods, especially as mean sea levels rise. There will also be consequences for biodiversity (see Chapter 8).

Nutrient cycling: Most importantly this concerns the fixation and cycling of nitrogen, which is the limiting nutrient in most ecosystems. Damage to the process can cause loss of naturally generated soil fertility or poisoning of water supplies if inputs exceed denitrifying capacity.

Waste treatment: Excreta and dead plants and animals are recycled naturally. The artificial treatment of waste is expensive and the consequences of failure to do so widespread and damaging.

Water supply and regulation: Forests and wetlands catch water and smooth out its runoff. Drainage and deforestation lead to poorer and erratic water supplies. During heavy rain, faster runoff can cause floods and soil erosion.

Soil formation and retention: The conversion of sterile mineral fragments to soils is a slow biological process that supplies the medium on which agriculture depends. The export of crop material, the exposure of devegetated soil to rain and sun and the salination derived from inappropriate irrigation damage and degrade soils. There are no realistic technical solutions for reversing soil loss, which is a major global problem.

Pollination: Most food crops are pollinated by bees or other animals, and would fail to set seeds or fruits in their absence. In much of the United States, domestic bees have to be used to support natural pollination but this is becoming harder as a result of bee diseases and ongoing losses due to insecticides.

Pest control: Globally, some 25–50% of crops are lost as a result of pests. Predators regulate numbers of potential pests but they have become scarcer where, for instance, their field margin refuges have been removed to make more cropland, or pesticides have killed them. Though pesticides cost some US$25 billion per annum, and have such side effects as killing 220,000 people per annum, the same proportion of crops is lost as in pre-pesticide times (Naylor & Ehrlich 1997).

Production of food and raw materials: Food gathered from the wild is still important to much of humanity, provided by biodiversity as a free good. Such products rely on the continued integrity of their habitats, including key refugia such as spawning grounds for fish. Over-harvesting in the majority of commercial fisheries and the consequent loss of jobs and opportunities is the obvious pointer to the under-valuation of such services.

The genetic library: Millennia of evolution have generated a range of chemical defences especially in plants and sessile marine organisms. Knowledge acquired from the study of these bioactive compounds provides the potential to supply new drugs or pesticides. Genes for tolerance of different stresses may be needed for future crop breeding.

Recreation and cultural: Natural habitats are in demand for outdoor adventure, enjoyment, scientific study, inspiration, relaxation and other human needs.

Valuing ecosystem services

The need for evaluation of ecosystem services derives from the need to make choices about change. The voice for change will generally be based on a market assessment that the change will be beneficial. Net future gains will exceed costs. A mangrove forest will be cleared to develop a profitable shrimp farm. A cost–benefit analysis can show whether or not costs, including loss of ecosystem function, exceed benefits in terms of profit. Ethical values cannot be quantified and are thus difficult to argue for. Marginalisation or omission of the environmental costs generally flaws cost–benefit arguments. It should be noted that the beneficiaries would be known and limited in number. Costs will be incurred more widely across the impacted society and may also be deferred to the future. The deadly and damaging flood caused by poor coastal protection from a typhoon may not come for years. The shrimp farmer will not alone pay these costs. In many cost–benefit assessments, profitability will depend on subsidy aimed at supporting development. Thus in managed markets, society often not only fails to ensure that environmental costs are properly anticipated and paid but also tips the scales in favour of damage. If the analysis was done properly with environmental costs included and subsidy excluded, the resulting shrimps would have to be sold at higher prices and the enterprise might be shown to be non-viable.

There are three main ways to estimate the values of ecosystem services. All require knowledge of what the service is and how it works, particularly how it responds to change. Thus in the case of the mangrove clearance we need to understand the frequency and severity of typhoons in the region and how they interact with coastal deforestation. Knowledge about ecosystem function is all too rare. The required studies are interdisciplinary and thus fail to appeal to the personal ambition of individual researchers. Most directed research is focused on profit generation rather than risk avoidance.

Direct market costs can be used where the service is the provision of goods such as fresh water for irrigation, pollination of crops, or marine fish catches. Loss of irrigation water might be compensated by a project to deliver an alternative supply or farmers might have to accept lower yields and greater risk of total crop failures. Loss of natural predators of crop pests can be compensated by the use of more pesticides, or accepted as causing greater crop losses. These alternatives can be valued in the market.

Where there are no markets, such as the maintenance of wildlife habitat, valuation has to be inferred by indirect methods. The most common is contingent valuation, which simply asks people what they would be prepared to pay to keep the service or how much they would accept in compensation for its destruction. An example might be the preservation or destruction of a particular block of habitat. The question refers to the marginal cost or value of a small unit of change. The question of the value of all wildlife habitats is meaningless because it would change with quantity surviving and rise perhaps to infinity. Critics of contingent valuation would argue that people might say anything when they do not actually have to pay (and, in general, willingness to accept is higher than willingness to pay). Added over many possible scenarios, people might say they were prepared to pay more than they actually owned or could pay. There is also the difficult question of who to ask and how to weight the answers of different stakeholders. What about the poor whose willingness to pay money is necessarily low even if they would feel a huge loss? What about future generations who cannot be

asked directly? Many of the issues involved in ecosystem services are very complicated. This raises questions about how to get the views of people who do not fully understand. Should the views of experts be weighted more heavily? In spite of all the criticisms, contingent valuation is often the only way of measuring value so the pragmatist would argue for better development and understanding of this approach.

For non-consumptive use values such as birdwatching, the travel cost method can be used. The idea is that you can interview visitors to a bird-watching site and find out what they paid to make their visit. Their costs will have been travelling, accommodation and entry fees. Summed over all visitors this gives a minimum value of the site. Were the area to be damaged and become less attractive, people would stop visiting when they considered that the appeal was no longer worth the cost of a visit.

Global values of ecosystem services

For the reasons given, valuing ecosystem services has not proved easy. Costanza et al. (1997) make a first attempt at bringing together a range of previous estimates and filling gaps. They considered 17 ecosystem functions and estimated their marginal annual values per hectare within a hierarchy of major biomes. The most valuable services, each estimated at over one trillion US dollars (US$$10^{12}$) per annum were nutrient cycling, cultural, waste treatment, disturbance regulation, water supply, food supply, gas regulation, and water regulation. The most valuable biomes per unit area were estuaries, sea-grass and algae beds, and swamps and flood plains all worth near, or over US$20 thousand per annum.

Overall, the annual global value of ecosystem services was estimated as US$33 trillion (range 16–54). The world's gross national product (GNP) is about US$18 trillion. These figures will no doubt change with better understanding of the functioning of ecosystems and their response to change as well as the methods of valuing non-marketed goods. The safe bet, and certainly the wise precaution, would be to believe that they would probably increase with better understanding.

So, estimates of global ecosystem values exceed current GNP. This means that we simply could not afford to replace them with artificial substitutes even if this were technically possible. If the derived services were properly accounted for, the prices of many man-made goods and services would rise considerably. Pricing ecosystem service values makes it possible to include them in national accounts. This would focus attention on the question of the sustainability of current growth of apparent prosperity.

The extent to which ecosystem services are dependent on biodiversity is arguable. In many cases, such as flood protection or carbon sequestration, it may be biomass rather than biodiversity that is important. A single-species plantation may function just as well as the diverse natural forest it replaced. Agriculture shows that greatly simplified ecosystems can be effective in producing food. Other services such as pollination, pest control or recreation and culture are more obviously dependent on biodiversity.

THE VALUES OF BIRDS

Birdwatching

The economics of birdwatching has been best studied in the United States, where periodic national recreational surveys date back to 1983 (Cordell *et al.* 1996, 1999). Bird-watching was the fastest growing outdoor recreational activity in 1995. The growth was mainly among those with just a few days of participation each year. Compared with the average American, birders tend to be older, white, employed and educated, so they fit with the model of growing need for recreation in a prosperous society. Over 54 million people (27% of the population) participated in some birding, more than twice the level of 12 years earlier; 12.4 million of these devoted more than ten days a year to the hobby.

From a sample of those 43,000 participating in Christmas Bird Counts, it was estimated that annual expenditure on birding averaged US$1,852 (Wiedner & Kerlinger 1990). The total expenditure would be near US$80 million in the sampled population. If these were representative of the estimated 12.4 million keen birders then their total annual expenditure would be US$23 billion. Kerlinger & Eubanks (1995) argue that birders could better exploit the value of their activities to argue the case for conservation.

In South Africa a penguin colony near Cape Town attracted 200,000 people in the 1996–97 season and generated a gate revenue of R680,000 (US$102,000) and a return to the regional economy of over US$2 million. The annual value of birding-related activities in the whole country was estimated at US$15–33 million (Turpie & Ryan 1998).

Hunting

Hunting and fishing are very popular pastimes in the US with numbers totalling about 40 million individuals of whom 14 million are hunters. The hunters spent US$17.7 billion in 1996 (US Fish & Wildlife Service 1997).

Hunters and non-consumptive users of wildlife have increasingly used economic arguments to reverse the anti-wildlife trend which was successful in the early 1990s in portraying conservation as opposed to employment.

Ecotourism

Tourism has been among the fastest growing commercial sectors around the world in recent decades. For many countries it ranks highly as a source of foreign revenue. People travel to wild places for many reasons including adventure, enjoyment of scenery and nature, and more specific interests in wildlife. Valuation of nature tourism or ecotourism is obstructed by difficulties of definition. The Ecotourism Society has defined ecotourism as 'Responsible travel to natural areas that conserves the environment and improves the well being of local people'. Clearly the conditions in such a definition exclude quite a lot of tourism that derives at least some of its value from biodiversity.

In 1992, 7% of American travellers stated that they had taken at least one ecotourism holiday and 30% (35 million people) declared that they intended to take one in the next three years (US Travel Data Center 1992). The annual sum earned by developing countries has been estimated at US$2–12 billion. Tourism provides 17% of GDP and 60% of foreign exchange earnings in the Republic of the Maldives where upscale international tourism is primarily attracted by the coral reefs (Sawkar *et al.* 1998). The dominant economic activity in the Seychelles is tourism, which employs about 30% of the labour force and accounts for more than 70% of export earnings (newafrica.com 2001).

The size of these numbers supports the notion that wildlife or ecotourism might contribute to sustainable development and biodiversity conservation, especially in biodiversity-rich developing countries.

Honey (1999) reviews the principles that will be necessary to make the shift from a general theme of nature tourism to sustainable ecotourism. She proposes seven criteria against which to judge the records of a range of projects and countries:

- Involves travel to natural destinations
- Minimises impact
- Builds environmental awareness
- Provides direct financial benefits for conservation
- Provides financial benefits and empowerment for local people
- Respects local culture
- Supports human rights and democratic movements

Against these quite strict criteria, the record to date is patchy as several of Honey's (1999) examples show. The hardest to satisfy relate to provision of benefit to local people. Much of the tourism industry rests in large corporations and it is quite possible for the major revenues and benefits to accrue largely outside the areas of destination. Local people may not be well placed to provide facilities of internationally attractive standard or to market what they can provide. Governments, where it is in their power, may not always be eager to allocate benefits locally. The tourism industry itself has lobbied vigorously, on grounds of fair trade, against the kinds of financial instruments such as taxation, which might help to redistribute benefits. There are grounds, too, for concern about the direct impact of tourism on the target wildlife (Roe *et al.* 1997), not to mention the environmental costs of air travel to ecotourism destinations.

COSTS AND VALUES OF CONSERVATION

Nature conservation itself is a source of employment and economic impact that may be more significant than competing development options in more traditional areas of economic activity. Nature conservation interest is often high in marginal rural areas that are vulnerable to social and economic deprivation. The fact of unemployment and declining opportunities for rural communities being combined with biodiversity loss is a clear sign of non-sustainability with both natural and social capital in decline. New policy thinking needs to look with greater integration across sectors to reverse these trends.

In the United Kingdom, it is estimated that there are between 10,000 and 20,000 full-time (equivalent) jobs directly in nature conservation. Four to six times more jobs may be supported by the fact that nature reserves attract visitors to rural areas (Rayment 1995). Throughout Europe, there are abundant case examples showing that policies supporting biodiversity conservation can be good for rural employment and rural communities (Cuff & Rayment 1997; Rayment 1997). Many of these opportunities are dependent on public subsidy but so, often, are the competing alternatives, be they agriculture or even industry, attracted to remoter areas by development grants.

In the US, opponents of the Endangered Species Act have often made their arguments on the basis of short-term analyses of impact on jobs displaced from critical habitats. But what is the value of saving these rare or threatened species? In a meta-analysis, Loomis & White (1996) found average annual willingness to pay for keeping threatened species amounts to

US$10–100 for birds and other charismatic vertebrates. The cost per US household of ensuring the survival of the northern spotted owl (*Strix occidentalis caurina*) has been estimated at US$3.4 (Hagen *et al.* 1992). Thus the spotted owl is well worth keeping; the cost of doing so is far less than the benefit. Opposition to the Endangered Species Act comes from interests that perceive that they bear an undue share of the costs, such as private landowners whose economic opportunities are foreclosed. This is an issue of the equitability of distribution of costs and benefits that could be tackled by a fair subsidy system.

The forest industry has been effective in arguing that environmentalists are threatening logging jobs and economic growth. The revenues and employment generated by birdwatching (and other natural services) depend on the continued existence of natural habitats. So the counter-argument has validity. Logging threatens jobs and the economy surrounding wildlife.

If conservation can be an economically attractive proposition, what might it cost and how might we pay for more? James *et al.* (1999) estimated the global costs of an adequate conservation programme. They considered the prospects of ensuring that 10% of the Earth was strictly protected and the existing 5% in multiple use reserves maintained. Extra costs would be incurred in survey, purchase and annual management. In a fair market, purchase costs would compensate for loss of future opportunity to use the land – this is how the current owner would estimate a fair sale price. For existing reserves, James *et al.* (1999) suggested the payment of compensation for lost opportunity to local communities. Over the next 30 years such a programme would cost US$27.5 billion per annum, about four times higher than current expenditure on protected areas. Regional variations are large but overall this would be a cost of US$1335 km^{-2}. While protected areas will always be a foundation of conservation effort, it is clear that the maintenance of biodiversity in human dominated landscapes is also important. James *et al.* (1999) estimate this cost as US$290 billion per year. Agriculture would be the largest demand – it is estimated that greening agriculture in the UK would cost about US$2.4 billion per annum (Pretty 1999). Thus greening the wider environment will be ten times more expensive than an adequate protected area system.

BIRDS AS INDICATORS

The drive for sustainability demands the integration of the environment into all sectors of social and economic activity. This in turn drives a demand for biologists to be more explicit about the location and status of biodiversity. Birds have proved to have a powerful value as indicators (Furness & Greenwood 1993).

We know where the major centres of endemism, and thus of unique value for birds, are (ICBP 1992; Stattersfield *et al.* 1998) and there is evidence that this is quite a good indication of the patterns for other terrestrial biodiversity (see also Chapter 5). In Europe, Africa and the Middle East and partly elsewhere in the world, we know where the most important sites for birds are (Evans 1994; Heath & Evans 2000; Fishpool 2001). Such information is of critical importance if conservation is to set itself a proactive agenda and reach out to a wider audience. For the rest of biodiversity, major conservation organisations are still debating and working on where to set their priorities at a very broad scale (Olson & Dinerstein 1998; Myers *et al.* 2000) and have yet to tackle the problem of making more information-explicit priorities at a finer scale.

For birds, there has been an explicitly documented list of globally threatened species for more than a decade (Collar *et al.* 1994; BirdLife International 2000). This has yet to be achieved for any other major group of organisms (IUCN 1996). In Europe and the Americas, there is documented evidence on the status of all bird species, which provides information on general trends in numbers and distributions (Tucker *et al.* 1994; Stotz *et al.* 1996). In Europe, these are the only formally documented facts on trends in biodiversity which support otherwise qualitative indications of widespread losses. The adoption of a biodiversity measure based on birds as one of the indicators for quality of life in the UK is a significant step in the political process (Anon. 1999a).

It is outside the scope of this chapter to discuss in detail just how good these indicators are. It would be wrong to claim that they are either complete or ideal. They have, however, contributed in a major way to making some facts about the status and location of biodiversity more explicit and thus more susceptible to political discussion.

There are several reasons why birds have proved to be good indicators. In part these are biological. It helps that birds are conspicuous and relatively easy to find and identify, and that their taxonomy is relatively well agreed. It also helps that they are widespread in most terrestrial habitats and there are a tractable number of species to work with (about 10,000 globally compared with perhaps 300,000 plants). I believe, however, that a more powerful reason is their symbolic value and importance to humans that dates back across millennia and transcends national and cultural boundaries.

We possess the data because people have been sufficiently interested in birds to observe and record them on a scale that has simply not been achieved for frogs or trees, for example. The data have power partly for scientific reasons but just as importantly because they are significant to the many people who care. Concern about an 80% decline in skylarks in the UK is demonstrably shared by nearly 2% of the population who support the Royal Society for the Protection of Birds.

CONCLUSIONS

There is a view that seeking to value birds or biodiversity is inappropriate. Were a different ethic to prevail, then environmental decision-making would be more favourable to biodiversity. There is a good case to be made for the development and teaching of a new environmental ethic and awareness on a global scale. However, there is at least a growing understanding of the need for sustainability as a political issue that balances material, social and natural capital values. Arguments about the measurable utility of biodiversity are worth developing because they speak in the language of political and economic debate.

Ecosystems provide services of value to humanity on a scale comparable to the total gross national product. In other words, we do not earn enough money to repair by technical means the damage done to the natural environment. So it would make good sense to look after ecosystem functions that in part are dependent on biodiversity.

Birds have considerable measurable values to birdwatchers and hunters who spend money on equipment and travel to pursue their hobby. Tourism is a fast growing sector and the part that is dependent on nature and wildlife is significant as a potential source of revenue especially in connection with protected areas.

Far from being an obstacle to development, conservation itself can be a significant economic activity (and the development which it is obstructing may itself be unsustainable because it is quarrying a natural resource or is only apparently economically beneficial because of subsidy). The global costs of an adequate conservation strategy are surprisingly good value in relation to the ecosystem services that would be safeguarded.

Nor need the payment of the bill be difficult. Non-sustainable practices are promoted by huge public subsidy. It would take only a small proportionate redirection of such subsidy so that agriculture, for instance, was not purely growing crops but was being supported to meet social and environmental objectives as well.

All the numbers presented here could be debated but it is likely that to order of magnitude they will turn out to be correct. A small redirection of subsidy would be a very wise investment in securing the future of biodiversity. Failure to do so runs a very high risk of incurring large costs in the future.

If the argument for conservation is so clear in economic terms, it is interesting to ask why things continue as they are. Clearly the beneficiaries of environmental degradation are enjoying benefits for which they have not fully paid. Societies are unjust in the way in which they allocate costs and benefits. This can be seen in the huge wealth of a small segment of humanity and the great poverty of vast numbers. To the powerful and rich, there is vested interest in continued inequity.

A second reason for inertia is the optimistic belief that we will find technical solutions to emerging problems. A wise investor managing the world's portfolio of environmental capital would take steps to deal with risk. The problem is that there is not a single investment manager. In the short term, it is cheaper to continue in the hope that things will not go too wrong, to take no insurance, not to hedge investments, to spend natural capital rather than just the interest (Costanza *et al.* 2000). The idea of the precautionary principle would make sense to the wise manager. Whatever may be the risk of things actually going wrong, if they do the consequences will be disastrous.

Perhaps another reason that economic arguments for conservation have not been very successful is that they are relatively new and contentious, and have yet to be made with convincing and widespread power. In part this might be because conservationists have been reluctant to accept the idea of reducing biodiversity to numbers and joining what some see as the unattractive debates about politics and economics.

Attributing to birds a value as indicators talks of a different kind of value. But perhaps there is a connecting theme. The people who enjoy birds and who see their population declines are very well placed as a social and political force to promote concern for conservation, not just of birds but of the environments on which they depend. A new awareness will need to be based on a new ethic that gives greater value to the natural environment and to the fair sharing of its costs and benefits. But it will also need to be based on the application of political and economic argument at all levels of society where environmental decisions are made. Birdwatchers who know and care about biodiversity have a powerful role to play.

3

Mapping and monitoring bird populations:
their conservation uses

LES UNDERHILL & DAVID GIBBONS

INTRODUCTION

Accurate and up-to-date distribution maps and a good numerical insight into population sizes and trends are a prerequisite for effective conservation. The conservation status of a species hinges on three questions: 'Where are they?', 'How many are there?' and 'What is their trend?' This chapter focuses on providing answers to these questions. We cannot conserve what we do not understand.

This chapter provides a series of examples and case studies into conservation applications of bird inventories and bird monitoring. However, even the best inventories and perfect monitoring make no contribution to conservation on their own. This information simply allows an assessment of the status of a species or a site: it will not, for example, halt a species' decline. Explanations need to be found for trends, and management and action plans need to be compiled and implemented. Monitoring needs to be built into these actions, otherwise we have no measure of the impact of conservation interventions.

One of the most outstanding conservation successes of the twentieth century – the widespread removal of organochlorine insecticides from the environment – showed clearly the role that monitoring plays in bird conservation. These harmful chemicals caused direct mortality of adult birds of prey, most notably peregrines (*Falco peregrinus*), through accumulation in body tissues, and caused indirect mortality through thinning of their eggshells leading to reduced hatching success and poorer breeding performance. Consequently, peregrine populations declined worldwide, and only recovered when organochlorine usage was reduced.

This story shows, in a microcosm, the role of monitoring in identifying and solving a big conservation challenge. It was the *monitoring* of peregrine populations, their eggshells and breeding success, that highlighted the problem. As a consequence the species became a high conservation *priority*. *Research* showed that population declines and shell-thinning commenced soon after the introduction of DDT, that these compounds were accumulating in adult tissues, and that the amount of thinning – and thus success of individual clutches – was closely linked to the amount of chemical residue in the shells. The knowledge gained from this research was turned into conservation *action* by non-governmental conservation organisations and governmental agencies that campaigned for the removal of these chemicals from the environment. Subsequently, many governments implemented bans on their use. *Monitoring* showed that these actions had been successful as peregrine populations recovered dramatically (Newton 1998).

Thus monitoring comes at the beginning and end of a conservation circle that leads from monitoring to prioritisation, research, action and back to monitoring. Even within the 'research' stage, monitoring is used to assess the success of small-scale trials that test potential solutions. This circle of activities is fundamental to conservation and monitoring plays a vital role.

This chapter discusses the manner in which bird distribution, population size and trend information is collected, and its uses. As numerous texts have reviewed bird monitoring methods, these are considered only briefly here, and instead we focus on the uses of such data. Because reviews of methods to determine distributions (principally 'atlases') are much less well documented (but see Bibby *et al.* 2000), these are discussed at greater length.

WHERE ARE THEY?

Bird inventories

A distinct vocabulary has grown up around answering the question 'Where are they?' A 'bird atlas' has come to mean a collection of distribution maps, in which the geographic ranges of the avifauna of a given area no longer have the smooth and overconfident shapes shown in field guides and handbooks. Atlas maps usually display the distributions as presence or absence of a species on a rectangular grid system, and increasingly they also show abundance. The verb 'to atlas' has come to mean doing the fieldwork to create these maps. Although some terminology has been developed, there is no 'theory' of atlasing, and there are few useful resources to provide practical guidance on how to run a bird atlas project. The following paragraphs provide some first steps in this direction. If you are ever called upon to run a bird atlas the best advice we can give is to tell you to read the 'methods' sections of as many published atlases as you can assemble!

Choice of region and choice of grid for a bird atlas

The choice of the region in which to conduct fieldwork is frequently determined politically. Most often, these are countries, or administrative regions within countries. More rarely, they cover several countries and even subcontinents. However, other areas may be appropriate for specific purposes, such as a place of impending development. Such areas tend to be near people, so there is a high probability of good coverage and the data may be very relevant to a particular conservation case, the development itself.

The choice of grid is usually driven by pragmatic expediency. For any potential grid, the critical question that needs to be asked is, 'How many grid cells does the choice of grid generate?' More than any other decision, it is the number of grid cells that determines the complexity of an atlas project. In an analysis of 25 bird atlas projects, Donald & Fuller (1998) showed that there was a strong positive correlation between the size of grid cells and the total area being covered; atlases covering larger areas used larger grid cells. Such questions as 'What level of coverage is being aimed for? How many observers are available, and how much effort can they devote to the project?' will all influence the choice of grid. Thinking in the longer term, it is necessary to consider how many years the project will last, and what resources will be available to capture and process the data.

The authors of this chapter played key roles in the two atlas projects with the largest numbers of grid cells (Table 3.1), the atlases of southern Africa (Harrison *et al.* 1997) and Britain and Ireland (Gibbons *et al.* 1993), both of which had nearly 4,000 grid cells. Without substantial funding and a complex support infrastructure, this is probably near the upper limit of what can be attained in a 4- or 5-year bird mapping project. Although the scope of the European Atlas (Hagemeijer & Blair 1997) encompassed an area of 4,400 grid cells, not all were systematically covered.

Within Europe, atlas grids are almost invariably based on the Universal Transverse Mercatour (UTM) grid system (a system of grid reference lines called parallels of latitude and meridians of longitude); the most frequently used grid intervals are 2 km and 10 km, but 1 km, 5 km and 50 km grid intervals have also been used (Table 3.1). One exception was an atlas of northeast Scotland, where grid cells were subdivided into polygons

Table 3.1. *Numbers of grid cells of a selection of published atlases*

Region	Number of grid cells	Grid size	Reference
Britain and Ireland	3858	10 km	Gibbons *et al.* 1993
Southern Africa	3973	15 minutes	Harrison *et al.* 1997
'southwestern Cape'	76	15 minutes	Hockey *et al.* 1980
The Netherlands	1767	5 km	SOVON 1987
Hertfordshire, UK	491	2 km	K.W.Smith *et al.* 1993
Hampshire, UK	1031	2 km	Clark & Eyre 1993
Essex, UK	1068	2 km	Dennis 1996
Northumbria, UK	1410	2 km	Day *et al.* 1995
Austria	2624	5 min × 3 min	Dvorak *et al.* 1993
Swaziland	100	7.5 minutes	Parker 1994
Sul do Save, Mozambique	250	15 minutes	Parker 1999
Europe	4400	50 km	Hagemeijer & Blair 1997
Kenya	228	30 minutes	Lewis & Pomeroy 1989
Switzerland	468	10 km	Schmid *et al.* 1998

encompassing particular habitat types (Buckland, *et al.* 1990). In Africa and Australia, the natural grid is geographical, with intervals of 1 degree, 30 minutes and 15 minutes of both latitude and longitude being most frequently used (Table 3.1). In Swaziland, a 7.5-minute grid was used (Table 3.1); however, it is recommended that, when grid intervals less than 15 minutes are needed, the most sensible alternatives are 5 minutes, 3 minutes and 1 minute. The geographical grid is satisfactory in equatorial regions, and produces cells which are approximately square to about 40° N and 40° S. Closer to the poles, the convergence of the lines of longitude results in grid cells which are narrow rectangles. The lines of latitude remain 104 km apart. However, adoption of an UTM-based grid does not solve the problem when the north–south extent of the project is large, as for the European Atlas (Hagemeijer & Blair 1997).

It is acceptable for the scale of the grid to change over the region being covered. The breeding bird atlas in Ontario, for example, used a 10 km grid in southern Ontario and a 100 km grid in northern Ontario, this decision being based largely on the number of potential observers (Cadman, *et al.* 1987). Similarly, for the Southern African Bird Atlas Project (Harrison *et al.* 1997), a half-degree grid was used in Botswana, and a quarter-degree grid for the remaining five countries involved. Although the decision to operate in this way was taken for pragmatic reasons, it could equally well have been made for scientific reasons, because the environmental gradient over most of Botswana is not steep. In fact, a future atlas of southern Africa would probably use a variety of grid scales, as appropriate to the rate of change of habitat types. Complete coverage of a larger grid may well be more desirable than partial coverage of a smaller grid.

The scale of grid adopted will also be dependent upon the aims of the project. If the data are to be used, for example, to support a conservation case dealing with individual pieces of built development, then a large grid scale would be entirely inappropriate. Thus the scale must reflect the aims.

Atlases that are not based on grids

Not all atlases have been based on grids or polygons. The two atlases of birds of North America, one of wintering (Root 1988) and one of summering birds (Price *et al.* 1995), are based on extrapolating bird densities from individual bird census plots. The data for these came from the two long-running bird monitoring schemes in North America, the Christmas Bird Count and the North American Breeding Birds Survey, respectively. These two atlases have the great merit of providing geographical patterns of abundance (rather than just presence or absence in grid cells) across an entire subcontinent: however, they do not give precise distributions within grid cells, just probabilistic ones.

Uneven distributions of observers

One of the biggest problems that all atlases have had to overcome is the uneven distribution of observers. More species are likely to be found in areas with more observers, simply because the probability of recording a given species increases with time, and more observers can spend more time. Thus the recorded distribution of a species in an area with more (or keener) observers may be more likely to reflect its 'true' distribution, than in an area with fewer (or less keen) observers. There is no simple way of overcoming this problem. Some atlases set themselves targets for the number of species that are 'likely' to be present within each grid cell, and then stop fieldwork when at or near this target. Such an approach, though pragmatic, is not ideal and has somewhat circular logic. Another approach is to reduce the grid size in less well covered parts of the survey area. A further, more sophisticated approach is to build in some measure of observer effort into the fieldwork. This is especially the case when producing a quantitative atlas (see below) that shows geographical variation in abundance, rather than simple presence or absence in grid cells. The repeat atlases of Britain and Ireland (Gibbons *et al.* 1993) and Switzerland (Schmid *et al.* 1998) produced maps of both distribution (uncorrected for observer effort) and abundance. The latter were corrected for effort by instructing observers to count for specified periods of time (Britain and Ireland) or undertaking simplified territory mapping in grid cells (Switzerland).

Quantitative atlas methods

Most atlases simply collect presence or absence information in each grid square although, for breeding atlases at least, this is qualified by the level of proof of breeding (possible, probable or confirmed) obtained for each species. Increasingly, however, there is a trend towards quantitative atlases, based on the relative abundance of species in each grid square. A variety of methods have been used for quantitative atlases.

Perhaps the simplest is to ask observers to estimate how many of each species they think are in each grid square. Generally, such estimates are broken down into categories, e.g. 1–10 pairs, 11–100, 101–1000, 1001–10,000, 10,001–100,000 etc. (Hagemeijer & Blair 1997). Though simple, this method can be inaccurate and may not provide much detail on a map of geographical variation in abundance for a given species because most species will probably only vary over two or three orders of magnitude between grid squares.

Another commonly used approach is frequency of occurrence, either temporal or spatial. The southern African atlas (Harrison *et al.* 1997) used the frequency of occurrence of species on record cards (the 'reporting rate') as a measure of relative abundance. Thus if all record cards for a given grid square reported a given species, its reporting rate was 100% (or 1.0); if only half did so, its reporting rate was 50% (0.5). Such an approach requires a grid square to be visited several times to ensure that a reporting rate can be calculated at all. Despite this, the simplicity of this method has much to commend it.

Where multiple visits cannot be made to a grid square, an alternative is to use record cards covering a limited time period, e.g. one hour. Observers produce checklists of all species recorded during each hour in each square. A reporting rate can then be calculated as the proportion of one-hour periods in which the species was recorded in the square. Such an approach is being used for the second atlas of breeding birds in Portugal. The third approach, used for the repeat atlas of Britain and Ireland (Gibbons *et al.* 1993), is to record the proportion of yet smaller grid squares in which a species was recorded. Thus if an observer visited twelve 2 km squares in a given 10 km square and recorded a species in six of these, its frequency of occurrence would be 0.5 for that 10 km square. An advantage of recording in this manner is that very fine resolution information can be captured – 2 km square in this case. None of the methods based on frequency of occurrence is particularly efficient at measuring relative abundance of very common species. This is because the frequency of occurrence (or reporting rate) will always tend to be high, thus not allowing much geographical variation in abundance to be distinguished. To overcome this problem, fieldworkers for the repeat Swiss atlas (Schmid *et al.* 1998) undertook simplified, three-visit, territory mapping in each of ten 1 km squares in each 10 km square, thus allowing the calculation of relative densities for many species in each 10 km.

Another approach, used for the atlas of wintering birds in Britain and Ireland (Lack 1986), was the timed count. Observers were asked to travel around their grid square counting all birds they noted. They also recorded time spent in the field. Because some observers would only have spent one hour in the field, and others 12 hours, this needed to be corrected for in the analyses. Thus, all counts were standardised to a 6-hour time period by producing regression equations relating numbers of individuals counted and time in field for each species. Such relationships could not always be produced, however, especially for species with clumped distributions where the same number of individuals would be counted, irrespective of the length of the count. Nevertheless, the final maps did reveal a great deal of within-species variation in abundance, and the method is highly repeatable. The downside of the approach, however, is that every individual bird of each species needs to be counted, which can become onerous for very abundant species.

More sophisticated quantitative methods, such as point counts in sample areas, have been used – for example, in selected squares in Britain and Ireland (Gibbons *et al.* 1993) and in each grid square for the repeat atlas of breeding birds in The Netherlands. However, such quantitative methods are not always warmly received by volunteer birdwatchers. Despite this, point counts can provide very useful information for more abundant species.

Comparing atlas distributions with those in field guides

True atlas-derived species distributions are usually smaller than shown in field guides. Distribution mapping is a modern concept; for example, the first distribution maps for southern Africa were produced in 1957 (McLachlan & Liversidge 1957). Professor Jack Winterbottom (1966) has described the process whereby those early maps were generated: 'To take an exaggerated example, suppose a species has been recorded in Windhoek, Pretoria and Port Elizabeth; are we justified in joining these three places together and filling in the area so enclosed as the range of that species? In default of more detailed information, that way of mapping ranges is all too common in South Africa,' and doubtless 'shading the triangle' has been used in many other parts of the world, too. Once the first range maps have been produced, there is inertia to change them, and modifications usually only incorporate observed range extensions. Range contractions, or over-optimism in the original maps through 'shading the triangle', are less easily implemented. Failure to see a species in areas where it is shown as present is seldom reported, and consequently errors of absence are not corrected until an atlas project has been published.

This pattern is clearly seen in *The Birds of the Western Palearctic* (e.g. Cramp & Perrins 1994), which, apart from Russia, had the benefit of atlas projects in most European countries. For many species, the distributions in Russia are shown as continuous, whereas in western and central Europe, distributions appear fragmentary. In reality, an atlas project in Russia is likely to demonstrate that distributions there show the same complex pat-terning as in the remainder of Europe.

Presentation of distribution maps

In many bird atlases, the published maps are so 'busy' that it is hard to con-centrate on any single theme. The use of a large collection of different sym-bols in the grid cells, with variations to indicate current records, historical records, relative abundance, breeding status or the existence of museum specimens, generates maps that are difficult to interpret. Maps that confine themselves to a single theme (e.g. Gibbons *et al.* 1993; Harrison *et al.* 1997; Schmid *et al.* 1998) are easier to interpret than those representing a variety of data themes (e.g. Hagemeijer & Blair 1997).

Repeat atlases

An increasing number of regions now have completed second bird atlas projects, for example Britain and Ireland (Sharrock 1976; Gibbons *et al.* 1993), and Switzerland (Schifferli *et al.* 1980; Schmid *et al.* 1998), each with two decades between pulses of fieldwork. Whilst temporal comparisons can be revealing, they require caution if, for instance, fieldwork methods or lev-els of coverage differed. Increased coverage could convey the impression of changed ranges for species that in reality were stable. To overcome this, some measure of fieldwork effort can be incorporated, as outlined above for the repeat atlas in Britain and Ireland.

The conservation applications of atlas data

The applications of atlas data are numerous, and can be broadly categorised into: education and recreation, conservation casework, taxonomy, species and site prioritisation, survey design, and determining the underlying causes of distributions and their change. A comprehensive review is given by Donald & Fuller (1998).

Most purchasers of the published form of atlases probably do so to learn about the avifauna of their region, and to help them decide which species they are likely to find in their local area, or in areas that they wish to visit. Enthusing and teaching people about wildlife – a role successfully filled by atlases and atlasing – will clearly have long-term conservation benefits.

A common use of atlas data is in conservation casework, for example environmental impact assessments (EIA). Frequently, however, the resolution of the information is not of a sufficient scale to investigate the potential impact of some developments, which will often be on a much finer scale than that provided by an atlas. Nevertheless, atlas data can give an indication of the sort of species that are likely to be present, and can act as a basis for a more detailed site inventory. One potential downside is that atlas data of insufficient resolution may be used in an EIA rather than undertaking a site-specific – and inevitably more expensive – survey.

Distributional information can help in cases of taxonomic uncertainty. Using DNA studies, Crowe et al. (1994) revealed that the two 'subspecies' of the black korhaan (*Eupodotis afra*) were distinct. The southern African atlas (Harrison et al. 1997) supported this taxonomic split as, apart from one small area of overlap, the ranges of the two 'subspecies' were disjunct (see Harrison et al. 1997, p. 355). The early distribution maps, produced on the 'shade-the-triangle' principle, had been totally misleading in showing the black korhaan to occur throughout the Karoo. There are several other examples in the southern African bird atlas of ranges of 'subspecies' which have been revealed as disjunct, and which molecular and morphological studies have shown to be 'species', and there are several more similar, uninvestigated cases.

Atlas data are also widely used in species prioritisation exercises, in at least three separate ways: estimation of overall range size, population size and contraction of range. First, the overall range of a species (its 'area of occupancy') is a criterion within the IUCN Red List categories, such that species with very small global ranges are considered a higher priority than those with larger ranges. A similar approach has been adopted in the United States as part of the 'Partners in Flight' prioritisation plan (Carter et al. 2000). Second, population sizes are frequently assessed by calculating densities in either individual grid squares, or survey plots within grid squares, then extrapolating to an overall population size based on the 'species range' documented by an atlas (see e.g. Gates et al. 1993; Stone et al. 1997). Finally, contraction of range (assessed following a repeat atlas) is often used as a criterion in its own right alongside population decline. Thus, for example, in the species prioritisation process adopted in the UK, a 50% loss of range over a 20-year period was grounds for red-listing (Avery *et al.* 1994; Gibbons *et al.* 1996a). Similarly, Tucker & Heath (1994) used range change as one criterion when assessing the conservation status of all European birds.

Atlas data are being increasingly used in the selection of sites for bird conservation. Thus, for example, Williams *et al.* (1996) and Brown *et al.* (1995) used atlas data to select priority areas for bird conservation in Britain and the English uplands, respectively. Southern African atlas data were key to the selection of Important Bird Areas in this region (Barnes 1998). On a broader geographical scale, Balmford *et al.* (2001) have used distribution data to locate areas of high species richness of African birds, mammals, snakes and amphibians; worryingly, they note that these areas often co-incide with high human population densities. Selection of sites for bird conservation is covered more comprehensively in Chapter 5.

Because atlases provide detailed information on the overall range of a species, they have proved invaluable in further survey design by ensuring that such surveys can be undertaken within the species' range. Several recent surveys in the UK have used atlas data in their design. Thus, for example, a survey of the red-throated diver (*Gavia stellata*) (Gibbons *et al.* 1997) was based on a randomised selection of grid squares from within its distribution documented by the most recent breeding atlas (Gibbons *et al.* 1993). The distribution of this species encompassed 1,400 5 km squares in mainland Scotland and the Hebridean Islands, 147 of which were comprehensively surveyed in 1994. A total of 39 breeding pairs were located, and the overall population was thus calculated by extrapolation as 370 breeding pairs (95% CI 250–505).

More sophisticated designs may seek to stratify atlas data to ensure that effort is concentrated in areas where most birds are likely to be found. Thus, for example, the distribution of the rapidly declining black grouse (*Tetrao tetrix*) in Britain was split into two strata: those grid squares that were likely to still hold the species (based on the most recent atlas), and those which had probably lost it in recent decades (based on a comparison of the distributions in the first and second atlases). For the survey a higher proportion of squares were sampled from within its current than its lost range. This maximised efficiency but ensured that areas in which it had previously been were recorded were actually checked, thus – in the event – confirming its marked contraction in range (Hancock *et al.* 1999).

The distributions of atlas observers, rather than birds, can also be used in survey design. In Poland, the location of randomly allocated 1 km² survey plots for a new common bird monitoring scheme is based on the distribution of observers that took part in the Polish atlas. This stratification ensures that the number of survey plots in a given region is related to the number of potential surveyors, but is still randomised within each region.

Atlas data can also be used to help interpret the underlying causes of bird distributions and their change in distribution. Though often fraught with statistical problems, not least those of spatial auto-correlation and discriminating between true causation and simple correlation (Buckland & Elston 1993; Donald & Fuller 1998), such analyses can be very revealing. For example, Gibbons *et al.* (1995) showed that the geographical patterns of relative abundance of the buzzard (*Buteo buteo*) and raven (*Corvus corax*) were strongly negatively correlated with the distribution of moorland managed for sport shooting of red grouse (*Lagopus lagopus scoticus*). However, they could only infer, rather than prove, that this was a consequence of persecution of buzzards and ravens by the managers of grouse moors.

More revealing, perhaps, has been the modelling of bird distributions in relation to climate. By comparing the first and second British breeding atlases, Thomas & Lennon (1999) showed that the ranges of southerly-distributed British birds may have shifted northwards by nearly 20 km between 1970 and 1990, a shift they attributed to climate change.

HOW MANY AND WHAT IS THEIR TREND?

These two questions, though separate, are often answered using similar methods, so are covered simultaneously here.

Methods of counting birds have been comprehensively described elsewhere, though a brief review is given here. Gibbons *et al.* (1996b) introduces bird-counting methods, while Bibby *et al.* (2000) is the most contemporary and authoritative text on the subject. Gilbert *et al.* (1998) provide a highly practical set of monitoring techniques for UK species, while Buckland *et al.* (1993) introduce the method of 'distance sampling'. Greenwood (1996) provides one of the most comprehensive reviews of basic techniques and sampling design, while Sutherland (1996a) covers census techniques for a wide variety of taxa.

One of the most fundamental decisions to make before undertaking a survey is to decide what is to be measured, whether an estimate of absolute population size or an estimate of the change in population over time (the trend). The former can be obtained by a single survey, the latter requires monitoring over time. Furthermore, population trends can be measured by an index, rather than by estimating absolute population size every year. For most site monitoring, however, an index is insufficient, as a site manager will need to know the population size of each species on the site, not least to allow an assessment of the site's importance.

The Common Birds Census in the UK (CBC; Marchant *et al.* 1990), the UK Breeding Bird Survey (BBS; see Noble *et al.* 2000) and the North American Breeding Bird Survey (Robbins *et al.* 1986) are examples of long-running monitoring schemes that monitor year-on-year changes in population with an index. Although all use different field methods – the CBC territory mapping, the UK BBS line transects and the North American BBS roadside point counts – each uses a standardised method that is repeated annually. This is the essence of monitoring, i.e. a well-defined activity repeated at regular intervals. Increasingly, monitoring is used to assess trends in relation to predetermined targets, such as a desired population level or trend.

Designing and undertaking a survey

Several important decisions need to be made when designing and undertaking a survey: where will the count be undertaken; will it be a full census or a sample, if a sample, to what design; what field method will be used; who will undertake the counts, and how will the results be made known?

The decision on where to count will largely be based on the objectives of the survey. If, for example, it is to assess the size of a species' population within a given region, then the count should be undertaken within the species range boundary, preferably based on its atlas distribution. If the objective is to obtain information on many species on a particular site or in a political region, then the count should clearly be undertaken within the site or political boundary.

The next step is to decide if the survey is to be a complete census – all individuals counted – or a sample survey. Rare species, and those that are colonial or highly clumped in distribution, are much more amenable to complete censuses because either the numbers to count are small (rare species) or the great bulk of the population occurs at a small number of traditional sites. Examples of such species are colonial breeding seabirds and non-breeding waterfowl. 'Seabird 2000' and its predecessors (Cramp *et al.* 1974; Lloyd *et al.* 1991) are 15-yearly complete censuses of breeding seabirds in Britain and Ireland, while the Wetland Birds Survey (e.g. Pollitt *et al.* 2000) is an annual census of nonbreeding waterfowl in the UK. The International Waterbird Census (Delaney *et al.* 1999) collates the results of national mid-January censuses to provide estimates of population size and trends for all European and Asian waterbirds.

For more common and widespread species, it is both impractical and unnecessary to count all individuals in the population to estimate sizes and trends. In general, it is more effective to count samples of the population. If these samples are truly representative then the trend of the sample will be the same as that of the overall population, and the size of the population can be estimated by extrapolation. It is crucial, however, that the samples are truly representative. Greenwood (1996) and Bibby *et al.* (2000) provided a series of theoretical and empirical examples of ways of ensuring that sampling bias is not introduced into survey design. Some simple rules are: ensure that the sample is representative of the whole (e.g. don't just sample at the edge of a species range or a colony); do as many samples as you can; ensure the samples are selected by non-subjective means (e.g. don't just survey in the most convenient areas) and stratify the sample if necessary to make the survey more efficient.

Some surveys involve a mixture of census and sample. The 1994 survey of the red-throated diver in Britain (see above) was based on a complete census at the core of its range – the islands of Orkney and Shetland – but a sample of randomised grid squares elsewhere in its range on mainland Scotland and the Hebridean islands (Gibbons *et al.* 1997). The census of Orkney and Shetland located 484 pairs, the sample elsewhere in its range 370 pairs (95% CI 250–505); the overall British population was thus estimated as 855 pairs (95% CI 735–990). Hen harriers (*Circus cyaneus*) were surveyed in a similar manner in the UK in 1998 (Sim *et al.* 2001).

After deciding upon count location, the next step is to decide upon the field method. This will depend upon the sorts of species that are to be counted, the number to be counted simultaneously and the habitat they live in. If several species are to be counted, then a generic method is required. This may not be ideal for any one species, but is the best 'on average'. The most commonly used generic methods are territory mapping, line transect and point count (= point transect), though each can also be used for single-species survey work.

Territory mapping involves repeated visits to a survey plot by an observer who marks observations of territorial and other behaviour on a large-scale map of the plot. At the end of the season, these registrations are used to estimate the number of breeding territories of each species on the plot. For a line transect an observer travels (often walks) along a transect, recording all birds seen and heard on either side of the line. For a point count, an observer records all birds seen and heard while standing at a particular spot. Line transects tend to be favoured in large areas of homogeneous, open habitat where bird densities may be low (e.g. moorland and sea), while point counts are favoured in patchy or closed habitats (e.g. woodland).

Territory mapping yields absolute population sizes of each species on a plot yet is labour intensive. Line transects and point counts are simpler to do, but are often used to estimate relative abundance only. However, they can be used to estimate densities and thus population sizes (see e.g.

Gregory & Baillie 1998; Arendt *et al.* 1999). There are two ways to do this. Traditionally, an observer would count up to a set distance from the line or point (e.g. 10, 25 or 50 m) and assume that all birds present were actually recorded. Commonly, however, this assumption may not be met and increasingly a method known as 'distance sampling' is being used to estimate densities (Buckland *et al.* 1993). This method assumes that all birds present actually on the line or at the point are recorded, but that more distant birds, though present, may be missed. By recording distances to each bird, or at least recording birds in distance bands, and by assuming that birds are distributed evenly across the landscape (an assumption which also may not be met) it is possible to estimate densities. Line transects are probably more suitable for distance sampling than point counts for two main reasons. First, any errors in distance estimation by the observer will influence the results more for point counts. Second, as the observer is static during a point count, birds are more likely to move into the 'plot' during counting thus possibly inflating densities of highly mobile species (e.g. Arendt *et al.* 1999).

Such methods are most suitable for reasonably common and widespread species that are easy to detect. Many species are not so amenable, and a plethora of methods has been developed to survey such species. These involve: recording vocalisations to discriminate between individual bitterns (*Botaurus stellaris*) (Gilbert *et al.* 2001); using tape-playback to elicit a response from burrow-nesting storm petrels (*Hydrobates pelagicus*) (e.g. Ratcliffe *et al.* 1998); using droppings as an index of goose abundance; counting nests of northern gannets (*Morus bassanus*) from aerial photographs and censusing African penguins (*Spheniscus demersus*) using moult counts. All these examples underline the concept that counting techniques require a sound knowledge of a species' natural history; the more that is known, the better the census technique.

Monitoring methods need not be complex. For example, bird lists for nature reserves usually contain all species ever recorded, including vagrants. One way of turning such data into useful monitoring information is to collect 'reporting rates', the proportion of observers that reported the species in the reserve. Common species will have high reporting rates, rare species lower rates. This reporting rate approach was used, with a great degree of success, to measure geographic patterns of abundance for the southern African atlas (Harrison *et al.* 1997). Such reporting rates have more than simple academic interest, as they are exactly the sort of information that ecotourist guides require: a realistic assessment of the likelihood of recording a species at a site.

Monitoring tends to be an expensive undertaking. There are a number of ways of overcoming this. One option is to reduce the sampling intensity, although this will inevitably make the results less reliable. Another approach is to use volunteers to help with the fieldwork. In the UK, many parts of northwestern Europe, southern Africa and North America, there has been a huge growth in the involvement of volunteers – 'citizen scientists' – in survey and monitoring. Compared with many other taxa, birds are mostly readily identifiable and detectable, are not so species diverse that the observer is overwhelmed, are well described in field guides and are much loved. Consequently, amateur birdwatchers are keen to become involved in survey and monitoring. The UK and North American BBSs, the UK Wetland Bird Survey and the atlases of Britain and Ireland, The Netherlands (SOVON 1987) and southern Africa all involved several thousand volunteers in data collection.

The results of any survey or monitoring scheme need to be reported. In some instances it is entirely appropriate that this is via the scientific literature. In other cases, however, especially when large numbers of volunteers are involved, feedback of results – even interim ones – is necessary on a regular basis to maintain their enthusiasm and interest. Such feedback could take the form of an annual report (e.g. Drennan 1996; Noble *et al.* 2000; Pollitt *et al.* 2000; Upton *et al.* 2000) or, increasingly, via the Internet and World Wide Web (see e.g. www.bto.org/birdtrends and www.im. nbs.gov/bbs). Undoubtedly the most sophisticated website for bird survey and monitoring information is the National Audubon Society/Cornell Laboratory of Ornithology's 'BirdSource' site (www.birdsource.cornell.edu). This is used both to disseminate bird monitoring information and collect data from observers. During 2000, more than 60,000 people submitted data on-line for the National Audubon's Great Back Yard Bird Count. Similarly, Birds Australia is collecting data for the second Australian atlas via the web (www.birdsaustralia.com.au).

Although most bird monitoring is of trends in population levels and distribution, increasingly schemes seek to monitor demographic parameters, most notably breeding success and survival. Monitoring demography can provide a forewarning of adverse population trends to come, as well as retrospectively helping to unravel the causes of population declines by highlighting the demographic mechanisms responsible. Typically, such mechanisms would be reduced adult or juvenile survival, or declining breeding success.

A widely used method for monitoring demographic parameters involves catching birds in nets under standardised conditions, for example: the

Constant Efforts Sites (CES) scheme, developed in the UK (Peach *et al.* 1996) and adopted in ten or so other European countries; the Mettnau-Reitz-Illmitz (MRI) scheme in Austria and Germany (Berthold *et al.* 1986); and the Monitoring Avian Productivity and Survival (MAPS) scheme in the USA (DeSante *et al.* 1993). For CES, bird ringers erect a set of mist-nests in the same positions, for the same length of time, during a dozen morning visits in the breeding season. Precisely the same location and times are adopted in subsequent years. Year-to-year changes in the numbers of adults caught can be used to measure population trends, while the proportion of young birds in the catch late in the season can be used to monitor changes in breeding success. Survival rates can be calculated from between-year retraps of ringed birds (e.g. Peach *et al.* 1996). Because capture probability does not vary between years, constant-effort ringing greatly simplifies survival rate analyses.

While there are numerous species-specific methods for monitoring productivity (see e.g. Gilbert *et al.* 1998), one generic method that has been adopted to monitor the breeding performance of a wide range of species is the Nest Record Scheme, initially developed in the UK (Crick & Baillie 1996). In such schemes, observers complete nest record cards for each nest they find, giving details of the nest site, contents of the nest at each visit and evidence for success or failure. From this information it is possible to calculate date of laying, clutch and brood size and daily nest failure rates, the latter using the Mayfield method (Mayfield 1961, 1975).

The Commission for the Conservation of Antarctic Marine Living Resources (CCAMLR 1992) has developed and standardised an innovative range of monitoring methods that are applied by all research stations in the Antarctic. For example, there is a protocol to estimate the parameter 'adult weight on arrival at breeding colony' for three species of *Pygoscelis* penguins. This provides an index of feeding conditions during winter. Likewise, 'chick weight at fledging' measures the feeding conditions during the breeding season. The protocols specify the sample sizes and other procedures. Motivations for, and early results from these (and other) monitoring tools can be found in Williams & Croxall (1990, 1991).

Suites of national schemes

Several countries have developed sophisticated sets of monitoring schemes, covering population, demography and distribution. Leaders in this field are probably the UK, the USA, South Africa and The Netherlands, though several other countries are close behind. Table 3.2 lists one such set of national schemes, that for the UK. Analogous schemes, sometimes identical but

Table 3.2. *Bird monitoring schemes in Britain*

Scheme	Lead partner	Others	Season	Species covered	Scope	Distbn	Popn	Demog	Start	Freq	Sample or census	Vols (V) or profs (P)
Common Birds Census (CBC)	BTO	JNCC	breeding	common, terrestrial	UK		✓		1962	1 y	sample	V
Waterways Birds Survey (WBS)	BTO	JNCC	breeding	riparian	UK		✓		1974	1 y	sample	V
Breeding Bird Survey (BBS)	BTO	JNCC, RSPB	breeding	common, terrestrial	UK	(✓)	✓		1994	1 y	sample	V
Wetland Birds Survey (WeBS)	WWT	BTO, JNCC, RSPB	non-breeding	waterfowl	UK	✓	✓		1993 (1947)	1 y	census	V
Rare Breeding Birds Panel (RBBP)	–	BB, BTO, JNCC, RSPB	breeding	rare species	UK	(✓)	✓		1973	1 y	census	V
Statutory Conservation Agencies/RSPB Annual Breeding Bird Scheme (SCARABBS)	RSPB	JNCC, EN, SNH, CCW, DoENI	breeding	'red data'	UK	(✓)	✓		1998 (1961)	1 y	variable	V & P
Seabird 2000, Seabird Colony Register, Operation Seafarer	JNCC	Seabird Group, RSPB, SOTEAG	breeding	seabirds	B & I	✓	✓		1969	15 y	census	V & P

Scheme	Org	Org	Season	Scope	Region	Distbn	Popn	Demog	Started	Freq	Method	V & P
Seabird Monitoring Programme (SMP)	JNCC	Seabird Group, RSPE, SOTEAG	breeding	seabirds	B & I	(√)	√		1986	1 y	sample	V
Breeding Atlases	BTO	IWC, SOC	breeding	all	B & I	√	(√)		1968	20 y	census	V
Winter Atlas	BTO	IWC	winter	all	B & I	√	(√)		1981	>20 y	census	V
Nest Record Scheme (NRS)	BTO	JNCC	breeding	most	UK			√	1939	1 y	sample	V
Constant Effort Sites ringing (CES)	BTO	JNCC	breeding	various	UK		(√)	√	1983	1 y	sample	V

Organisations: BTO, British Trust for Ornithology; WWT, Wildfowl and Wetlands Trust; RSPB, Royal Society for the Protection of Birds; JNCC, Joint Nature Conservation Committee; BB, *British Birds*; EN, English Nature; SNH, Scottish Natural Heritage; CCW, Countryside Council for Wales; DoENI, Department of the Environment for Northern Ireland; SOTEAG, Shetland Oil Terminal Environmental Advisory Group; IWC, Irish Wildbird Conservancy (now BirdWatch Ireland); SOC, Scottish Ornithologists' Club.

Scope: UK, United Kingdom; B & I, Britain and Ireland.

Distbn, monitoring of distributions; Popn, monitoring of populations; Demog, monitoring of demographic populations. √, measured by scheme; (√), measured by scheme in part. Freq, frequency of scheme, e.g. 1 y = annual, 20 y = every 20 years. Vols (V) or Profs (P); if V, majority of fieldwork is by volunteers; if P, majority is by professionals.

Taken from Gibbons & Avery (2001).

more often developed along similar lines, are present in the other countries mentioned.

The conservation applications of population size and trend data

As with atlas data, the conservation uses of population data are numerous. They include: species and site prioritisation, fulfilling legal obligations, understanding the causes of changing species status, monitoring environmental change, monitoring conservation actions and the generation of summary statistics ('indicators').

Species prioritisation

Population size and trend data are central to species' prioritisation exercises that have been adopted at global, continental and national levels. The widely accepted global criteria developed, and continuously up-dated by IUCN (e.g. Mace & Stuart 1994) classify species as Critically Endangered, Endangered, Vulnerable or of Lower Risk (see Chapter 4). A Critically Endangered species is, for example, one whose population has declined by at least 80% over the last 10 years (criterion A1), or whose population numbers fewer than 250 mature individuals in the wild and has declined by at least 25% over a 3-year period (criterion C1).

Two continent-wide prioritisation exercises have adopted similar criteria. Tucker & Heath (1994) classified all European birds (or at least those that were not globally threatened) as being of either favourable or unfavourable conservation status. The information used to assess this was based on their population size and extent of decline. Thus, for example, a species whose European population was 10,000 pairs or more and was not declining was considered to be in favourable conservation status, while one whose population numbered fewer than 2,500 pairs and was declining rapidly was considered to be in an unfavourable conservation status. The species' overall classification was then weighted by the proportion of the species' global population in Europe, and received a higher (more worrying) classification for a species whose population was concentrated in Europe. This assessment thus required a knowledge of population trends and sizes of each species in each European country, from which Europe-wide trends could be approximated, European populations calculated and the proportion of each species' global population in Europe estimated (Tucker & Heath 1994; Heath *et al.* 2000a).

Land bird conservation priorities in the United States have been set by the 'Partners in Flight' consortium (Beissinger *et al.* 2000; Carter *et al.* 2000). Partners in Flight (PIF) was created, in 1990, in response to the declining populations of Neotropical migratory songbirds (Askins *et al.* 1990). The PIF exercise recognised seven criteria for prioritisation, and each species was assigned a score from 1 (low priority) to 5 (high priority) for each criterion. These scores were then summed to indicate an overall conservation priority that could range from 7 to 35, from which was produced a National Watch List for the US (Pashley 1996). Two of the criteria, Relative Abundance (RA) and Population Trend (PT) were assessed for each species using North American BBS data (Robbins *et al.* 1986). RA was assessed on the mean number of birds recorded per BBS route. Thus, for example, a species with an average of 100 or more birds per route received an RA score of 1, while a species with less than one bird per route received an RA score of 5. A species PT score was based on both its population trend, and the statistical significance of the trend. Thus, for example, a species whose population had increased (or decreased) by 1% or more per annum, and whose trend was significant at the $p < 0.1$ level received a PT score of 1 (or 5). By contrast one whose population had increased (or decreased) by 1% or more per annum, but whose trend fell short of significant at the $p > 0.11$, but $p < 0.35$ level received a PT score of 2 (or 4).

Finally, Avery *et al.* (1994) and Gibbons *et al.* (1996a) provide an example of a national prioritisation exercise for birds. This assessment, 'Birds of Conservation Concern in the UK', split all species occurring in the UK into one of three classifications: red, amber or green. Red-listed species were of greatest conservation concern, deserving urgent and effective conservation action; amber-listed species were of medium concern, while green-listed species should, it was suggested, be monitored. One of the most important criteria for red-listing was if a species had undergone a population decline of 50% or more over the previous 25 years. Similarly, species that had undergone a more moderate decline of 25–49% were amber-listed. There were, however, other grounds for amber-listing, for example if the species' overall population in the UK was small, specifically 300 breeding pairs or fewer per annum. The notion of international importance was also incorporated; a species was amber-listed simply if the UK held a substantial proportion (more than 20%) of the European population.

It is clear from this brief review of species prioritisation processes at a range of geographic scales that data on population sizes and trends is fundamental to such assessments.

Site prioritisation

Though dealt with more fully in Chapter 5, some of the most important uses of population size data are in determining which sites are most important for birds and, ultimately, in designating those sites as protected areas.

Various site prioritisation exercises are based on information on population size. Examples are sites that qualify as Important Bird Areas (IBAs, e.g. Heath *et al.* 2000b) under BirdLife's IBA programme, as Ramsar sites under the Ramsar Convention, and as Special Protection Areas (SPA) under the European Union's Birds Directive (see Chapter 12). All of these assessments have used broadly similar criteria for site selection. Priority sites are those with significant populations of globally threatened species, and those that hold important congregations of, for example, migratory waterbirds or colonial-nesting seabirds. Numerical thresholds are set for each species, and sites at which one or more species pass these thresholds are included in the priority set.

One of the most widely used criteria is the 1% level. Thus, for example, a site qualifies as an IBA, SPA and Ramsar if more than 1% of the flyway population of a waterbird species congregates at that site at some time in the year. There is no more justification for this 1% criterion to measure 'significant' waterbird concentrations than there is for the tradition of using the 5% 'significance' level as a golden rule between deciding to accept or reject the null hypothesis in statistical testing. Both have evolved as sensible measures that facilitate consistent decision-making.

Legal obligations

Governments and their agencies sometimes argue that the reason bird monitoring is undertaken at all is to fulfil legal obligations. Countries within the European Union, for example, are legally obliged to locate, designate and protect the most important areas for birds and to ensure that each relevant species maintains a favourable conservation status within their country. Governments can only fulfil these obligations through survey and monitoring. This argument, however, confuses 'means' and 'ends' objectives. The 'ends' objective is to ensure favourable conservation status for as many species as possible. Imposing legal obligations on Governments is merely one of the means to this end, albeit an extremely important one.

Monitoring as research

Monitoring tells us whether a species' (or site) population is increasing, stable or declining. An entirely separate programme of research may be needed to understand the causes of a species' decline. However, if a monitoring programme is sufficiently well designed it can provide a research function. Typically, this is done by integrating environmental information alongside the bird survey and monitoring data. Donald *et al.* (2001) provide an excellent example of this, assessing whether differences in population trends of farmland birds in European countries reflected differences in their agricultural intensity (see Box 8.3, Chapter 8).

Demonstrating whether depredation has been the cause of a species' decline is not simple. Often the only way to prove a causal link is to undertake an experiment to monitor trends in populations of prey in areas in which predators have and have not been removed (see e.g. Cote & Sutherland 1996). Such experiments can prove difficult and expensive. An alternative approach can be to use long-term monitoring data. Using 30 years of bird monitoring data from several hundred CBC plots, Thomson *et al.* (1998) investigated the impact of two bird predators, the magpie (*Pica pica*) and sparrowhawk (*Accipiter nisus*), on populations of songbirds in the UK, following concerns that the declines of songbirds were linked to increases in numbers of these two predators. The authors compared population trends of 23 songbird species on CBC plots that held these predators, with those that did not. Trends of songbirds were broadly the same on CBC plots with and without these predators, providing no support for a causal link between increasing numbers of predators and declining numbers of their prey.

Davidson & Delany (2000) examined the impact of dams on waterbirds, for the International Commission on Large Dams. They used count data from the waterbird monitoring programmes in Switzerland, the UK and South Africa to undertake a desk study that enabled them to contrast bird populations on dammed and natural lakes, and to draw conclusions on the impact of large dams on waterbirds. The key point here is that no additional data needed to be collected to investigate the new problem on hand; Davidson and Delany were able to use existing data sets creatively to address these concerns.

These studies are examples of how important questions that might otherwise require a large programme of research to answer, have been investigated by the clever application of long-term population monitoring data.

A word of caution, though; when data collected for one purpose are used for other purposes, some of the niceties of statistics and the scientific method are violated. In particular, the underpinning assumptions of the theory of statistical hypothesis testing frequently do not apply. The probability values calculated from statistical tests need to be treated as guidelines and pointers, rather than absolute truth.

Applications of demographic monitoring

As discussed earlier, the monitoring of productivity and survival can allow a retrospective examination of the causes of population declines by highlighting the demographic mechanism that caused it, such as reduced survival or declining productivity. Once the demographic mechanism has been clarified, research can subsequently focus on the relevant parameter in order to understand the environmental causes of its change.

A good example of this is provided by a study of seed-eating birds on farmland in Britain (Siriwardena *et al.* 2000). In this study the annual breeding performance of a dozen granivorous bird species was analysed with respect to blocks of years during which their populations were increasing, stable or declining. The study showed that most species' population declines were not associated with poor breeding performance per attempt. Thus, for the declining turtle dove (*Streptopelia turtur*), skylark (*Alauda arvensis*), tree sparrow (*Passer montanus*), yellowhammer (*Emberiza citrinella*) and corn bunting (*Miliaria calandra*), breeding performance was actually higher during periods of population decline. It is thus tempting to conclude that if variations in breeding success are not the demographic mechanism underlying the decline of such species, then it must be caused by changes in survival, either post fledging or of first year or adult birds. Such interpretations, however, need to be tempered with caution. In this study, it was only possible to measure breeding success (e.g. clutch and brood size, and daily nest failure rates) for each individual nesting attempt. More recent studies have shown that changes in the number of nesting attempts, rather than success per attempt, may be an underlying demographic mechanism. Among turtle doves in Britain, which declined by 75% in the last quarter of the twentieth century, the number of nesting attempts per pair in the 1960s was two to three times that at the end of the twentieth century, even though the success per attempt had changed little (Miles 2000). The cause of this demographic change is unknown, but may be attributed to reduced food supplies because of the loss of weed seeds through increased herbicide use and the earlier ripening of cereals.

The wandering albatross (*Diomedea exulans*) breeding population on South Georgia declined at a rate of about 1% per annum from the early 1960s to the end of the twentieth century (Croxall *et al.* 1990). Detecting this change at a statistically significant level in such a long-lived species with low reproductive and mortality rates required nearly ten years of data, thus highlighting the importance of long-term data. Similar declines have occurred elsewhere, such that the species is considered Globally Threatened.

Using long-term monitoring data from South Georgia on breeding success, breeding frequency and survival and recruitment rates, Croxall *et al.* (1990) were able to determine the demographic mechanism underlying this population decline. Over the period, breeding success actually increased (by 1.2% per annum) while breeding frequency remained constant. By contrast, recruitment into the breeding population fell from 36% (of a cohort) in the 1960s to 30% in the late 1980s, while adult survival fell from about 96% to 94% over the same period. Although small, these changes alone were sufficient to account for the observed population decline.

Not only did this study reveal the demographic mechanism: it also found the cause of the changes in recruitment and survival. Wandering albatrosses are frequently caught as an incidental by-catch of long-line fishing for tuna. This fishery accounted for an annual mortality of 2–3% of adults and 14–25% of juveniles from the South Georgia population. This was easily sufficient to establish the long-line fishery as the single most important cause of death of the South Georgian albatrosses, and the most likely cause of the population decline. Similar studies carried out over the past three or four decades at Crozet and Kerguelen Islands in the Indian Ocean indicate that a population decline there was mainly the result of increased adult mortality, and secondarily of low recruitment (Weimerskirch *et al.* 1997). Satellite tracking of breeding birds and ring recoveries of non-breeding birds showed that these birds foraged in areas in which Japanese long-line fisheries were operating. This study showed that the rate of decline of each of five wandering albatross populations was closely correlated with the number of long-line fish hooks set in the central foraging area of each population; more hooks led to faster rates of decline.

Monitoring of the environment

Birds can be excellent monitors of the changing environment. Furness & Greenwood (1993) give a useful review of this subject; here we provide a few recent examples of the use of birds as monitors of environmental change. Examples of birds as monitors of climate change are provided in Chapter 8.

Operating on a suggestion that the preferred prey of cape gannets (*Morus capensis*) was the sardine (*Sardinops sagax*), scientists at the marine fisheries research unit in Cape Town set up a gannet diet monitoring programme in 1977; the project is still continuing. Diet samples can easily be obtained by non-destructive methods. Monthly diet samples are obtained from two breeding colonies; birds are readily caught with a gannet hook as soon as they have landed after feeding, are inverted over a bucket, and regurgitate the stomach contents. The sardine fishery off South Africa collapsed. Berruti *et al.* (1993) demonstrated that a recovery of the sardine was detected in the gannet diet before it was detected in conventional acoustic surveys conducted by expensive fisheries research cruises. The monitoring of gannet diets provided a variety of other insights relevant to the fishing industry that were not detected by ship-borne instruments. The gannet diet study thus monitors not only the diet of the birds, but is a useful tool for managers of the fishery in the extremely complex and unstable Benguela ecosystem for monitoring and understanding patterns in fish biodiversity.

Another apparently bizarre form of monitoring consists of patrolling the shoreline for dead seabirds. Feathers absorb oil readily, and beached seabirds that are oiled need not have died because of being oiled at sea, but have picked up the oil as they drifted to shore. The proportion of dead seabirds in regular beach patrols thus provides one of the most sensitive measures available to estimate the extent of oil spills at sea, and is far cheaper than any other form of survey, either by ship or by aircraft. The shortcoming of beach patrols is that the lag between a spill and birds being found with oil on the beach is too long to be able to locate the culprits. The value of beach patrols for dead seabirds is that they can provide an index of long-term trends in oil pollution (e.g. Furness & Camphuysen 1997; Camphuysen 1998).

Neither of these long-term studies was set up to monitor environmental change; both, however, do so in one way or another.

Monitoring of conservation actions

As outlined earlier, monitoring needs to be built into all conservation actions, otherwise we have no measure of their impact. In addition, if the monitoring is designed suitably, it can be used to further improve these actions.

A good example is provided by the monitoring of the recovery of cirl bunting (*Emberiza cirlus*) populations in the UK (Peach *et al.* 2001). The cirl bunting is a small seed-eating farmland bird that suffered a major decline in population and contraction of range during the twentieth century (A.D. Evans 1997a). Research indicated that low intensity mixed farming provides cirl buntings with two key foraging habitats: rough or semi-improved grasslands as a source of invertebrate prey in summer, and weedy cereal stubbles as a source of seed in winter (A.D. Evans 1997b). To halt the decline of this species, an agri-environment scheme, the Countryside Stewardship Scheme (CSS), was tailored to meet the needs of this species and introduced within its range in southwest England. The CSS provides payments to landowners who manage their land for cirl buntings in a number of ways, principally by introducing low-intensity grazed grassland and weedy winter barley stubbles.

Monitoring showed that this conservation action was extremely successful; cirl bunting numbers increased by 83% on land entering CSS agreements between 1992 and 1998, compared with an increase of just 2% on adjacent countryside not managed under CSS. Further analyses (Peach *et al.* 2001) confirmed the results of the earlier research and showed that those agreements that provided grass margins around arable fields gained cirl buntings, while those that lacked winter barley stubbles remained uncolonised. Interestingly, the analysis also showed that CSS agreements that were more than 2 km away from extant populations of cirl buntings remained uncolonised, irrespective of how well the habitat had been managed for them. While the mechanism for this is undoubtedly the highly sedentary nature of the species, it does allow conservation actions to be targeted more exactly; there is no point entering land into a CSS agreement if it is more than 2 km away from the nearest cirl bunting population.

Indicators

Bird population monitoring provides a great wealth of data: long-term trends for many species across a wide geographical area. Although ornithologists and conservationists may be fascinated by such trends, politicians and their advisors will be unmoved unless this mass of data can be summarised into simple statistics that can be understood readily by them and members of the public alike. If they are not, then other environmental statistics, such as air and water quality, will be used to monitor Governmental environmental policy, overlooking their impacts on wildlife. To this end, highly summarised statistics of bird population trends have recently been developed (Bibby 1999).

An indicator based on highly summarised bird population trend data has become one of the UK Government's 15 headline indicators of

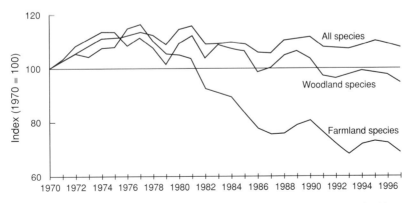

Fig. 3.1. The UK Government's headline wildlife indicator: populations of wild birds. (Anon 1999a.)

sustainable development and the 'Quality of Life' (Anon. 1999a). This indicator sits in a small set, most of which measure more traditional social, economic and environmental trends, such as life expectancy, educational qualifications and river quality. The 'wild bird index' (Fig. 3.1) is a summary of the population trends of 139 of the more common native species that breed in the UK (Gregory et al. 1999). The index for each group of species (all species, or farmland and woodland species separately) was constructed by aggregating the individual population indices, each based on 1970 = 100, with each species given equal weight in the index. The index was constructed using a logarithmic transformation of each species series and then taking the exponential of the average to form the overall index. This transformation was necessary because of the skewed nature of the distributions (i.e. because species can only decline by 100%, but can increase infinitely). Populations of birds in a group whose index rose from 100 to 200 will have doubled, on average, while those whose index fell from 100 to 50 will have halved. As is clear from this indicator, populations of birds on farmland have declined markedly in the UK since the mid-1970s. The UK Government has committed itself to reversing these declines by 2020, and will use this indicator to assess its performance.

4

Priority-setting in species conservation

GEORGINA M. MACE & NIGEL J. COLLAR

INTRODUCTION

Problems in the environment are recognised long in advance of solutions; and since money tends to be parted with only when compelling evidence of an effective solution is presented, it is an inevitable circumstance – or at least perception – that the resources available for conservation are always fewer than the number of issues for which they are judged to be needed. It follows that priorities have to be set.

The move towards setting priorities in conservation began with formal initiatives to record and rank species threatened with extinction. Red Data Books, which undertook this documentation, were first produced within IUCN in the early 1960s (Scott *et al.* 1987). Over the ensuing 30 years the IUCN Red Data Book programme, except for birds, was regrettably replaced by a simple Red List (Collar 1996), although Red Data Books have continued to be central to planning at national levels, and the proliferation of such books in the past 30 years has been remarkable (Burton 1984; hence Gärdenfors *et al.* 1999). Since conservation actions directed at species are nearly always directed at their habitats, a logical consequence was the rapid growth in priority-setting systems directed at areas. One simple and cost-effective solution was to identify key areas of overlap between threatened species (Collar & Stuart 1988; Wege & Long 1995). However, the paucity of high-resolution distribution data for species other than birds has limited this approach and much attention has been afforded to the development and use of indicator or surrogate measures (see Chapter 5). In the 1980s and 1990s, algorithms and computing power combined to take area-based priority-setting to a level of sophistication which species-based approaches have never matched (Pressey *et al.* 1996, 1997; Csuti *et al.* 1997; Margules & Pressey 2000) (see Chapter 5).

In this same period, increasing awareness of the relevance of environmental management for economic growth and development caused an appreciation of the value of explicit conservation planning. Such planning became formalised through legal instruments at both national and international levels. The most important of the latter was the Convention on Biological Diversity (CBD), which requires countries that are signatories to make plans for the conservation of their own biological diversity. As a result, many governmental environment agencies began to develop more explicit approaches to biodiversity conservation, often supported by non-government organisations (NGOs) (Wynne 1998). Such approaches emphasise the importance of setting targets and goals, and of developing policies and plans that enable the targets to be met. However, while much thought has been given to planning methods and decision analyses (Margules & Pressey 2000), rather less has been given to the problematic nature of the decisions that have to be made with respect to species. This is perhaps surprising, since species-based approaches are at the heart of biodiversity conservation, and provide the philosophical starting points for many conservation plans. However, any review of the methods and merits of different species-based approaches must be prefaced by a review of certain key factors which frame the analysis but which rarely receive the attention they deserve, even though they bear significantly on the results.

CONTEXT: SCALE, SCOPE, SPECIES CONCEPTS AND OBJECTIVES

The scale and scope of the priority-setting to be undertaken are perhaps the most fundamental considerations. They can reflect two kinds of axes: geographical or political, and taxonomic or biotic. So, priority-setting can be done globally, regionally, nationally or (at several levels) subnationally; and it can include all species, or some taxonomic subset (e.g. all birds, all vertebrates), or some other biotic subdivision (e.g. all terrestrial vertebrates, all freshwater invertebrates, etc.). Hence, of course, it can be done in various combinations of these hierarchical levels – all species in Bavaria, all birds in the world, Galliformes in Asia, pheasants in China, and so on. This scaling down is in many ways both desirable and inevitable. Conservation actions, education programmes, legislation and enforcement are all much more effective at local scales. However, taken to extremes the trend to localisation presents both difficulties and conflicts. Local conservation priorities do not necessarily translate up at larger scales, and the lack of a 'big-picture' view can result in some important priorities being missed (see e.g. Mares 1992).

Scaled-down exercises also have the scope – because addressing self-containing subjects, with no apparent impact outside themselves – to modify widely adopted standards and techniques to suit their context (e.g. by the adoption of a different classification principle). They also often have an advantage for interested parties – people or institutions with biases towards particular areas or species – and this may drive both the exercise itself and the funding and implementation of the resulting proposed actions. It must therefore be obvious that, as these exercises become more restricted in geographical and biological scale, so they risk yielding results that are increasingly idiosyncratic and difficult to reconcile. As a consequence, conflicts of interest arise. While the most frequent complaint is that scaled-down exercises get ignored in dominant 'bigger-picture' studies, it is also true that sectorally-linked funding agencies can push through their priorities (at least a queue-jump and at worst a hijack) long before those identified through a more dispassionate evaluation of a more extensive suite of candidates. Since there is not now, and is unlikely ever to be, a single global authority for biodiversity priorities, resolving this kind of conflict of interests is a far-off target.

A second decision relates to taxonomy, particularly in exercises where species have been identified as the unit of concern. In recent years, there has been a growing academic interest in determining species limits through explicit cladistic methods based around parsimony and the distributions of shared characters – the so-called phylogenetic species concept (PSC) (see Zink 1997). These methods have challenged the biological species concept (BSC), where species limits are determined by patterns of geographic distribution and reproductive isolation (Mayr 1940, 1942). The PSC tends to reject subspecies, recognising all diagnosably distinct taxa outside clines as species. In theory, therefore, the PSC avoids the arbitrariness with which the BSC ascribes hierarchical status to forms in which geographic isolation prevents the test of reproductive isolation. However, an important consequence of the general adoption of the PSC will be to increase species numbers considerably (e.g. Cracraft 1992) – among birds in general probably by a factor of over two (Zink 1997) to approximately 20,000. It will also reconfigure priority taxa lists. For example, a recent revision of the albatrosses raised the number of species in the family from 14 to 24 (Robertson & Nunn 1997), although on further advice BirdLife International (2000) admitted only 21. Even so, under the old taxonomy the number of species threatened with extinction would have been 11, whereas under this new arrangement the number is 16 (A.J. Stattersfield *in litt.* 2001). An increase in the number of threatened species will not be the only consequence; in Mexico, a new species concept identified new areas high in country-endemics, which might therefore become high priority conservation areas (Peterson & Navarro-Siguënza 1999). A major increase in the number of PSC 'species' requiring evaluation and conservation may be inconvenient and unwelcome to already overstretched evaluators and conservationists, but is not a good reason to reject the concept. However, the fact that the great majority of the 'new' species will be near-identical taxa certainly is a drawback, since it can be predicted that pressure will mount from various quarters for a list of species that better reflects evolutionary distinctiveness (Collar 1997). Moreover, in practice the PSC is no less arbitrary, albeit at a finer scale, than the BSC, often resulting in highly unstable, somewhat inconsistent and frequently controversial faunal listings, with serious implications for national and international legislation (Collar 1997; Snow 1997).

However this debate is resolved – we set out our view in the final section–the problem of subspecies will not be removed overnight. Subspecies are difficult because they tend to be ephemeral entities (accepted, rejected, disputed or merged by different taxonomists), their ranges are often badly known, and they frequently reflect only very minor levels of distinctiveness (slightly paler colour of a feather, slightly longer wing, etc.). Their unquestioned acceptance into priority-setting exercises can lead (as with their elevation to species under the PSC) to some serious inequalities with respect to individual evolutionary history. Their omission, on the other hand, can lead (as with their submergence under the BSC) to an elevated risk of extinction through simple lack of awareness. However, it has long since been pointed out that a very large proportion of subspecies share habitat with threatened species, and that the preservation of the latter's habitat almost certainly benefits the former in equal measure. Moreover, scope exists to identify those subspecies that fall outside this pattern and to make the case at least at the national level for the preservation of such forms (Collar 1997; see also Collar et al. 1999, pp. 37-39).

A third decision concerns the *object* of the priority-setting. Targets that aim to increase the total diversity of species within a country almost certainly predicate different actions from targets that aim to increase the long-term viability of existing species. The former would require countries to devote resources to increasing the number of species that are recorded there (perhaps by re-establishment of recently extinct or non-breeding species); the latter would dictate actions to increase the population size and improve reproductive success of the most threatened species or those exhibiting the greatest declines in abundance. Similarly, there may be tension between creating long lists of species, all of which are monitored and mapped, versus short lists that are all the objects of some kind of intensive management.

A consideration so obvious that its influence in decision-making tends to be forgotten is *feasibility*, the main determinants of which are political and financial. Forests on the Scarp of Angola were ranked as high in importance by Collar & Stuart (1988) as that on Mount Oku (Kilum) in Cameroon, but while the latter has benefited from a long-term ICDP (integrated conservation and development project) since that time, the former have languished as Angola continues to endure the torment of civil war. For many years, the kagu (*Rhynochetos jubatus*) in New Caledonia emerged as the highest avian conservation priority, based on degree of endangerment multiplied by taxonomic uniqueness, but political instability, coupled with very high costs on the island, deterred interest in pursuing the matter. Many other islands in the Pacific are even more prohibitively expensive to work in; and several other countries or areas around the world continue to remain outside the ambit of conservation attention owing to problems of regime, insurgency, and so on.

Finally, it needs to be stressed that because priority-setting is based on information, and because information is a resource that is constantly changing, priority-setting itself must be understood as a *process*, subject to constant modification and upgrading. The level of assumption present in this process is higher than most people suspect, and one of the stated priorities in any priority-setting exercise must be for the process to engender a self-optimising component that seeks to recognise and, over time, minimise uncertainty. Rather than regarding uncertainty as an inconvenience and attempting to hide it, we recommend newer approaches that embrace uncertainty and deal with it explicitly in planning excercises (Taylor *et al.* 1996; Todd & Burgman 1998; Akçakaya *et al.* 2000).

KINDS OF PRIORITY

Deciding on priorities can appear straightforward and there are many published systems and lists. Surprisingly, rather few of these discuss or justify the system that they use and almost all published systems use traits or combinations of traits (see Table 4.1). Here we outline the different systems that have been applied, and briefly review their merits and demerits.

Probably the commonest measure of priority is the severity of the threat the species is facing. Usually this is translated into the relative likelihood of extinction. The IUCN Red List continues to be a standard source, with categories of threat reflecting an increasing severity of extinction risk (Vulnerable, Endangered, etc.) (Fitter & Fitter 1987). Despite a common nomenclature, this system has in fact evolved over time from subjective, 'expert-led' assessments of a subset of species to an explicit, quantitative system that aims to be both comprehensive and systematic (Mace & Lande

Table 4.1. *Summary of traits recommended or used for between-species priority-setting*

Trait used for priority-setting among species	Priority given to	References
Severity of threat/ extinction risk	Most threatened species	Collar & Stuart 1985
Recent decline rate	Most depleted in recent years	Siriwardena *et al.* 1998
	Most depleted and trends in declines	Fewster *et al.* 2000
	Most depleted and importance (proportion of regional population	Tucker & Heath 1994
	Declines in extent of occurrence	McGowan & Gillman 1997
Rarity	Low population density	Terborgh & Winter 1980; Poulsen & Krabbe 1997
	Low population density, rare habitat types, small extent of occurrence	Kattan 1992; Reed 1992
Endemism	Species restricted to a particular region	ICBP 1992; Peterson *et al.* 2000
Restricted range	Species with small global distributions	Bibby 1998
Range size rarity	Areas with most restricted ranges of species	Williams *et al.* 1996
Evolutionary uniqueness	Species with most unique characters	Vane-Wright *et al.* 1991
	Species with greatest genetic distinctiveness	Crozier 1992; Nee & May 1997
	Species in clades undergoing evolutionary radiations	Erwin 1991
Phenotypic traits	Maximising diversity of phenotypic traits	Owens & Bennett 2000b
Protection status	Species poorly represented in protected areas	Scott *et al.* 1993; Cassidy *et al.* 2001
Land use change	Species in areas susceptible to destruction	Menon *et al.* 2001
Ecosystem role	Species important in ecosystem, e.g. as pollinators	Allen-Wardell *et al.* 1998
Multi-species interactions	Maximal phylogenetic diversity within a set of interacting species	Witting *et al.* 2000
Regional status	Highest priority within a region	Dinerstein & Wikramanayake 1993; Avery *et al.* 1995; Berg & Tjernberg 1996; Freitag & van Jaarsveld 1997

1991; IUCN 1994). However, while the system for placing species into categories of threat was evolving, the Red Data Book concept from which the system grew itself deteriorated from being a comprehensive review of information on the conservation status of species to simple lists of species compiled from networks of experts (Collar 1996). Consequently, whereas the original approach outlined key circumstances affecting a species' threatened status and allowed conservation to be appropriately addressed, the newer lists simply present relative assessments of the threat level. This is insufficient for prioritising conservation actions. Threat level is clearly a necessary element in priority-setting, but on its own, and as it is currently used, the system is too coarse-grained and does not incorporate other important elements such as feasibility, reversibility and relationships with other species.

Assessing the severity of threat facing a species can be done in a variety of ways ranging from the subjective, expert-led assessments described above, through various rule-based and scoring systems to the outcomes of explicit population viability analyses (PVA). Any of these approaches has both positive and negative aspects, and the best method to use will depend on the quality and quantity of information on the species and the purpose of the analysis. For example, using PVAs for large-scale species-based analyses would be problematic, because of the considerable data needs for robust PVAs (Beissinger & Westphal 1998; Brook *et al.* 2000; Coulson *et al.* 2001; see also Chapter 9), but probably also unnecessary since the desired outcome is for a simple ranking on which to build further plans. On the other hand, while the simpler systems may give relatively robust rankings between species, they are unlikely to give precise estimates of risk for any one species (Mace & Hudson 1999).

All kinds of extinction risk assessments have some drawbacks in terms of their predictive accuracy (Taylor 1995; Beissinger & Westphal 1998; Ludwig 1999; Coulson *et al.* 2001), and an alternative explicit approach has been to use recent rates of decline as a measure of priority. In its simplest manifestation, species can be categorised as increasing, decreasing or stable (Tucker & Heath 1994) – information that can be quite easily gathered for large numbers of species over large areas. Slightly increased precision is introduced by classifying species into categories according to the percentage decline in a specified period. For example, Gibbons *et al.* (1996b) used three decline rate categories over a 25-year period to assess decline rates of British birds from census data. This approach has the advantage of being both simple and quantitative, and of leading to measurable targets to assess the effectiveness of conservation actions. Furthermore, it complements a structured approach to devising conservation actions based on the analysis of causes of decline in a species (Green 1995; see also Chapter 7) or among sets of species (Siriwardena *et al.* 1998). These latter examples have used the exceptional data on distribution and abundance for United Kingdom birds, but a related approach has been developed for less well known avifaunas using locality data from both museum records and sightings. The point data can be converted to an extent of occurrence and the reduction in a species' extent of occurrence used to assess relative priorities (McGowan & Gillman 1997).

Although threat analyses are commonly applied, many other single-species traits have been used for priority-setting. Genetic variability within species is a source of evolutionary innovation, and either populations showing high levels might be favoured (Kark *et al.* 1999), or areas such as ecotones, which are associated with high variability, might be high priorities (T.B. Smith *et al.* 1993; Siriwardena *et al.* 1998). Genetic data can also be used to identify conservation units for management and to assess recent demographic changes – equivalent to assessing decline rates (Moritz 1994a, 1999; Crandall *et al.* 2000). 'Rare' species have long received attention from both conservationists and naturalists and, despite the apparent simplicity of this as a concept and its close relationship to conservation goals, both the assessment and management of 'rare' species are fraught with difficulties (Gaston 1994). Rarity can be measured by a species' overall or local abundance, its overall or local range area or its habitat specialisation, and each of these is distributed continuously so that arbitrary cut-offs must be used to identify 'rare' species (Rabinowitz *et al.* 1986; Gaston 1994). In fragmented woodlots in São Paulo state, Brazil, the birds that had gone extinct locally were all either extreme specialists or low-abundance species (Terborgh & Winter 1980). Various authors have suggested using the scheme of Rabinowitz *et al.* (1986) to determine priorities, though not necessarily in the same way (see Kattan 1992; Reed 1992). However, the utility of this approach appears limited. The three axes of rarity tend to co-vary so as to make it likely that species share rarity in its different forms, and may not represent other attributes of species or habitats that are important, such as threat intensity or ecological structure (Swain 1995; Poulsen & Krabbe 1997). A relationship between rarity and threat certainly exists, but it is not absolute. Rarity is a natural feature of many species' life histories and, while they might be vulnerable and therefore require protection, there is no sensible objective to stop them being rare. Species that are rare but were once common are a different matter, and it remains an open question whether or not some species are adapted to rarity and therefore persist in this state for longer than those reduced to it by recent anthropogenic events (Lawton 1995). To complicate matters further, some rare species are judged to be relics of previously wide-ranging forms now restricted to suboptimal habitats (Thiollay & Probst 1999), making it unlikely that they will respond to site-specific conservation actions.

Endemism is another commonly applied trait in priority-setting that is defined in various ways. Most simply it refers to species that are restricted to a particular locality, although the locality may vary from a single habitat or small island to an entire country or even continent. In some area-based analyses, its quantification is confounded with the range area of species in a locality, making it a combination of both range size and rarity (Williams *et al.* 1996). At various spatial scales, endemic species tend to be aggregated in particular areas (ICBP 1992; Fjeldså 2000), and this circumstance can be used to identify biodiversity 'hotspots', which are increasingly advocated as a general target for conservation actions (Myers *et al.* 2000). However, areas of high endemism may not reflect other important attributes, such as threat or evolutionary diversification, and may be unstable under altered species concepts (Peterson & Navarro-Siguënza 1999; Fjeldså 2000). Endemics are clearly high priorities for regional conservation plans, on which their persistence depends, but over large areas, a single focus on endemics can result in a skewed distribution of effort, with areas of high richness or threat being under-represented.

Not all species are equal. From an evolutionary perspective, species that represent a long history of independent evolution, such as single representatives of a family or genus, or those found at the tips of long phylogenetic branches, might be afforded a higher value than those that are members of large genera or families, or part of a 'bushy' clade (Vane-Wright *et al.* 1991). In theory, with a cladogram or a dated phylogeny, the relative contribution of each species to the overall evolution of an entire clade can easily be quantified and used in priority-setting (Crozier 1992). The difficulty arises over how this information is best applied. While the most intuitively obvious approach is to favour the long branch species with all their unique evolution (Vane-Wright *et al.* 1991; Crozier 1992; Nee & May 1997), these species are by definition the ones that have failed to radiate and adapt to prevailing conditions – they may in reality be the last relics of an evolutionary lineage that is in decline and nearing total extinction. In the face of a changing world, therefore, it is regularly argued that conservation actions might better be focused on the species associated with successful lineages that have shown the ability to adapt and diversify into a range of available niches – those at the evolutionary fronts (Erwin 1991; Soltis & Gitzendanner 1999). The drawback here is that such a strategy could simply be to support outcomes that will occur without any interventions – and increase the relative number of 'weedy' species generalists at the expense of highly adapted niche specialists.

Finally, there is a range of other kinds of values that have been suggested for priority-setting exercises, some of which are highly specific to particular interests or perspectives, for example, maintaining an overall range of particular phenotypic traits (Owens & Bennett 2000b), maximising productivity (Vermeij 1993), minimising costs to achieve a certain target (Ando *et al.* 1998), minimising extinction risk among a set of interacting species (Witting *et al.* 2000), and focusing on species ('flagships') that are of particular social, aesthetic or economic value. All of these may have merit within a particular context, but in general simply raise another question about why these particular attributes should be more highly rated than fundamental values such as are measured by species counts or evolutionary distinctiveness.

One significant but difficult area of priority-setting relates to those species upon which other species or even whole communities depend. Some such 'cornerstone' or 'keystone' species are easily recognised – for example, hornbills as dispersers of figs, or hummingbirds as the sole pollinators of particular plants. However, there appear to be some species that are more important than others to ecosystem stability and productivity, although in many cases these may not be particularly obvious (e.g. those at the highest trophic levels or the most abundant or widespread) (Power *et al.* 1996; Purvis & Hector 2000). As a conservation target, therefore, this principle has practical difficulties but it should not be forgotten.

Perhaps the most obvious conclusion from this discussion is that there is no single measure on which priorities should unequivocally be based (although as the scale of the exercise approaches global, so the measure of threat is likely to rise in importance). We should not be surprised: for nor is there a single way of measuring or valuing biodiversity overall (Purvis & Hector 2000), and our difficulties here simply reflect the fact that there are multiple goals of biodiversity conservation that may be used by planners. The problem has been widely recognised, and planners have responded to it in two major ways. Some have recognised that there are many, different and often not well correlated variables that need to be taken into account, and they have developed quantitative point-scoring systems that attempt to summarise a range of different measures. Others have focused only on the criteria that seem, in their own specific context, to be of overwhelming importance, and have ignored the multiplicity of possible alternatives (Margules & Pressey 2000; Jepson & Canney 2001).

USING MULTIPLE MEASURES

At regional levels, there have been numerous instances where point-scoring systems have been developed to quantify conservation priorities, taking into account a range of significant parameters. The range of parameters is broad but characteristically includes endemism, protection status, population size and perhaps human-related measures such as threat and values (Mace 1994). All these variables can be scored, their scores weighted and an overall value determined from their sum or multiple. Some highly elaborate systems exist (Millsap *et al.* 1990), while others include only a few variables (Dinerstein & Wikramanayake 1993; Freitag & van Jaarsveld 1997), but all are appealing since they imply a quantitative and objective assessment of elements, minimise the influence of special interests, and result in a clear ranking of species.

Nevertheless, we believe that this approach can be quite misleading. First, many of the variables included are positively correlated with one another, while others are negatively correlated and still others are completely independent. The final score for a species may well be highest for a species that scores at a midpoint on many variables – the priority then being a species that does not meet any particular objective. This cannot be what was intended. Second, different variables may be explicitly or implicitly weighted differently. Explicit weightings may be used when a particular trait is felt to be of great importance, and may be introduced *post hoc* when a system fails to deliver the 'right' kind of result. Implicit weightings can result when many independent variables are positively related, or when for reasons of convenience one variable is scored on a longer scale (e.g. 1 to 10) than another (e.g. 1 to 5). In either case, the weighting is driving the assessment and may or may not reflect what the assessors really intend to measure. Finally, and most fundamentally, this approach results in a set of ranked priorities that have no clear relationship to goals, targets or conservation actions. Therefore, it will be impossible to assess the success of plans put in place as a result of the priority-setting exercise.

Ideally, planners would determine one or two clear objectives at the outset and base the entire planning cycle around them (Margules & Pressey 2000). Unfortunately, there are usually several considerations and, with multiple stakeholders, it can be very difficult to reduce to one or two measures. However, we suggest that the parameters of interest are reduced to the smallest number of unrelated variables that can then be scored independently. Then, instead of producing a composite score, the precise situation for each combination of scores is considered in terms of the kinds of conservation actions it requires. For example, Avery *et al.* (1995) scored bird species as high, medium or low according to three variables, global threat, regional threat and importance in the region, which gives a total of 27 possible states for a species. Although the overall scores might be the same if added, allowance was made for priorities to be different for species with high global threat than for those with high regional threat. Therefore each of the 27 states is considered independently and the appropriate conservation priority determined for each. Similarly, Menon *et al.* (2001) scored areas high or low for both protection status and future vulnerability and prescribed appropriate actions according to which of the four possible states an area may have.

This kind of approach seems to us to be more relevant in most circumstances, and has the advantage that it forces some clear strategies to be considered, leads to appropriate and relevant actions, and provides for the objective evaluation of the success of those measures. However, getting to this point is not easy and depends critically on a thoughtful analysis of what exactly the priority-setting is intended to achieve.

PRIORITY-SETTING FOR WHAT?

Priority-setting is a necessary process in the development of a non-random response to environmental problems, and it can be seen as serving a sequence of purposes. Primarily its role is to identify, rationalise, rank and fix the programme of practical actions to be undertaken by the institution that commissioned the exercise. Second, it frames the fund-raising strategy of the commissioning institution, and therefore aims to demonstrate rigour (comprehensiveness, detail, system) and hence merit to the programme's anticipated sponsors (which then release money both to the institution and to the priority targets). Third, it also seeks to fix the programme as far as possible in the agendas of *other* conservation institutions, as a means of spreading the load and buying in further resources.

It is important to recognise that priority-setting is therefore a sectoral exercise, and inevitably reflects the preferences and predispositions of the commissioning institution, including (almost inevitably) the way in which the institution contemplates its funding opportunities. The strengths of priority-setting may be obvious; but its latent weaknesses become most apparent when the link to sponsors is made. The fact is that priority-setting is seriously problematic and potentially divisive, with each commissioning institution promoting the merits of its own rationale, methods and data sets, but none comfortable to admit the limitations of its own exercise or, worse, the actively competitive and aggressive position underlying the adoption of its results. Inevitably, however, priority-setting involves both the conscious and unwitting exclusion of species, phenomena, habitats and issues which do not fit the declared remit of the commissioning institution. 'The hotspots approach is more comprehensive than the first two [priority-setting analyses]', wrote Myers *et al.* (2000), 'because it combines five categories of species, and it is more closely focused than the third' – thereby, in a single sententious remark, very publicly consigning three other painstaking, expensive and long-term institutional reviews to the margins of relevance.

What biodiversity conservation most urgently needs now – its highest priority, perhaps – is agreement among the major priority-setting institutions on the global agenda (Mace *et al.* 2000). This can only be achieved by accepting the sectoral nature of priorities and by seeking to integrate them in a manner that builds common ownership and increases their status as the most objective and comprehensive suite of remedies available. Work is urgently needed to develop systems for achieving this synergy. Such behaviour is, of course, required throughout the priority-setting universe, and it applies equally to taxonomic matters, where the best way forward is clearly through a mutual accommodation (Avise 2000). Certainly the steady 'unlumping' of the world's avifauna, which has been in progress for perhaps 20 years, and which has been given important momentum by proponents of the PSC, will result in a distinct upturn in the number of broadly recognised species, even under the BSC; the Asian avifauna, for example, might be expected to increase its species complement by 5–10% (N.J. Collar, unpublished data).

In ideal circumstances, flexibility needs to be built into any priority-setting procedure not only to take cognisance of other such exercises, but also to accommodate new information and to acknowledge the central role played by opportunity in conservation. We have seen how considerations of political and logistical feasibility, and the plain matter of cost, can completely subvert a hierarchy of priorities based solely on biological criteria; equally, however, unusually favourable circumstances can arise which propel relatively lowly projects to the head of the queue. There *are* no unambiguous answers to the priority-setting process, but instead there is the need for the broadest possible consensus and ownership. What is *not* appropriate, of course, is that this process should become so flexible that it allows opportunity to dominate biologically determined priorities. Once that happens, the institution in question starts to assume the identity of an environmental consultancy.

5

Selecting sites for conservation

ANDREW BALMFORD

INTRODUCTION

Over the past decade, the issue of identifying where we might best focus limited conservation resources has received enormous attention from conservation practitioners and academics alike. The result has been an impressive raft of real-world priority schemes (see Box 5.1, p. 77), the development of powerful techniques for systematic site selection, and the collation of several substantial data sets to which these tools can be applied. This chapter aims to review these developments, examining how priorities are currently set, and exploring how prioritisation might be further improved in future. The focus throughout is on identifying priority areas for conservation (rather than priority species, as in Chapter 4) – with a particular emphasis on the identification of the most appropriate sites for reservation (rather than on the wider landscape issues addressed in Chapters 8 and 10). For an excellent account of how the selection of priority sites fits into a broader framework of conservation planning, including the design, management and subsequent monitoring of conservation areas, see the review by Margules & Pressey (2000).

I begin by considering why prioritisation is necessary, before outlining the importance of establishing *a priori* the goals and scale of any priority-setting exercise. The bulk of the chapter then sets out a series of biological and human-linked concerns that need to be addressed in selecting priority sites, and examines how recent theoretical tools and real-world priority schemes tackle these concerns. Wherever possible, these examples deal with birds, but in the next section I consider the crucial question for bird conservation organisations of how far focusing on priority areas for birds is likely to help conserve biodiversity in other taxa as well. The chapter closes with a brief overview of some of the challenges that lie ahead if priority-setting is to realise its full potential for helping conservationists maximise the impact of their field activities.

WHY WE NEED TO IDENTIFY PRIORITY AREAS FOR CONSERVATION

Two fundamental facts dictate that conservationists must be prudent in deciding where to conserve. First, biodiversity is in deep trouble – indeed, a comparison with background extinction levels suggests that humans are now driving species to extinction at a rate unprecedented since the end of the last mass extinction event, 65 million years ago (Pimm *et al.* 1995). According to the latest IUCN Red List, 12% of all bird species are already threatened with global extinction in the short to medium term (BirdLife International 2000); rates of loss of populations are of course far higher (Hughes *et al.* 1997). Moreover, both genetic and phenotypic diversity are being eroded more rapidly than the species figure suggests, given that threatened species are disproportionately concentrated in small, phylogenetically and phenotypically distinct genera (McDowall 1967; Gaston & Blackburn 1997; Hughes 1999; Russell *et al.* 1999; Owens & Bennett 2000b; Purvis *et al.* 2000). One other sobering thought is that birds are probably among the least threatened of all groups: by comparison, threat rates for thoroughly assessed freshwater groups in North America run at 39–68% of all species (The Nature Conservancy 1997).

A second reason why prioritisation is essential is that, while establishing and maintaining protected areas can be tremendously valuable in stemming the loss of biodiversity (Brandon *et al.* 1998; Oates 1999; Terborgh 1999), we clearly cannot hope to reserve all remaining natural habitat. The human population is likely to rise above 10 billion before 2100 (Lutz *et al.* 1997) and per capita consumption rates seem set to grow even faster (Ehrlich 1994; Czech 2000). Currently, around 7.9% of the Earth's land surface lies in some form of protected area (IUCN 1998). Being realistic about both the amount of land that will be required for future food production (Musters *et al.* 2000), and the level of financial resources required to offset the immediate, local-scale opportunity costs of strict reservation (James *et al.* 1999; Godoy *et al.* 2000), it seems unlikely that reserve networks will expand beyond, at most, 15% of land area in the coming century. Application of the classic species area relationship ($S = cA^z$, with z set to a conservative value of 0.25) tells us that if those reserves are selected non-systematically, then even if they were contiguous with each other they would probably

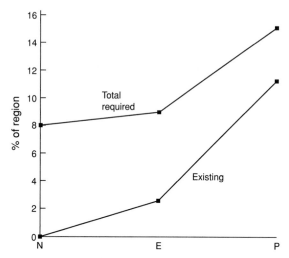

Fig. 5.1. An example of *ad hoc* reserve selection. The extent of existing reserves, and the total reserve area required to represent 5% of each land system in the Western Division of New South Wales, both expressed as percentages of the total land area. Area required is identified from a complementarity-based algorithm, (N) starting from the pre-1960 situation of no reserves, (E) starting with all reserves existing in 1993, and (P) starting with all existing and proposed reserves in 1993. Existing reserves do little to reduce the amount of extra land required to achieve the representation goal; the existing and proposed reserves cover more than the minimum area required to achieve the goal, but fall far short of meeting that goal. (From Pressey 1996, Adison Wesley Longman Limited 1996, reprinted by permission of Pearson Education Limited.)

retain no more than *c.* 60% of currently extant species (after Mayer & Pimm 1998).

Hence it is imperative that protected area systems are planned as carefully as possible. Despite this, there is considerable evidence that in some parts of the world, reserves have been established on an essentially *ad hoc* basis, in areas of low value for other land uses (Leader-Williams *et al.* 1990; Pressey 1994, 1996; Pressey & Tully 1994). The resulting networks are frequently inefficient, in that they conserve relatively few species for their size (Fig. 5.1; Pressey & Nicholls 1989). More importantly, existing systems commonly leave many natural features (such as species or habitats) unprotected (see e.g. Khan *et al.* 1997; Jaffre *et al.* 1998; but see also Rodrigues *et al.* 1999). Hence, a more systematic approach to reserve selection is often needed.

Box 5.1. Some global priority systems (see also Box 5.3).

BirdLife's Endemic Bird Areas - 218 regions with at least two bird species with global breeding ranges of less than 50,000 km² (for details see Figs. 5.3, 5.9; Stattersfield *et al.* 1998).

Conservation International's Megadiversity Countries - the 17 biologically richest countries (see Fig. 5.2; Mittermeier & Werner 1988; Mittermeier *et al.* 1997).

Conservation International's Hotspots - 25 areas each possessing as endemics at least 0.5% of the global total of plant species (minimum of 1,500 species), and having lost at least 70% of their natural habitat (Mittermeier *et al.* 1999; Myers *et al.* 2000; and www.conservation.org/xp/CIWEB/ strategies/hotspots/hotspots.xml). Note CI's use of 'hotspots' is distinct from that of many authors, who define hotspots simply as the richest areas for particular groups of species (Reid 1998).

Conservation International's Major Tropical Wilderness Areas - areas of high biodiversity tropical ecosystems where more than 75% of the habitat remains (Mittermeier *et al.* 1998; and www.conservation.org/xp/CIWEB/strategies/ tropical_wilderness/tropical_wilderness.xml).

World Resource Institute's Frontier Forests - largely undisturbed forests considered big enough to maintain all of their biodiversity in viable populations, and whose structure and composition are determined primarily by natural events (Bryant *et al.* 1997; and www.wri.org/wri/ffi/).

World Wide Fund for Nature and World Conservation Union's Centres of Plant Diversity - 234 'first order' sites each with ≥ 1,000 vascular plant species including ≥ 100 species endemic to their phytogeographic region (for mainland sites); or with ≥ 50 endemic species or ≥ 10% endemism (for islands) (see Fig. 5.9; WWF & IUCN 1994–97; and www.si.edu/botany/projects/centres/menutemp.html).

World Wildlife Fund-USA's Global 200 Ecoregions - of nearly 1,000 ecoregions worldwide, these comprise all the Biologically Distinctive Ecoregions, plus ecoregions which represent rare habitats, large areas of undisturbed habitat, major migrations of large mammals, or high concentrations of endemic families or genera (Dinerstein *et al.* 1995; Olson & Dinerstein 1998; Ricketts *et al.* 1999; Abell *et al.* 2000; and www.worldwildlife.org/global200/).

ESTABLISHING GOALS, TARGETS AND SCALES

The first step in systematic priority assessment is to establish its scope (Williams 1998; Margules & Pressey 2000). What is the conservation goal of the exercise? This might be the conservation of all species, or of a subset of species, such as birds, or threatened species, or narrow endemics. The target could be traditionally defined biological species, or groupings that meet the phylogenetic species concept (for divergent views on whether this makes a practical difference, see Peterson & Navarro-Siguënza 1999; Fjeldså 2000). One may equally well focus on genera, or even families, especially when data on species are not available (Gaston & Williams 1993; Williams & Gaston 1994). Moving on, alternative, non-taxonomic goals might be the conservation of habitats, or of key biological processes, such as pollination, or migration.

Next, having identified the conservation goal, one must establish targets: how many species, how many representations of habitats, how much process, will be enough? Targets must be explicit in order for selection to be efficient, and for progress towards goals to be measurable.

Third, one must be clear about two aspects of the scale of any planning exercise. What is the grain size, i.e. how big are the units of land under assessment? Assigning priorities to large political units – such as countries, or counties – can be important in informing decisions over where to invest financial resources, or effort in capacity building; similarly, priority-setting using large equal-area grids can establish key areas for finer-grained assessments. But in order to identify specific sites for field-based initiatives, one must eventually work with much smaller units, representing individual parcels of land.

Besides grain size, one must also be clear about the extent of the area across which one is trying to achieve a stated conservation goal: this might be the world or a continent, but it could equally well be a country or habitat type. All scales are legitimate. The Convention on Biological Diversity requires countries to develop national plans capable of maintaining all species that occur within their borders, including those that are found elsewhere (Glowka et al. 1994); this may be particularly valuable where neighbouring countries have relatively weak conservation legislation (Abbitt et al. 2000). At a more parochial scale, attempting to ensure the local persistence of all features still extant in an area can be important in conserving the genetic diversity of broad-ranging species, and in fostering grassroots support for conservation (Hunter & Hutchinson 1994). That said, whenever the areal extent of a prioritisation exercise is defined geopolitically rather than biogeographically, it will tend to contain species or habitats which are rare locally but widespread elsewhere. Attempting to conserve all such features in each political unit they inhabit will inevitably increase the resources required for conservation quite considerably (see Erasmus et al. 1999 and Brooks et al. 2002 for worked examples). There may therefore be merit in giving differential weight to wide-ranging and locally restricted species (Csuti et al. 1997; see below).

BIOLOGICAL CONSIDERATIONS

In the following two sections, I explore biological and human issues relevant to identifying sets of priority areas for conservation. All the approaches share a common broad goal of maximising the persistence of biodiversity given finite conservation resources, although the examples used to illustrate them differ in scale as well as in their precise targets and objectives. In reviewing these ideas, it is worth bearing a couple of caveats in mind. First, both the information available and the status of species and habitats are dynamic; consequently, the costs and benefits of different conservation actions will also change through time. To be sensitive to these changes, priority-setting should be viewed as an ongoing process, subject to regular review (Margules & Pressey 2000). Second, for some species – particularly those whose populations range very widely or unpredictably, or which can persist in reasonable numbers on conventionally managed land – reserve-based conservation efforts may not be especially helpful, or even relevant (Chapter 8; Woinarski *et al.* 1992; Pain *et al.* 1997; Pain & Pienkowski 1997). In establishing targets for area selection, it may be sensible to exclude such species, while making sure their needs are assessed and, where necessary, met by alternative conservation initiatives (see Chapter 8).

Biologically rich areas

Perhaps the most obvious issue to be addressed in priority-setting is the fact that diversity is not distributed evenly across the planet (Gaston & Williams 1996). Tropical latitudes, intermediate altitudes, and certain habitat types support greater densities of species than elsewhere (Rosenzweig 1995). Other things (such as the costs of conservation) being equal, it therefore makes sense to concentrate conservation efforts in areas of high species richness.

Besides its intuitive appeal, targeting areas of high richness has the added advantage of having relatively limited data requirements. For several groups, including birds, summary data on species richness are already available for countries (WCMC 1994), as well as for biogeographical units such as ecoregions (Dinerstein *et al.* 1995; Ricketts *et al.* 1999; Abell *et al.* 2000). Where total richness figures are considered unreliable because of differences in sampling effort, if effort can be estimated, one can still calculate scores of relative richness that are independent of effort (see Gaston 1996b for a summary of techniques).

But while richness is an attractive and readily available measure for priority-setting, it has one crucial drawback: it completely ignores

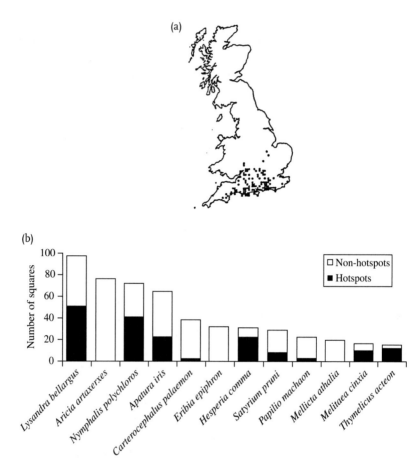

Fig. 5.2. (a) Britain's 5% richest 10 km × 10 km squares ('hotspots', *sensu* Prendergast *et al.* 1993) for butterflies. Note these are very clustered in the warmer south. (b) Butterflies occupying <100 10 km × 10 km squares are in some cases absent from such hotspots altogether. (Reprinted by permission from *Nature*, Prendergast *et al.* 1993, *Nature* **365**: 335–337, copyright 1993, Macmillan Magazines Ltd.)

differences in the composition (rather than size) of the biotas of candidate conservation areas. It is quite possible for all the richest areas under consideration to belong to just a few, very rich, habitat types: while these would be well represented in a richness-based priority set, poorer but distinctive habitats would be ignored (see Fig. 5.2 for an example). Hence, richness alone is unlikely to identify a set of conservation areas that between them represent all of a region's biodiversity.

Areas of high endemism

A second, popular approach to priority-setting which pays explicit attention to biological differences between areas involves focusing on parts of the world which are particularly rich in narrowly distributed species (Caldecott *et al.* 1996). Like overall richness, endemism is more pronounced in some places – such as mountains, remote islands, and low latitudes – than in others (Stevens 1989; Gaston & Williams 1996). These areas are often not rich in other, more widespread species – and so may be missed by prioritisation based simply on overall richness. Yet, because they contain many species found nowhere else, their conservation is evidently essential if global extinctions are to be avoided.

This thinking stimulated BirdLife International (then the International Council for Bird Preservation) to set about mapping the distribution of all 2,561 extant bird species with historical breeding ranges below an arbitrarily chosen threshold of 50,000 km^2 (roughly the size of Costa Rica – ICBP 1992; Crosby 1994). The result of this unprecedentedly detailed global exercise was the identification of 218 Endemic Bird Areas (EBAs), defined as areas where the distributions of at least two of these restricted-range species overlap (Fig. 5.3; see Stattersfield *et al.* 1998). Between them, EBAs encompass the entire ranges of 93% of restricted-range birds (25% of all bird species), as well as parts of the ranges of a further 2% of restricted-range species and of many, more widely distributed birds. This priority set is efficient in terms of area: the remaining natural habitat in all EBAs combined covers only *c.* 5% of the Earth's land surface, and three-quarters of the restricted-range species (20% of all birds) are nowadays confined to just 1% of land area (Stattersfield *et al.* 1998; but see Fjeldså *et al.* 1999).

In addition to generating efficient priorities, focusing on narrow endemics concentrates conservation efforts on species that are particularly vulnerable to extinction (Manne *et al.* 1999; BirdLife International 2000). As a consequence both of their small range size, and of the tendency of narrowly distributed species to be locally scarce as well (so-called 'double jeopardy' – Lawton 1993; Gaston 1994), restricted-range birds are over seven times more likely than other birds to be be globally threatened (with threat rates of 31% and 4%, respectively; data from Stattersfield *et al.* 1998). Over 73% of all currently threatened birds have restricted ranges, as did 80% of those species that have gone extinct since 1800 (Stattersfield *et al.* 1998). Targeting areas of high endemism will evidently reap disproportionate dividends in terms of slowing species loss.

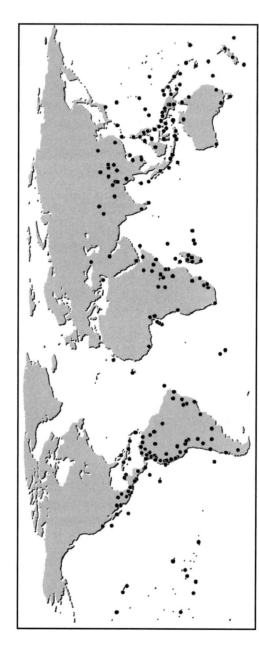

Fig. 5.3. The locations of BirdLife's Endemic Bird Areas. (From Stattersfield *et al.* 1998.)

Complementarity: integrating richness and endemism

Several quantitative techniques have been developed since the mid-1980s, which simultaneously address both richness and endemism. These are mostly centred around the concept of complementarity. At its simplest, complementarity is about biological distinctiveness, and can be expressed in terms of an average similarity index between an area and all others, or its distance from all others in multivariate space (Faith & Norris 1989; Colwell & Coddington 1994). In the context of priority-setting, complementarity can be usefully viewed as a dynamic property, summarising the contribution of an area to a representational target, taking into account the contributions of all previously selected areas (Margules & Pressey 2000).

The majority of prioritisation techniques incorporating complementarity do so by a series of iterative steps, at each of which all candidate areas are compared in terms of how well they complement those areas which have already been chosen (see Pressey *et al.* 1993; Williams 1998 for reviews). The most straightforward approach – known as a 'simple greedy' algorithm – starts off by picking the richest area of all, then that with the highest complementary richness to that area, then the area with the most features not found in either of the first two selections, and so on (see Box 5.2). Alternatives include various rarity-weighted algorithms, which pick first those sites that are essential because they contain features found nowhere else, and several algorithms that check that early choices remain appropriate after the inclusion of later ones.

Any of these approaches can be run until the conservation goal (say, representing all species once) has been met, thereby identifying a near-minimum set of areas capable of meeting this target. After this, the members of this set can be re-ordered according to various criteria, yielding a prioritisation sequence in case not all members of the near-minimum set can be conserved at once. Software for running these procedures is now available in user-friendly packages for the PC, such as WORLDMAP (Williams 1996; www.nhm.ac.uk/science/projects/worldmap/), C-plan (Finkel 1998; Pressey 1998, and MARXAN (www.ecology.uq.edu.au/marxan.htm).

Strictly speaking, even algorithms which include back-checking do not necessarily identify truly optimal priority sets which represent, for instance, the maximum number of species in a fixed set of areas, or all species in the minimum total area (Underhill 1994): this requires evaluating the performance of all possible priority sets. Such optimisation can now be achieved even on desktop machines using recently developed linear-programming

Box 5.2. Why addressing complementarity improves efficiency.

Imagine being asked to select the smallest set of sites capable of representing all of the five species whose distribution is summarised in the matrix below. If we paid attention simply to richness, we would pick site 1 first (giving us three species from one site), then sites 2 and 3 (with two species each), and only after that, sites 4 and 5: it would take us five whole sites before we had all five species represented at least once. Paying attention to complementarity greatly improves the efficiency of site selection. Adopting a 'simple greedy' algorithm, for instance, we would again start off by picking the richest site first, but after that, we then focus just on species which are complementary to those present at site 1. The only sites with any complementary species are sites 4 and 5, so that after choosing just three sites we would already have all our five species represented once. A complementarity-based approach also highlights flexible choices: in the example below, if site 1 was unavailable for conservation, the representation goal could still be achieved by replacing site 1 with sites 2 and 3 together.

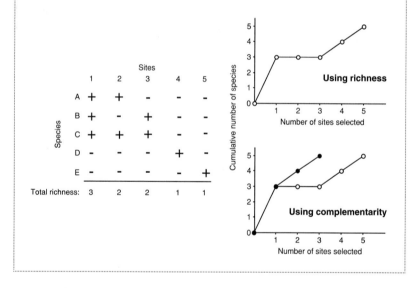

packages such as CPLEX (ILOG 1999). Nevertheless it appears that in many real-world examples, the more straightforward iterative algorithms yield priority sets which are very nearly as efficient as these optimal solutions (Pressey *et al.* 1996; Csuti *et al.* 1997).

The main advantage of employing quantitative, complementarity-based techniques is clearly illustrated by a priority-setting exercise for greater South Africa (Lombard 1995). Here the richest 5% of all quarter-degree grid-squares (97 out of 1971) represent over 90% of all of the region's 595 breeding bird species. However, applying a simple greedy algorithm to the

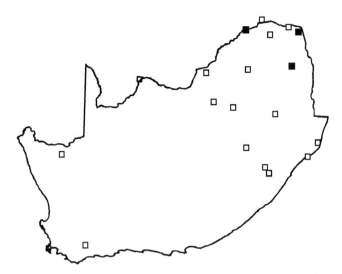

Fig. 5.4. The locations of 20 quarter-degree grid-squares capable of representing all of greater South Africa's 595 breeding bird species at least once, as identified by a complementarity-based algorithm. Solid squares are irreplaceable: they contain species found nowhere else; open squares are flexible: their species can be conserved elsewhere. (From Lombard 1995.)

same data identifies a near-minimum set that collectively contains 100% of species at least once in just 20 grid-squares (see Fig. 5.4). This dramatic difference in efficiency between richness- and complementarity-based approaches is typical (Pressey & Nicholls 1989). In the UK, for instance, the richest 5% of 10 km × 10 km grid-squares for breeding birds contain 89% of all 218 species, yet a rarity-based complementarity algorithm picks a priority set which represents all species in just 1% of squares, and in 5% of squares, one can represent each species at least six times over (or every time they occur, if this is less often; Williams *et al.* 1996).

Programmes such as WORLDMAP and MARXAN highlight other advantages of complementarity-based algorithms. They can make clear why each area is picked (or not) in terms of its contribution to a representation goal – and hence increase the accountability of the priority-selection process to decision-makers. Because complementarity techniques can select areas even though they have no species unique to them (see Box 5.2), there will commonly be flexibility in priority sets. This flexibility can be made explicit (see Fig. 5.4), enabling planners to choose between a range of land-use options all of which may achieve the overall conservation goal. The extent to which areas are flexible members of priority sets can be summarised in scores such as irreplaceability (which can be defined as the proportion of all sets meeting the conservation target in which an area is a member – Pressey *et al.* 1993; Ferrier *et al.* 2000), giving a clear indication of an area's overall biological importance. Last, systematic prioritisation techniques are themselves flexible, and can be modified to incorporate other measures of biological value besides the presence or absence of particular features, as well as human-related concerns (see below).

Two problems can arise from using complementarity-based algorithms. First, they tend to select widely scattered areas. Second, they often pick areas which represent many species efficiently because they straddle two or more habitat types, yet where each habitat patch may be too small to retain viable populations of its species (Branch *et al.* 1995; Nicholls 1998). However, to the extent that these selection patterns pose a real problem – which will depend on the scale of the analyses – they can be addressed by adding constraints to the algorithms. Thus selection procedures can be modified so that they give differential weight to areas abutting those that have already been chosen (promoting clumping); they only consider representations of species in the core (rather than the margins) of their ranges; or they preferentially select areas where the target species are most likely to be present in viable numbers (see below; and Nicholls & Margules 1993; Nicholls 1998; Williams 1998; Williams & Araújo 2000, for examples).

A more fundamental problem is that all these systematic procedures assume equal sampling effort across all candidate areas, and require information on the distribution of each feature of conservation concern. Only by having access to information on the identity (and not just the number) of such features in each area can the complementarity of all areas to the growing priority set be recalculated at each iteration of the procedure. This information need not, of course, be on species, or even on biodiversity *per se* – it could be on more readily surveyed proxies for biological diversity, such as the distribution of landforms (Faith & Walker 1996 – although note that the performance of such abiotic surrogates is still unresolved). Moreover, a series of worked examples has recently revealed that the costs of acquiring detailed distributional information – even down to the level of species – are considerably less than the benefits obtained through the efficiency gains of complementarity-based priority assessment (Balmford & Gaston 1999).

Other types of species of particular conservation concern
Species occurrences are the most common currency used in identifying priority areas for conservation, yet, as Chapter 4 explored in detail, not all species are of equal conservation concern. For example, narrowly

distributed species are disproportionately vulnerable, and we have already seen how they may be directly targeted in priority assessment, either by focusing on endemics alone, or using complementarity driven algorithms, which may in addition be weighted by species' range-size rarity. But endemics are not the only species of special interest to those devising networks of reserves. There are at least three other types of species that may merit greater conservation attention than others.

(1) **Threatened species.** Area prioritisation may focus solely on species that are in danger of extinction. This was the case for the Key Areas programme of BirdLife International, which identified sites essential for the conservation of red-listed species (e.g. Wege & Long 1995), and which has since become one element of BirdLife's Important Bird Areas programme (see below). High threat is also one criterion – alongside high plant endemism – in defining Conservation International's 25 Hotspots (Myers *et al.* 2000; see Box 5.1). A rather different approach is to give threatened species disproportionate weighting in quantitative selection procedures that include data on other species as well. If the goal is to represent all species, this will not alter the near-minimum set of areas, but it can substantially affect the priority attached to sites within the set (because threatened species are commonly confined to scattered, relatively depauperate areas – see Dobson *et al.* 1997; Reyers *et al.* 2000 for examples). One limitation of any attempt to focus on threatened species is that threatening processes may change unpredictably over time, in terms of their relative importance, their interactions, and their geographical spread (Myers 1995; Balmford *et al.* 1998; cf. Abbitt *et al.* 2000).

(2) **Species that are evolutionarily distinct.** The non-uniform nature of diversification and extinction means that extant species differ in the amount of evolutionary history they now represent (Vane-Wright *et al.* 1991). Species with few close relatives – such as the kagu (*Rhynochetos jubatus*) – represent more evolutionary history than others – such as any one of the very many white-eyes (*Zosterops* spp.) that have undergone marked radiation only recently. With this in mind, several authors have developed measures of phylogenetic diversity that score each species according to the unshared phylogenetic branch length that it represents (for different approaches see May 1990; Vane-Wright *et al.* 1991; Faith 1992, 1994). Because phylogenetic diversification does not correspond directly to phenotypic diversification – some lineage splits are associated with greater phenotypic change than others – Owens & Bennett (2000b) have recently devised a technique

which complements phylogenetic diversity measures by generating scores for how much phenotypic diversity each taxon represents. Results so far for birds suggest both approaches give similarly disproportionate weight to ancient, distinctive lineages. Of course, both the phenotypic and the phylogenetic diversity approaches yield weightings entirely at odds with the alternative suggestion that conservation efforts should preferentially target currently diverging taxa which may have the greatest potential to evolve new lineages in the future (Erwin 1991; Brooks *et al.* 1992). Incorporating any of these procedures into systematic area selection is essentially straightforward (provided the information needed to derive the weights is available). However, it is as yet unclear whether areas differ sufficiently in the average distinctiveness of their species for priority sequences to alter much once evolutionary history is taken into account (see e.g. Erasmus *et al.* 1999; Whiting *et al.* 2000; cf. Owens & Bennett 2000b).

(3) **Species whose conservation can enhance that of others.** Included in this group might be keystone species – which exert an ecological influence out of proportion to their contribution to a community's biomass; umbrella species – whose requirements for area or management are so demanding that if met, they would underpin the simultaneous conservation of most sympatric species; and flagship species – whose plight can serve as a rallying point for raising funds, awareness and action (for reviews see Caro & O'Doherty 1999; Leader-Williams & Dublin 2000). Birds in general are widely promoted as conservation flagships, and particular species, such as the northern spotted owl (*Strix occidentalis caurina*) and the California condor (*Gymnogyps californianus*) may act as both flagships and umbrellas. Despite this, identifying area priorities for broad regions based solely on the distribution of small groups of particularly significant species leads to predictably large gaps in overall representation (Kerr 1997; Andelman & Fagan 2000; Williams *et al.* 2000).

Ecological and evolutionary processes

This final suite of biological concerns to be addressed in priority-setting is probably the least tractable, yet ensuring the continuation of key ecological and evolutionary processes is vital to achieving long-term conservation goals (see Balmford *et al.* 1998 for a review). To pick a well-worked example, reserve networks must be designed not only to represent species, but also to maintain them in populations that are sufficiently large to be resilient, over reasonable time-frames, to stochastic genetic and demographic threats.

Other process-linked concerns include the maintenance (where relevant) of metapopulation dynamics, of dispersal, and of large-scale migration and nomadism; the retention of the capacity for adaptive evolution; and the continuation of key ecological interactions, through the persistence of competition, herbivory, predation, parasitism and pollination, as well as the maintenance of prevailing hydrological, fire, and other disturbance regimes. All of these processes are part of business-as-usual for wild species and communities. In addition, several – such as adaptation and large-scale range shifts – are likely to be prove essential in enabling species to persist in the face of novel anthropogenic threats such as climate change (see Chapter 8 and Huntley 1998).

Each of these concerns can in principle be addressed in systematic priority-setting, but to do so one must identify the spatial requirements for the maintenance of each process: how large an area is needed for population viability, how extensive and predictable is a species' migration route, what is the scale over which an ecosystem's fire regime is determined, and so on. We are a long way from being able to answer many of these questions in depth, yet conservation planners have nevertheless begun taking the first steps in developing rules-of-thumb for incorporating process-linked concerns into area prioritisation. For instance, pragmatic approaches to address population viability include constraining algorithms to select cells adjacent to one another, cells in the core of species' ranges, multiple cells per species, and cells where species have high population densities or high real or modelled probabilities of persistence (see Nicholls & Margules 1993; Winston & Angermeier 1995; Nicholls 1998; Williams 1998; Araújo & Williams 2000; Rodrigues et al. 2000; Williams & Araújo 2000). Likewise, recent evidence suggests that one way to maximise future evolutionary potential may be to target ecotones, where divergent selection pressures generate novel adaptations (Smith et al. 1997; Schneider et al. 1999). Resilience to climate change may be enhanced by selecting areas with sufficient topographical variation to encompass broad climatic gradients (Huntley 1995, 1998; Pounds et al. 1999).

A recent, groundbreaking study from southern Africa's Succulent Karoo has explored the consequences of simultaneously incorporating several process-linked concerns in a single prioritisation exercise (Cowling et al. 1999; see Fig. 5.5). Each of the reserves proposed in this scheme is judged big enough to contain viable populations of large mammals and nomadic birds (as well as less demanding species), and maintain small-scale disturbance regimes. In addition, each reserve encompasses large and steep climatic gradients, and clusters of distinct, juxtaposed habitats associated

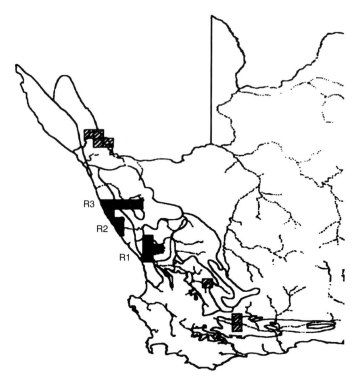

Fig. 5.5. A hypothetical reserve system designed to conserve key ecological and evolutionary processes in the Succulent Karoo. Quarter-degree squares selected fall into three clusters (R1–R3). Squares covered by existing reserves are hatched. Other lines denote watershed and bioregion limits. (From Cowling *et al.* 1999, *Diversity and Distribution* 5, 51–71.)

with ongoing adaptive radiation. Large-scale disturbance regimes are also represented: one reserve includes the whole of a major watershed, one incorporates an entire corridor for the inland movement of marine sands, and one covers the complete route of a seasonal ungulate migration.

Yet, predictably, addressing these processes comes at a high price (even ignoring the costs of acquiring meaningful process-linked information). For the Succulent Karoo, the process-based system covers the same area as one that represents all red-listed species at least once, yet the former fails to capture 63% of red-listed species (Cowling *et al.* 1999; see Nicholls 1998 for other examples). Given real-world constraints on conservation resources, it may prove difficult to represent all currently extant species in reserves that simultaneously capture the fundamental biological processes on which their long-term future depends. This prospect in turn highlights the fundamental importance of conservation measures in the matrix between reserves.

HUMAN CONSIDERATIONS

While biological considerations are obviously essential for area prioritisation, addressing human concerns is equally vital if conservation actions are to be supported, are to be affordable, and are to succeed over the long term. The importance of factoring people into conservation planning is underlined by a cruel irony emerging from several recent studies: human populations and their impacts tend to be higher in areas of particular biological value. Thus, across the tropical Andes, human densities peak in or near areas of high avian endemism (Fjeldså & Rahbek 1998). Globally, countries with greater concentrations of endemic forest birds are experiencing higher deforestation rates than elsewhere (Balmford & Long 1994). Across sub-Saharan Africa, densities of people, vertebrate species as a whole, and narrowly restricted species, all co-vary (Balmford et al. 2001). These patterns are yet poorly understood, but they appear pervasive (see also Cincottta et al. 2000), and highlight the need to incorporate human-linked concerns directly into area selection.

Financial costs

Shortage of money often limits the extent and success of reserves and other conservation initiatives (James et al. 1999). However, the costs of conservation vary enormously, across both global and local scales (James et al. 2001). Systematic prioritisation techniques can be readily modifed to address such variation, for instance by selecting at each step not the site with the highest complementary richness, but that with the highest ratio of complementary richness to cost. In one of the first attempts to do this, Ando et al. (1998) showed that the relative importance of different US counties for conserving endangered species changed markedly when variation in land price was taken into account (cf. Dobson et al. 1997). However, the cost of land is only one element of the overall cost of conservation – maintenance costs and opportunity costs to local communities are also substantial (James et al. 1999). Considering all these costs can again re-order conservation priorities quite dramatically, and greatly increase how far a given goal is achieved within a fixed budget (for a worked example based on true optimisation, see Balmford et al. 2000). These early results suggest building economic information into area selection may have considerable merit; the constraint at present is the lack of area-specific data on conservation costs.

Threats

Giving explicit consideration to the nature and spread of threats will enhance both the long-term success and the affordability of reserve-based conservation. This is important in the design and management of individual reserves (see Peres & Terborgh 1995), but can also be addressed in selecting networks of priority areas. The key is wherever possible to avoid areas that are likely to be difficult or expensive to conserve (in so far as this is predictable – see above). As with considerations of cost, this is not to advocate triage, with the complete abandonment of highly threatened areas: where such areas have very high biological value, they may still be targeted by conservation. Nevertheless, by paying explicit attention to threat (and costliness), the challenges associated with selecting difficult areas are made clear at the planning stage.

Key data layers that might be examined in considering exposure to threat include information on existing or predicted habitat conversion, and on human population density and growth. Selection algorithms can then be adjusted to exclude any areas where habitat modification or population parameters exceed a certain threshold (Nantel et al. 1998; Wessels et al. 2000), or (as with cost) to select at each step the area with the highest ratio of biological value to population density or land conversion (see Balmford et al. 2001). These systematic approaches to threat avoidance extend the total area required to meet representation goals (Nantel et al. 1998; Wessels et al. 2000; Balmford et al. 2001), but will also increase the probability of selected areas persisting, and reduce long-term conservation costs. Other ways of enhancing the resilience of reserves to threats might be to preferentially pick areas encompassing entire watersheds (which in areas where most transport is by river will then be more defensible – Peres & Terborgh 1995), and to select areas with marked altitudinal variation (thereby increasing the probability of species persisting through climate change – Huntley 1995, 1998; Pounds et al. 1999).

Existing reserves

Although some protected area networks may be flawed (see above), others are not (see e.g. Rodrigues et al. 1999). Moreover, even replacing those that are poorly designed with entirely new reserves would generally be prohibitively expensive, both financially and politically. Hence, it usually makes good sense to consider existing protected areas as a baseline from which to expand reserve systems (see Fig. 5.6). This can be achieved by prefacing systematic priority-setting with an initial gap analysis, which identifies those features that are adequately represented in current reserves, and then

Fig. 5.6. The results of a gap analysis for Britain's breeding birds. Crosses mark those 10 km × 10 km squares which are >50% covered by Sites of Special Scientific Interest. Solid squares represent a near-minimum set of extra areas needed to represent each Red Data species at least once. (From Williams *et al.* 1996.)

excludes them from the selection of new areas (Scott *et al.* 1993). Such pre-filtering inevitably reduces the requirements for achieving a conservation goal (and can also establish those features for which existing reserves are particularly important). Across South America, for instance, excluding species in those one-degree squares judged to be already adequately protected reduces from 177 to 109 the number of extra squares needed to represent 913 passerine species at least three times over (Fjeldså & Rahbek 1998). Nevertheless, because biologically rich or distinctive areas are in some cases disproportionately close to dense human settlement (see above), but existing reserves have generally been established in areas with few people, gap analyses may not greatly reduce the requirement for new reserves in areas of potentially high conflict (Balmford *et al.* 2001).

Local support

Ultimately, conservation and development concerns can only be resolved successfully if conservation initiatives have the support of the communities they affect. In terms of criteria used for site selection, this means weight might be given to areas which contain locally valued species or landscapes, which have high potential for conservation education, or where prospects for successfully linking conservation and development are especially promising (see Howard 1991 for an example).

More generally, the need for local support has profound consequences for the process of how priorities are set. Rather than being determined by top-down decision-making, it is vital that conservation planning is conducted as far as possible by local or regional experts on biodiversity, development and land use (da Fonseca *et al.* 2000). Thus local input lies at the core of BirdLife's Important Bird Areas (IBA) scheme, which aims to identify all sites which are of importance to narrowly distributed, threatened or migratory birds, via in-country consultation (see Box 5.3 and Fig. 5.7). One route to achieving consensus and hence ownership in conservation planning is through regional and local priority-setting workshops (Mittermeier *et al.* 1995); the systematic approaches to priority-setting discussed here can play an important part in such meetings, by providing interactive platforms for establishing alternative options and examining the consequences of different decisions (Ferrier *et al.* 2000; Margules & Pressey 2000). The continued development of prioritisation workshops presents opportunities for capacity-building, empowerment of local experts, and repatriation of biodiversity data, as well as playing a key role in generating lasting conservation initiatives (da Fonseca *et al.* 2000).

Box 5.3. Important Bird Areas (see also www.birdlite.org/sites/index.cfm).

In contrast to the schemes outlined in Box 5.1, BirdLife's Important Bird Areas programme is focused at the level of individual sites. It aims to identify all areas of global importance for threatened, narrowly distributed or migratory species. Sites can qualify by meeting any of four criteria (Bennun & Fishpool 2000):

1 They hold significant numbers of a globally threatened bird species, or other species of global conservation concern.
2 They contain a significant part of the breeding range of the species whose distributions define an Endemic Bird Area.
3 They hold a significant portion of the distribution of those bird species restricted to a biome.
4 They are important congregation sites, regularly holding $\geq 1\%$ of the biogeographic populations of waterbirds, $\geq 1\%$ of the global populations of other congregatory species, $\geq 20,000$ seabirds or waterbirds, or (for bottleneck sites) exceeding other specific thresholds for migratory species.

Central to the IBA designation process is the need for sites to be identified, wherever possible, by local experts. The building of local support, capacity and networks are thus a key output of the IBA programme. IBA assessment has already been conducted for the Middle East, most of southern and eastern Africa, and Europe (Evans 1994; EWNHS 1996; Barnes 1998; Bennun & Njoroge 1999; Baker & Baker 2001; Byaruhanga *et al.* 2001). For Uganda, forest IBAs (which qualify mostly under criteria 1–3) represent species in other groups remarkably efficiently (Balmford *et al.* unpublished data.); across East Africa as a whole, cross-taxon coverage is also good, although in this latter case not significantly better than in randomly selected networks of the same total area (Brooks *et al.* 2001).

USING BIRDS AS BIODIVERSITY INDICATORS

Having explored in some depth how biological and human-linked data can be used to identify robust priorities for conservation, I turn now to the issue of how far focusing on birds will help conserve the rest of biodiversity. This is an important question because for most of the world we know relatively little about other groups, the public generally care more about the conservation of birds than that of, say, fungi or flies, and (in consequence) much of the legislation underpinning conservation is bird-oriented (e.g. the EU Birds Directive, 79/409/EEC, see Chapter 12). We are interested here specifically in the performance of birds as what is termed biodiversity indicators – which is not be to be confused with other potential surrogacy roles, such as indicating ecosystem health or population trends, or acting as

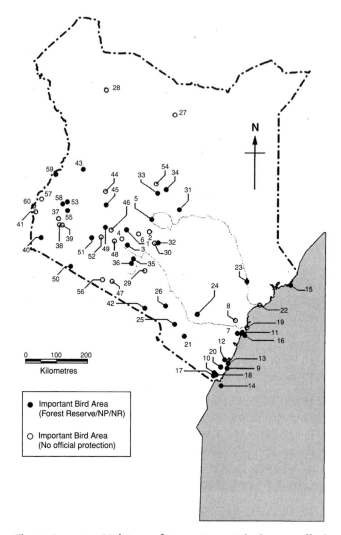

Fig. 5.7. Important Bird Areas of Kenya. Open circles have no offical protection. Thirty-three of 60 sites mapped here are judged to be severely or critically threatened. (From Bennun & Njoroge 1999.)

umbrellas or flagships (see above, and the review by Caro & O'Doherty 1999).

Birds appear to meet some but not all of the broad-brush criteria proposed for identifying suitable biodiversity indicators (see Pearson & Cassola 1992; Kremen *et al.* 1993; Kremen 1994; Caro & O'Doherty 1999). On the one hand, the distribution of birds is unusually well documented, and birds are relatively stable taxonomically, easy to survey, and (as a group) widely distributed across a broad range of habitat types. On the other hand, flight means that birds disperse quite readily, and consequently have relatively large distributional ranges. Hence, their biogeography is more coarse-grained than that of many other groups, so that area priorities for birds may fail to adequately capture biodiversity in taxa exhibiting higher spatial turnover.

In practice, proper assessment of the performance of birds as biodiversity indicators requires quantitative analysis. Two types of questions can be asked. How well do distribution patterns of birds mirror those of other groups, and how far will priority areas for birds conserve other groups?

Do distribution patterns of birds mirror those of other groups?

How far spatial richness patterns coincide across taxa varies, depending both on the ecological similarities of the groups under consideration, and the scale of the analysis (Curnutt et al. 1994; Gaston 1996c, d; Gaston & Williams 1996; Flather et al. 1997; Reid 1998; Pearson & Carroll 1999). Thus across Australia, species richness for birds correlates reasonably well with that of marsupials, but neither correlates well with richness patterns for reptiles, which are far better adapted to arid conditions (Schall & Pianka 1978). In terms of scale, at global and continent-wide levels, there is often reasonable agreement in the relative richness of countries or other large areas for different groups (Fig. 5.8; see also Pearson & Cassola 1992; Caldecott et al. 1996). However, at regional levels, congruence in species is typically somewhat weaker, and at fine scales, it can break down altogether (see Pomeroy 1993; Prendergast et al. 1993; Lombard 1995; Gaston 1996c, d; Kerr 1997; Howard et al. 1998; Lawton et al. 1998; Oliver et al. 1998; but see also Weaver 1995, who reports greatest congruence at finest scales).

Similarly mixed findings emerge from studies of congruence in patterns of endemism, and patterns of threat. At coarse scales, there is quite good cross-taxon overlap in the richness of different areas for range-restricted species (Thirgood & Heath 1994; Balmford & Long 1995; Caldecott et al. 1996). For instance, despite some obvious exceptions (such as mediterranean regions, which are very rich in plant endemics, yet typically support rather few restricted-range birds), there is a broad match in the locations of EBAs and of Centres of Plant Diversity (see Fig. 5.9; Stattersfield et al. 1998). Likewise, Conservation International's 25 Hotspots, defined in part by high plant endemism, also support large numbers of endemic vertebrates (Myers et al. 2000). There is reasonable cross-taxon agreement

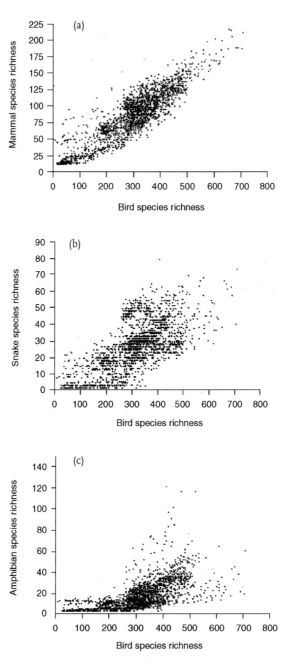

Fig. 5.8. Varying continent-wide patterns of congruence in species richness, across 1962 1° grid cells of sub-Saharan Africa. (a) Mammals vs. birds ($r_{s\ corr} = 0.84$). (b) Snakes vs. birds ($r_{s\ corr} = 0.65$). (c) Amphibians vs. birds ($r_{s\ corr} = 0.69$). (Data from the African biodiversity databases compiled by the Zoological Museum, University of Copenhagen.)

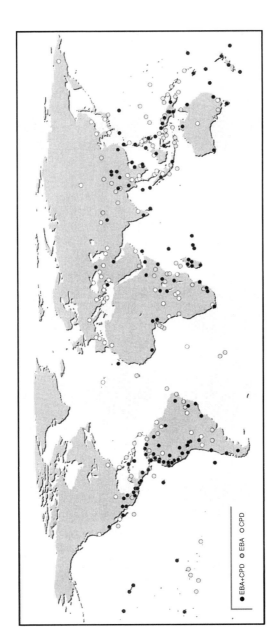

Fig. 5.9. The locations of Centres of Plant Diversity (CPD) and Endemic Bird Areas (EBA) compared. (From Stattersfield *et al.* 1998.)

in the large-scale distributions of threatened species too – for example, countries with many threatened birds generally contain many threatened mammals as well (Baillie 1996). However, congruence in both endemism and threat breaks down at finer scales (Lombard 1995; Dobson *et al.* 1997).

This heterogeneity in cross-taxon congruence, whether measured in terms of overall richness, endemism or threat, is important in conservation planning, because it means that at the sorts of fine scales used for selecting individual reserves, outstanding sites for one group (such as birds) cannot be safely assumed to be equally important for other groups. This is not good news for those who need to select areas for protection using data limited to one or two groups. However, thinking about complementarity teaches us that what really counts is the overall representation achieved by entire networks of reserves (Csuti *et al.* 1997; Balmford 1998). Comparing the richness of individual sites may not give us the whole picture.

Will priority areas for birds conserve other groups?

Given that efficient conservation networks comprise not simply rich sites, but ones that complement one another, how well individual taxa perform as biodiversity indicators cannot be properly inferred from richness correlations across all areas, but rather requires the assessment of each group's priority sites (Csuti *et al.* 1997; Balmford 1998). One way to do this is to look at the extent of overlap in complementarity-derived priorities for different taxa. Most studies adopting this approach suggest the correspondence of sites is poor. For example, there is typically only limited overlap between areas selected for birds and those chosen to represent other groups (Ryti 1992; Saetersdal *et al.* 1993; Kitching 1996; van Jaarsveld *et al.* 1997; Eeley *et al.* 2001; but see Reyers *et al.* 2000).

Yet weak area overlap still does not necessarily refute the biodiversity indicator concept, and a richer, more encouraging picture emerges if one considers instead how fully a taxon's priority areas capture other groups' species. Recent work covering a suite of different scales, study areas and taxa, shows that complementarity-derived choices for one group can collectively represent diversity in other taxa remarkably well (Csuti *et al.* 1997; Howard *et al.* 1998; Reyers *et al.* 2000; Virolainen *et al.* 2000; Eeley *et al.* 2001; Moore *et al.* 2002; see also Box 5.3). In Uganda, for instance, the top 20% of the country's forest estate selected to represent bird richness contains as many species of birds, small mammals, large moths, butterflies and woody plants as an equivalent area chosen using data on all groups at once (Fig. 5.10; Howard *et al.* 1998). This arises despite low cross-taxon congruence in patterns of species richness. The reason – here and in some other

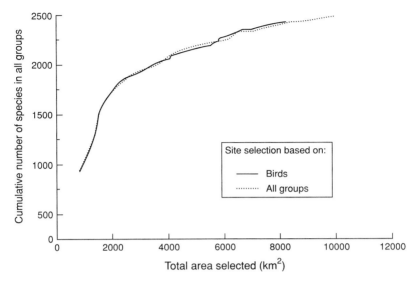

Fig. 5.10. Cumulative number of species of birds, small mammals, large moths, butterflies and woody plants represented in sets of Ugandan forests picked by applying a simple-greedy algorithm to data on all groups, and just on birds. (For further details, see Howard *et al.* 1998.)

cases (Eeley *et al.* 2001) – appears to be that different taxa have responded in broadly similar ways to abiotic factors shaping their biogeography. Hence, there is good cross-taxon agreement in patterns of complementarity, so that sites that are collectively efficient in representing the distributional patterns of one group in turn capture richness in other groups efficiently too.

However, these results are drawn from a limited number of studies, and there are several caveats concerning the performance of birds as fine-scale biodiversity indicators. Obviously, priority areas for birds will not fully represent diversity in other groups where these are ecologically very different, or where they exhibit much finer grained spatial turnover (Ryti 1992; Saetersdal *et al.* 1993). It also appears that cross-taxon species capture is particularly weak for narrowly distributed and threatened species. Such species often show markedly divergent distribution patterns across groups (Dobson *et al.* 1997), and are more likely than other species to be omitted from the priority areas of other taxa (Reyers *et al.* 2000; Moore *et al.* in press). The needs of these species will often not be identified by unrelated indicator groups. Last, no studies have yet examined how far paying attention to process-linked concerns for one group will improve persistence of other taxa. The relatively large scale over which birds operate means that areas considered large enough to retain them are also likely to support viable populations in many other groups. Conversely, groups with more limited dispersal than birds are likely to be more sensitive to problems such as habitat fragmentation and climate change.

Overview

To sum up, findings to date argue for the cautious use of birds as biodiversity indicators. At coarse scales, information on birds generates priorities which meet the needs of other groups reasonably well, with obvious exceptions: for example, birds are unreliable surrogates in mediterranean regions, and are presumably poor at representing marine diversity. At finer scales, although results to date are encouraging, more studies examining the crucial issue of cross-species capture are clearly needed. Given that data on birds are often more readily acquired than those on other groups, and that birds are a legitimate focus of conservation concern in their own right, it seems sensible to use bird information in priority selection. However, wherever possible, this should be supplemented with data on other relatively tractable groups – in particular, those (such as flowering plants, freshwater fish and invertebrates) that are likely to exhibit different biogeography, face different threats, and hence have different conservation requirements.

CHALLENGES TO FUTURE PRIORITISATION

Clearly, our ability to identify efficient and robust priority areas for conservation has improved considerably in the past decade. Nevertheless, more work is needed on several pressing issues.

Obtaining better distributional data

Differences in sampling effort and hence knowledge present a serious challenge to identifying the most appropriate sites for conservation action. However, at a coarse level, many large-scale data sets have recently been compiled, and we are now only a few years away from seeing summaries of the distributions of all terrestrial vertebrates worldwide, on at least a one-degree resolution (T. Brooks, pers. comm.). Descriptive distributions and taxonomies for all such groups except birds are already in the public domain (for mammals: www.nmnh.si.edu/msw/, reptiles: www.embl-heidelberg. de/~uetz/LivingReptiles.html, amphibians: research.amnh.org/cgi-bin/ herpetology.amphibia). At finer scales, much scattered information exists in museum records, in the literature, and in people's heads and notebooks. This urgently needs to be collated, made publicly accessible, and supplemented by new field surveys. Such work will not be cheap (and will require improved support for chronically underfunded museums and herbaria – Collar 1997; Wilson 2000), but it would be cost-effective (Balmford & Gaston 1999). As a parallel to this, we also need to explore techniques for predicting fine-scale distributions from coarser data (Boitani *et al.* 1999). But while we need to make progress on all these fronts, we cannot afford to delay planning for want of better data: rather, priorities should be set now, on the basis of current knowledge, and upgraded as new data become available.

Building consensus

At present, several international NGOs are promoting somewhat divergent global conservation priorities (see Box 5.1). While some diversity is inevitable and healthy, establishing a commonly accepted set of priority areas may do much to facilitate action by governments and the private sector alike (Mace *et al.* 2000). More importantly, at local scales, seeking consensus between all the major stakeholders involved is fundamental to conservation planning (see above). In this context, there is an evident need to identify and disseminate best practice on how to achieve broad-based local ownership and support.

Meeting the needs of highly localised species

Several studies suggest that very narrowly distributed or highly threatened species may be poorly served by systematic priority-setting. They may not occur in areas of highest priority for more widespread species, or for narrowly endemic or threatened species from other groups (Prendergast *et al.* 1993; Lombard 1995; Dobson *et al.* 1997). Consequently, sites containing them may be among the last irreplaceable areas to be picked (Reyers *et al.* 2000). In some cases, the conservation of such species in dedicated, medium- to large-sized reserves may be unaffordable. Instead, their needs may be best accommodated in small species-specific reserves, or by land management agreements between conservation organisations and individual land-holders (Cowling *et al.* 1999; Reyers *et al.* 2000; Wessels *et al.* 2000).

Better integrating human- and process-linked considerations

While techniques now exist for incorporating information on costs, land use, and some aspects of biological processes into quantitative prioritisation, several challenges remain. There are evidently many gaps in the data needed to factor-in these concerns. In some cases – such as the issue of population persistence – we are not even clear what the most relevant data are. Such problems demand that conservation planners work more closely than in the past with experts in these areas – many of whom are not biologists. In the case of ecological and evolutionary processes, a further likely difficulty is that the areas required to maintain viable systems (see e.g. Soulé & Sanjayan 1998) into the future may greatly exceed feasible limits for reserve networks.

Conserving the wider landscape

For many parts of the world, the most promising solution to the question of how to maintain large-scale biological processes in restricted reserve systems will lie in softening the matrix surrounding protected areas. This can have immediate benefits in terms of reducing edge effects and maintaining disturbance regimes, and it seems likely to be important in enabling species to shift their ranges in the face of climate change (Janzen 1986; Franklin 1993; Huntley 1998; Chapter 8). Extending conservation initiatives into semi-natural habitats is also essential for many species that are dependent on exploited landscapes (Pain et al. 1997; Pain & Pienkowski 1997; Chapter 8). With this in mind, the techniques discussed here for selecting protected area networks have considerable potential for identifying the most important places for wider, off-reserve action as well.

6

Critically endangered bird populations and their management

BEN D. BELL & DON V. MERTON

INTRODUCTION

Some bird populations have declined in abundance to critically low levels or have become highly localised. For example, during the period 1979-81 the Chatham Island black robin[1] was reduced to only one effective breeding pair, while by the early 1970s the Mauritius kestrel (*Falco punctatus*) had declined to four known individuals. Despite such extreme endangerment, both species were saved from the brink of extinction and restored to viability in the wild by conservation management (Jones 1998; Merton 1990). In this chapter, we review the variety and characteristics of critically endangered species, and outline the threats they face and how they are managed. Endangered bird conservation successes and failures are examined, as well as ongoing programmes where the fate of taxa on the brink of extinction remains in balance. To provide reference material for practitioners, lecturers and students, we examine key management techniques before presenting individual case studies covering a diverse range of species and situations. While we focus on birds, the management techniques that we review apply (to a greater or lesser extent) to other taxa.

WHICH ARE THE WORLD'S CRITICALLY ENDANGERED BIRDS?

Within the last 500 years, 128 bird species are known to have become extinct, 103 of these since 1800 (BirdLife International 2000). Currently 1,186 bird species (12% of all birds) are considered threatened with extinction

[1] Latin names not given in the text are in Appendix 6.1.

within the next 100 years. Of these, 182 are Critical (15%), 321 Endangered (27%) and 680 Vulnerable (57%); a further three are Extinct in the Wild (BirdLife International 2000). Human activity, either directly or indirectly, has accounted for virtually all such losses and declines, and there are many justifications for stemming the tide of extinctions and conserving remaining avian diversity (see Chapter 2). This requires commitment to recovery and restoration of biodiversity across a range of ecological levels from the individual through the population and species to the community up to bio-regions (Atkinson 1999).

The 2000 IUCN Red List adopts five main criteria (A–E) for determining the status of threatened species. Of the 182 bird species listed as critically endangered, 135 (74%) were classified by a single criterion, 30 (16%) by two criteria, 10 (5%) by three criteria and seven (4%) by four criteria (Table 6.1). Criterion D (very small population or range) was used most often – 77 species (30%); next was criterion C (small population and declining) – 74 species (29%); then criterion B (small range and fragmented, declining or fluctuating) – 70 species (28%); and finally criterion A (rapid population reduction) – 32 species (13%). No critically endangered species were classified using criterion E (quantitative analysis indicating the probability of extinction in the wild to be at least 50% in ten years or three generations).

In selecting species for inclusion in this chapter, we focus on those birds currently, or formerly, listed as critically endangered or extinct in the wild. The orders and global distribution of those birds listed as critically endangered (182) or extinct in the wild (3) in *Threatened Birds of the World* (BirdLife International 2000) are summarised in Table 6.2. Nineteen of the 27 avian orders (Morony *et al.* 1975) are represented with most species being in the Passeriformes (39%), then the Psittaciformes and Procellariiformes (each 8%). Most are from South America (47 species), then Asia (42) and North & Central America, including Hawaii (35), followed by Africa and Oceania (each 29 species). Europe has only two listed species and Antarctica only one.

Proving beyond reasonable doubt that a species is extinct, or that it still survives, can be problematical and some species listed as critically endangered (BirdLife International 2000) may already be extinct, for example several Hawaiian forest birds: 'o'u (*Psittirostra psittacea*), nukupu'u (*Hemignathus lucidus*), O'hau 'alauahio (*Paroreomyza maculata*) and po'o-uli (*Melamprosops phaeosoma*).

Table 6.1. *Summary of criteria by which birds classify as 'Critical' (critically endangered) in* Threatened Birds of the World *(BirdLife International 2000)*

The five criteria (A–E) are defined in *Threatened Birds of the World*. Sub-criteria are omitted from the table.

2000 IUCN Red List Criteria	No. (%) of species
A = Rapid population reduction	14 (8)
B = Small range & fragmented, declining or fluctuating	32 (18)
C = Small population & declining	32 (18)
D = Very small population or range	57 (31)
E = Quantitative analysis	0 (0)
Criteria A & B	3 (2)
Criteria A & C	3 (2)
Criteria B & C	20 (11)
Criteria B & D	1 (1)
Criteria C & D	3 (2)
Criteria A & B & C	1 (1)
Criteria A & B & D	1 (1)
Criteria A & C & D	3 (2)
Criteria B & C & D	5 (3)
Criteria A & B & C & D	7 (4)
Total critically endangered bird species	182

The three species that are listed as extinct in the wild are the Alagoas curassow from Brazil, the Guam rail from Micronesia and the Socorro dove from Mexico. In 2001, Spix's macaw was probably the most recent bird species to become extinct in the wild with the disappearance of the last remaining wild bird, though some 66 individuals exist in captivity (BirdLife International 2001). The Bali myna is also almost extinct in the wild, though about 1,000 are believed to exist in captivity (BirdLife International 2000; Nicholson-Lord 2000).

WHAT THREATS DO CRITICALLY ENDANGERED BIRDS FACE?

Many of the threats faced by endangered species are faced by all birds, including common and widespread species (see Chapter 8). Such threats embrace habitat loss and fragmentation (see Chapter 10), predation and competition, disease and parasites, human exploitation, chemical toxins,

Table 6.2. *The orders and global distribution of those 185 birds listed as critically endangered (CE) or extinct in the wild (EW) in* Threatened birds of the world *(BirdLife International 2000)*

Hawaiian species are included under North & Central America, while those from the Indian Ocean islands (e.g. Madagascar, Mascarenes, Seychelles) are included under Africa, except for Christmas Island, which is listed under Asia.

Avian order	EW	CR	Africa	Antarctica	Asia	Europe	N & C America	Oceania	S America	Total
Tinamiformes	0	2	–	–	–	–	–	–	2	2
Podicipediformes	0	2	1	–	–	–	–	–	1	2
Procellariiformes	0	14	2	1	–	1	3	6	1	14
Pelecaniformes	0	2	–	–	2	–	–	–	–	2
Ciconiiformes	0	4	2	–	2	–	–	–	–	4
Anseriformes	0	5	1	–	2	–	–	1	1	5
Falconiformes	0	9	2	–	3	–	3	–	1	9
Galliformes	0	8	1	–	1	–	1	1	4	8
Gruiformes	1	6	1	–	1	–	–	4	–	6
Charadriiformes	0	6	–	–	3	1	1	1	–	6
Columbiformes	1	13	–	–	7	–	2	3	1	13
Psittaciformes	0	15	1	–	3	–	1	4	6	15
Cuculiformes	0	2	–	–	2	–	–	–	–	2
Strigiformes	0	7	4	–	2	–	–	1	–	7
Caprimulgiformes	0	3	–	–	–	–	2	1	1	3
Apodiformes	0	9	–	–	–	–	2	–	7	9
Coraciiformes	0	2	–	–	2	–	–	–	–	2
Piciformes	0	3	–	–	1	–	2	–	–	3
Passeriformes	0	73	14	–	11	–	18	7	23	73
Total	3	185	29	1	42	2	35	29	47	185

pollutants and other environmental hazards (Appendix 6.1). When bird populations are numerically small or limited in distribution, such factors become increasingly problematical. Caughley (1994) reminds us of the distinction between two paradigms in conservation biology: the small population paradigm that deals with the effect of smallness on the persistence of a population, and the declining-population paradigm that deals with the cause of the smallness and its cure. With respect to critically endangered species, both paradigms are relevant, but conservation of commoner species focuses on the latter paradigm, in attempting to explain causal factors behind population declines. Note, however, the comments of Hedrick *et al.* (1996).

Critically endangered species generally have small distributions or populations, so stochastic events, introduced species and genetic factors represent actual or potential threats to survival and contribute to the so-called 'extinction vortex' (Ballou 1995). Moreover, there is a distinction between species with naturally small populations and distributions, and those resulting from declines from factors summarised in the upper sections of Appendix 6.1. For example, the Lord Howe rail has always had a limited distribution – on Lord Howe Island – while the shore plover, now limited to a few islands of New Zealand, was formerly much more widespread, having become a 'biological refugee' like the little spotted kiwi (*Apteryx owenii*), kakapo, and stitchbird (*Notiomystis cincta*), amongst others (Bell 1991; BirdLife International 2000).

The situations in which many critically endangered bird species occur may have made them inherently vulnerable – for example, 54% of the world's endangered birds live on islands (Temple 1985b, 1986), where they evolved in the absence of many of the pressures they now face following human settlement and development. As well as understanding the threats listed in Appendix 6.1, we must understand why some birds are more threatened than others, and consider inherent, evolved traits. Island endemics are particularly prone to endangerment and extinction, having a tendency for specialisation and/or for *K*-selection (Pianka 1970; King 1980; Temple 1985b). About half of the New Zealand land birds are now extinct. Predictably, both the extinct group and many currently threatened species are characterised by high degrees of endemism and trends towards *K*-selection, i.e. tameness, flightlessness and large size (gigantism), increasing their risk to hunting and predation, together with protracted maturation and breeding cycles, and small clutch size, resulting in low productivity potential and a lack of ability to recover quickly from adversity (Bell 1991; Merton 1992).

HOW ARE CRITICALLY ENDANGERED BIRD POPULATIONS MANAGED?

The scope of endangered species management

Diverse management techniques have been developed over the last 40 years to help conserve and restore critically endangered species. These have covered the spectrum from retaining all surviving individuals in captivity (e.g. Guam rail, California condor), through partial captive breeding (e.g. whooping crane, black stilt) or control of specific threats (e.g. Tahitian monarch), to integrated close-order management entirely in the field (e.g. black robin, Seychelles magpie-robin). These can be broadly categorised as follows:

1 Maintenance within natural historic range and habitat, through securing habitats and addressing issues of habitat quality, e.g. Taita thrush (*Turdus helleri*) in Kenya; kaka (*Nestor meridionalis*) and other threatened forest birds in New Zealand;

2 Where (1) is no longer a viable or practical option, translocation to more secure or appropriate locations within or beyond natural historic range, e.g. the two races of New Zealand saddleback (*Philesturnus carunculatus*), North Island kokako, noisy scrub-bird (*Atrichornis clamosus*);

3 Where (1) and (2) are no longer practicable, captive management has often been regarded the only other alternative, at least in the immediate term, e.g. Alagoas curassow;

4 However, over the last two decades, intensive 'close-order' management at the individual level in some free-living species has proved highly effective in boosting productivity and rebuilding populations to a level where less intense, longer-term strategies can be applied, e.g. black robin, kakapo, kakerori, Seychelles magpie-robin.

A wide range of avian conservation management techniques has developed over the last 40 years (Halliday 1978; Temple 1978). In the United States, Mauritius and New Zealand, for example, they include largely field-based management and population manipulation, with varying degrees of captive-propagation, sometimes none at all (e.g. black robin). Increasingly, new technologies, such as electronics and molecular genetics, are becoming important in conservation programmes. Atkinson (1999) noted, 'the level of science and technology now applied to the kakapo problem is second to none in New Zealand (and possibly the world)'.

Management of critically endangered species complements other initiatives such as scientific research, education programmes, political action and protective legislation. Management is intervention and manipulation in order to (i) arrest the slide to extinction; (ii) rebuild numbers; and (iii) reinstate free-living, self-sustaining populations. Inaction can be a form of management (i.e. passive management) in some cases – e.g. for the black tit (*Petroica macrocephala dannefaerdi*) and subantarctic snipe (*Coenocorypha aucklandica huegeli*) on near-pristine Snares Island south of New Zealand. Here, populations are monitored but otherwise left unmanaged, apart from legislative protection of the island and minimising risks of introducing mammalian predators (such as rats from fishing boats moored offshore). Active management can be 'aggressive' – for instance, where a competing species needs to be controlled or eradicated to protect a more vulnerable one. For example, on Mangere Island (Chatham Islands) the rare Forbes parakeet was protected from hybridisation with the more numerous Chatham Island red-crowned parakeet (*Cyanoramphus novaezelandiae*) by culling hybrids and red-crowned parakeets (Nixon 1994). Passive management includes legislative protection of individuals and habitats and practical steps such as fencing to keep out animals (including humans).

The goals of wildlife management include both quality and quantity control. Quantity control addresses numbers, survival factors, recruitment factors and the spatial distribution of threatened species. Quality control addresses the population's ecological and genetic health including population age and sex structure, population dispersion, and management of genetic risks, for example inbreeding depression and hybridisation. While our emphasis is on species rather than the community, both should be foci of biodiversity conservation. Temple (1978) noted a broad dichotomy in threatened species management: on the one hand, management of factors reducing survivorship (e.g. over-harvesting, increased predation, habitat degradation, fragmentation or reduction); on the other, management of factors reducing fecundity (e.g. competition for nesting sites, reproductive dysfunction from toxins, breeding habitat reduction). As noted previously, Caughley (1994) made a further distinction between the two paradigms of the small-population (effect of smallness on the persistence of a population) and the declining-population (cause of the smallness and its cure). Townsend *et al.* (1999) note that a balanced approach to conservation requires a compendium of ecological 'health-care' measures: preventative and primary care (setting aside protected areas), emergency care (for critically endangered species), intensive care (captive breeding in zoological and botanical gardens), and reconstructive surgery (restoration ecology). The ultimate goal, however, must be 'to provide for ongoing, long-term survival and evolution in an unmanaged, free-living state'. Recovery programmes lacking this longer-term goal, might better be described as 'maintenance' rather than 'recovery' plans. The future of life forms in the latter group is precarious since the vital, ongoing human prop is essentially a temporary measure (i.e. to 'buy time') that will eventually be withdrawn.

In New Zealand, the government's Biodiversity Strategy (Anon. 2000) reflects a focus on natural habitats and ecosystems as a means of conserving species and the diversity within them, in keeping with the International Convention on Biological Diversity emphasis on conserving biodiversity in its natural surroundings (i.e. *in situ* conservation). Maintaining viable populations of indigenous species across their natural ranges should largely be achieved by maintaining a full range of natural habitats and ecosystems. However, New Zealand notes that within the life of its Strategy, it is likely that the survival of some indigenous species will continue to require an individual species recovery focus beyond just maintaining and restoring the habitats and ecosystems to which these species belong (Anon. 2000).

With a rapidly increasing global human population placing ever increasing pressures on remaining natural resources of all kinds, even in New Zealand this idealistic concept has its limitations. The options for perpetuating some more sensitive, threatened life forms 'within their natural habitats' or even within their historic range no longer exist. This highlights a dilemma which threatened species managers will inevitably have to face with increasing frequency: the necessity to look for solutions beyond traditional boundaries – to explore all options that might provide for continued survival and evolution in a free-living state, independent of ongoing, often expensive human props. In addition to ecological issues, this poses the ethical question of whether or not in certain critical circumstances it is justifiable to establish a threatened life form in an alien environment, perhaps even beyond its historic biogeographic range, rather than to assign it to long-term captivity – or to extinction. A number of precedents already exist. In New Zealand, the two races of saddleback, little spotted kiwi, Eastern weka (*Gallirallus australis*) and kakapo have all proved incapable of coexistence with the diverse range of predators that have been introduced to the mainland, and owe their existence to the fact that they have been translocated to new locations beyond their natural range.

Successful management of threatened bird populations requires a basic knowledge of the biology of the species, including maturity and recruitment rates, survival rates, longevity, habitat requirements (including food, nest sites and shelter) and social behaviour. The degree to which a particular species is tolerant to management manipulation can also be critical. For instance, it was fortuitous that the black robin and the kakapo, like many island endemics, proved very resilient to extensive manipulation, for example translocations, egg or brood manipulation and nest protection and, in the case of the black robin, transfer of nests into the security of nest-boxes (Merton 1990; Butler & Merton 1992).

The principal conservation management techniques used for a selection of 25 critically endangered species (or formerly critically endangered species) are summarised in Appendix 6.2.

We use a range of selected case studies to illustrate in more detail the conservation management of particular species, comparing and contrasting species threats and management techniques across a range of situations in different parts of the world (Boxes 6.1–6.5).

Management techniques for critically endangered birds

Habitat, nest, shelter and food management

Management of the physical and/or ecological environment, for instance habitats, nests, shelter, food and water, are variously important for the survival of endangered species in the wild. Habitat protection can embrace reservation through local, national, state or private agencies, but in practical management terms, it involves such activities as fencing, installing buffer zones around sensitive habitats and protection against fire. Habitat restoration may be necessary, such as re-vegetation of forest or recreation of wetland sites, control/eradication of alien (and in some instances native) predators and food competitors. Atkinson (1999) points out that management associated with island restoration includes: identification of a restoration goal (i.e. perceived condition, and assemblage of animals and plants present at some point in time), the recovery or reintroduction of threatened species, the replacement of locally extinct taxa, the restoration of biotic communities and processes, and ecological engineering i.e. the creation of a contrived habitat that suits the need of endangered species, for example planting exotic fruit trees or food crops to provide supplementary food and conditions where breeding can occur for the kakapo (Box 6.3). While islands can provide sanctuary for threatened 'refugee' species (Bell 1991), mainland restoration projects are alternative options. For instance, in New Zealand 8.6 km of mammalian predator- and herbivore-proof fencing has been constructed around the Karori Wildlife Sanctuary, Wellington, to provide a more secure mainland 'island' in which exotic mammals have been eradicated and excluded, to allow future restoration through reintroduction of threatened species formerly likely to have occurred there (Anon. 1999b). Endangered migratory species offer particular challenges for conservation for their habitat management spans their migratory range, for example the whooping crane (Box 6.1) and eskimo curlew in North America, and the slender-billed curlew (*Numenius tenuirostris*) in Europe (Hayman *et al.* 1986; Lewington *et al.* 1991; BirdLife International 2000).

Box 6.1. A migratory species requiring an international management endeavour: whooping crane (*Grus americana*).

Locality: United States and Canada.
Status: Migrant.
IUCN Red List category & criterion: EN D1.
Main cause of decline: Over-hunting, habitat conversion and general human disturbance in the nineteenth century were the main causes of this species' decline.
Future threats: Possibly long-term effects of genetic drift through the severe population bottleneck that has occurred. Environmental risks include predation by golden eagles (*Aquila chrysaetos*), collision with power lines, oil and chemical pollution of the important wintering grounds, problems of boat traffic, wave erosion and dredging at the winter grounds. Deteriorating breeding habitat owing to drought is also causing concern.
Minimal world population: 14 in 1938.
Recent world population: *c.* 300 in 1999.
World population trends: The only self-sustaining wild population breeds on the border of Northwest Territories and Alberta, Canada, and winters at and near Aransas National Wildlife Refuge, Texas, USA. This population is increasing slowly (*c.* 5% per year since 1966), with the 1998 population represented by 183 birds (including 49 pairs). A pre-1870 peak population of 1,300–1,400 birds has been estimated with this being reduced to just 14 adults in 1938. An additional wild (reintroduced) non-migratory flock is present in Florida numbering *c.* 60 in 1999 (including six territorial pairs), with more birds reintroduced annually from captivity. An experimental, non-reproductive flock cross-fostered by sandhill cranes (*Grus canadensis*) aimed at establishing a population in Idaho, and wintering south to New Mexico, has dwindled to 1 or 2 birds (in 1999) – the experiment has been discontinued. Captive flocks total 124 birds held at three main locations in the USA: 67 birds at Patuxent, Maryland, two pairs at San Antonio, Texas; 30 birds at Baraboo, Wisconsin; and 19 birds at Calgary, Alberta (all figures from 1998).
Principal management: Close-order management including captive breeding, cross-fostering and behavioural manipulation.
Commentary: This species qualifies as Endangered due to its extremely small population but as the natural wild population continues to increase (and will soon reach 200), and the reintroduced resident flock is likely to be self-sustaining, it could soon be down listed to Vulnerable. The transnational recovery plan has focused on increasing the captive population to supply birds for release; ecological research and monitoring; experimental release; establishing additional wild populations; and teaching captive-bred birds to migrate, following light aircraft or vehicles on the ground. The problem of collision with power lines is being addressed by use of markers to increase the visibility of power lines.
Sources: R. McClellan, *in litt.*; BirdLife International 2000.

Management of nest sites has been a critical aspect of conservation measures for many threatened species. This includes: fencing off breeding sites (from the public, larger predators, domestic stock or wild herbivores); provision of additional artificial nest sites in boxes, burrows or on ledges; wardening or nest guarding to deter interference; use of anti-predator devices such as traps, poison bait stations or collars on nest trees; and attention to nest-site hygiene (e.g. treatment or replacement of nests or nest material in order to avoid fungal disease and the treatment of parasite infections). Protection of shelter sites can also be important, for example positioning of roost boxes above the ground to reduce threats of rat predation was used with outstanding success for the saddleback (Lovegrove 1996). Provision of supplementary foods and water has been part of management programmes for winter feeding of cranes (Archibald 1978), crested ibis (*Nipponia nippon*) (Yamashina 1978), California condor (Wilbur 1978), takahe (*Porphyrio mantelli*) and kakapo (Box 6.3 – Mills *et al.* 1989; Merton *et al.* 1999), Mauritius kestrel, pink pigeon, echo parakeet (Box 6.4 – Jones *et al.* 1999) and Seychelles magpie-robin (Watson *et al.* 1992; BirdLife International 2000).

Pest and disease management

The deliberate or unintended introduction of exotic predators or competitors has had a profound impact on endemic bird populations, especially on islands formerly without such threats (Merton 1978; Veitch & Bell 1990). Two examples illustrate the dramatic impact that exotic predators can have on endemic birds. Guam 'has recently been the scene of what may become the greatest avian disaster of this half-century' (Engbring & Pratt 1985). This was due largely to the introduction of the brown tree snake (*Boiga irregularis*). All 12 species that made up the entire native forest bird fauna of Guam went extinct in the wild. The Guam rail survives through captive propagation (BirdLife International 2000). The second example is the invasion of Big South Cape Island in southern New Zealand by ship rats (*Rattus rattus*) (Bell 1978; Galbreath 1993). Despite the efforts of wildlife conservation officers at the time, the endemic Stead's bush wren (*Xenicus longipes variabilis*), the Stewart Island snipe (*Coenocorypha aucklandica iredalei*) and the greater short-tailed bat (*Mystacina robusta*) all went globally extinct, together with a number of local extinctions.

Control of both exotic and native predators and competitors can be a crucial aspect of endangered species management, particularly on islands without introduced mammalian predators that have become the sole remaining habitats of 'refugee' species (Bell 1991). Predator and competitor management includes exclusion, eradication, reduction of pest numbers and biological control. A dramatic recovery of the kakerori on Rarotonga, Cook Islands, was due to ongoing control each year of predators (*Rattus rattus*) in the breeding habitats and guarding of nests with rat-proof metal bands (Box 6.2 - McCormack & Künzle 1990; Robertson 1999). Predator control is pivotal to the survival and ongoing management of Chatham Island taiko (*Pterodroma magentae*): since the first nesting burrows were found in 1987/88, 204 feral cats (*Felis catus*), 3,053 brushtail possums (*Trichosurus vulpecula*), 1,572 weka and 589 rats (Rattus sp.) were killed in 109,892 trap-nights to March 1993 (Imber *et al.* 1994). Total eradication of some

---

Box 6.2. Management of a critically endangered island passerine: kakerori (*Pomarea dimidiata*).

Locality: Rarotonga, Cook Islands.
Status: Resident.
IUCN Red List category & criterion: EN D1.
Main cause of decline: Introduced mammalian predators (especially *Rattus rattus*); habitat loss.
Future threats: Cyclones.
Minimal world population: 29 in 1989.
Recent world population: 183 in 1999.
World population trends 1987–99:

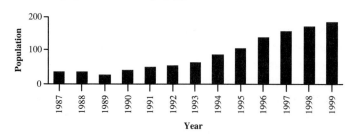

Principal management: Predator control with nest tree protection; habitat protection.

Commentary: In 1989, the kakerori and the related Tahiti monarch flycatcher (*Pomarea nigra*) were among the ten rarest bird species in the world. An example of effective 'research-by-management' with a dramatic recovery of the species due to ship rat (*Rattus rattus*) control in the breeding habitats and guarding of nests with rat-proof metal bands. A special feature of the recovery programme is that all the management has taken place within the natural habitat of the kakerori. Local landowners are involved. No captive breeding but translocation to another site in Cook Islands being considered.

Sources: McCormack & Künzle 1990; IUCN 1997; Robertson 1999; BirdLife International 2000; E. Saul & H.A. Robertson, pers. comm.

13 animal pest species from some 60 important islands off New Zealand has been achieved to the benefit of endemic birds, reptiles, invertebrates and plants (Merton 1978; Veitch & Bell 1990; Empson & Miskelly, 1999). Adaptive management-by-research on kokako at Mapara, New Zealand, addresses cost – benefit aspects of predator/competitor control, attempting to maximise benefits within a managed 'mainland island' forest area (see Chapter 7 for details of 'adaptive management').

Diseases and parasite infections can have dramatic impacts on critically endangered bird populations. Disease and parasite screening and control has been an integral part of recovery programmes for such birds, for example the echo parakeet and pink pigeon in Mauritius (Mauritius Wildlife Appeal Fund 1990; Swinnerton *et al.* 1998), the black robin (Tisdall & Merton 1988), black stilt, kakapo and takahe in New Zealand (Reed *et al.* 1993; Crouchley 1994; Merton *et al.* 1999) and the whooping crane in the United States (Kuyt 1996). Disease management is an integral part of captive propagation programmes in zoos and aviaries, for example Bali myna (van Balen & Gepak 1994; Partington *et al.* 1989).

Parasite and disease management includes quarantine control. The management of disease has been of particular concern in the Hawaiian Islands, where many endemic birds are highly susceptible to avian disease and extinctions and endangerment are attributed to this cause (see Chapter 8).

Disease management is an important part of translocation programmes, and disease screening of both the birds to be translocated, and the species present at potential translocation sites, should be conducted. Practical disease prevention measures need to be undertaken, for instance effective hygiene protocols at supplementary feeding stations. Also important is effective biosecurity control at national borders, especially for vulnerable island nations, to prevent arrival of unwanted organisms.

Genetic management

There are genetic threats to small populations due to declining genetic diversity from the effects of genetic drift and inbreeding depression (see Chapter 1). Theoretically, their long-term survival is jeopardised since they gradually lose the genetic diversity necessary for them to continue to evolve, and their short-term survival is jeopardised by the likely effects on survival and reproduction (Lovejoy 1978; Ballou 1995). However, Craig (1991) argues that inbreeding has long been part of the mating systems of small populations of island birds, as in New Zealand, with no apparent detrimental effects over the short term. Where known, levels of inbreeding far exceed the 1–3% suggested by Soulé (1987) as the maximum allowable before loss of genetic variability occurs with consequent deleterious effects (Craig 1991). DNA profiling by Professor David Lambert and associates at Massey University in New Zealand has shown just how intense this is in some island forms. For instance, virtually no detectable variability was found in the Chatham Island tit (*Petroica macrocephala chathamensis*), black robin, Campbell Island teal and kakapo. Having survived an intense bottleneck throughout the twentieth century, culminating in a single viable pair in the early 1980s, the black robin now (2001) numbers *c.* 300 individuals. Although all are derived from a single pair, there is no indication of the classic negative consequences of prolonged, high levels of inbreeding (Ardern & Lambert 1997; Merton 1990, 1992), although this may not become apparent for many years.

Hybridisation is a genetic threat to some endangered populations and requires management (Pierce 1984; Nixon 1994; Triggs & Daugherty 1996). In Europe, the introduced North American ruddy duck (*Oxyura jamaicensis*) hybridises with the vulnerable white-headed duck in Spain (Peterson *et al.* 1993), threatening the integrity of the rarer European species. Steps have been taken to minimise pairing between critically endangered black stilts and the commoner pied stilts on the South Island, New Zealand. Hybridisation has also resulted from cross-fostering programmes: two instances occurred during the rescue and recovery of the black robin, in which over 100 robin nestlings were fostered by Chatham Island tits (Box 6.3).

Population manipulation

Population manipulation is a core aspect in the management of critically endangered species, embracing translocation of free-living individuals (to other areas) and manipulation of pairings, fertilisation, and egg clutches or broods (Cade 1978). The black robin recovery programme involved most of these field-based techniques (Box 6.3).

Translocation of free-living individuals or populations to new sites (often islands, beyond a species' natural range) has been the key element in the conservation management for many critically endangered birds. Successful examples in New Zealand, which has pioneered this type of management, include both the Eastern and North Island weka, the two races of saddleback, Chatham Islands snipe, black robin (Box 6.3), brown teal (*Anas aucklandica chorotis*), kakapo (Box 6.3), kokako, North Island brown and little spotted kiwi, stitchbird and takahe (Bell 1975, 1991; Merton 1975a, b, 1990, 1992; Flack 1978; Mills & Williams 1978; Butler & Merton

Box 6.3. Close-order management in two endangered New Zealand birds: black robin (*Petroica traversi*) and kakapo (*Strigops habroptilus*).

1. Black robin
Locality: Chatham Islands, New Zealand.
Status: Resident.
IUCN Red List category & criterion: EN D1.
Main cause of decline: Introduced mammalian predators, habitat loss and degradation.
Future threats: Predatory mammals, especially rats, reaching the species' island refuges, the long-term consequences of high levels of inbreeding.
Minimal world population: 5 in 1979–80.
Current world population: *c.* 300 in 2001.
World population trends 1972–2001:

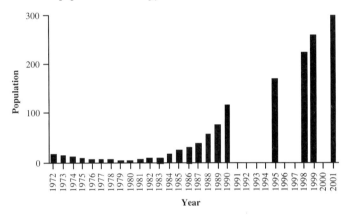

Principal management: Close-order management: habitat restoration by re-vegetation, predator and competitor eradication and control, translocation to two islands, supplementary feeding of breeding pairs to induce earlier laying [and] production of enlarged clutches and permit raising of enlarged broods, nest protection and reconstruction, cross-fostering of eggs and broods to two species (initially Chatham Island warbler (*Gerygone albofronta*), later – and more successfully – to the congeneric Chatham Island tit), clutch and brood manipulation, genetic and behavioural management of offspring to minimise the effects of inbreeding and imprinting respectively (Butler & Merton 1992; Merton 1990, 1992; Galbreath, 1993).
Commentary: In 1980 the species was regarded the rarest in the world, with only five individuals including just one viable pair. The survival of the species represents one of the most dramatic recoveries from the brink of extinction. It has demonstrated that manipulative management of a free-living, critically endangered species is practicable, and that even in the extreme case (one remaining viable pair: female 'Old Blue' and male 'Old Yellow') recovery is possible (Merton 1990). The recovery occurred without resort to captive breeding.

Box 6.3. (*cont.*)

Sources: Flack 1978; Merton 1990, 1992; Reed & Merton 1991; Butler & Merton 1992; BirdLife International 2000.

2. Kakapo
Locality: New Zealand.
Status: Resident.
IUCN Red List category: CR D1.
Main cause of decline: Introduced mammalian predators, competitors (mammalian herbivores), habitat loss and degradation, commercial collecting.
Future threats: Acute scarcity of suitable (mammal-free) habitat, introduced mammalian predators or food competitors reaching its island refuges, conservation-dependence in suboptimal habitats to which it has been confined, impacts of demographic, physiological and genetic factors.
Minimal world population: 51 in 1995–96.
Recent world population: 62 in 2000 (36 males, 26 females).
World population trends 1977–2000:

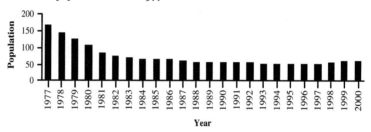

Principal management: Close-order management.
Commentary: The first conservation efforts on kakapo were the pioneering translocations of 350–400 birds to predator-free Resolution Island (Fiordland, NZ) by Richard Henry over the period 1894–1910. Regrettably, his efforts were in vain, as stoats reached the island and eliminated the kakapo (Hill & Hill 1987). The current attempt to save the species was launched in 1974. At first, the prognosis was poor because the remnant, fragmented population in Fiordland was found to comprise only old males, of which 18 were found. A major breakthrough came in 1977 when a new population was found on Stewart Island. In 1980, females were confirmed within this population – the first seen in more than 70 years! Monitoring revealed that feral cats on Stewart Island were killing adult kakapo at an alarming rate – over 50% of birds fitted with radio-transmitters were killed within 12 months. Cat control measures were immediately set in place, and during the following ten years, the 61 remaining kakapo found on Stewart Island have been relocated to three smaller, cat-free islands. Although effectively destroying the last natural population, this drastic step provided safe refuges for the survivors: once settled on the new islands adult mortality fell to less than 2% per year (Clout & Merton 1998). Sixty-two kakapo, including six juveniles from the 1999 season are known to survive – 26 females and 36 males. Fifteen (9 males, 6 females) are the progeny of translocated birds. The

remainder (47) are from Stewart Island, with the exception of an aged male known as 'Richard Henry' – the last known surviving individual from the New Zealand mainland. Only one adult death is known to have occurred in the period 1994–2001, but many of the birds are now old and some may be during incapable of breeding. Only six females have been added to the world population since 1981; the remainder are at least 18 years old and most are probably much older than this (Merton 1999; see also note on p. 131.). An intensive three-pronged management strategy, involving (i) support of all breeding females through supplementary feeding, (ii) protection of nests from rats, and (iii) monitoring of nests coupled with intervention as necessary, was instigated in 1995 and has brought spectacular results. Management is highly specialised and technical, including radio-telemetry, automatic weighing, monitoring food consumption, predator alarm systems at nests, intensive nest monitoring via IR video throughout the c. 4 months incubation/nestling stages, computer-logged data at lek sites, mapping of individual home ranges, hormonal studies, supplementary feeding and diet research, captive hatching/rearing, modern communication systems for observers and substantial logistic support for personnel.

　　Sources: Merton *et al.* 1984, 1999; Hill & Hill 1987; Butler 1989; Reed & Merton 1991; Clout & Merton 1998; Atkinson 1999; Merton 1999; BirdLife International 2000.

1992; Galbreath 1993; Merton *et al.* 1999). Failed attempts include kakapo (1895–1910), Eastern and North Island weka (to mainland sites), Stead's bush wren, Stewart Island snipe, shore plover and Antipodes Island parakeet (*Cyanoramphus unicolor*). A range of species has been translocated in other parts of the world. Island-to-island translocations include the Seychelles magpie-robin from Frégate to Cousin, Cousine and Aride (Watson *et al.* 1992; BirdLife International 2000), the Seychelles brush warbler (*Acrocephalus sechellensis*) from Cousin to Aride and Cousine (Komdeur 1994), the Laysan finch (*Telespiza cantans*) from Laysan to Midway (where subsequently destroyed by rats) at Pearl and Hermes Reef (Halliday 1978; Pratt *et al.* 1987) and the Marquesas ultramarine lorikeet (*Vini ultramarina*) from Ua Pou to Ua Huka (Pratt *et al.* 1987). The Mauritius kestrel has been translocated to various sites within Mauritius and to Ile aux Aigrettes since rats were eradicated (Jones 1990), and the noisy scrub-bird (*Atrichornis clamosus*) of Western Australia from its sole surviving population in the southwest of the state to a number of mainland sites and one island (Young 1983; Comer 2000). Reintroductions of a variety of less threatened species have occurred elsewhere in the world. Britain, for example, has seen the return of species such as the capercaillie (*Tetrao urogallus*) (Perrins 1987), and white-tailed eagle (*Haliaeetus albicilla*) (Dymond *et al.* 1989), with supplementary reintroductions of red kite (*Milvus milvus*) and goshawk (*Accipiter gentilis*) (Perrins 1987; Heinzel *et al.* 1998; Svensson & Grant 1999).

Box 6.4. Close-order management: Mauritius pink pigeon (*Columba mayeri*).

Locality: Mauritius.
Status: Resident.
IUCN Red List category & criteria: EN B1+2c;C2b.
Main cause of decline: The species has experienced severe loss of habitat, compounded by nest predation by introduced rats and monkeys, with feral cats taking newly fledged young and adult birds. Late winter food shortages also threaten the species.

Future threats: Disease threatens all populations, particularly on Ile aux Aigrettes. Cyclones also destroy some nests and accelerate habitat degradation. Possible genetic bottleneck effects.

Minimal world population: 10 in 1990 (in the wild, not including captive birds).

Current world population: 364–375 (in the wild) in 2000 (plus captive birds).

World population trends 1991–2000: Although once common, declined to its lowest number of 10 individuals in the wild in 1991, with captive populations in Mauritius and at Jersey Zoo. Since then the population has recovered as a result of intensive management. Between July 1987 and October 1992, 51 captive-bred birds were released at Brise Fer such that by September 1993, the introduced population stood at 28 (12 pairs and 4 juveniles), and by May 1994, this population was 52 (half of which were hatched in the wild), with the original wild population at *c.* 25. In 1994 the release programme was extended to the 25 ha predator-free Ile aux Aigrettes and to a lowland site at Bel Ombre. In 1997 the known population was 330 individuals, more than half of which had been bred in the wild, comprising 76 at Pigeon Wood, 102 at Bel Ombre, 102 at Plaine Lièvre and 50 on Ile aux Aigrettes, with some limited movement between the three mainland populations. In January 2000, there were 364 individuals (86 in Pigeon Wood, 88 at Bel Ombre, 98 at Plaine Lièvre and 71 on Ile aux Aigrettes). However, it is doubtful that these numbers could be maintained without the present intense management (BirdLife International 2000).

Principal management: Close-order management.

Commentary: In 1991 the species was one of the rarest birds in the world. It is doubtful whether current populations could be maintained without the current intense habitat management. Native habitat has been restored (exotic plants removed and replaced with native species), and exotic mammals are controlled (rats, mongooses and cats) or excluded (deer, pigs and people). There are also predator control grids at some sites. A captive-breeding and reintroduction programme to the three mainland sites and reintroduction to the predator-free (cats and rats having been eradicated) Ile aux Aigrettes, combined with habitat restoration, supplementary feeding, nest guarding, clutch and brood (fostering) manipulations, rescue of eggs and young from failing nests and control of disease, helped to improve the breeding success and hence chances of survival of this species. An introduced population at

Combo is composed of captive-bred birds and individuals translocated from other subpopulations. All populations are currently monitored to establish survival and productivity. Research is ongoing into present and historic genetic variation of the species so that the effects of the population bottleneck can be quantified and current populations managed to preserve maximum genetic diversity. The newly created Black River National Park partly covers the species' distribution and habitat.

Sources: C. Jones *in litt.* to BirdLife International; Jones *et al.* 1999; R. McClellan, *in litt.*; BirdLife International 2000.

Care is required with translocations to avoid detrimental impact at release sites (Atkinson 1990). When the Laysan finch was introduced to Midway Island the birds initially survived but at the expense of some of the resident birds, whose eggs they ate (Bailey 1956; Halliday 1978). In New Zealand, the opportunistic and predatory weka has now been removed from some of the islands to which it had been introduced (e.g. Codfish Island, Trios Island, Chetwode Islands, Maud Island). In reaching decisions on translocations, Atkinson (1990) recognised a triangle of potential conflicts in the management of islands resulting from their use for (i) protecting relict species of the mainland, (ii) recovery of endangered mainland species not originally present on the island, and (iii) ecological restoration of particular biotic communities. Potential conflict might be avoided by way of an integrated, national strategy incorporating threatened animals and plants, and biologically important islands.

Fyfe (1978) reviewed the introduction of endangered birds to the wild and proposed five requirements: (i) prior identification of the species' requirements; (ii) concentrating releases to promote mating; (iii) minimising mortality in released birds; (iv) releasing birds that are fit for the wild; (v) monitoring the survival of released birds.

Breeding enhancement can involve pair manipulation, artificial insemination and clutch or brood manipulation, including egg harvesting to induce re-laying, fostering or cross-fostering, chick transfer for fostering or cross-fostering, and the rescue of eggs or chicks from failing nests (see e.g. Reed & Merton 1991; Merton 1990; Butler & Merton 1992; Kuyt 1996; Jones *et al.* 1999). Examples are given in Appendix 6.2.

The Re-introduction Specialist Group of the International Union for the Conservation of Nature (IUCN) produced guidelines for species reintroductions. Adhering to these is important both for maximising the chances of success of reintroductions and minimising impacts on other biodiversity (Soorae 1996).

Captive propagation

Captive propagation, though often viewed as a last resort, has been important in many recovery programmes for endangered birds. Four bird species – Alagoas curassow, Guam rail, Spix's macaw and Socorro dove – are extinct in the wild and depend on captive propagation for their continued survival (BirdLife International 2000, 2001; Luis Baptista, pers. comm.). Zoos have recently become the centre of a spirited debate (Townsend et al. 1999). At one extreme, some see zoological and botanical gardens (and germ banks and seed banks) as small arks that provide refuge for endangered species from a flood of species extinctions; others see them as living museums – once a species enters a zoo it is essentially dead (Ginsberg 1993). Such arguments could be extended to include species like the kakapo (Box 6.3), now a 'refugee' species extinct throughout its natural range and confined to a number of safe New Zealand islands (Bell 1991; Clout & Merton 1998; Merton 1999). It is flightless and thus in effect 'captive' on these islands where it is intensively managed.

Plans for integrated breeding and release amongst bird stocks are developing to improve captive management programmes. Fyfe's (1978) five requirements (above) include reintroductions from captivity. Captive propagation has been entirely responsible for the survival of extinct-in-the-wild species like the Guam rail and California condor, though for other species captive breeding is incorporated into integrated programmes of wild population management – 'captive breeding in the wild' is a phrase used for this approach in the recovery of the echo parakeet in Mauritius (Greenwood 1996). Eggs and/or chicks may be collected from the wild and then incubated/reared in captivity, with care being taken to use models of adults to avoid imprinting on humans. Such 'head starting' has proved valuable for species like takahe, kakapo (Box 6.3) and black stilt in New Zealand as well as, for instance, with Mauritius kestrel and whooping crane (Box 6.1). The Bali myna (Box 6.5) is the only critically endangered passerine to have been substantially maintained in captivity, with about 1,000 in captivity but only about a dozen remaining in the wild.

Relatively few avian species have been successfully reintroduced and established from captive stock – hopefully the current California condor programme will provide one exception. The Mauritius kestrel 'represents one of the most dramatic examples of the effectiveness of intensive breeding and management of an endangered species' (Carl Jones, p. 31 in Cossons 1992). Captive stock may have poor survival, or may differ behaviourally or genetically from original wild stock, for example in the nene (*Branta sandvicensis*),

Box 6.5. Problematic management of a critically endangered Asian passerine: Bali myna (*Leucopsar rothschildi*).

Locality: Bali, Indonesia.

Status: Resident.

IUCN Red List category & criteria:
CR A1a,d;A2b,d;B1+2e;C1;C2b;D1.

Main cause of decline: Habitat destruction, and illegal capture and sale to pet market.

Future threats: Further habitat loss (fuel wood), human encroachment and poaching.

Minimal world population: *c.* 12 in wild.

Current world population: *c.* 12 in wild (plus captive birds).

World population trends 1925–2000: Hundreds in 1925 (von Plessen 1926) but population had shrunk dramatically by 1960s as agriculture developed; by 1990 numbers had declined to as low as 13 and remains at only 12–14 (van Balen & Gepak 1994; Nicholson-Lord 2000).

Commentary: In the wild the Bali myna is one of the rarest birds in the world, the estimated population being about a dozen (Anon. 1998, Nicholson-Lord 2000). It is the only threatened passerine to have been substantially maintained in captivity, with *c.* 1,000 in zoos and on studbooks. The forest habitat is legally protected (Bali Barat National Park) but there is little knowledge of the species' requirements or effective management on the ground. Illegal poaching is a major problem; an armed gang recently stole virtually all breeding Bali mynas in a captive-breeding facility in West Bali National Park. Given the problems the species faces in the wild, captive management offers the species the best hope in the short term, though ultimately secure habitats without poaching and interference are needed to ensure its future survival (with captive releases) in the wild. An Appendix I species under CITES. In 1991, the myna was adopted by the Indonesian government as the provincial symbol of Bali and since has become a conservation symbol in Indonesia.

Sources: von Plessen 1926; de Iongh 1983; Mackinnon & Mackinnon 1991; van Balen & Gepak 1994; IUCN 1997; Anon. 1998; Nicholson-Lord 2000; BirdLife International 2000.

reintroduced to Hawaii, in which positive selection for one feature (fertility or 'wildness') in captivity can increase another less desirable genetic trait (young with meagre 'cottony' down – Kear & Berger 1980). Captive release may require behavioural manipulation to enhance survival of released birds, for example pre-release aversion training in the California condor to avoid power lines and humans or post-release training to induce migration in the whooping crane (Box 6.1 – Lewis 1995, 1997; US Fish & Wildlife Service 1996; BirdLife International 2000).

Integrated management

Various management terms for endangered species recovery have been
used to describe an integrated approach, covering a range of techniques,
such as 'integrated management', 'clinical ornithology', 'close-order management', 'management-by-research' and 'adaptive management' (Plunkett
1978; Merton 1992; Greenwood 1996; Atkinson 1999). Greenwood (1996)
notes that Stanley Temple coined the term 'clinical ornithology' to describe
the type of intensive conservation management of wild birds that began with
attempts to save peregrine falcon (*Falco peregrinus*) populations of North
America. A combination of nest-site protection and reconstruction, habitat restoration, supplementary feeding, pest control and manipulation of
breeding biology has been applied to a number of critically endangered
birds across the world. He notes that this has probably developed to its highest level in Mauritius and New Zealand. Close-order management similarly
embraces many management activities: it is the manipulation of behaviour
and/or physiology of free-living individuals, based at the individual rather
than the population level with the aim of boosting productivity through enhancement of production and survival (Merton 1992). Examples of species
to which such management has been applied are the black robin, black stilt,
kakapo and takahe of New Zealand (Box 6.3), the kestrel, pink pigeon and
echo parakeet of Mauritius (Box 6.4) and the magpie-robin of the Seychelles
(BirdLife International 2000).

Recovery plans and population viability analyses

Species recovery plans are prepared and regularly reviewed for many of the
world's endangered species, addressing the status of the species, reviewing
recovery options, and recommending management action.

Population Viability Analysis (PVA) is a modelling approach to extinction risk and is defined as 'a systematic evaluation of the relative importance of factors that place populations at risk' (Soulé 1987). Many factors
facing small populations result from random, stochastic events so their exact effects cannot be predicted with total accuracy, yet conservation strategies need to address these situations (see Chapter 9 for details of PVA).
Amongst threatened bird species for which PVA has been used are the black
stilt (Box 6.3), the blue duck (*Hymenolaimus malacorhynchos*), the Nihoa
finch (*Telespiza ultima*), the Nihoa millerbird (*Acrocephalus familiaris kingi*)
and the whooping crane (Box 6.1 – O'Driscoll & Veltman 1992;
Henderson 1994; Morin *et al.* 1998). Brook *et al.* (2000) examined the predictive accuracy of population viability analysis in conservation biology
and concluded that, despite considerable scepticism, PVA predictions are

surprisingly accurate, given adequate data, and are useful in the conservation contexts in which they are currently applied (but see Coulson *et al.* 2001).

Advocacy, education and community involvement

Legislative protection facilitates management and includes listing species in CITES Appendix I, international protective treaties, protective national and state law, the arrest and prosecution of poachers, the creation of reserves, national parks and other protected areas. Public advocacy through education curricula in schools, educational films and documentaries, environmental and wildlife conservation societies, clubs and charities, the media, and through field-based socio-economic community initiatives is of critical importance. Steps to encourage the local community and land owners to identify with critically endangered species have been responsible for important advances in recovery programmes, for example the kakerori in Rarotonga (Box 6.2), the noisy scrub-bird in Western Australia, the helmeted honeyeater (*Lichenostomus cassidix*) of southeastern Australia, critically endangered parrots of some Caribbean nations, and a raft of Chatham Islands endemics. However, this approach has worked less well for others (e.g. Bali myna in Indonesia–Box 6.5).

DISCUSSION

While ideally threatened species management should be based on scientific principles, the practice of saving the most endangered bird species has been as much an art as a science. It has often required not only a knowledge of the species concerned, but also carefully integrated management involving the skilful application of a range of management techniques. Although well suited to a team approach, repeatedly, the survival and recovery of some of the most critically endangered life forms can be attributed to the extraordinary commitment, determination and practical innovation of just one, or a few individuals. The extreme urgency to intervene in (some very) critically endangered situations often precludes meaningful preliminary study. The conservation manager of endangered species faces a dilemma. While every reasonable effort must be made to acquire a full knowledge of a species and its evident requirements before applying conservation management, too long a delay in management could place the species at even greater risk. Michael Soulé has pointed out that 'the luxuries of confidence limits and certainty are ones that conservation biologists cannot now afford. Constructive criticism is welcome, but to embrace the purist's motto of "insufficient data" is to abandon the bleeding patient on the operating table.'

In future priority-setting exercises, the cost and cost-effectiveness of different approaches to critically endangered species management requires consideration. For example, the California condor project is relatively expensive, with high ongoing costs, while the Seychelles warbler management and translocation project was relatively cheap.

Common-sense decisions by personnel familiar and sensitive to the species' plight were a major factor in the success of the black robin rescue and recovery (Butler & Merton 1992). Fortunately, research and management increasingly act to save species in a coordinated, complementary way. For instance, Robertson (1999) describes the successful research-by-management approach to the recovery of the kakerori in the Cook Islands.

It is of concern that relatively few critically endangered species have been pulled from the brink of extinction to persist as self-sustained free-living populations, though some appear to have done this, at least in the short term (Table 6.3). While there have been some spectacular successes, there have also been failures despite management action being taken. Other species have gone extinct through lack of action or lack of attention, while the fate of many critically endangered species still hangs in the balance, for example some of the Hawaiian endemic birds. Spectacular successes include Chatham Islands black robin, Mauritius kestrel, Seychelles warbler, noisy scrub-bird and both North Island and South Island saddlebacks. Notable success has also been seen in recovery programmes for the California condor, echo parakeet, kakerori, Forbes parakeet (*Cyanoramphus forbesi*), nene, pink pigeon, Seychelles magpie-robin, takahe, kakapo and whooping crane. The jury is still out on species like the 'alala, Bali myna and Guam rail. Even when we have averted extinction and rebuilt a population to a safer level, the battle may be won but the war is not necessarily over – the goal of long-term sustainability presents a further and perhaps even more daunting challenge. In the face of an ever expanding human population, natural systems, communities and habitats are under ever increasing pressures. Moreover, the number of life forms that are now, to varying degrees, dependent for their survival upon ongoing, often costly, labour-intense human props is increasing at an alarming rate. The challenges facing conservation biologists are daunting:

- To avert extinction;
- To rebuild depleted populations; and
- To find lasting solutions whereby conservation-dependent life forms might be given a second chance to survive in a free-living state without the need for ongoing intervention.

Table 6.3. *Examples of the relative degree of success and failure in conservation management of threatened bird species listed in Appendix 6.2, with an assessment of success (or otherwise) in re-establishing self-sustaining populations*

Species	Success (+) or failure (−) in the wild	in captivity	Has management resulted in one or more free-living, self-sustaining populations
'Alala	?	?	No
Bali myna	−−	+++	No
Black robin	+++		Yes
Black stilt	+	++	No
California condor	+	++	No
Chatham Is. taiko	+		No
Echo parakeet	++	++	No
Guam rail	−−−	++	No
Gurney's pitta	−		No
Kakapo	++	−	No
Kakerori	++		No (dependent on ongoing rat control)
Mauritius kestrel	++	++	Yes
Montserrat oriole	?	?	Not applicable
Nene	+	+++	Yes
Noisy scrub-bird	+++		Yes
Northern bald ibis	−−	+	No
Pink pigeon	++	++	No (dependent on on-going supplementary feeding)
Saddleback	+++	+	Yes
Seychelles magpie-robin	++		Yes
Seychelles warbler	++[+]		Yes
Slender-billed curlew	−−		No
Spix's macaw	−−−	++	No
Stitchbird	+[+]	+	Yes (translocated populations are precarious)
Takahe	++	+	No
Whooping crane	++	++	Yes

Ecological, genetic, social, economic and political constraints will continue to influence threatened species research and management in the forseeable future.

In concluding remarks to a symposium on management of endangered birds at the University of Wisconsin-Madison in 1977, Ian Nisbet (1978) remarked: 'Since endangered species management has long-term goals, we need to look ahead periodically at the future state of the environment... the world is in a state of dramatic and rapid change. During the next

30 years . . . we can expect to see a fundamental transition of the earth from a generally natural state to a generally disturbed and degraded state in which even semi-natural ecosystems will become sparse and fragmented. At the same time, we can expect to see a change in social attitudes to the natural world, although these are less easy to predict.' Most of those 30 years are now past and indeed there have been major global changes with burgeoning human populations, accelerated loss of tropical rainforests, global climate change and increased traffic in endangered species, and losses of many more birds to extinction over that time. Times are not any easier, but despite the problems that face us, many critically endangered birds have been rescued from the brink. Such successes provide hope for further recovery of the world's threatened avian biodiversity despite the even more daunting political, social, economic and ecological challenges that lie ahead.

Note added in proof:

In January 2002 the world population of Kakapo stood at 62 individuals, with no eggs laid over the last three years. Breeding is believed to coincide with mast-fruiting of the rimu tree Dacrydium Cypressinum. This year has been a major rimu fruiting year on Codfish island, and all 21 breeding female kakapo were on, or taken to, the island. At the time of writing (15 February 2002), the females had laid 47 eggs. The New Zealand Department of Conservation carried out two successful massive eradication operations to get rid of possums (1989) and rats (1997) on Codfish island, and there are consequently no predators left on the island to attack the kakapo nests and eggs. We hope that by the time this book is in print, the world population of the species portrayed on the cover of this book will have significantly increased.

Appendix 6.1. *Examples of threats or potential threats faced by critically endangered or endangered birds*
EW, extinct in the wild; CR, critically endangered; EN, endangered

Threat	Popular name	Scientific name	Status (rarer taxa)	Location	Source
A. THREATS APPLYING TO MANY BIRDS, NOT JUST ENDANGERED SPECIES					
Habitat loss					
Natural events					
Volcanism	Montserrat oriole	*Icterus oberi*	CR	Montserrat Is.	Arendt et al. 1999
Drought & desertification	Raso lark	*Alauda razae*	CR	Cape Verde Is.	Bird Life International 2000
Cyclones & storms	Cape Verde cane warbler	*Acrocephalus brevipennis*	EN	Cape Verde Is.	Hazevoet et al. 1999
	Kakerori	*Pomarea dimideata*	EN	Cook Is.	Robertson 1999
	Cozumel thrasher	*Toxostoma guttatum*	CR	Mexico	BLI 2000
	Chatham albatross	*Thalassarche eremita*	CR	New Zealand	BLI 2000
	Tahitian monarch	*Pomarea nigra*	CR	Tahiti Is.	BLI 2000
Direct human impact					
Deforestation	Alqagoas curassow	*Mitu mitu*	EW	Brazil	BLI 2000
	Plain spinetail	*Synallaxis infuscata*	CR	Brazil	BLI 2000
	Ivory-billed woodpecker	*Campephilus principalis*	CR	Cuba	BLI 2000
	Sumatra ground-cuckoo	*Carpococcyx viridis*	CR	Indonesia	BLI 2000
	Amami thrush	*Zoothera majori*	CR	Japan	BLI 2000
	Okinawa woodpecker	*Sapheopipo noguchii*	CR	Japan	BLI 2000
	Liberian greenbul	*Phyllastrephus leucolepis*	CR	Liberia	BLI 2000
	Short-crested coquette	*Lophornis brachylopha*	CR	Mexico	BLI 2000
	Faichuk white-eye	*Rukia ruki*	CR	Micronesia	BLI 2000
	Black-hooded coucal	*Centropus steerii*	CR	Philippines	BLI 2000

Appendix 6.1. (cont.)

Threat	Popular name	Scientific name	Status (rarer taxa)	Location	Source
	Visayan wrinkled hornbill	*Aceros corrugatus*	CR	Philippines	BLI 2000
	Bulo Burti boubou	*Laniarius liberatus*	CR	Somalia	BLI 2000
	Gurney's pitta	*Pitta gurneyi*	CR	Thailand	Round 1996; BLI 2000
Wetlands drainage	Siberian crane	*Grus leucogeranus*	CR	Eurasia	BLI 2000
	White-shouldered ibis	*Lophotibis cristata*	CR	SE Asia	BLI 2000
	Giant ibis	*Pseudibis gigantea*	CR	Cambodia & Laos	BLI 2000
	Sakalava rail	*Amaurornis olivieri*	CR	Madagascar	BLI 2000
Human settlement, urbanisation & industry	Sapphire-bellied hummingbird	*Lepidopyga lilliae*	CR	Colombia	BLI 2000
	Tumaco seedeater	*Sporophila insulata*	CR	Colombia	BLI 2000
	Northern bald ibis	*Geronticus eremita*	CR	Morocco	Bowden 1998
	Seychelles Scops-owl	*Otus insularis*	CR	Seychelles	BLI 2000
Hydroelectric development	Junin grebe	*Podiceps taczanowskii*	CR	Peru	BLI 2000
Fire	Night parrot	*Geopsittacus occidentalis*	CR	Australia	BLI 2000
Rising sea levels	Tuamotu sandpiper	*Prosobonia cancellata*	EN	Tuamotu Is.	BLI 2000
Intensified agriculture	Socorro mockingbird	*Mimodes graysoni*	CR	Mexico	BLI 2000
Open-cast mining	Abbot's booby (formerly)	*Papasula abbotti*	CR	Christmas Is.	Nelson 1975; Merton 1983
Predators & competitors					
Predation	Abbot's booby by yellow crazy ant(?)	*Papasula abbotti*	CR	Christmas Is.	BLI 2000
	Christmas Is. frigatebird by yellow crazy ant(?)	*Fregata andrewsi*	CR	Christmas Is.	BLI 2000

	Species		Location	Reference
Christmas Is. white-eye by yellow crazy ant(?)	*Zosterops natalis*	CR	Christmas Is.	BLI 2000
Lord Howe rail by pigs, cats, dogs, people	*Gallirallus sylvestris*	EN	Lord Howe Is.	BLI 2000
Guam rail by brown treesnake	*Gallirallus owstoni*	EW	Guam Is.	Engbring & Pratt 1985
Guam swiftlet by brown treesnake	*Collocalia sawtelli*	EN	Guam Is.	BLI 2000
Alaotra grebe by carnivorous fish	*Tachybaptus rufolavatus*	CR	Madagascar	BLI 2000
Fatuhiva monarch by ship rat	*Pomarea whitneyi*	CR	Marquesas Is.	BLI 2000
Mauritius fody by rats & crab-eating macaque	*Foudia rubra*	CR	Mauritius Is.	BLI 2000
Kakapo formerly by Pacific rat, feral cat & stoat	*Strigops habroptilus*	CR	New Zealand	Merton et al. 1999
Socorro dove by cats	*Zenaida graysoni*	EW	Mexico	Baptista & Martinez-Gomez 1996; BLI 2000
White-chested white-eye by ship rat	*Zosterops albogularis*	CR	Norfolk Is.	BLI 2000
Zino's petrel by ship rat & cats	*Pterodroma madeira*	CR	Portugal	BLI 2000
Semper's warbler by mongoose	*Leucopeza semperi*	CR	St Lucia	BLI 2000
Seychelles magpie-robin	*Copsychus sechellarum*	CR	Seychelles Is.	BLI 2000
Cahow by white-tailed tropic bird	*Pterodroma cahow*	EN	Bermuda	Wingate 1978
Millerbird by rabbits (habitat loss)	*Acrocephalus familiaris*	CR	Hawaiian Is.	BLI 2000
Kokako by brushtail possum	*Callaeus cineria*	EN	New Zealand	Leathwick et al. 1983

Competition

Appendix 6.1. (*cont.*)

Threat	Popular name	Scientific name	Status (rarer taxa)	Location	Source
	Takahe by red deer	*Porphyrio mantelli*	EN	New Zealand	Mills *et al.* 1989; Lee & Jamieson 2001
	Puerto Rican parrot by pearly-eyed thrasher	*Amazona vittata*	CR	Puerto Rico	Jackson 1978; Low 1994
	Seychelles magpie-robin by Indian myna	*Copsychus sechellarum*	CR	Seychelles Is.	BLI 2000
Disease & parasites					
	Hawaiian forest birds		CR,EN	Hawaiian Is.	Pyle 1990
	Mauritius echo parakeet	*Psittacula echo*	CR	Mauritius Is.	Mauritius Wildlife Appeal Fund (unpublished)
	Pink pigeon	*Columba mayeri*	EN	Mauritius Is.	Mauritius Wildlife Appeal Fund (unpublished)
Human exploitation					
Hunting	Pink-headed duck	*Rhodonessa caryophyllacea*	CR	India & Bangladesh	BLI 2000
	Javanese lapwing	*Vanellus macropterus*	CR	Indonesia	BLI 2000
	Madagascar pochard	*Aythya baeri*	CR	Madagascar	Madge & Burn 1988
	Eskimo curlew	*Numenius borealis*	CR	North America	BLI 2000
Collecting (pet-trade)	Bali myna	*Leucopsar rothschildi*	CR	Bali	Nicholson-Lord 2000; BLI 2000
	Lear's macaw	*Anodorhynchus leari*	CR	Brazil	BLI 2000
	Spix's macaw	*Cyanopsitta spixii*	EW	Brazil	BLI 2000
Use of gill-nets for fishing	Alaotra grebe	*Tachybaptus rufolavatus*	CR	Madagascar	BLI 2000

Chemical toxins, pollutants, environmental hazards

Category	Common name	Scientific name	Status	Location	Reference
Pesticides	Northern bald ibis	*Geronticus eremita*	CR	Morocco	Bowden 1998
	California condor	*Gymnogyps californianus*	CR	North America	Snyder 1983
Pollutants	Brazilian merganser	*Mergus squamatus*	CR	Brazil, Argentina	BLI 2000

B. THREATS APPLYING PARTICULARLY TO ENDANGERED SPECIES

Inherent evolutionary traits

Category	Common name	Scientific name	Status	Location	Reference
K-selected endemics cf. r-selected congenerics	Black stilt (cf. pied stilt)	*Himantopus novaezelandiae*	CR	New Zealand	Fleming 1962
	Takahe (cf. pukeko)	*Porphyrio mantelli*	EN	New Zealand	Bell 1991
Flightlessness & giantism	Kakapo	*Strigops habroptilus*	CR	New Zealand	Atkinson & Millener 1991; Bell 1991
	Takahe	*Porphyrio mantelli*	EN	New Zealand	Atkinson & Millener 1991; Bell 1991
Tameness & vulnerability	Galapagos cormorant	*Phalacrocorax harrisi*	EN	Galapagos Is.	BLI 2000
	Kakerori	*Pomarea dimideata*	EN	Cook Is.	Robertson 1999
	Kakapo	*Strigops habroptilus*	CR	New Zealand	Butler 1989

Demographic or spatial risks
Limited or declining population

Category	Common name	Scientific name	Status	Location	Reference
Rapid population decline	Erect-crested penguin	*Eudyptes chrysolophus*	EN	New Zealand	BLI 2000
	Galapagos petrel	*Pterodroma externa*	CR	Galapagos Is.	BLI 2000
Extreme fluctuations	Nihoa finch	*Telespiza ultima*	CR	Hawaiian Is.	BLI 2000
	Raso lark	*Alauda razae*	CR	Cape Verde Is.	BLI 2000
Very small population size	São Tome fiscal	*Lanius newtoni*	CR	São Tome Is.	BLI 2000
	Rodrigues warbler	*Acrocephalus rodericanus*	EN	Rodrigues Is.	BLI 2000

Appendix 6.1. (*cont.*)

Threat	Popular name	Scientific name	Status (rarer taxa)	Location	Source
Limited distribution					
Small extent of occurrence	Lord Howe rail	*Gallirallus sylvestris*	EN	Lord Howe Is.	BLI 2000
	Shore plover	*Thinornis novaeseelandiae*	EN	New Zealand	BLI 2000
Severe fragmentation	Forest owlet	*Athene blewitti*	CR	India	BLI 2000
	Orange-bellied parrot	*Neophema chrysogaster*	CR	Australia	BLI 2000
Genetic & demographic risks					
Genetic drift and/or inbreeding	Black robin	*Petroica traversi*	EN	New Zealand	Merton 1992; Ardern & Lambert 1997
	Campbell Island teal	*Anas aucklandica*	CR	New Zealand	Ardern & Lambert 1997
	Kakapo	*Strigops habroptilus*	CR	New Zealand	Ardern & Lambert 1997
	Whooping crane	*Grus americana*	EN	North America	BLI 2000
Hybridisation	Spix's macaw (× blue-winged macaw)	*Cyanopsitta spixii*	CR	Brazil	BLI 2000
	White-headed duck (× ruddy duck)	*Oxyura leucocephala*	EN	Spain	Peterson *et al.* 1993
	Hawaiian duck (× mallard)	*Anas wyvilliana*	EN	Hawaiian Is.	Pratt *et al.* 1987
	Black stilt (× pied stilt)	*Himantopus novaezelandiae*	CR	New Zealand	Pierce 1984
	Forbes parakeet × red-crowned parakeet	*Cyanoramphus forbesi*	EN	New Zealand	Nixon 1994; Triggs & Daugherty 1996
Systematic oversight	Orange-fronted parakeet	*Cyanoramphus malherbi*	EN	New Zealand	Boon *et al.* 2000; BLI 2000

Appendix 6.2. *The principal conservation management techniques used for a selection of 25 critically endangered species (or formerly critically endangered species)*

Species	Locality	Red list highest classification	Site reservation	Habitat protection	Habitat restoration	Nest site management	Roost site	Supplementary	Pest control	Disease management	Genetic management	Translocation	Pair manipulation	Artificial insemination	Clutch manipulation	Brood manipulation	Cross fostering	Nest rescue	Head starting	Captive breeding	Captive release	Behavioural	Close-order
'Alala	Hawaii	CR A1a,e;B1+2a,b,c,d,e; C1;C2b;D1	✓						✓	✓					✓					✓	✓	✓	
Bali myna	Indonesia	CR A1a,d;A2b,d;B1+2e; C1;C2b; D1	✓			✓				✓	✓									✓	✓	✓	
Black robin	New Zealand	EN D1	✓	✓	✓			✓	✓		✓	✓			✓	✓	✓	✓					✓
Black stilt	New Zealand	CR C2b;D1	✓	✓	✓			✓	✓		✓	✓			✓	✓	✓	✓	✓				✓
California condor	United States	CR D1	✓	✓	✓				✓		✓		✓			✓	✓		✓	✓	✓	✓	✓
Chatham Is. taiko	New Zealand	CR A1e;B1+2e,C2b	✓	✓	✓	✓		✓	✓							✓		✓	✓			✓	✓
Echo parakeet	Mauritius	CR D1	✓	✓	✓			✓	✓	✓	✓				✓	✓		✓		✓	✓	✓	✓
Guam rail	Micronesia	EW	✓				✓					✓								✓	✓	✓	
Gurney's pitta	Thailand	CR A2b,c,d;B1+2a,b,c,e; C1;C2b;D1	✓		✓																		
Kakapo	New Zealand	CR D1	✓	✓		✓		✓	✓	✓	✓	✓			✓	✓		✓	✓			✓	✓
Kakerori	Cook Islands	EN D1	✓	✓		✓		✓	✓	✓	✓	✓										✓	✓

Appendix 6.2. (*cont.*)

Species	Locality	Red list highest classification	Site reservation	Habitat protection	Habitat restoration	Nest site management	Roost site	Supplementary	Pest control	Disease management	Genetic management	Translocation	Pair manipulation	Artificial insemination	Clutch manipulation	Brood manipulation	Cross fostering	Nest rescue	Head starting	Captive breeding	Captive release	Behavioural	Close-order
Mauritius kestrel	Mauritius	VU D1;D2	✓	✓	✓	✓		✓	✓	✓	✓				✓	✓			✓	✓	✓		✓
Montserrat oriole	Montserrat	CR A1b,c,e; B1+2a,b,c,d,e	✓	✓		✓		✓	✓	✓	✓								✓	✓	✓	✓	
Nene	Hawaii	VU D1	✓		✓			✓	✓											✓	✓	✓	
Noisy scrub-bird	Australia	VU D2	✓	✓		?					✓									✓	✓	✓	
Northern bald ibis	Africa, Europe	CR B1+2e;C2b	✓	✓	?	✓	✓	✓	✓		✓	✓								✓	?		
Pink pigeon	Mauritius	EN B1+2c;D1	✓	✓	✓	✓	✓	✓	✓			✓				✓				✓	✓	✓	✓
Saddleback	New Zealand	LR (nt)	✓	✓	✓	✓	✓	✓	✓		✓	✓			✓	✓		✓	✓	✓	✓		
Seychelles magpie-robin	Seychelles	CR D1	✓	✓	✓	✓			✓			✓											
Seychelles warbler	Seychelles	VU D2	✓	✓	✓							✓											
Slender-billed curlew	Eurasia	CR C2b;D1	✓	?																			
Spix's macaw	Brazil	EW	✓	✓	✓	✓		✓	✓			✓	✓		✓	✓	✓			✓	?		✓
Stitchbird	New Zealand	VU D1;D2	✓	✓	✓	✓		✓	✓			✓	✓		✓	✓	✓		✓	✓	✓	✓	✓
Takahe	New Zealand	EN D1	✓	✓	✓	✓		✓	✓		✓	✓	✓		✓	✓	✓		✓	✓	✓	✓	✓
Whooping crane	North America	EN D1	✓	✓				✓	✓		✓	✓	✓	✓	✓	✓	✓		✓	✓	✓	✓	✓

7

Diagnosing causes of population declines and selecting remedial actions

RHYS E. GREEN

INTRODUCTION

Conservationists seek to prevent the global extinction of species and local extinctions that lead to loss of geographical range. Although populations of some species listed as threatened with global extinction are not declining (IUCN 1994), preventing the extinction of any species requires the ability to identify action that will arrest or reverse future population declines. Practical conservationists often rely on experience and common sense to identify remedial actions, but this approach runs a serious risk of misapplying conservation effort and delaying the implementation of effective measures (Green & Hirons 1991; Caughley & Gunn 1995; Sutherland 2000). Scientific study of the causes of population declines and the responsiveness of populations to conservation actions has been advocated as a means of improving the effectiveness of conservation action (Caughley 1994: Caughley & Gunn 1995), but ecology is a complicated science and it is usually difficult to achieve a detailed understanding of the factors driving population processes without expensive and long-term studies. The challenge of conserving global biodiversity is urgent and resources for conservation are limited, making such research seem an expensive luxury to many. This chapter examines the kinds of scientific investigations that conservation biologists can conduct that are rigorous enough to reduce the risk of serious error, but also cheap and rapid enough to aid recovery before the population has declined to the point where only heroic efforts can hope to sustain it.

WHY DIAGNOSE THE CAUSES OF PAST POPULATION DECLINES?

It would be possible to devise an effective programme of conservation measures for a threatened bird population without any understanding of the causes of its past decline. Except in populations that are already very small, population changes arise because of changes in external factors that cause a shift in the relative magnitudes of demographic rates. It is feasible to reverse a population decline that has been caused by a change in one demographic rate by management to cause a counteracting change in another rate (Green 1995). Hence, if one knew how to improve any demographic rate it would, at first sight, seem good policy to implement such management without further ado. However, there is at least one good reason why diagnosis of the causes of a population decline in the recent past often provides a more rapid and practical route to the identification of effective conservation actions. Management actions that are effective in improving a selected demographic rate may not lead to population recovery if they lead to compensating adverse changes in other rates because of density-dependence. Predicting this without trial and error would require a more detailed knowledge of population processes than is likely to be obtained with the limited time and resources available to most studies of threatened birds. However, if a change in a particular demographic rate is known to have caused a recent population decline, then management that reverses that change can be expected to reverse the decline, provided that the nature of density-dependence in the population has not changed. It may also be necessary for political reasons to have a convincing diagnosis, even in cases where reversing the cause of a past decline is not a practical option. For example, a species may have become rare because land use by humans has destroyed or degraded its habitat to an extent that is economically impossible to reverse. A clear diagnosis may then be needed to help the people who use the land, those with a duty to regulate their activities, and the general public to decide where the responsibility for other remedial action lies.

DIAGNOSING CAUSES OF POPULATION DECLINES USING THE COMPARATIVE METHOD

This widely used approach depends upon identifying correlations between rates of population change and potential external causes. The variations used for these correlations can be among time periods for the same geographical area, among areas within the same time period or, best of all, a combination of the two. The approach is outlined in Box 7.1, which synthesises and expands upon schemes suggested by Green & Hirons (1991), Caughley (1994), Caughley & Gunn (1995), Green (1995) and Sutherland (2000). Numerous pitfalls in the approach are noted here. The publications cited and the case studies mentioned therein can be consulted for illustration of the difficulties encountered.

The steps in Box 7.1 can be divided into two groups. Steps 1–4 constitute the comparative method and aim at a provisional diagnosis or narrowing of the list of candidate causes based upon correlation alone. Unless all four steps can be carried out it will be impossible to get even that far. Like all conclusions based upon correlation, those derived from this first group of steps can easily be erroneous because the real cause of the decline has not been thought of or quantified adequately and the supposed cause is merely correlated with it. Steps 5–7 are supplementary checks to reduce the risk of such errors. Although it would be ideal to pursue all of them, this may be impractical.

A diagnosis of the cause of the decline of the world population of the wandering albatross (*Diomedea exulans*), which includes most of the steps in Box 7.1, is presented as an illustrative example in Box 7.2. There was one strong candidate cause, mortality of albatrosses caused by long-line fishing, and published studies have concentrated on testing the hypothesis that it alone has caused the decline. This seems reasonable in this case, but it is usually desirable to test several candidate causes with equal rigour, even though there may be great practical difficulties in doing so. Uneven coverage of candidate causes of population declines is a particular problem in studies of birds because of their mobility. There are often phases of the life cycle that birds spend in places remote from ornithologists where there may not even be anecdotal information about possible factors that might be adversely affecting demographic rates. Even the whereabouts of the entire population of certain globally threatened bird species is unknown at some times of year. For example, the breeding grounds of the slender-billed curlew (*Numenius tenuirostris*) are unknown (Gretton 1991), and there is only sketchy information on wintering grounds of the aquatic warbler (*Acrocephalus paludicola*) (Curry-Lindahl 1981).

THE IMPORTANCE OF TESTING DIAGNOSES BASED UPON THE COMPARATIVE METHOD USING SUPPLEMENTARY INFORMATION

A diagnosis based upon correlation alone may be incorrect for the reasons given in the last section, so it is essential to regard the first four steps of the comparative method as the beginning of an iterative process in which supplementary studies can refute or support their outcome. Rejection of a diagnosis by these studies should lead to further expanded comparative

Box 7.1. Steps in diagnosing the external causes of a population decline and identifying effective remedies.

Step	Important questions	Frequent pitfalls
1. Assess the evidence for a decline in population or range.	• Can periods with differing population or range trends be identified reliably? • Can populations in separate areas be identified which have different trends?	• Population or range data are unreliable because methods are not comparable. • No surveys were conducted until after the perceived decline began. • So few repeat surveys exist that declines cannot be distinguished from fluctuations.
2. Study the species' natural history and ecology.	• Which habitats, nest sites, roost sites, foods etc. are utilised and preferred? • Which external factors affect survival and breeding success? • Do patterns of distribution and abundance correlate with distribution of certain resources or adverse factors?	• Anecdotal information, small or unrepresentative samples and poor analysis methods lead to a distorted picture. • Some factors are inconspicuous and difficult to study, e.g. cryptic pollutants, diseases and parasites or factors operating in remote or unknown non-breeding areas.
3. List plausible external causes of the decline.	• Can objective criteria be identified for deciding which factors to include and exclude?	• Inadequate knowledge either excludes an influential factor (if threshold for inclusion set high) or makes the list of candidates impractically long (if threshold set low).

Step	Important questions	Frequent pitfalls
4. Obtain data on candidate external causes and test for correlations of these with population trend.	• Which external factor(s) is (are) correlated with variation in population trend?	• Data on some candidate causes are lacking or unreliable. • Some of the candidate causes are intercorrelated making identification of real causal factors problematical.
5. Check whether variation in demographic rates supports conclusions from step 4.	• If the candidate external factor(s) selected by step 4 could only have its effect via certain demographic rates, do those rates vary among populations or periods in the expected way?	• Data on demographic rates lacking, biased or of low precision.
6. Check whether the magnitude of a change or difference in the external factor is sufficient to cause the observed population effect.	• Could the increase in e.g. predators, hunters or decrease in habitat kill sufficiently more birds to produce the observed decline?	• Data on external factors are insufficiently quantitative. • The available simulation model of population processes is too vaguely defined to permit a reliable assessment.
7. Carry out replicated field experiments with adequate controls to test the effectiveness of the most promising remedies.	• Do treatments based upon the diagnosis produce the predicted effects on demographic rates or populations?	• Only feasible to apply treatments to small areas so immigration/ emigration obscures results. • Area or resources insufficient for adequate replication.

Box 7.2. Use of the comparative method to diagnose the cause of the decline of wandering albatross (*Diomedea exulans*) populations in the Southern, Indian and South Atlantic Oceans.

Background

This case study is based mainly upon Weimerskirch *et al.* (1997). Wandering albatrosses have a world population of about 21,000 breeding pairs and nest colonially on oceanic islands in the Southern Hemisphere. Breeding adults fly thousands of kilometres from the colony to forage, principally on cephalopods. Immatures and non-breeding adults range throughout the oceans between 30° S and the Antarctic Circle.

Step 1. Evidence for a decline

A marked and widespread decline in the breeding population of wandering albatrosses, based upon reliable counts covering a high proportion of the breeding distribution, was first detected in the 1970s. Rates of decline varied over time and among colonies. At some colonies it is not clear when the decline began.

Steps 2 and 3. Do studies of the natural history of the species suggest candidate external causes of the population decline?

Observers on fishing vessels catching tuna with baited hooks set on long lines noticed that substantial numbers of albatrosses, including both immature and adult wandering albatrosses, were caught and drowned when they attempted to take bait from hooks as the lines entered the water. Long-lining for profitable species such as for southern blue-fin tuna (*Thunnus maccoyii*) and Patagonian toothfish (*Dissostichus eleginoïdes*) increased substantially in the late twentieth century in many parts of the range of the wandering albatross. It seemed that the extra mortality caused by fishing might have caused the population decline. Other changes that could have such widespread effects were not apparent.

Step 4. Do changes over time in the rate of change of albatross population size correlate with changes in the candidate external cause?

Counts of breeding pairs of wandering albatrosses at Possession Island in the Crozet Islands (southern Indian Ocean) showed that the population was stable in the 1960s, declined rapidly by 7% per year between 1970 and 1976, continued to decline by 1.4% per year from 1977 to 1985 and then recovered at 4% per year from 1986 to 1995. Long-lining within the foraging range of the breeding birds from this colony increased markedly during the 1960s and remained at a high level until the mid-1980s when it became less intensive and took place in a smaller part of the albatross foraging area. Hence, there was a broad agreement between changes in population size over time and the extent of long-lining in the relevant area.

Step 4. Do differences in trend among albatross populations correlate with geographical variation in the candidate external cause?

Most breeding populations of wandering albatrosses declined during the late twentieth century, but the rate of decline varied widely among five populations studied, from 1% per year for South Georgia (South Atlantic) to 8% per year for Macquarie Island (Southern Ocean, south of New Zealand). Recaptures of ringed birds showed strong natal and breeding philopatry, so differences in trends should reflect variation among subpopulations in survival or breeding success rather than net immigration or emigration. The rate of population decline was significantly correlated with the extent of the area used by long-liners and the number of hooks set per year within the breeding season foraging range of each population. For example, the number of 5° squares used by long-liners around Macquarie Island was about four times greater than for South Georgia.

Step 5. Do studies of demographic rates support the diagnosis?
If long-lining was the cause of the population decline then it would be expected that annual survival rates of albatrosses would be negatively correlated with the prevalence of long-lining, whilst breeding success and the probability of attempting to breed would not be reduced in declining populations. Mark–recapture studies of ringed birds at Possession Island (Crozets) showed that survival rates of both immatures and adults were low during the period when long-lining was most prevalent, but breeding success was not. These findings were replicated at South Georgia (Croxall *et al.* 1990). Variation in the annual survival rate of adults at Possession Island was shown by multiple regression analysis to be significantly negatively correlated both with the extent of the area used by long-liners in the breeding season foraging range around the Crozet Islands and the number of hooks set in waters south of Australia frequented by many non-breeding birds. Albatrosses tended to breed for the first time at a younger age after long-lining increased, perhaps because settling to breed became easier when the number of competing adults declined.

Step 6. Is the magnitude of the effect of the external factor sufficient to account for the observed population decline?
The changes in survival rates observed during the period of expanded long-lining activity were sufficient, when incorporated into simulation models of albatross populations, to produce rates of population decline comparable with those actually observed. Measurements by observers on fishing vessels of the number of wandering albatrosses killed per million hooks set, when combined with statistics on the number of hooks deployed per year in the relevant areas, yield estimates of numbers of albatrosses killed per year that are broadly consistent with the number of deaths, in excess of those from natural mortality, that would be required to account for the observed declines in breeding population (Croxall & Prince 1991; Weimerskirch *et al.* 1997).

analysis and a revised diagnosis. Steps 5–7 of Box 7.1 outline ways in which this can be done. Careful consideration should be given to which combination of these approaches to adopt. It might be thought that an experimental test (step 7) should always be preferred. Manipulative experiments have high status in ecology because they increase its resemblance to 'hard' laboratory science. However, practical limitations often make ecological experiments expensive to implement and difficult to interpret. A particular problem of spatial scale occurs with experiments designed to detect effects of manipulations of external factors on the population size of mobile animals. Here the ideal field experiment involves plots, each of which should contain a naturally closed population uninfluenced by flows of individuals to or from elsewhere. If the treated and control populations are not closed, then false positives can arise if the treatment merely attracts individuals rather than affecting demographic rates. False negatives can also occur if density-dependent recruitment and/or dispersal smears away an effect of treatment on a demographic rate, which would translate into an increase in population density if applied to a closed population. For these reasons experiments in which the response variable is a demographic rate rather than population size are often easier to design, replicate and interpret, though on their own they do not test the effect of the manipulation on population size.

Given the difficulty of manipulative experiments on birds with population size or trend as the response variable, it should be more widely recognised that manipulation is not an essential feature of the experimental approach. Observational studies that test hypotheses generated by a diagnosis based upon the comparative method can be treated as mensurative experiments (Krebs 1991) and practical considerations may make them a more stringent test of the diagnosis than a manipulative experiment. Comparative studies of demographic rates, as suggested in steps 5 and 6 of Box 7.1, allow hypotheses about the demographic mechanism(s) underlying a population decline to be refuted or supported. In the wandering albatross example the robustness of the diagnosis is enhanced by the supporting information from studies of demographic rates (steps 5 and 6). Had survival rates been found not to vary over time in the way expected from the long-lining mortality hypothesis, this would have refuted that diagnosis. Similarly, if the maximum possible number of albatrosses killed by long-lining estimated from observations on fishing vessels had been too low to account for the observed rate of population decline, then this too would overturn the diagnosis. For a long-lived species like this a robust manipulative experiment with population trend as the response variable would take decades to complete even if it were practicable.

ESTIMATES OF DEMOGRAPHIC RATES AS A GUIDE TO CONSERVATION ACTION

The previous section identified a role for studies of demographic rates in testing and checking diagnoses made by the comparative method. However, the reverse approach is sometimes employed in which estimates of demographic rates are used in the first stages of a diagnosis to identify the demographic mechanism of a population decline. This may exclude some possible external causes of the decline that could only affect other demographic rates. For example, long time series of estimates of breeding success and survival rates based upon data collected by amateur ornithologists enabled Peach *et al.* (1999) to show that the demographic mechanism of a large decline in the breeding population of reed buntings (*Emberiza schoeniclus*) in Britain was probably a decline in survival. This finding implicated changes in farming methods that affect food supplies in winter, rather than factors that affect breeding success, as the most probable external cause of the decline. However, estimates of breeding success and survival are rarely available for threatened bird species and are usually single average estimates of each rate rather than time series. Modern statistical methods allow accurate estimates of breeding success (Aebischer 1999) and survival (Lebreton *et al.* 1992) to be made from nest check and radio-tracking, mark–resighting or mark–recovery data. However, reliable annual or period-specific estimates of all demographic rates, for several years, from study areas representative of the whole range of the population, are available for only a tiny proportion of threatened species (Green & Hirons 1991). What use can be made of the limited information that is usually available?

IDENTIFICATION OF THE DEMOGRAPHIC MECHANISM OF A POPULATION DECLINE FROM AVERAGE DEMOGRAPHIC RATES

Can the average values of demographic rates observed during a population decline indicate which rate has changed to produce the decline without comparison with rates in stable populations? It is first worth noting that frequently population studies of threatened species only advance to the stage of collecting demographic data after a decline has occurred and the population has stabilised at a low level. In these circumstances, the rates observed are those for a stable population and may provide no insight into the demographic mechanism of a past decline. However, suppose that representative and accurate average estimates of demographic rates are available for a population that is in decline. It might be hoped that a particular rate would be identifiable as being lower than expected and that this would indicate the mechanism of the decline. The problem is to know what values to expect. Stable bird populations show considerable variation in all of the three principal demographic rates: adult fecundity, adult mortality, and survival over the entire pre-reproductive period (Fig. 7.1). Variation is especially large in the first two of these parameters, which are positively correlated with

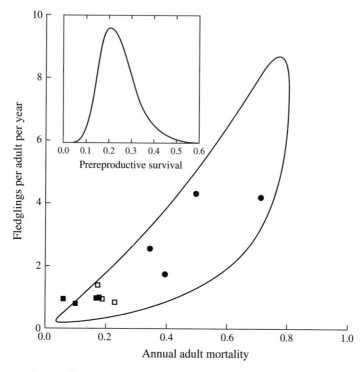

Fig. 7.1. The curved shape in the main diagram is an envelope containing adult fecundity and mortality estimates from 34 studies of approximately stable populations of 32 bird species (Ricklefs 2000). Symbols represent estimates for different populations of two exemplar species. Blue tit (*Parus caeruleus*) populations in Belgium, France and Corsica are represented by circles (Dhondt 1989; Blondel *et al.* 1992) and populations of mute swans (*Cygnus olor*) in the UK and Denmark are represented by squares (Bacon & Andersen-Harald 1989; Perrins 1991). Stable or increasing populations are shown by filled symbols and declining populations ($\lambda <= 0.95$) by open symbols. The envelope on the main diagram is a back-transformed 90% tolerance ellipse fitted to log-transformed fecundity and logit-transformed adult mortality values from Ricklefs (2000), which were kindly supplied by the author. The inset shows a log-normal frequency distribution fitted to data on survival for the whole of the period from fledging to reproductive age for the 34 populations considered in the main diagram.

one another (Ricklefs 2000). This pattern of variation and correlation of rates makes it difficult to identify which of the three principal demographic rates is abnormal in data for a single declining population. Suppose that the values for a declining population fell below the lower bound of the envelope shown in Fig. 7.1. Because of the shape and orientation of the envelope it is almost certain that adult fecundity and adult mortality would both still be within the wide range observed in stable populations. Hence, it would not be possible to say whether such a population had abnormally low adult fecundity, abnormally high adult mortality, or both. A change in either rate could move the population back into the envelope.

It has been suggested that average demographic rates for a declining species can be compared with those for related species with stable populations (Temple 1986), but rates vary widely among stable populations of closely related bird species and even among populations of the same species. For example, studies of stable populations of mute swans (*Cygnus olor*) and blue tits (*Parus caeruleus*) in different parts of Europe show considerable variation in adult fecundity and adult mortality (Fig. 7.1). Although declining populations of mute swans in the United Kingdom tended to have higher adult mortality than self-sustaining ones because of lead poisoning (Perrins 1991), the scatter of points for stable populations of both species makes it seem unlikely that comparison of demographic rates for a single declining population with those of stable populations of other species would give a reliable indication of the demographic mechanism underlying a decline.

There are extremes of adult mortality that would implicate changes in this rate as a mechanism of a population decline. The number of fledglings produced annually per adult cannot exceed a limit imposed by species-specific physiological constraints. Assuming an even sex ratio, maximum productivity of fledglings per adult per year is the product of maximum successful brood size and the maximum number of successful broods per year divided by two. The probability of a fledgling bird surviving to reproductive age rarely exceeds 0.5 (Ricklefs 2000; Fig. 7.1, inset). The combination of these two constraints leads to a maximum rate of recruitment to the breeding population that is the maximum number of fledglings that can be reared per adult per year divided by two. If the observed annual mortality rate of adults is higher than this then high adult mortality must at least be contributing to a population decline because recruitment could not realistically be any higher.

This rule is obviously useless for any species that can fledge more than two young per adult per year and is most likely to be helpful for those whose maximum annual rate of production of fledglings is much lower. For example, the maximum possible number of fledglings per adult per year for wild California condors (*Gymnogyps californianus*) was 0.333 (the clutch size is one egg and successful breeding can occur in two years out of three; Snyder & Snyder 2000). Adopting the maximum pre-reproductive survival rate (0.5) from the study of other species (Fig. 7.1 inset) gives a maximum possible recruitment rate of 0.167. The annual adult mortality rate for wild condors observed in the 1980s, when the population was declining rapidly, was 0.268, well in excess of this estimate of maximum recruitment (Snyder & Snyder 2000). Even with recruitment at its maximum possible rate the adult population would have been declining by 10% per year. Hence, even if nothing had been known about the actual fecundity and prereproductive survival rates of wild condors at the time, knowledge of the adult mortality rate alone would have been sufficient to identify its high level, due mainly to lead poisoning, as an important mechanism underlying the population decline, and one which could not have been completely compensated for by management of the wild population to improve the other demographic rates.

Extremes of survival from fledging to reproductive age can be identified more readily because this rate is less variable than adult mortality and fecundity (Fig. 7.1 inset) and is not correlated with either of them (Charnov 1993; Ricklefs 2000). As a consequence, it is possible to be more confident that an average value of pre-reproductive survival is unusually low compared with stable populations of other species and that it is probably at least contributing to a population decline. A log-normal distribution fitted to the data presented by Ricklefs (2000) indicates that less than 1% of stable populations would be expected to have a probability of a fledgling surviving to breeding age less than 0.09. Hence, if pre-reproductive survival in a declining bird population is lower than this, it would be reasonable to regard a change in this rate as a strong candidate for a mechanism of the decline. It would be desirable to base this rule upon a larger set of estimates with more even phylogenetic coverage than is used here, but it provides a useful rule-of-thumb none the less.

In conclusion, examination of a set of average demographic rates for a declining population is only likely to yield reliable clues about its mechanism in extreme cases where pre-reproductive survival is very low or adult mortality exceeds the maximum possible recruitment rate.

PROSPECTIVE USE OF ANALYSIS OF THE ELASTICITY OF POPULATION MULTIPLICATION RATE λ AS A GUIDE TO THE DEMOGRAPHIC RATES WHICH HAVE THE STRONGEST INFLUENCE ON POPULATION RECOVERY

Given a set of estimates of average, time-invariant, age-specific survival and fecundity rates, a measure of their relative influence on population growth can be calculated as the proportional effect on the population multiplication rate λ of a small proportional change in each of the rates in turn. This is the elasticity of λ with respect to a particular demographic rate a_i and it is given by the partial derivative $\partial\log(\lambda)/\partial\log(a_i)$ obtained from the Leslie population matrix (see de Kroon *et al.* (2000) for a review of methods). Elasticity analysis of λ, using simple life table data and assuming that adult survival does not vary with age, yields a general conclusion that population growth is most strongly affected by a proportional change in adult survival when the average adult survival rate is high (>0.5) and is more strongly affected by a change by the same proportion in fecundity or pre-reproductive survival when adult survival is low (<0.5).

It has been suggested that elasticity analyses of this type can be of considerable value for conservation practitioners because they allow the identification of the demographic rate whose manipulation would have the largest effect on λ. Although elasticity analysis has been applied to bird conservation problems (Wisdom & Mills 1997) there are some important limitations on its usefulness. First, it does not take into account the feasibility or cost of altering a particular demographic rate by management. Elasticity analysis for a bird species with long-lived adults would indicate that measures to increase adult survival by a given proportion would have a larger effect on population growth rate than increasing fecundity by the same proportion. However, the causes of death of adults might be such that it would be impractical or very expensive to increase adult survival, whilst there might be cheap and effective ways to increase breeding productivity or the survival of immatures, even though the proportional increase required to achieve a given effect on population size might be larger for recruitment than adult survival. This problem might be overcome by quantifying the relationship between the level of each demographic rate a_i and expenditure c_i on conservation management to alter that rate. If ways to improve a rate by management are unknown or do not seem feasible, c_i could be set to a high level chosen to represent the minimum cost of research and development. The effect on population growth rate of a small absolute change in expenditure on improving each rate, the partial derivative $\partial\lambda/\partial c_i$, would then be a more useful index of the relative merits of different management options under these circumstances. For example, Green & Hirons (1991) show a function relating adult fecundity of stone-curlews (*Burhinus oedicnemus*) to annual expenditure on wardens to prevent losses of nests and chicks from losses caused by farming operations. Such functions are rarely reported.

A second problem with analysis of the elasticity of λ is more difficult to resolve. Prospective analysis of the elasticity of λ assumes time- and density-invariant demographic rates. If some demographic rates are density-dependent, so that the population stabilises at or about an equilibrium level, then it will usually be unrealistic to use the elasticity of λ to guide conservation objectives. Most bird populations that have been studied show at least one and often several density-dependent demographic rates (Newton 1998, Table 5.1, pp. 104–105). It can be argued that populations of threatened species are usually below the capacity of the habitat to support them and density-dependence might be less important, but this is a weak argument and it seems likely that density-dependent rates due to resource limitation or density-dependent predation would also be frequent in such populations (Caswell 2000). Where there is density-dependence the elasticity or sensitivity of the average or equilibrium population size or the risk of population extinction, rather than of λ, is likely to be of more value for conservation. These response variables are clearly connected to the objectives of conservation practitioners. Grant & Benton (2000) showed that conclusions about priority demographic rates for conservation management based upon analyses of the elasticity of λ on populations with density-dependent rates would often not be the same as those from an elasticity analysis with equilibrium or average population size as the response variable. This was especially likely when a demographic rate was dependent on the density of a particular age class or stage, rather than the whole population. The way in which density-dependence can lead to misleading conclusions being drawn from an elasticity analysis is illustrated by a hypothetical example in Box 7.3.

Box 7.3. Consequences of basing conservation management decisions on an analysis of the elasticity of λ that assumes that demographic rates are invariant when they are really density-dependent.

A stable population of a hypothetical forest bird has a density-independent adult mortality rate of 0.2. The number of fledglings produced per adult per year declines with increasing adult population size because of limited numbers of suitable trees for successful nesting sites. Fledglings suffer a density-independent mortality rate of 0.5 and the surviving yearlings all breed. This produces the top curve in panel 1 relating the number of recruits per breeding adult per year to adult population size. A long-term deterioration in the breeding habitat begins in year zero because of selective logging of the best kinds of trees for nesting, the effect of which is to cause the slope of the density-dependent adult fecundity vs. adult population curve to become 3% steeper each year. Panel 1 shows the original form of this curve and its downward shift after 20, 40 and 60 years. The forest habitat otherwise remains suitable for the species, so survival rates of adults and immatures are unaffected. Consider three scenarios for the fate of the population.

- **Scenario A.** No conservation action is attempted. The adult population declines to extinction, with λ stabilising at 0.97 by about year 15 (line A on panel 2).
- **Scenario B.** A field study is carried out in years 15–19 and measures demographic rates. These are found to remain constant over the short study period (panels 3 and 4). The elasticity of λ for adult survival is found

to be 0.82 and that for adult fecundity is 0.18. This finding stimulates studies of adult mortality which reveal that hunting of adults for their bright plumage is common. This is banned immediately and adult mortality is thereby halved from year 20 onwards (line B in panel 3). The causes of variation in breeding success are not studied because elasticity with respect to fecundity is low. Adult population size responds strongly and immediately to the hunting ban, so the biologists win prizes and go elsewhere. However, the recovery is short-lived because the unchecked deterioration of the breeding habitat, exacerbated by the temporary increase in adult density, leads to a rapid drop in fecundity. From about year 30 onwards the population continues its decline to extinction.

- **Scenario C.** Biologists carry out the field study in years 15–19 exactly as in scenario B, but they also discover an archive of research on the species' demography that was done shortly before the population decline began. They notice that the mean number of fledglings produced per adult per year has declined from 0.40 to 0.34, whilst other rates have not changed. Simple calculations that assume no density-dependence show that the change in fecundity is sufficient to account for the drop in λ from 1.0 to 0.97. This finding stimulates studies of nesting success and the importance of particular trees for nesting is discovered. A ban on the logging of the best species and age classes comes into immediate effect. This freezes the fecundity vs. adult population relationship in the form it reached in year 20 (panel 1), but regeneration of the best nesting trees is not forthcoming, so it does not restore the situation to that found in year zero. The adult population continues to decline for a few more years, which causes density-dependent fecundity to improve (line C in panel 4) until the adult population reaches a new stable equilibrium at 56% of the original level (line C in panel 2).

Changes in equilibrium adult population sizes can be visualised using panel 1. The horizontal lines show the per capita adult death rates before (solid line) and after (dashed line) the hunting ban was introduced. The adult population is at equilibrium when the death rate curve and the recruitment curve cut one another, i.e. when recruitment rate equals death rate. The continuous decline in equilibrium population in scenario A is expected because the place where the solid horizontal death rate line cuts the density-dependent per capita recruitment curves labelled 0, 20, 40 and 60 shifts to the left over time (i.e. to lower population size) as the recruitment curve shifts downwards because of logging of the best trees. In scenario B the equilibrium population starts off declining as in A, but the death rate curve is shifted downwards to the dashed horizontal line in year 20, so it cuts the year 20 recruitment curve further to the right at a higher adult population level. Hence the population starts to increase. However, the recruitment curve continues to shift downwards as logging continues, so the cut point of the broken death-rate line on the recruitment curve moves to the left again, i.e. the population decline resumes. In scenario C the equilibrium population starts off declining as in A, but the recruitment curve is prevented from shifting its position any further downwards by the selective logging ban. Hence, the equilibrium population stabilises at the place where the solid horizontal line cuts the year 20 recruitment curve.

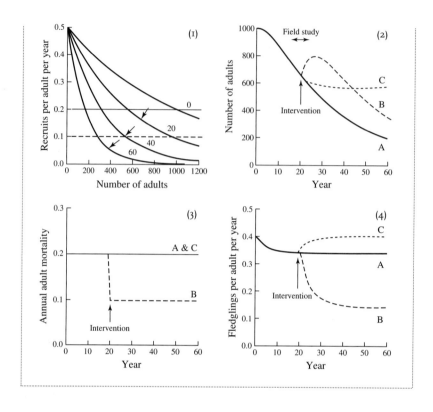

An improved approach that allows for density-dependence is illustrated by an elasticity analysis by Heppell *et al.* (1994) for red-cockaded woodpeckers (*Picoides borealis*) in the southeastern United States. They found that the number of cooperatively breeding groups of woodpeckers was limited by the availability of suitable habitat for foraging and of old (>80 years) living pine trees in which the birds excavated cavities in the heartwood for nesting and roosting. Logging of old trees, take-overs of cavities by other animals and deterioration and fragmentation of suitable foraging habitat were all contributing to population declines by reducing the number of suitable sites for group territories (Walters 1991). Competition occurred for territories, so numbers of breeding groups were regulated by density-dependent processes at a level set by the availability of suitable territories. Heppell and colleagues assessed the effects of various management options by an elasticity analysis in which they took average time- and density-invariant demographic rates and transition probabilities estimated for males in their woodpecker population and assessed the effect on λ of changing each parameter. They used a stage-structured model in which males of reproductive age could be floaters, helpers or breeders and their model included the transition probabilities for moving between stages: for example, the chance of a helper becoming a breeder. They showed that λ was most sensitive to management that increased the chance of transition from fledgling to breeder and from helper to breeder. The management options that had the largest effect on the transitions were the drilling of new nest cavities in otherwise suitable habitat and the removal of hardwoods to maintain habitat suitability. Although the model did not explicitly include density-dependence it actually included its effects by incorporating the effect of nest site and habitat availability on the chances of non-breeding and helping birds being able to become new breeders.

It is concluded that the value of elasticity analysis of λ to conservation practice is limited. It can be made more relevant by incorporation of the costs and feasibility of management options and the influence of density-dependence.

ADAPTIVE MANAGEMENT UNDER UNCERTAINTY

How can decisions be made about which conservation actions to implement? The earlier parts of this chapter outline a procedure in which the most likely causes of a past decline are identified by the comparative method and the validity of the diagnosis checked using supplementary information on demographic rates or management experiments. However, there are likely to be deficiencies, both in the data used and the scope of the hypotheses considered, so considerable uncertainty will probably remain about the most effective course of action. How should biologists and conservation managers balance the need for urgent action with a reluctance to make mistakes? A flexible approach is to use the knowledge obtained from diagnostic studies to build a simulation model of the population that describes its main density-dependent and density-independent processes. The model is then used to evaluate the effect on population size or the probability of extinction of various feasible management options. The model used can be based entirely on empirical data on demographic rates and population trends taken from field observations and experiments (e.g. Potts & Aebischer 1995), but it might alternatively derive some demographic rates from the aggregate of the behaviour of individual birds acting to optimise their performance under prevailing conditions of resource availability and density (Goss-Custard & Sutherland 1997).

Whatever the details of their construction, such models are usually subject to considerable uncertainty about both the form of the relationship of demographic rates to external variables and the values of model parameters. For example, for many populations of threatened birds it might only be possible to make an informed guess about the nature of density-dependence. A useful response to this uncertainty is to produce variants of the population model which incorporate different but plausible ranges of parameter values and forms and then to see whether conclusions about which management actions are most likely to be effective vary markedly or are similar no matter which of the plausible variants is used. One way to implement this approach is described by Drechsler and colleagues, who built simulation models of a threatened parrot population with a plausible variety of forms and parameter values and evaluated the extent to which uncertainty influenced conclusions about the effectiveness of various management options in reducing the probability of extinction (Drechsler *et al.* 1998; Drechsler 2000). The great virtue of analyses of this kind is that they draw attention to aspects of the population ecology of the species concerned for which lack of detailed knowledge has a critical effect on the usefulness of the advice given by biologists to conservation managers. This should stimulate the biologists to identify critical observations and experiments that would narrow down the uncertainty and encourage the conservation managers not to gamble too heavily on management options with weak scientific support and to build into their programme of conservation action further research to evaluate its effectiveness. The idea of an iterative relationship between research and management is the underlying principle of an adaptive management strategy (see also Chapter 9), an example of which is the interaction between scientific research and the legal regulation of duck hunting in North America (Nichols *et al.* 1995). Conservation scientists and conservation managers need effective two-way communication with each other. The development of an adaptive management strategy for a threatened bird population may offer a mechanism that encourages this to happen more often.

8

Outside the reserve: pandemic threats to bird biodiversity

DEBORAH J. PAIN & PAUL F. DONALD

INTRODUCTION

The identification of the most threatened species and the prioritisation of the most important sites for protection are, and will remain, essential to the conservation of bird biodiversity (Chapters 4 and 5). The uneven distribution of threatened biodiversity is highlighted by the fact that less than 5% of the Earth's land surface holds almost 75% of the world's threatened bird species (BirdLife International 2000).

On a global scale, however, protected areas are small; nationally protected areas cover less than 5% of the Earth's land surface and far less of marine habitats (Ryan 1992). It is generally accepted that site protection is inadequate to conserve existing populations of the majority of species whose ranges fall largely outside such areas (e.g. Pain & Dixon 1997). Some protected areas may even be insufficient to conserve those (often threatened) species for which they were designated. Relatively little work has been conducted on the long-term viability of such populations, especially important when reserves are isolated, although this is an expanding area of research[1] (see Chapter 5). In addition, protected status is often nominal rather than actual, especially in areas where the needs of local communities are in real or perceived conflict with the objectives of environmental protection (Terborgh 1999).

Reserves cannot be viewed in isolation, as many activities and population processes taking place outside protected areas can adversely affect conditions for species within protected areas (e.g. Baillie *et al.* 2000). Obvious examples include hydrological changes resulting from water extraction for

---

[1] See e.g. www.tws-west.org/pvaabstracts.html

agriculture, industry or tourism (e.g. Finlayson *et al.* 1992), pollution via water or the atmosphere (e.g. Dudley 1987; Pain *et al.* 1998), or the spread of alien or invasive species into reserves.[2]

There are also many biological reasons why reserves *alone* are inadequate. Many reserves are designated to protect species at critical stages of their life cycle, such as congregations of migratory birds, or important breeding or wintering sites. Although this is an efficient means of preserving such species, many of them use unprotected areas, or are dispersed over huge areas of unprotected land, at other stages of their life cycle. Manne *et al.* (1999) showed that the ranges of many threatened New World passerines, whilst on average much smaller than their non-threatened counterparts, are still too large for substantial amounts to be included within protected area networks. Over 90% of lowland passerines in the Americas have ranges larger than 100,000 km² and over 30% of threatened continental American passerines have breeding ranges of 1,000–100,000 km². Although a high proportion of restricted-range species are threatened, widespread species comprise a high proportion of bird biodiversity and biomass across most of the planet, and conservation strategy must consider this. Site protection may buffer species from threats such as local habitat loss and persecution, but many factors affect birds irrespective of their location, and these form the subject of this chapter. Threats covered elsewhere in this book, such as the introduction of alien species, predation, interbreeding (Chapter 6), and habitat loss and fragmentation (Chapter 10) are not discussed. In this chapter, we identify and discuss a number of threats faced by common and widespread birds. Many of these also threaten endangered species and, to varying degrees, the integrity and effectiveness of protected areas. We deal with one such threat, global climate change, in particular detail, as it has been identified as a particularly severe threat to biodiversity in the coming century (Peters 1991) and has been the subject of much recent research (e.g. Green *et al.* 2001; McCarty 2001). Other identified threats, some of which may prove equally serious, are discussed more briefly. The list of threats covered is not comprehensive, but includes those factors or activities that threaten the largest numbers of species. In each case we illustrate the processes involved using recent published examples from the scientific literature.

---

[2] See the Invasive Species Specialist Group website for numerous examples: www.issg.org

CLIMATE CHANGE[3]

Background

The temperature of the Earth's atmosphere is increasing, and global average surface temperature is projected to increase by 1.4–5.8 °C by 2100. The projected global mean sea level rise over this period is 9–88 cm, and precipitation patterns will change (IPCC 2001b; see also Watson *et al.* 1997). In addition, climate change may affect flow patterns of marine currents resulting in extreme local climate effects, although at present the nature and magnitude of such changes are difficult to predict. Climate change will result in new weather patterns all over the world, but the natural and social systems of some regions will be more vulnerable to the effects of climate change than others. Climate change is caused by increases in atmospheric CO_2 and other 'greenhouse gases' which absorb some of the long-wave radiation reflected from the Earth. Such increases result mainly from the release of stored carbon through, for example, the burning of fossil fuels for energy and transport and from deforestation. The Kyoto Protocol (an international treaty on climate change – see FCCP 1998) offers countries the opportunity to receive credits for a reduction in emissions or sequestration of carbon, for example through reforestation or afforestation (Schulze *et al.* 2000). Whilst potentially beneficial, such 'carbon accounting' creates risks to biodiversity as fast growing plantations could potentially be planted in areas of high biodiversity, such as natural grasslands, or primary forests (Noss 2001). In addition, there is uncertainty over how beneficial forests might be for long-term carbon sequestration (Davidson & Hirsch 2001).

The effects of climate change upon biodiversity can be evaluated most simply by assessing the likely effects of predicted changes in temperature and rainfall upon the climatic 'space' that a species can potentially occupy. Effects upon bird species are likely to vary enormously, depending upon the latitude or altitude at which they live, whether or not they are surviving at the extreme end of their temperature range already, and their ecological flexibility. An extreme case of habitat loss or alteration is likely to occur in the Arctic, where considerable loss of sea ice through thawing is anticipated in the Arctic Ocean. There will be major shifts in biomes such as tundra and boreal forests, and landscapes will be altered over large areas with impacts predicted for populations such as breeding water birds (Zöckler & Lysenko

---

[3] A detailed bibliography on the effects of global climate change on wildlife can be found at www.pacinst.org/wildlife.html

2001). Large areas of habitat will also be lost on low-lying islands through sea-level rise (IPCC 2001a).

However, the effects of climate change upon biodiversity will be far more complex and far-reaching than can be described by a species' 'climate space' alone; they will be related to the interaction between environmental, social and economic pressures. In 2001, Working Group II of the Intergovernmental Panel on Climate Change (IPCC 2001a) made an informed (but largely qualitative) assessment of the vulnerability of different regions to the effects of climate change. The most vulnerable systems or regions were considered those most sensitive to modest changes in climate, and with limited ability to adapt as a result of natural and/or social and economic systems. The African continent, Latin America and developing countries in Asia were considered to be particularly at risk, for instance from frequent droughts and floods along with heavy reliance on rain-fed agriculture (particularly in Africa), whilst adaptive capacity of human societies is low, due partly to lack of economic resources and technology. In all of these areas, threats to biodiversity from land use, land cover change and population pressure will be exacerbated by climate change. This is unfortunate, as it is just those parts of the world that harbour the greatest biodiversity and the majority of threatened species (ICBP 1992, BirdLife International 2000; Myers *et al.* 2000). Biome distributions and the distribution, composition and migration patterns of many species will change, and significant extinctions of plant and animal species are expected (IPCC 2001a, b).

Complex models incorporating all of these factors will eventually be needed to predict adequately changes in species' and habitat distributions and land-use changes, and plan mitigation measures for biodiversity. However, a first step is to assess how climate change, in the absence of social and economic pressures, is affecting or could affect birds. Birds are particularly good indicators of climate change as their ranges and population trends are well known. An illustrative set of examples is given below, summarised within the following (overlapping) categories: (i) the timing of life cycles, (ii) species' distributions and populations, (iii) migrants and migration, and (iv) effects on important sites.

Timing of life cycles

Many species of plant and animal depend upon signals such as temperature or photoperiod to time or trigger certain stages of their life cycle. The onset of egg laying by great tits (*Parus major*), for example, appears to be strongly related to spring temperatures (McCleery & Perrins 1998). Few monitoring schemes have been sufficiently long-term to give clear indications of trends resulting from changes in climatic variables that occur over many years. Here we discuss a few of the long-term data sets that have been used in this way[4].

Recent research has provided convincing evidence of large-scale impacts of rising temperatures on wildlife. Crick & Sparks (1999) used the British Trust for Ornithology's Nest Record Scheme, spanning 57 years (1939–95), to evaluate the relationship between median laying dates of 36 bird species and mean monthly temperature and rainfall. The authors identified the mean monthly weather variables that accounted for variation in laying date, weighted by sample size. They found that 17 of 19 species with long-term trends in laying date exhibited significant weather effects, with mean March and April temperatures being the key variables (Fig. 8.1). For seven of these 17 species, weather variables alone were sufficient to account for the long-term trends in laying date; these seven species are all widespread in Britain and their records may provide the best match with the weather data. This provides compelling evidence for the impact of rising temperatures upon the timing of birds' life cycles. Crick and Sparks also used a climate change scenario for the United Kingdom (Hulme & Jenkins 1998) to predict how laying dates may change by 2080. The average advancement was predicted at 8 days, with a maximum of 18 days.

So, if laying dates for some species in the UK are already earlier, and are predicted to become more so, what are the implications for breeding birds? If warmer spring temperatures affect vegetation phenology, food abundance and other cues that stimulate the onset of reproduction in a pattern entirely synchronous with the advancement of laying dates, then it is feasible that there would be a negligible, or even a positive, effect upon the breeding success of some species. However, there is evidence that this is not happening. Visser *et al.* (1998) investigated the relationship between the timing of reproduction in a population of great tits in The Netherlands and the timing of peak caterpillar availability for the young, over a 23-year period. Whilst spring temperatures had increased and peaks of caterpillar abundance become earlier, laying dates of the tits did not advance. However, 'Selection differentials', calculated for each female as laying date minus mean laying

---

[4] The UK Phenology Network was initiated in 1998 by the Centre for Ecology and Hydrology, which joined forces with the Woodland Trust to promote the scheme widely in 2000. The scheme aims to encourage people to record the timing of natural phenomena all over the UK, so that such events can be monitored particularly with respect to the impacts of climate change. Further information can be found on the website: www.phenology.org.uk/

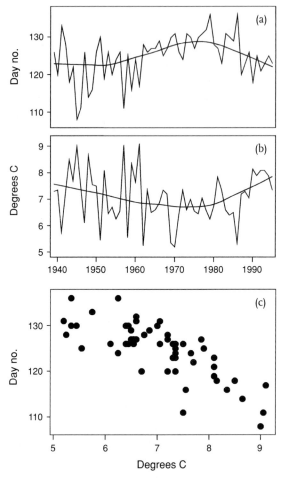

Fig. 8.1. Weather and laying dates of the chaffinch (*Fringilla coelebs*).
(a) temporal changes in annual median laying date. (b) Temporal changes in the mean of March and April monthly mean Central England Temperatures (CETs).
(c) Relation between annual median laying date and mean of March and April CETs ($r = -0.76$, $P < 0.001$). Laying date is numbered such that day 110 is 20 April and day 121 is 1 May. The smoothed lines are calculated using a LOWESS (locally weighted scatterplot smoother) method. (Reprinted by permission from *Nature*, Crick & Sparks, **399**: 423-424, 1999, Macmillan Magazunes Ltd.)

date for the population and weighted by the number of chicks produced, showed that selection for earlier laying became significantly stronger over the study period. For some species in Europe, however, warmer winters and/or springs have been associated with increased reproductive success (Sæther *et al.* 2000 and review by McCarty 2001).

Distributions and populations

Global climate destabilisation will result not only in changing air temperatures in many parts of the world but also changing sea temperatures, and
an increasing number of studies are assessing their likely effects on birds.
Sooty shearwaters (*Puffinus griseus*) breed in South America and Australasia
on a 9-monthly cycle, and large numbers (an estimated 5 million birds in
the late 1970s; Briggs & Chu 1986) winter in the productive California
Current System (CCS) of the eastern Pacific. Veit *et al.* (1997) examined
the relationships between sooty shearwater abundance, sea surface temperatures and zooplankton abundance at three widely separated localities off
the Californian coast. Sooty shearwaters declined in abundance in the CCS
by 90% between 1987 and 1994. Ocean temperatures increased by 0.8 °C
in the 500 m surface layer between 1950 and 1992, coinciding with a 70%
decline in zooplankton abundance. The analysis of Veit *et al.* showed a negative correlation between sooty shearwater numbers and increasing temperatures within the California current, and the correlation was strongest with
a temporal time lag of 9 months. Zooplankton and their predators form
the diet of sooty shearwaters, providing a link between climate change and
bird populations. Similar findings from a study of northern gannets (*Morus
bassanus*) suggested that even very slight changes in ocean temperature can
have profound effects on not only the distribution and numbers but also the
diet of seabirds over huge areas (Montevecci & Myers 1997).

During the last half-century, populations of several krill-eating Southern
Ocean predators, such as chinstrap penguins (*Pygoscelis antarctica*), have
increased. Until recently, this had been attributed to a presumed increase
in food availability following declines in baleen whale populations through
commercial whaling (Croxall *et al.* 1984). This hypothesis was based upon
the predominance of Antarctic krill in the summer diets of chinstraps and
whales. It therefore appeared anomalous that the Adélie penguin (*Pygoscelis
adeliae*), which overlaps in range with the chinstrap and shares a similar
summer diet, had not similarly increased in numbers. A multidisciplinary
expedition to the Scotia and Weddell seas in 1988 suggested that climate
change provided a better explanation for the population trends observed.
Fraser *et al.* (1992) analysed long-term biological and environmental data
sets and concluded that the retreat of pack ice due to oceanic warming was
benefiting species that feed in open water, like the chinstrap, but not pack
ice feeders like Adélies[5] (see also Ainley *et al.* 2001).

---

[5] The use of stable isotope technology, used only relatively recently in ecological studies, is
    likely to assist in future work linking marine wildlife population changes to climate.
    Isotope signatures in food webs are reflected in the tissues of consumers, and vary

Sorenson *et al.* (1998) illustrated the power of long-term data sets for predicting the effects of climate change. The most important breeding area for waterfowl in North America is the Prairie Pothole Region (PPR) of the Great Northern Plains, and the size of breeding duck populations has been correlated with spring wetland conditions. Using a range of long-term monitoring data sets, Sorenson *et al.* were able to predict the likely impact of climate change using what are currently considered the most likely scenarios (Box 8.1).

Box 8.1. Summary of Sorenson *et al.* (1998). Effects of climate change on breeding waterfowl in North America.

- Waterfowl and temporary wetlands were counted annually from aircraft along linear transects. Palmer Drought Severity Index (PDSI) values were obtained for 1955-96 from the National Climatic Data Center's archive of monthly weather data.
- PDSI was strongly correlated with the number of ponds in May and with breeding duck populations. The authors used this relationship to predict future numbers of ponds and ducks based upon PDSI values generated by sensitivity analyses and two General Circulation Model (GCM) scenarios of climate change (IPCC 1990).
- Whilst GCMs are in agreement with projected temperature rise assuming a doubling in CO_2, projections of changes in rainfall are less certain. Sensitivity simulations of PDSI were therefore performed using the range of values of temperature and precipitation changes predicted by the climate models for the region.
- PDSI values were found to be highly sensitive to changes in temperature, with a 1.5 °C rise in temperature giving rise to PDSI values corresponding to 'moderate drought' conditions. Using two GCM scenarios, assuming a doubling in CO_2 by 2060, a major increase in drought conditions is predicted for the Prairie Pothole Region, translating to a north-central US breeding duck population of only 42-54% of the present long-term mean of 5 million.

---

temporally and spatially according to a range of biogeochemical processes. For example, in oceans the carbon (C) isotope ratios in marine phytoplankton are related to cell growth rate, which itself varies with ocean temperature (see Schell & Abromatis 2000), and C isotope ratios will be reflected in the tissues of phytoplankton consumers, and so on up the food web. As these ratios are stable, historical specimens of marine wildlife can be used to explore changes in oceanic primary productivity. Other isotopes of use include oxygen (O) and nitrogen (N): O isotope ratios are related to temperature, and N to trophic level. A combination of N, C and O isotope ratios can give useful information on changes in diet, and how this might relate to changes in climate. For further information, see epswww.unm.edu/facstaff/zsharp/carbon_nitrogen_literature.htm

This type of predictive work is extremely important as it generates recommendations for policy and research to help mitigate potential effects, e.g. the gathering of data on the demography and habitat relationships of birds breeding outside the PPR region, and the targeting of conservation resources to the less drought-prone parts of the PPR.

Migrants and migration

Many factors associated with climate change could affect populations of migrants, particularly long-distance migrants, as summarised in Box 8.2.

Box 8.2. Ways in which climate change could adversely affect migrants (from P.R. Evans 1997).

- Increased energetic costs caused by, for example, increases in size of ecological barriers such as deserts and changes in wind direction.
- Increased navigational risks if, for example, adverse weather during migration is more frequent.
- Increased risks of predation if, for example, extra food is required because of increased energetic costs, and this is obtained at the expense of vigilance.
- Reduction in food availability if, for example, conditions change in the quality, size or location of refuelling sites such as oases in deserts, or if these become less predictable.
- Changes in the seasonal availability of food relative to timing of arrival at breeding or wintering grounds.
- Increased competition with residents for resources.

A key concern in Africa is that reductions in annual rainfall, runoff and soil moisture will exacerbate desertification (IPCC 2001a). This could have significant impacts upon trans-Saharan migrants. Peach *et al.* (1991) showed that fluctuations in population levels and estimated survival rates of sedge warblers (*Acrocephalus schoenobaenus*) between 1969 and 1984 in Britain were strongly correlated with rainfall in their west African wintering areas (Fig. 8.2), although such clear-cut results have not been observed for all species investigated (Marchant 1992). Drought in sub-Saharan west Africa may affect a wide range of Palaearctic migrants by restricting the availability or quality of wintering habitat (Cave 1983; Kanyamibwa *et al.* 1990), or by increasing the size of the Sahara–Saudia Arabian desert belt. Beiback (1992) calculated that the energy (largely fat) reserves of willow warblers (*Phylloscopus trochilus*) crossing or grounded in the desert are insufficient to allow them to reach the Sahel zone in still air without foraging en route,

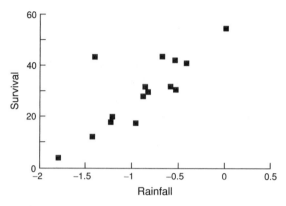

Fig. 8.2. Estimated annual survival rates (%) of adult sedge warblers trapped between 1969 and 1984 at two sites in southern England plotted against an index of annual rainfall for the previous wet season (May–October) in their West African winter quarters. Survival estimates were generated by program SURGE (Clobert *et al.* 1987) in which survival was modelled as time-dependent but site-independent, and recapture probability was site-dependent and constant over time. (Reprinted from Peach *et al.*, *Ibis*, **133**: 300–305, 1991.)

and foraging opportunities are very restricted. Beiback suggested that wind regimes in the autumn normally allow birds to profit from tailwinds, and that birds probably depend upon these for a successful crossing. If Beiback's energy/flight-range calculations are accurate, the safety margin for willow warblers and many other migrants is very small, and any changes in the size of the desert they have to cross, or the weather patterns at critical times of year, could profoundly influence successful migration. The ability of migrants to overcome these difficulties depends largely on their behavioural, ecological and genetic adaptability, which may be high (Berthold 1999).

Above we discussed the potential mismatch between peak laying dates of resident birds and peaks of food abundance. Migrants could be similarly affected, particularly if there is a mismatch between the advancement of vegetation leafing and invertebrate abundance on the breeding grounds, and arrival dates of migrants. Both & Visser (2001) found that the migratory pied flycatcher (*Ficedula hypoleuca*) has advanced its laying date over the past 20 years, but that the shift has been hampered by its spring arrival date, which has not advanced. Consequently, there has been increased selection for earlier breeding over the same period. The authors suggest that some long-distance migrants may suffer either because their migration strategy is unaffected by climate change, or because climate on breeding and wintering grounds are changing differentially. However, Coppack *et al.* (2001) showed that the advancement of laying dates in blackcaps (*Sylvia atricapilla*) leads to an advancement in autumn moult and migration of juvenile birds, and suggested that the photoperiodic control of migration may be maladaptive under novel environmental conditions resulting from climate change.

Sparks & Carey (1995) examined phenological records spanning two centuries in relation to central England monthly temperature and annual rainfall data. Regression models for all observed events showed highly significant responses. Sparks and Carey fitted a climate change scenario (IS92a – Houghton *et al.* 1992) to the regression models to predict the effect on first day of observation caused by a 3.5 °C rise in winter temperature, a 3 °C rise in spring, summer and autumn temperature, and a 10% increase in rainfall in the southeast of England by 2100. The estimated effects were for first leafing records for 13 tree species to take place 2–3 weeks earlier, and the arrival of swallow (*Hirundo rustica*) and cuckoo (*Cuculus canorus*) 4–5 days earlier.

It is difficult to predict how climate change will affect arrival dates of migrants. Migrants have no way of forecasting weather on arrival at breeding (or wintering) grounds, and departure times and duration of migratory period will be influenced by a range of factors, many of which may not be directly related to weather conditions at their final destination. Phenological data are being collected in some places to help monitor arrival times of migrants.[4] There is a range of potential effects and Berthold (1999) suggested that, in Europe, some partial migrant populations may shift to being sedentary, and short-distance migrants may shorten their migration distances. Long-distance migrants may then decline through increased competition from residents.

Important sites

Peters (1991) stated that 'What is clear . . . is that the climatological changes would have tremendous impact on communities and populations isolated by development and, by the middle of the next century, may dwarf any other consideration in planning for reserve management'. Climate change has occurred throughout the planet's history, but the current situation differs greatly in two respects; first, the rate at which the climate is warming probably surpasses anything in the last 2.4 million years (Huntley 1995) and, second, much of the world's threatened wildlife is now confined to small protected areas within otherwise hostile landscapes (see fragmentation discussions in Chapter 10). The Quaternary record suggests that in the past, most species' response was to gradually move into new areas, but many species in protected areas now have nowhere else to go. An extreme example of this is those species that inhabit tropical low-lying islands, many of which may suffer significant inundation, e.g. the Tuamotu sand-piper (*Prosobonia cancellata*), confined to several small atolls in the Tuamotu archipelago, southwestern Pacific (BirdLife International 2000). The problems posed to important protected sites by global warming are strikingly illustrated by threats to tropical montane cloud forests, which typically harbour large numbers of endemic species. Still *et al.* (1999) suggested that increased atmospheric CO_2 would lead to an altitudinal shift upwards in cloud formation, reducing cloud contact and increasing evapotranspiration in existing forests. Where such forests exist near the tops of mountains, there is no possibility for them to follow the cloud base upwards. Such changes have already been implicated in the massive declines in wildlife communities of an apparently unchanged cloud forest in Costa Rica (Pounds *et al.* 1999).

Until recently, predicted species' responses to likely climate change scenarios have not been considered within reserve selection criteria, and this presents a major challenge for the future. Balmford (Chapter 5) describes a suite of biological process-linked concerns, and human considerations, that need to be addressed in reserve selection. He notes that factors that affect population resilience and metapopulation dynamics will be essential in determining whether species can persist in the face of threats like climate change. It is important that the impacts of climate change on habitat and species' distributions and on the location and degree of resource exploitation by human communities are factored into reserve selection criteria. A range of options could be considered in the design of a protected areas network to minimise the impacts of climate change on the biodiversity for which they were designated. Noss (2001) suggested that for forest biodiversity protection, emphasis should be placed upon the protection of climate refugia (areas that harboured species during past climate changes), and on providing habitat connectivity parallel to environmental gradients. Protected areas could, for instance, be designed to run on a north–south axis and include a range of elevations, and 'wildlife-friendly' corridors or stepping-stones could be provided between protected sites. Ideally, however, protected areas need to be managed as parts of a dynamic landscape, and the matrix between reserves needs to be managed in a way that is sympathetic to both the current and likely future needs of a range of species.

AGRICULTURAL INTENSIFICATION

Few regions of the world are completely free from land dedicated to food production for humans and their domesticated animals, and in many areas agriculture comprises the dominant land-use type. Worldwide, the area of land given over to food production is now nearly 5 billion hectares, representing 38% of the planet's land surface (UN Food and Agriculture Organization statistics). It is predicted that in the tropics, a further 1 billion hectares of natural habitats will be lost to agriculture by 2050 (Tilman *et al.* 2001). A very large number of factors, principal amongst them population growth, economic pressure and improved technology, have meant that the intensity with which agricultural land is managed has increased greatly over the last half century. In this section, we assess the effects of land-use intensification on bird populations in two very different production systems: European agriculture and tropical coffee production.

European agriculture

After millennia of expansion across a continent with unusually favourable conditions for agriculture, farmland now occupies a higher proportion of total land area in Europe than in any other equivalent-sized landmass. As a result, much of Europe's remaining biodiversity is found on farmland (Krebs *et al.* 1999), which acts as a matrix connecting smaller habitat islands of generally higher biodiversity. Around 50% of the land surface of Europe is in agricultural production of one type or another, making this by far the most extensive wildlife habitat on the continent. In the UK, the area of cereals alone is 16 times greater than the area of all the country's nature reserves combined (Potts 1991). Despite its largely artificial nature and its often intensive management, farmland remains an extremely important bird habitat, supporting more bird Species of European Conservation Concern (SPECs) than any other (Tucker & Heath 1994). Nowhere in Europe is the problem of protecting dispersed species outside reserves more acute than in the protection of birds in agricultural habitats.

Across much of Europe, farmland bird populations declined greatly during the last quarter of the twentieth century, a trend well documented by several synoptic monitoring schemes (summarised in Tucker & Heath 1994 and Hagemeijer & Blair 1997). In the UK, declines of over 80% have been recorded in the populations of formerly common and widespread species with a long history of association with modified habitats (Siriwardena *et al.* 1998). During the same period, the intensity of management of farmland changed. In western Europe, agricultural intensity increased greatly through political economic support for the increased use of pesticides and fertilisers, increased mechanisation, changes in crop types and improved varieties (Pain & Pienkowski 1997). In contrast, in eastern Europe, agriculture in many countries has suffered a severe setback since the collapse of Communism in the late 1980s, reversing previous increases in productivity brought about by state support. Productivity has fallen and many previously farmed areas have been abandoned.

Although it has been possible to establish causative links in only a small number of cases, a large body of research (e.g. Campbell *et al.* 1997; Pain & Pienkowski 1997; Aebischer *et al.* 2000) points to the existence of direct links between agricultural intensification and farmland bird declines. Indeed there is strong evidence that agricultural intensification has had demonstrable negative effects on bird populations at a continental scale. Donald *et al.* (2001) examined variation between European countries in farmland bird population trends in terms of a number of indices of agricultural intensification (Box 8.3). They concluded that agricultural intensification is a major anthropogenic threat to biodiversity comparable with deforestation and climate change in its ability to affect bird populations over continental scales. Similar conclusions on the ecosystem effects of modern agriculture have emerged from North America (Matson *et al.* 1997).

Tropical coffee production

Coffee is the world's most valuable agricultural export commodity and the developing world's greatest source of income. The land area given over to coffee production is currently 11.5 million hectares, most of it on land formerly under primary forests. Traditional growing systems involved the

---

Box 8.3. Summary of Donald *et al.* (2001). The pan-European effects of agricultural intensification on farmland bird populations.

- The population trends of 52 species, identified by an independent assessment as being those most likely to respond to changes in agricultural intensity, were extracted for each of 30 European countries from the European Bird Census Committee/BirdLife International European Bird Database (EBD).
- The EBD places each species in each country in a trend category from -2 (>50% decline) to $+2$ (>50% increase). Each species/country trend score has a data quality code ranging from 1 (no quantitative data) to 3 (reliable quantitative data). An average farmland bird trend was calculated for each country, weighted by data quality.
- A number of indices of agricultural intensity were calculated, including cereal yield, milk yield, fertiliser use and levels of mechanisation. Bird population trends were modelled in terms of these indices.
- Many of the indices of agricultural intensity were negatively correlated with mean farmland bird population trend, the most strongly correlated being cereal yield.
- The results provided multi-country, multi-species support for the hypothesis that agricultural intensification has had significant deleterious effects on farmland bird populations, which are visible at continental scales.

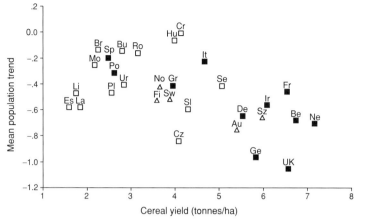

Scatterplots of weighted mean population trends of farmland birds,
1970–90 on cereal yields in 1993. □, eastern European countries; ■,
countries which joined the EU before 1990; △, countries which joined the
EU after 1990 or other western European countries which are not Member
States. $r_{28} = -0.54$, $p = 0.002$. Au, Austria; Be, Belgium/Luxemburg;
Br, Belarus; Bu, Bulgaria; Cr, Croatia; Cz, Czech Republic; De, Denmark;
Es, Estonia; Fi, Finland; Fr, France; Ge, Germany; Gr, Greece; Hu, Hungary;
Ir, Ireland; It, Italy; Ne, Netherlands; La, Latvia; Li, Lithuania; Mo, Moldova;
No, Norway; Pl, Poland; Po, Portugal; Ro, Romania; Se, Slovenia; Sl,
Slovakia; Sp, Spain; Sw, Sweden; Sz, Switzerland; UK, United Kingdom; Ur,
Ukraine. Figure reproduced from Donald, *et al.* 2001. *Proceedings of the Royal
Society of London B*, **268**, 25–29.

planting of coffee bushes under the thinned canopy of the original rainforest (shade-grown coffee), whereas more recently there has been a shift
in many coffee-producing areas towards removing the canopy completely
and growing the coffee under full sun. This system rewards growers when
prices are high, as the extra yields more than compensate farmers for the
higher costs of managing full sun systems. There is considerable concern
that the loss of shade trees will adversely affect bird populations, so the
bird populations of forest and the two forms of coffee production have been
the subjects of considerable recent research. The results of one such study
(Greenberg *et al.* 1997; Box 8.4) suggest that while coffee stands can under certain management regimes support diverse wildlife, they do not approach pristine forest in species richness. However, there is no doubt that
shade-grown coffee systems have prevented total forest clearance in many
areas.

Box 8.4. Summary of results of Greenberg *et al.* (1997). Bird species richness in forest, two types of shaded coffee and full sun coffee.

- Bird species richness was estimated in Guatemala in forest remnants, coffee plantations dominated by two types of shade tree (*Inga* and *Gliricidia*) and unshaded (full sun) coffee plantations.
- Forest remnants held higher species richness than *Inga*-shaded coffee, which held higher richness than *Gliricidia* and full sun coffee. Differences were largely due to differences in the number of resident species recorded (see table).
- Multivariate analyses showed that bird populations in coffee plantations were faunistically distinct from those in forest fragments, as well as being less rich.
- *Inga* is structurally more diverse than *Gliricidia*, which probably accounts for its higher species richness.
- While some forms of coffee plantation are better than others, none achieves the biodiversity of pristine forest.

	Species richness			Species per count[a]	
Habitat	All[b]	Mig.	Res.	Mig.	Res.
Forest remnant	72.2	23	63	2.9	5.8
Inga-shaded	55.5	23	42	2.0	3.2
Gliricidia-shaded	46.3	20	33	1.6	2.6
Full sun	49.2	22	33	1.9	1.5

Counts were made in March–April.[a] Average number of species recorded per 10-minute point count.[b] Based on rarefaction analysis (species per 400 individuals) to correct for different sample sizes from different habitats. Mig., migrant; Res., resident.

POLLUTION

A wide range of pollutants affect birds; their effect can be local or widespread, and they can affect both widespread and common species and critically endangered species, both within and outside protected areas.

Concerns about the effects of DDT on eggshell thickness and reproduction in birds began almost as soon as it was in widespread agricultural application in the 1940s and 1950s (Blus 1996). These concerns have been addressed in recovery programmes for a range of species including the bald eagle (*Haliaeetus leucocephalus*), California condor (*Gymnogyps californianus*), peregrine (*Falco peregrinus*) and Mauritius kestrel (*Falco punctatus*) (Peakall 1976; Barclay & Cade 1983; Grier *et al.* 1983; Snyder 1983; Jones

1987). A good recent example of the indirect impacts of agricultural chemicals upon birds is provided by research on the grey partridge (*Perdix perdix*). Experimental research has shown the decline in this species in the UK to be due to chick starvation resulting from shortages of insect food – brought about by the widespread use of herbicides (Potts 1997).

Another widespread source of pollution to wild birds is lead (Pb). Waterfowl and waders frequently ingest spent lead gunshot, mistaken for food or grit, whilst feeding, and predatory and scavenging birds are exposed to lead shot or bullet fragments in the flesh of prey and carrion (Pain 1995). In the USA, the ingestion of lead gunshot was considered to be responsible for the deaths of several million waterfowl annually before it was replaced with non-toxic shot, and lead shot is still widely used throughout Europe and many other regions. As well as affecting many common and widespread species, lead poisoning was also the most significant cause of mortality in the last few California condors remaining in the wild in the mid-1980s (Wiemeyer *et al.* 1988). Mercury (Hg) is another metal of concern. Mercury is released through a range of human activities, accumulates through the food chain, and has been shown to result in physiological damage in birds (see Thomson 1996).

Coastal and marine flora and fauna are constantly threatened by oil spills, from vessels colliding or running aground, and illegal cleaning of ships' bilge tanks at sea (Frost *et al.* 1976). Oil spills tend to cause problems at a relatively local scale, and their impact depends upon timing, proximity to important seabird breeding or feeding sites, and a range of environmental factors such as weather. A number of large-scale oil spills have had notable impacts on birds. The largest oil spill in US waters was that of the *Exxon Valdez* in Prince William Sound, Alaska, in March 1989. Following the spill, over 35,000 dead birds were retrieved, although actual seabird mortality could have been in the hundreds of thousands (Wiens 1995a). In 1994, a bulk ore carrier, the *Apollo Sea*, sank near Dassen Island off the coast of South Africa (33° 25′ S, 18° 05′ E) resulting in oiling of 10,000 African penguins (*Spheniscus demersus*), about 5% of the world population of this globally threatened species (Whittington 1999). In Europe, the crude oil tanker *Sea Empress* was grounded off the coast of southwest Wales in February 1996, discharging *c.* 72,000 tonnes of oil into the sea and affecting over 6,900 birds. More recently, tens of thousands of birds (largely wintering guillemots) were estimated to have been affected by oil from the *Erika*, which sank on 12 December 1999.

In the same way that oil spills contaminate marine and coastal habitats, chemical spills and accidents can contaminate freshwater and terrestrial habitats. The breach of the tailings dam of the Los Frailes pyrite mine in southwest Spain, on 25 April 1998, resulted in significant contamination of the Guadelquivir marshes, one of the most important wetland sites in Europe. Contaminated areas included those within the Doñana Natural and National Parks, and areas outside the parks also extremely important for bird conservation (Pain et al. 1998; Meharg et al. 1999).

Acidifying pollutants causing 'acid rain' are truly transboundary in nature, transported long distances by prevailing winds and often causing environmental problems far from the pollution source. This matter was highlighted in the 1960s when large numbers of Scandinavian lakes showed a decrease in pH, rain was observed to be more acid in much of Europe, and forest deterioration was linked to exposure to acidic pollution (ApSimon et al. 1997). Acid rain results from emissions of sulphur dioxide and nitrogen oxides that can be converted chemically into secondary pollutants like nitric and sulphuric acids. The majority of these are of anthropogenic origin, from the combustion of coal and other fuels. The resulting acidic pollutants return to Earth as acid rain, snow, fog, or as dry deposition. Areas with different soil types have different buffering capacities, but when this is exceeded aquatic ecosystems can be severely disrupted with loss of plankton, invertebrates, fish and their predators. Terrestrial ecosystems can be affected through direct effects on plant surfaces, and changes in soil chemistry such as increases in the availability of certain metals under more acidic soil conditions. Many bird species may be affected by acidification. One of the best documented species is the dipper (*Cinclus cinclus*), the abundance of which is negatively correlated with low stream pH, high stream aluminium (Al) concentration, and the scarcity of calcium (Ca) rich prey (Ormerod et al. 1988a, 1991; Ormerod & Tyler 1989; Reynolds et al. 1993). Kingfishers (*Alecedo atthis*) are also scarce or absent from acidic streams where fish populations have decreased (Ormerod et al. 1988b).

An increasing amount of work is being conducted on endocrine (or hormone) disruptors (EDCs) – chemicals that alter the function of the endocrine system and consequently cause adverse health effects (including reproductive problems). EDCs include a variety of chemicals, for instance natural and synthetic hormones, pesticides, additives used in the plastics industry, detergent components and breakdown products, and persistent environmental pollutants. Ecological effects potentially linked to EDC exposure include reproductive effects, altered immune function and altered population levels, and have been observed in a variety of taxa including birds. For example, research on bald eagles (*Haliaeetus leucocephalus*) in the Great Lakes of North America has indicated that EDCs may have been associated with reproductive and teratogenic effects (Bowerman et al. 2000).

HUMAN EXPLOITATION

Mankind has been exploiting birds for millennia, for food, for sport or to protect other species. Human exploitation resulted in the extinctions of such iconic species as the dodo (*Raphus cucullatus*) on Mauritius, the great auk (*Alca impennis*) in the north Atlantic, and 11 species of moa (and other flightless birds) in New Zealand (Greenway 1967; Atkinson & Millener 1991; Bell 1991; BirdLife International 2000). The ability of direct exploitation to affect populations of even very common and widespread species was most dramatically illustrated in the case of the passenger pigeon (*Ectopistes migratorius*). In around 300 years, it was reduced from being perhaps the world's commonest bird to extinction. It is possible that hunting reduced colony sizes to a level where reproductive output was reduced sufficiently to lead inevitably to extinction (Halliday 1980). Although hunting on this scale is rare today, largely through legal protection, it may still influence the populations of common and widespread quarry species. Around eight million hunters kill at least 70 million birds in Europe each year, and there is some evidence that this influences populations and annual survival rates at wide geographical scales (Aebischer *et al.* 1999).

Human exploitation does not always result in the death of birds. A number of formerly common species have suffered population declines partly because of trapping for the cagebird industry (e.g. Wright *et al.* 2001), and this continues to threaten endangered species such as Lear's macaw (*Anodorhynchus leari*) in Brazil and the Bali myna (*Leucospar rothschildi*) in Indonesia (BirdLife International 2000). Furthermore, impacts are not always intentional. In recent years, there has been alarm at the effects of certain fishing methods on seabird populations. Long-lining, where up to 12,000 baited hooks are put out on lines as long as 100 km, is known to snare and drown tens of thousands of albatrosses, petrels, shearwaters, skuas and gulls each year. Brothers (1991) estimated that in 1988, the Japanese long-line fishery alone killed around 44,000 albatrosses, including globally threatened species. Both demersal (bottom) and pelagic (near-surface) long-lining can cause mortality. The problem appears to be particularly severe (around 10 birds per 1,000 hooks set) at high latitudes in the north and south Atlantic, north Pacific and Southern Oceans. A number of preventative measures have been devised, but these are generally ignored by unregulated long-liners, which are estimated to kill 100,000 seabirds annually. Weimerskirch *et al.* (1997) modelled populations of two albatross species in the Indian Ocean and found that population trends were driven by trends in adult mortality. When long-lining was being carried out in the birds' feeding grounds, mortality increased and populations fell, but when the fishing fleets moved elsewhere, mortality declined and populations increased.

In addition to direct exploitation, birds face increasing disturbance from human activities, such as car traffic and shooting, particularly outside protected areas. Disturbance may be unintentional but can still have adverse effects as birds are made to take flight or hide and waste energy and feeding time or increase their likelihood of predation (e.g. Madsen 1995; Reijnen *et al.* 1996).

DISEASE

An increasing number of infectious diseases, of both humans and wildlife, have emerged in recent decades (Daszak *et al.* 2000). Human population densities are increasing and encroaching upon wildlife habitat, which increases the degree of human/wildlife contact and potential for disease transmission. Globalisation is resulting in increased movement of people around the world, and an increase in legal and illegal trade in domestic animals and wildlife. All of these factors will result in birds and other taxa being brought into contact with pathogens to which they have not previously been exposed, or to old pathogens under new circumstances (May 1995). Each such case is likely to present its own unpredictable problems. It has been argued that infectious disease is unlikely to result in extinctions as the ease of transmission falls with decreasing population density. However, this does not hold true when the pathogen has an alternative host or a saprophytic lifestyle.

A good example is that of the Hawaiian avifauna, of which 75% of historically recorded species are extinct or threatened with extinction. Malarial parasites (*Plasmodium* spp.) must have been sporadically present in Hawaii, in the tissues of waterfowl and waders migrating annually from North America and Mexico. However, the malarial vector, the mosquito, was absent in Hawaii until 1826, when the night mosquito (*Culex quinque-fasciatus*), the principal vector of avian malaria, was accidentally introduced to the island of Maui. Native Hawaiian forest birds are particularly susceptible to avian malaria (Atkinson *et al.* 1995), and malaria had devastating effects upon the avifauna at low elevations, where *Culex* breeds successfully (Warner 1968).

A further factor that will influence disease epidemiology is climate change, although the extent to which this will occur depends upon many factors and is relatively difficult to predict (see e.g. Dye & Reiter 2000; Rogers & Randolph 2000).

It is likely that disease is responsible for the dramatic declines in populations of two species of Griffon vulture (*Gyps* spp.) in the Indian subcontinent over the last decade. White-backed (*Gyps bengalensis*) and long-billed (*G. indicus*) vultures were common and widespread in the 1980s, but by 2000 were classified as 'Critical' threatened species (BirdLife International 2000). Declines were first noticed in the well-monitored Keoladeo National Park World Heritage Site (KNP), Rajasthan, where numbers of both species declined by over 90% between 1987/88 and 1997/98, and sick and dying birds were recorded with unusual signs of 'head droop' (Prakash 1999). Nationwide surveys in 2000 found that numbers of both species, both within and outside protected areas, had declined by >90% throughout India within a decade (Prakash 2000). Sick adult and juvenile birds appeared throughout the country. Autopsies revealed that birds were dying of enteritis and visceral gout resulting from the same infectious disease process – probably of viral origin (V. Prakash *et al.*, unpublished data). At the time of writing, the causal agent has not been identified, although intensive studies, funded by the UK Governments' Darwin Initiative for the Survival of Species, are under way. Only vultures of the genus *Gyps* are currently affected and, as *Gyps* spp. are found across Asia, Europe and Africa, there is concern that the disease will spread. There is already evidence of infected birds in Nepal and Pakistan, and the first signs of disease were reported in Eurasian Griffons (*Gyps fulvus*) in March 2001. Future research aims to identify the causal agent, its origin and mode of transmission. However, the most likely explanation is exposure of vultures to a (perhaps alien introduced) disease, or perhaps a vector for a disease from which the vultures were previously ecologically isolated.

Few regulations or systems of surveillance consider introduced disease threats to wild animals. Although guidelines exist to prevent the release of animals that may carry pathogens to new areas (IUCN 1995),[6] these are frequently not adhered to (Griffith *et al.* 1993). It is essential that such guidelines are followed and that animals are screened for disease prior to translocation. Further research is needed on the underlying causes of bird and other wildlife diseases, and the factors that influence their spread.

CONCLUSIONS

This chapter identifies and discusses a number of threats to birds both within and/or outside protected areas. The vast majority of these are anthropogenic; although a small number appear to be largely natural, they

[6] See also www.iucn.org/themes/ssc/pubs/policy/reinte.htm

might not have achieved importance were it not for human environmental modification. Few of the threats identified could be addressed through site protection measures alone.

The threats discussed above are not mutually exclusive and indeed are generally closely interlinked. For example, forest clearance for agriculture causes loss of bird biodiversity and the problems associated with fragmentation. It also contributes to global warming, further impacting on biodiversity. Intensification of the resulting agriculture can cause further problems for the birds that have survived there. Future conservation strategy therefore requires an integrated approach that addresses all such threats.

Over the next few decades, major changes to the landscapes of the world are expected, due to a combination of social pressure (such as increased population and resource demand), economic and political pressures (such as trade agreements), and environmental pressure (such as climate change). All of these factors will interact to influence both the extent and types of land use, at both local and landscape scales. Current projections (assuming that fertility in all major areas stabilises at population replacement level by 2050) are for the world population to increase from the 1995 estimate of 5.9 billion to 9.7 billion by 2050 (UN 1998). Projected rates of habitat loss are similarly dramatic. The remaining 8 million km² of tropical humid forests are currently being cleared at a rate of about 1 million km² every 5-10 years (Pimm & Raven 2000). These forests contain about half of the world's terrestrial birds and other biodiversity. Climate will affect all of these factors. Given such a socially and environmentally demanding scenario, it is inevitable that not all currently protected areas will remain intact, and it is certain that they will not conserve most of the planet's biodiversity.

Protection in many specific sites is currently ineffective, and even where protection remains effective over time, this is far from being a guarantee that the wildlife for which the site was designated will remain intact. The identification and protection of the most important areas for biodiversity conservation will always play a very significant part in helping to prevent species extinctions – this is undisputed. We hope, however, that in this chapter we have illustrated that the protection of specific sites covering only a very small proportion of the planet's surface is alone insufficient to protect avian biodiversity, and will certainly not be enough in future. A far more integrated approach to the conservation of bird species diversity is required. This requires improved scientific understanding of the requirements of species, and their responses to habitat fragmentation, isolation, and habitat changes brought about by factors like climate change. It also requires understanding of the social demands upon the environment, and how these are likely to change. The importance of long-term monitoring schemes, not just of bird populations but of anthropogenic inputs and environmental variables as well, is clearly illustrated by the examples cited in this chapter. An interdisciplinary approach to the management of landscapes, with projections of how human and wildlife populations and habitat or biome distributions are likely to change, is required if both human and wildlife populations are to have sustainable futures. This is particularly true in tropical developing countries, where the majority of threatened and other biodiversity remains, and where human pressures and needs are likely to be greatest.

9

Predicting the impact of environmental change

KEN NORRIS & RICHARD STILLMAN

INTRODUCTION

Much of modern conservation biology concerns understanding the impact of past and/or ongoing environmental change on animal and plant populations. This work has many facets including, for example, diagnosing causes of population declines at various spatial scales and managing critically endangered populations (see Chapters 6–8). Increasingly, conservation biologists are being asked to look into the future and assess how populations might respond to future environmental change. In this respect, environmental change might include the activity or inactivity of conservationists themselves, large-scale changes in the environment such as global warming (see Houghton 1997 for a review, and Chapter 8), or the direct impact of human activities on the environment at various levels of scale, for example habitat loss and fragmentation (see Chapter 10).

To look into the future conservationists need predictive tools. Without predictive tools, debate about the impact of future environmental change becomes dominated by dogma. However, to inform debate conservationists need reliable predictive tools that allow them to quantify and assess the impacts of environmental change on important populations. In this chapter, we critically review predictive tools (ecological models) that are becoming increasingly used by conservationists for forecasting how populations might behave in the future, in the face of a broad range of environmental changes. The chapter is structured so that particular ecological models are outlined in principle, before detailing their application to various bird conservation problems. Next, the reliability of models is discussed and suggestions made about how they might be used appropriately.

POPULATION VIABILITY ANALYSIS

What is a population viability analysis?

One way to approach the problem of predicting how a particular population may behave in the future is to attempt to quantify its risk of extinction over a given future time period. Demographic models have increasingly been used in conservation biology to make such an assessment, and this process is usually referred to as population viability analysis (PVA) (Gilpin 1996; for recent reviews see Lindenmayer *et al.* 1993; Beissinger & Westphal 1998). A PVA estimates the probability that a given population will go extinct within a given time period (usually 50, 100 or 200 years) or reach a specified low abundance value ('quasi-extinction'). PVA has increasingly been used by conservation biologists over the past ten years to assess extinction risk in endangered bird species (Appendix 9.1), and there are a number of commercially available software packages for constructing and analysing demographic models for PVA (detailed by Lindenmayer *et al.* 1993; Brook *et al.* 2000). Here, we describe the types of demographic model used for PVA, and discuss their application in bird conservation. For a more thorough discussion of PVA techniques and their problems, see the review by Beissinger & Westphal (1998). Details of specific models are given in the source material cited in Appendix 9.1.

Demographic models developed and used for PVA vary in their complexity (see Beissinger & Westphal 1998). The simplest type of model is deterministic and estimates the rate of population growth (usually as the population multiplication rate, λ) expected from the vital rates (i.e. births and deaths) measured for a single, closed population. The model can be structured by age or stage (e.g. distinguishing immature and adult birds). For example, Lande (1988) used the following simple deterministic model to estimate the multiplication rate of the northern spotted owl (*Strix occidentalis caurina*) population found in old-growth forests of the northwestern United States:

$$\lambda^a(1 - s/\lambda) = l_a b \tag{eqn 9.1}$$

where a = age at first breeding (years), s = adult annual survival probability, l_a = survival probability to breeding age, and b = rate of production of female offspring per adult female. This analysis showed that $\lambda = 0.96 \pm 0.06$, so abundance would be expected to decline at the rate of 4% per annum, although the confidence interval around this rate suggests that λ was not significantly different from a value of 1, indicating stable abundance over time.

Simple deterministic models provide a qualitative assessment of extinction risk; if $\lambda < 1$ then abundance will decline to extinction if this multiplication rate persists in the longterm. However, quantitative estimates of extinction risk require the incorporation of stochastic events that affect vital rates into a demographic model. It has been recognised for some time that small isolated populations are vulnerable to stochastic events such as storms, fire or disease, even if the average rate of population growth is positive (i.e. $\lambda > 1$) (Lande 1993; Mangel & Tier 1994). Therefore, it is important to incorporate variability in vital rates in PVA. Two types of stochasticity are recognised in PVA: demographic and environmental. Demographic stochasticity is the variation in vital rates among individuals at a given time, whereas environmental stochasticity is the variation in vital rates experienced by all individuals in the population over time or space (Shaffer 1987; Lacy 1993; Kendall 1998). The demographic model is then run a number of times, e.g. 500–1,000 (Beissinger & Westphal 1998), and vital rates are sampled for each individual in the population at each time step from distributions of potential values (rather than just using the mean value as in a deterministic model) within each model run. Since the outcome of each model run varies depending on the specific vital rates used at each time step, the data from all model runs allow the chances of extinction or quasi-extinction to be estimated. For example, Li & Li (1998) used a computer simulation application called VORTEX (see Lacy 1993) to estimate the extinction risk of the crested ibis (*Nipponia nippon*) population in China. This population has not exceeded 40 individuals since its discovery in 1981. The demographic model included stochasticity in birth and death rates, and the PVA suggested the population had a 19.7% risk of extinction in the next 100 years.

The deterministic and stochastic models outlined above are most routinely applied to single, closed populations, such as an island endemic species. However, anthropogenic changes to the environment often involve habitat loss and fragmentation (see Chapter 10 for a discussion of these issues). This means that particular populations can be subdivided into discrete (in space) subpopulations occupying habitat fragments, with dispersal of individuals between these subpopulations. Demographic models that include spatial components are referred to as metapopulation or spatially explicit models depending upon whether the spatial information is implicit or explicit within the model (Dunning *et al.* 1995b; Hanski & Simberloff 1997). Such models are much more complex than the single, closed population models, because each subpopulation in a spatial-demographic model functions in the same way as the single populations outlined above, with the exception that abundance in a particular subpopulation is also influenced by immigration from and emigration to other subpopulations. For example, the helmeted honeyeater (*Lichenostomus melanops*) inhabits riparian and swamp forest fragments in river catchments in Victoria, Australia. To construct a demographic model of this population, that incorporated spatial information, Akçakaya *et al.* (1995) used a geographical information system (GIS) to describe the landscape of forest fragments, and combined this with a metapopulation model that described the demography of the honeyeaters within and between forest fragments. This model was then used to assess population viability and examine the value of potential management, for example translocation of birds to new forest fragments.

How have people used population viability analysis in bird conservation?

Since PVA provides an estimate of extinction risk over a given time period, demographic models are becoming increasingly used to assess endangerment. The World Conservation Union (IUCN) criteria for assessing the status (i.e. Critical, Endangered, Vulnerable) of animal and plant species on a global scale includes a criterion based on an unfavourable PVA (Mace & Lande 1991). For birds, Collar *et al.* (1994) define critical status, based on PVA, as a >50% probability of extinction in the next five years, endangered as a >20% probability in the next 20 years and vulnerable as a >10% probability in the next 100 years, using this unfavourable PVA criterion (although this criterion was not actually applied in their endangerment assessment). The corollary of using PVA for assessing endangerment is that models provide a means of estimating the viability of a particular population in future if current environmental conditions are maintained (i.e. a 'do nothing' assessment).

The main use of PVA is in identifying appropriate future management for a population. Management in this sense falls broadly into three categories: demographic, population or environmental management. One way to manage a population is to determine the vital rate(s) that most strongly affect population growth and attempt to target management to that vital rate in the hope that population growth increases as a result (demographic management). This is usually termed elasticity analysis (Caswell 1978, 1989; critically reviewed recently by Mills *et al.* 1999; see also Chapter 7). An example of its application to endangered species management is given by Maguire *et al.* (1995) for red-cockaded woodpeckers (*Picoides borealis*).

An alternative approach to demographic management is to use a demographic model to predict population viability in response to future plausible changes in specific vital rates, and then compare viability with a 'no change' scenario. For example, the lesser kestrel (*Falco naumanni*) nests in urban areas surrounded by farmland in Europe, and the population has declined dramatically in the last 30 years. Using a stochastic demographic model, Hiraldo et al. (1996) showed that a plausible increase in the birth rate in a population in southern Spain would be sufficient to reduce extinction risk in this population from 98% in 200 years to 1.4% (Fig. 9.1). As a result, they argue that management initiatives should be designed to ensure that important farmland habitats are available for these birds while nesting.

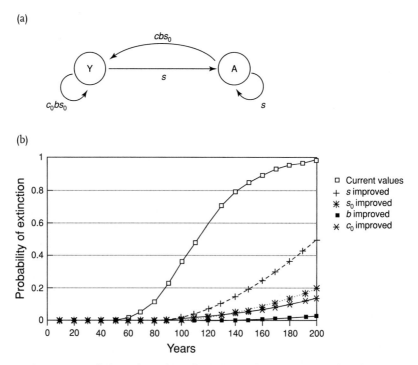

Fig. 9.1. PVA of a lesser kestrel population in southern Spain. (a) Life cycle diagram and vital rates included in the demographic model. A, adults ($\geq$ 2 years old); Y, yearlings; s, adult annual survival probability; s_o, juvenile survival probability (in first year of life); b, female progeny per reproductive female; c_o, proportion of yearlings attempting to breed; c, proportion of adults (2 years or older) attempting breeding. (b) Predicted extinction trajectories for different demographic management options. (Reproduced with permission from Hiraldo et al. 1996, *Journal of Applied Ecology*, Blackwell Science Ltd.)

Demographic management is designed to result in an increase in abundance within a particular population by targeting management to important vital rates. Population management changes abundance directly using translocation or reintroduction schemes. This is a relatively common technique in endangered species management (Cade & Temple 1995; see also Chapter 6). PVA can provide a way of estimating the viability of a population for alternative release programmes that differ in the number and frequency of releases. For example, the white-tailed sea eagle (*Haliaeetus albicilla*) became extinct in Scotland early last century. Between 1975 and 1985, 82 wild-bred birds from Norway were released into western Scotland, and Green *et al.* (1996) used PVA to assess whether supplementary releases were required to improve the viability of this population. They showed that the population had a high (60%) risk of extinction in 100 years without any further releases, but that this risk could be dramatically reduced by the additional release of 60 juveniles. They also showed that viability was not significantly affected by a range of plausible release rates. PVA can also be used to assess the impact of translocation or captive breeding/release programmes on the source population (e.g. Bustamante 1996). This is important if the source population itself is also endangered or necessarily small, as in many captive populations.

Rather than managing the population directly (using either demographicor population management), PVA can also be used to assess the impact of alternative forms of environmental management on an endangered species. For example, the Florida scrub jay (*Aphelocoma coerulescens*) has declined dramatically in abundance following the loss (due to human population expansion) and modification (due to fire suppression) of its scrub habitat. Root (1998) used the computer application RAMAS GIS to examine the importance of habitat quality and connectivity on extinction risk (i.e. a spatially explicit demographic model), and showed that the viability of the population depended crucially on the restoration of high quality scrub habitat. Without this restoration, extinction risk within a short time period (<30 years) was highly likely. Comparable PVAs have been conducted to assess habitat management measures for other endangered species, for example snail kites (*Rostrhamus sociabilis*) (Beissinger 1995) and red-cockaded woodpeckers (Heppell *et al.* 1994).

How reliable are population viability analyses?

PVA clearly has an important role in bird conservation, and this role has increased not least because of the availability of computer software to design and run a PVA. This pattern in birds mirrors the role of PVA in general conservation biology. But, is PVA reliable? Over recent years a number of authors have highlighted both specific and general problems associated with PVA (see Lindenmeyer *et al.* 1993; Wilson *et al.* 1994; Hamilton & Moller 1995; Taylor 1995; Brook *et al.* 1997; Beissinger & Westphal 1998; Kendall 1998; Mills *et al.* 1999). Here, we limit our discussion to a number of important points that crucially affect the use of PVA in bird conservation.

Any demographic model is only as good as the data on which it is constructed and on the ecological importance of parameters for which values are uncertain or largely unknown. In birds, and most other vertebrates, there is a general paucity of data on vital rates in endangered species (Green & Hirons 1991). Although there are ways of obtaining plausible values for use in PVA for certain vital rates (see Beissinger & Westphal 1998), life history parameters such as dispersal are generally poorly known for birds, in terms of both actual immigration and emigration rates, and factors affecting these rates.

Probably the most serious problem for PVA is the paucity of data on density-dependence in wild populations, in terms of either impact of density upon specific vital rates, or how density imposes a ceiling on abundance (i.e. carrying capacity), both of which can be included in demographic models used in PVA. This is important because the degree of density-dependence can have an impact on population viability estimated using PVA. For example, Brook *et al.* (1997) showed that PVA of density-independent models of the Lord Howe Island woodhen (*Tricholimnas sylvestris*) population substantially over-estimated observed population size, compared with models that included density-dependence as a ceiling on abundance (Fig. 9.2). However, they also showed that carrying capacity could only be assessed accurately in retrospect, using observed abundance data as the population has increased in size. This shows how difficult it is to estimate important density-dependent parameters in endangered species whose abundance may be considerably lower than the carrying capacity of the environment.

The usual way of dealing with uncertainty in a PVA is to undertake a sensitivity analysis to determine how sensitive estimated extinction risk is to the demographic model's parameters. Studies using PVA generally do this (Appendix 9.1). Furthermore, statistical methods are available for undertaking sensitivity analyses of relatively complex models, which would otherwise be cumbersome and difficult to interpret (see McCarthy *et al.* 1995, 1996). However, it should be noted that the results of a sensitivity analysis are specific to the parameter values included in the model. This means that uncertainty in particular parameter values could have an important impact on its results, and thus could influence subsequent management decisions.

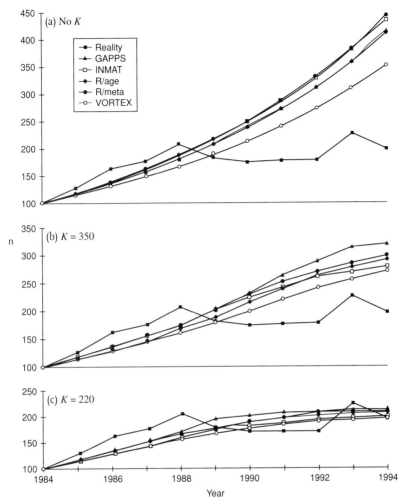

Fig. 9.2. Predicted population trajectories for the Lord Howe Island woodhen population using a range of PVA software packages (detailed in the legend). Actual population size is shown for comparison (filled squares). (a) No density-dependence (i.e. no carrying capacity), (b) density-dependent model, with the carrying capacity K set at 350 birds, and (c) K set at 220 birds. (Reprinted from *Biological Conservation*, **82**, B.W. Brook *et al.*, © Elsevier Science (1997), with permission from Excerpta Medica Inc.)

How should conservationists use population viability analysis?

The advantage of PVA is that it forces conservationists to make explicit the ecological principles they are using to guide management decisions. However, because the reliability of demographic models is so difficult to assess, certain authors have advocated using *relative* rather than *absolute* values of extinction risk as a guide to management (Beissinger & Westphal 1998). This view questions the use of PVA in assessing endangerment because it relies on absolute values of extinction risk. It is debatable whether PVA contributes much to endangerment assessment in any case. The PVA criterion (see p. 183) has had little impact on the assessment of endangered birds (see Collar *et al.* 1994), and existing IUCN criteria such as small population size and population decline already quantify extinction risk indirectly.

How should PVA be applied to demographic, population and environmental management? The examples outlined above show how PVA can be used to compare extinction risk between different management options. The option selected is then the one that provides the lowest estimated extinction risk (i.e. decisions are made using relative extinction risks). Although intuitively appealing, this approach is not without its problems. First, the rank order of management options can be affected by uncertainty in model parameters and how this uncertainty is incorporated within a demographic model (e.g. Drechsler *et al.* 1998). Second, in using PVA for environmental management decisions, assumptions have to be made about how demography is likely to respond to particular future environmental change. As discussed later in this chapter, demography, particularly density-dependence in vital rates, is very sensitive to environmental modification. Given that it is difficult to describe current demography in wild populations, assessing how demography might respond to future environmental change is extremely difficult using the current PVA framework.

Should conservationists stop using PVA? The answer to this is 'no', but PVA needs to be applied to management problems critically and with caution. What does this mean in practice? PVA should be viewed as part of an iterative process (see also Chapter 7). First, it is important to assess the basic information required to construct a model, viewed in the light of the ecology of the species in question. This initial assessment should include an evaluation of the timescales necessary for collecting the data to construct a basic model viewed against the timescales considered necessary for the implementation of conservation action. Second, a model is constructed and its behaviour critically explored using sensitivity analysis. This might result in further data collection to measure more precisely important parameters, or to determine parameter values that might be important but have as yet remained largely unknown. Third, the model can be applied to assess a range of management options. The efficacy of the ranking should further be explored by critically evaluating the behaviour of the model using a sensitivity analysis. Finally, if the model produces a consistent ranking of management options across a wide range of plausible parameter values, then its predictions can be used to prioritise management. However, once started, management initiatives should be monitored in a way that allows the response of the population to management to be compared with its expected behaviour from the PVA.

In conclusion, PVA has a role to play in modern conservation biology, but it is important to use demographic models critically. This is a substantial challenge given the ease with which models can be constructed using readily available computer software. It is also important to use longer-term data sets to retrospectively analyse PVA predictions as a means of building up general insights into the behaviour of demographic models (and software) used for PVA. To date, retrospective analyses across a range of taxa are encouraging (see Brook *et al.* 2000). However, the reliability of PVA predictions from a range of taxa that differ widely in life history and population ecology might not be comparable to the reliability of predictions made for the same population experiencing different management schemes (see also Coulson *et al.* 2001). This is particularly true when environmental change in the future alters vital rates (and their density-dependence) in ways that are not easily predictable from past population behaviour.

BEHAVIOUR-BASED MODELS

What is a behaviour-based model?

Behaviour-based models are designed to overcome one of the major limitations of traditional PVAs, their reliance on empirical estimates of vital rates and in particular density-dependence in vital rates. The problem is that there is no way of knowing whether the empirical relationships on which these models are based, typically measured over a relatively narrow range of population sizes or environmental conditions, will remain the same as conditions change greatly – for example, when a population declines close to extinction or when habitat loss greatly reduces the amount of resources available. This is important because prediction to new circumstances is one of the major uses of PVAs. Behaviour-based models avoid this problem by predicting vital rates from basic properties of a system, rather than requiring them as input.

Behaviour-based models have as their framework the optimality and game theory approaches developed by behavioural ecologists (see e.g. Maynard Smith 1982; Krebs & Davis 1997). Their central assumption is that each individual within a population always behaves in a manner that maximises its own fitness. For example, they nest in locations where their chances of successfully fledging young are greatest, feed in locations or on prey which minimise their chances of starving, or adopt migration strategies which maximise their reproductive success. By following the behaviour and ultimate fate of each individual within the population, a behaviour-based model is able to predict the population consequences of the optimal decisions made by each individual (e.g. Lomnicki 1988; Sutherland 1996b; Goss-Custard & Sutherland 1997). Game theory is used by these models because the behavioural decisions of individuals depend on the decisions made by all other individuals within the population. For example, a behaviour-based model of the non-breeding season might follow the optimal foraging decisions (e.g. choice of patch and prey which maximise intake rate) of each individual within a population as each attempted to meet its daily energy requirements. The intake rate achieved by each individual might depend on its own foraging efficiency, the density of prey remaining in the habitat and the strength of interference from competitors. The predicted mortality rate would be the proportion of animals that failed to meet their requirements and starved, even though they were attempting to minimise the chance of this happening. Recent reviews of behaviour-based models are given in Sutherland (1996b), Goss-Custard & Sutherland (1997) and Pettifor *et al.* (2000b); Goss-Custard (1996) describes a detailed system-specific model.

Why are behaviour-based models useful?

Behaviour-based models have two main advantages over traditional demographic models. First, because they are based on the mechanisms underlying population ecology, the process of developing and parameterising them is likely to force more precise thinking into the workings of a system; traditional models describe what changes happen to populations through time, whereas behaviour-based models explain how changes occur.

Secondly, their real strength is that they should produce more accurate predictions outside the range of conditions for which they are parameterised. The empirical relationships from which demographic models derive their predictions may or may not change as the environment does, but there is no way of knowing this in advance. In contrast, the basis of predictions of behaviour-based models – fitness maximisation – does not change, no matter how much the environment changes (Goss-Custard 1996; Goss-Custard & Sutherland 1997). Animals in behaviour-based models are likely, therefore, to respond to environmental change in the same way as real ones would. The real value of behaviour-based models is likely to be as tools to predict to future environmental conditions, brought about, for example, by climate change, or changes in habitat quantity or quality resulting from building developments or changes in farming practices.

Examples of behaviour-based models and their application

Contrasts in the natural histories of different study systems and the types of questions posed, has meant that a range of different behaviour-based models has been developed. At one extreme are models designed to provide general insights into the processes underlying population ecology (e.g. the general model of migration developed by Sutherland & Dolman 1994), while at the other extreme are detailed models of specific systems which aim to accurately predict the consequences of habitat change for population size, mortality or reproductive rate (e.g. the model of the Exe estuary oystercatcher population developed by Goss-Custard *et al.* 1995a–c). Although varying in detail, all behaviour-based models are based on the same underlying principle of fitness maximisation. All have their value, but here we emphasise those models that have been applied to specific systems and address real conservation problems. To date, most behaviour-based models have been developed for the non-breeding period and used to predict the number of individuals an area of habitat can support or to predict the mortality rate of a population. Our emphasis is, therefore, on this season, and how these models have been used to predict the consequences of environmental change (e.g. habitat loss or change of quality, human disturbance or shellfishing), on the sustainable population size or mortality rate within a population.

The simplest behaviour-based models are the spatial depletion models, originally developed by Sutherland & Anderson (1993). These models assume that all individuals within a population are identical (i.e. when feeding in the same place, they all consume prey at the same rate), that interference (the short-term, reversible decline in intake rate due to the presence of competitors (Goss-Custard 1980)) is absent and that individuals always feed in those locations where their intake rates are maximised. They predict the manner in which a predator or herbivore population spreads out between patches as successive ones are depleted. They are used to answer questions such as 'What is the maximum number of birds that a habitat can support over the course of winter, and how would this number be changed if the habitat was to change?'

Spatial depletion models have been used to address a number of conservation problems, mainly in wildfowl and waders. Sutherland & Allport's (1994) model showed how the stock grazing regime and intensity of grazing from a competing species, the wigeon, interacted to determine the number of days a population of bean geese could be supported on a grazing marsh.

Percival *et al.* (1996, 1998) used a similar model to determine the consequences of sea-level rise, removing habitat from the bottom of the shore, and encroachment of *Spartina anglica*, removing habitat from the top of the shore, for the number of days a brent goose population could be supported in an intertidal area. K. Norris *et al.* (unpublished data) used a spatial depletion model to predict the consequences of shellfishing for the population size of oystercatchers supported in the Burry Inlet, South Wales. They showed that current levels of shellfishing in this estuary do not reduce the number of days that the bird population can be supported, but that large increases in fishing effort could adversely affect the population.

Spatial depletion models are clearly of value to conservation, but do have limitations. In particular, they are not used to predict the mortality rate within a population. This is because, as they assume that all individuals are identical, they predict that either all die or all survive. The predicted density-dependent mortality is therefore a step-function. Instead of mortality, they predict the number of bird-days that can be supported by a habitat. But bird-days do not distinguish whether a small population is supported for a long time, or a large population supported for a short time. Real populations seldom show an all-or-nothing response because individuals differ in their competitive abilities. Because of this some die before others and so a more gradual density-dependent curve is found. Spatial depletion models also assume that interference is absent or negligible, but this will not always be the case. Other models have been developed which do not make these assumptions, and so can be applied to a wider range of systems. These models can answer questions such as 'How will the mortality rate in a population change if its size increases by 50% or if 50% of the habitat is lost?'

The most detailed behaviour-based model developed to date is that of Goss-Custard and co-workers (Goss-Custard *et al.* 1995a–c; Stillman *et al.* 2000), which has been used to simulate a population of oystercatchers overwintering on the Exe estuary, and feeding primarily on mussels. This model contains many detailed aspects of the real system (e.g. the seasonal change in the quality of mussels, the successive ebb and flow of the tide and differences in the feeding methods used by oystercatchers to open mussels), but its central assumption is still the same as other behaviour-based models. Individuals within the model differ in a number of ways which influence their intake rates, including their age, feeding method on mussels, dominance and foraging efficiency while feeding on mussels and supplementary prey on upshore flats and fields surrounding the estuary. Although all individuals base their decisions on the same principle, intake rate maximisation, the actual decisions made by each differ and depend on its own particular characteristics. Whether an individual survives is determined by the balance between its daily rates of energy expenditure and acquisition. When daily energy acquisition exceeds daily expenditure, individuals add to their energy reserves or maintain them if a maximum level has already been reached. When daily requirements exceed daily acquisition, individuals draw on their energy reserves. If energy reserves fall to zero, an individual dies of starvation.

This model has demonstrated the ability of behaviour-based models to predict to circumstances outside the range of conditions for which they are parameterised (Fig. 9.3). The model was developed by comparing its predicted overwinter mortality rate with the observed rate on the Exe estuary during 1976–80. Successive components were added or removed until the discrepancy between prediction and observation was reduced. By the end of development the model described the system with a reasonable degree of accuracy. However, this may have arisen because too many

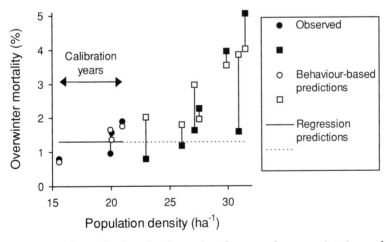

Fig. 9.3. Observed and predicted mortality of oystercatchers overwintering on the Exe estuary. Predictions are from a behaviour-based model of the oystercatcher population (Stillman *et al.* 2000) and a simple regression model. Both models are developed for the calibration years 1976–80, during which time overwinter mortality was independent of oystercatcher density. During 1980–91, the oystercatcher population increased in size and there was an associated density-dependent increase in mortality. The behaviour-based model predicts this increase in mortality, even though it is only developed for the years during which mortality was density independent. The simple regression model does not predict this increase in mortality, because it simply extrapolates the density independent mortality rate. (Adapted from Stillman *et al.* 2000).

parameters had been added to the model and it had become over-fitted to the data. As a test of the model the predicted mortality rate was compared with the observed rates during 1980–91, a period in which the oystercatcher population had increased and there was a density-dependent increase in the mortality rate. The model successfully predicted this increase, even though it was only developed to predict the mortality rate when the population size was lower. A demographic model, only developed during 1976–80, would have not predicted this increase in mortality (Fig. 9.3). Furthermore, the Exe model predicted, with a reasonable degree of accuracy, the underlying oystercatcher behaviour, such as the amount of time spent feeding on mussels, the distribution of birds throughout the estuary and the changes in body mass through the season. This demonstrates the potential of this model in particular, and behaviour-based models in general, to accurately predict to circumstances outside the range of conditions for which they are parameterised. This model has been used to predict the impact of habitat loss and shellfishing on the oystercatcher populations of the Exe estuary and Burry Inlet (Goss-Custard et al. 2000; Stillman et al. 2001).

The models considered so far are restricted to single sites (e.g. an estuary), and predict mortality rate or the number of bird-days supported. They assume that birds can move freely between the different patches within a site and have perfect, or near-perfect, knowledge of the quality of different patches. These assumptions become less realistic as the spatial scale increases. The behaviour-based models developed by Pettifor et al. (2000a) for brent goose and barnacle goose, and by Clark & Butler (1999) for western sandpiper, are at the continental scale and consider the time and energy costs of moving between sites and uncertainty in the quality of sites. The model of Pettifor et al. (2000a) predicted how habitat loss or changes in the composition of crop types affected the population size of barnacle and brent geese. In the brent goose model, birds moved between a number of wintering sites in response to depletion of their feeding areas and habitat loss. This model therefore incorporated the knock-on consequences for habitat loss in one site for the population density and mortality rate of birds at another site. Again these models generated population-level predictions from the realistic behaviour of birds within the model population (e.g. brent geese switched between feeding on intertidal *Zostera* beds and terrestrial fields at the same time as was observed).

Limitations and future model development

The general principle of behaviour-based models means that they are expected to accurately predict to environmental conditions outside the range of conditions for which they are parameterised. This is their main advantage over PVAs based on demographic models. However, to date this has only been tested for one model, applied to one system (Stillman *et al.* 2000). Furthermore, this model was based on one of the most intensively studied bird species, in one of the most intensively studied systems. As a result, many specific details of the species and system could be added to the model; this would not be possible for most other species or sites. Although this test was encouraging, further tests of the ability of behaviour-based models to predict to new circumstances are clearly required in order to properly judge their value as predictive tools. In particular, it is important to assess the amount of system-specific information that needs to be included in models in order for them to predict accurately.

Most behaviour-based models developed to date have been applied to the non-breeding systems. They have predicted the number of bird-days supported by a habitat or the mortality rate within a population, and have used intake rate maximisation as their measure of fitness. The migration model of Clark & Butler (1999) is an exception to this that uses the behaviour-based approach to predict both mortality rate and breeding success. The models of Pettifor *et al.* (2000a) and Stillman *et al.* (2001) do predict year-round population size, but are only behaviour-based in winter and spring; they use empirical demographic models to predict reproductive rate based on the numbers and/or body condition of birds returning to the breeding grounds. More models encompassing the full annual cycle and geographical range of populations are needed to fully explore the potential of the approach.

In summary, behaviour-based models have the potential to predict the form of density-dependent relationships, which PVAs require as input. However, these models are in their infancy, and have only been applied to a narrow range of systems to date. Although they cannot, as yet, replace traditional PVAs, we encourage their development for a wider range of systems.

GENERAL CONCLUSIONS

Population viability analysis and behaviour-based models have developed in isolation, yet are clearly complementary tools for enabling conservation biologists to estimate how populations might behave in the future. PVA has primarily been used for the management of endangered species (Appendix 9.1), whereas behaviour-based models have been applied to the management of relatively common species (Appendix 9.2). How can these techniques be brought together?

One weakness of PVA is that viability is strongly influenced by density-dependent processes that are extremely difficult to measure in wild

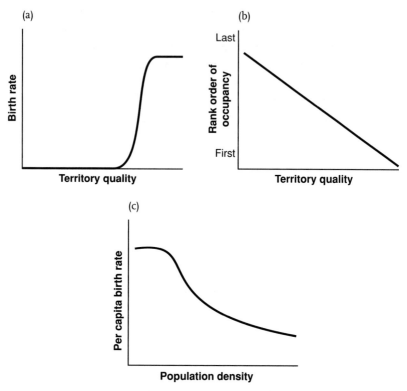

Fig. 9.4. An example of how a simple behaviour-based model can be used to generate a function describing density-dependence in the birth rate in an endangered species. The model describes a territorial species in which the birth rate is affected by territory quality (a). As a consequence, birds preferentially occupy the best quality territories that are currently available (b). That is, birds behave in an ideal despotic way. As population density increases, birds are forced to occupy poorer and poorer quality territories, so the per capita birth rate declines (c). Density-dependent changes in the birth rate can then be estimated for any combination of territory qualities by assuming that territories are occupied in order of their quality (the best one first) and that the birth rate increases with increasing territory quality as shown in (a).

populations. This is exacerbated in endangered species, in which there is a paucity of demographic information (Green & Hirons 1991), and because populations, due to their endangerment, may be at levels of abundance considerably below the carrying capacity of the environment. For example, consider an island bird population whose abundance has been reduced by the introduction of an alien predator. Clearly management should aim to remove the predator, but what is the long-term viability of the population after predator removal? This is very difficult to estimate because it will depend on how density-dependence regulates population growth to some extent. This might be impossible to assess directly because the recent abundance history of the population might be well below abundance levels at which density-dependent processes are evident. In such cases, a behaviour-based approach can provide valuable insights into density-dependent processes that might otherwise be unmeasurable (see Fig. 9.4 for a hypothetical example).

Most existing behaviour-based models are essentially deterministic, whether constructed to examine local abundance (e.g. Percival *et al.* 1996) or global equilibrium population sizes (e.g. Sutherland & Dolman 1994) (although see Goss-Custard & West 1997 for an example of a behaviour-based model predicting population size with stochastic year-to-year variation in the food supply). Most population viability analyses, in contrast, are based on stochastic models. This is important because populations can still decline in abundance in the face of stochastic processes, even when a deterministic model predicts positive population growth rates (Lande 1993; Mangel & Tier 1994). It seems important, therefore, for behaviour-based models to consider the impact of stochastic processes on both quality and quantity of available habitat, but also directly on particular vital rates derived from behaviour-based processes.

In this chapter, we have attempted to highlight the advantages and disadvantages of different approaches to predicting the impact of environmental change. It is crucial to remember that models are only as good as the data with which they are constructed. This means that they should always be used critically and their behaviour thoroughly examined on an ongoing basis.

Appendix 9.1. *Examples of the application of population viability analysis to various bird conservation problems*

Species	Year of Publication	Details of Demographic Model				Conservation Management Issues Addressed by Model			Source
		Stochastic?	Spatially Structured?	Sensitivity Analysis?	Software Used?[a]	Demographic	Population	Environmental	
Red-cockaded woodpecker	1993	Yes	No	Yes	Yes	No	Yes	No	Haig et al. 1993
Red-cockaded woodpecker	1994	No	No	Yes	No	Yes	No	Yes	Heppell et al. 1994
Helmeted honeyeater	1995	Yes	Yes	Yes	No	Yes	No	No	McCarthy et al. 1995
Sooty shearwater	1995	Yes	No	Yes	Yes	Yes	No	Yes	Hamilton & Moller 1995
Helmeted honeyeater	1995	Yes	Yes	No	No	No	Yes	No	Akçakaya et al. 1995
Snail kite	1995	Yes	Yes	Yes	No	No	No	Yes	Beissinger 1995
Red-cockaded woodpecker	1995	Yes	No	Yes	Yes	Yes	No	No	Maguire et al. 1995
Helmeted honeyeater	1996	Yes	Yes	Yes	No	Yes	No	Yes	McCarthy 1996
Bearded vulture	1996	Yes	No	No	Yes	No	Yes	No	Bustamante 1996
Lesser kestrel	1996	Yes	No	Yes	No	Yes	No	No	Hiraldo et al. 1996
White-tailed sea eagle	1996	Yes	No	Yes	No	No	Yes	No	Green et al. 1996

Species	Year								Reference
Lord Howe Island woodhen[b]	1997	Yes	No	No	Yes	Yes	No	Yes	Brook et al. 1997
Orange-bellied parrot	1998	Yes	No	No	No	No	Yes	Yes	Drechsler et al. 1998
Hawaiian stilt	1998	Yes	Yes	Yes	Yes	Yes	No	No	Reed, Elphick & Oring 1998
Crested ibis	1998	Yes	No	No	Yes	Yes	No	No	Li & Li 1998
Northern spotted owl	1998	Yes	Yes	Yes	Yes	Yes	No	Yes	Akçakaya & Raphael 1998
Florida scrub jay	1998	Yes	Yes	Yes	Yes	Yes	No	Yes	Root 1998
Capercaillie	1998	Yes	No	No	No	Yes	Yes	No	Marshall & Edwards-Jones 1998
Kirtland's warbler	1998	Yes	No	No	No	No	No	Yes	Marshall et al. 1998
Capricorn silvereye	1998	Yes	Yes	Yes	Yes	Yes	Yes	Yes	Brook & Kikkawa 1998
Piping plover	2000	Yes	No	No	Yes	Yes	No	No	Plissner & Haig 2000

[a] This refers to non-specific software such as VORTEX or RAMAS for undertaking PVA.

[b] This study was a retrospective analysis of various demographic models and computer software, so did not address specific management issues.

Appendix 9.2. *Examples of behaviour-based models and their application*

Species	Incorporates Interference	Individuals Vary	Single or Multiple Sites	State Dependent	Predicts Mortality	Conservation Issues Addressed	Source
Goshawk	Yes	Yes	Single	No	Yes	–	Kenward & Marcström 1988
Bean goose	No	No	Single	No	No	Habitat management	Sutherland & Allport 1994
Wigeon	No	No	Single	No	No	Habitat management	Sutherland & Allport 1994
Brent goose	No	No	Single	No	No	Interspecific competition, habitat loss	Percival et al. 1996, 1998
Wigeon	No	No	Single	No	No	Interspecific competition, habitat loss	Percival et al. 1996, 1998
Brent goose	Yes	Yes	Multiple	No	Yes	Habitat loss	Pettifor et al. 2000a
Barnacle goose	No	Yes	Multiple	No	Yes	Habitat loss and change of quality	Pettifor et al. 2000a
Pink-footed goose	No	No	Single	No	No	Human disturbance	J.A. Gill, unpubl.
Oystercatcher	Yes	Yes	Single	No	Yes	Density-dependent mortality and habitat loss	Goss-Custard et al. 1995a–e
Oystercatcher	Yes	Yes	Single	No	Yes	Density-dependent mortality and shellfishing	Goss-Custard et al. 2000

Species							Source
Oystercatcher	Yes	Yes	Single	No	Yes	Density-dependent mortality	Stillman *et al.* 2000
Oystercatcher	Yes	Yes	Single	No	Yes	Shellfishing and habitat quality	R.A. Stillman *et al.*, unpubl.
Oystercatcher	No	No	Single	No	No	Shellfishing and habitat quality	K. Norris, unpubl.
Western sandpiper	No	No	Multiple	Yes	Yes	–	Clark & Butler 1999
Black-tailed godwit	No	No	Multiple	No	No	Habitat quality	Gill *et al.* 2001

10

Fragmentation, habitat loss and landscape management

PAUL OPDAM & JOHN A. WIENS

INTRODUCTION

Fragmentation of natural habitats is a central concern of biodiversity conservation. Indeed, it has been labelled 'the principal threat to most species in the temperate zone' (Wilcove *et al.* 1986) and 'the single greatest threat to biological diversity' (Noss 1991). Our central thesis in this chapter, however, is that fragmentation is only one of several ways that human activities can affect the distribution and availability of habitat to organisms. The major conservation issue, in fact, is land use (Meyer & Turner 1994; Dale 1997; Laurance & Bierregaard 1997), and solutions to the threat of fragmentation may be ineffective unless they are placed within a broader framework of changing land use and its impacts on entire landscapes. To develop this thesis, we first consider the physical template of fragmentation and the mechanisms of organism responses. We then address how these points affect our ability to predict the consequences of landscape change, and how this knowledge can contribute to finding solutions to the conservation issues raised by land use and fragmentation.

THE PHYSICAL TEMPLATE

Habitat fragmentation and habitat loss

In its most elementary state, the pattern of fragmentation is unambiguous: bits and pieces of habitat (e.g. forests, grasslands, wetlands) are scattered through a background matrix of non-habitat. This simple 'habitat/non-habitat' conceptualisation of fragmentation has been fostered especially by island biogeography theory (MacArthur & Wilson 1967). If one views fragments as counterparts of islands isolated in an inhospitable ocean, then all the power and predictions of the theory can be brought to bear on fragmentation issues and their resolution. This was the premise behind attempts to design nature reserves according to the principles of island biogeography (e.g. Wilson & Willis 1975; Diamond 1986; Shafer 1990). In the end, however, the analogy between islands and fragments is flawed, and insights derived from island biogeography theory, while initially useful, are ultimately incomplete and misleading (cf. Zimmerman & Bierregaard 1986; Wiens 1995b; Haila 1999).

One reason for the failure of the island analogy is that island-like fragmentation is but one stage on a continuum of habitat patterns that result from human land use. Envision a scenario in which an unbroken expanse of habitat is progressively developed (Fig. 10.1; Forman 1995; Hunter 1996). Initially, roads may be constructed that *dissect* the habitat. Isolated patches of habitat may then be converted to non-habitat, through timber harvesting, clearing for agriculture, low-density human settlement, or the like; the habitat has become *perforated*. As development continues a point is reached at which the habitat is *fragmented*; habitat continuity has been disrupted, and habitat patches are physically isolated from one another (Norton & Lord 1990). Further development may result in a reduction in fragment size (*shrinkage*) and a loss of some fragments from the landscape (*attrition*).

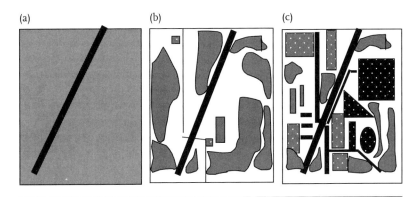

Human land-use pressure

Fig. 10.1. A diagrammatic representation of the variety of changes produced by human activities in an idealized landscape. (a) A railroad is constructed dissecting a forest. Fragmentation, no habitat loss. (b) Subsequently, agriculture comes in by two farms and a farm road. Habitat loss and, consequently, increased fragmentation. (c) Urban development takes over, the total forest coverage has decreased and is dissected into a few scattered patches, within a matrix of housing, major roads and other urban area.

In highly developed landscapes, only scattered remnants of natural habitat may remain (Saunders *et al.* 1987; McIntyre & Hobbs 1999).

This scenario reveals an important distinction. As soon as development or disturbance begins, habitat is lost, and habitat loss continues as development proceeds. Fragmentation, however, occurs only when disturbance or development reaches a thresholdat which habitat continuity is broken. As a result, patches of suitable habitat become isolated, and population dynamics vary among patches. Exactly where on the development/disturbance continuum the fragmentation threshold may occur is difficult to predict. Simple percolation theory (Gardner *et al.* 1989) predicts a critical threshold at about 60% remaining coverage of habitat, but elaborations of the theory (e.g. Pearson *et al.* 1996; Pearson & Gardner 1997; With 1999) indicate that under different assumptions the fragmentation threshold occurs at lower coverage values. The empirical studies on birds and mammals summarised by Andrén (1994, 1996; but see Mönkkönen & Reunanen 1999; Andrén 1999) suggest that fragmentation effects may set in when perhaps 30% of the original habitat remains, although the critical proportion of remaining habitat differs among species. The response of species populations to landscape change is also non-linear (Andrén 1996; Hanski & Ovaskainen 2000; Vos *et al.* 2001). Territory occupancy by nuthatches (*Sitta europaea*), for example, varies non-linearly with the degree of fragmentation, given a fixed amount of habitat (Verboom *et al.* 1993) (Fig. 10.2), and the probability of persistence of populations of northern spotted owls (*Strix occidentalis caurina*) shows a sharp threshold with changes in the coverage of old-growth forest habitat in the landscape (Lamberson *et al.* 1992). Because there are stochastic elements in such responses, however, it is difficult to predict exactly when a threshold of habitat occupancy or population persistence will be passed.

Theoretical views of fragmentation, such as those portrayed in island biogeography or percolation theory, consider both habitat and the non-habitat matrix to be internally homogeneous. Natural landscapes, however, are really heterogeneous mosaics of vegetation types that undergo continuous change as a result of ecological succession and natural disturbances such as windfall, fire or erosion (Wiens 1995c, 2001a). The baseline for thinking about habitat loss and fragmentation should therefore be the dynamically heterogeneous landscape mosaic, not a static and homogeneous abstraction (Haila 1999). Moreover, the bird populations and communities that occupy these landscapes are themselves dynamic; natural systems rarely exhibit the sort of equilibrium configuration assumed by traditional ecological theory (Wiens 1977; Pickett *et al.* 1992).

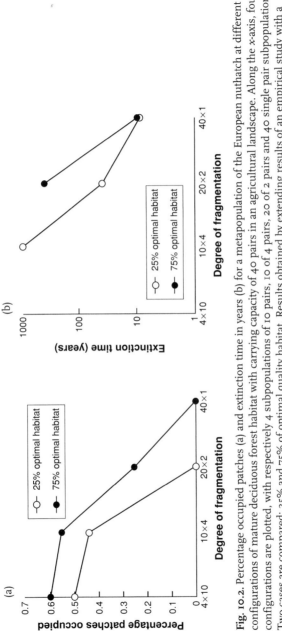

Fig. 10.2. Percentage occupied patches (a) and extinction time in years (b) for a metapopulation of the European nuthatch at different configurations of mature deciduous forest habitat with carrying capacity of 40 pairs in an agricultural landscape. Along the *x*-axis, four configurations are plotted, with respectively 4 subpopulations of 10 pairs, 10 of 4 pairs, 20 of 2 pairs and 40 single pair subpopulations. Two cases are compared: 25% and 75% of optimal quality habitat. Results obtained by extending results of an empirical study with a metapopulation model. (From Verboom *et al.* 1993.)

There are three immediate consequences of recognising the natural dynamics and heterogeneity of habitats and populations. First, because fragmentation may occur through natural as well as anthropogenic disturbances, organisms may be adapted to the changes in landscape configuration and habitat distribution that occur naturally. These adaptations may determine how sensitive organisms are to different forms of anthropogenic disturbance, and knowledge of natural patch dynamics may provide guidelines for evaluating and mitigating the ecological effects of human-induced habitat loss and fragmentation (Hunter 1993; Spies & Turner 1999). Second, different places in a naturally heterogeneous landscape will differ in their suitability for human activities, and therefore in their probability of disturbance. The magnitude and spatial pattern of non-random habitat loss or fragmentation will differ among portions of a landscape as a result of underlying differences in pre-disturbance heterogeneity. Without consideration of these differences, simple predictions of the likelihood or consequences of fragmentation are not likely to hold. And third, because populations and communities are themselves dynamic, the conclusion that changes in abundance, distribution or community composition are due to anthropogenic changes in habitat distribution or availability may not be justified. The assumption that an observed change in landscape pattern is the cause of an observed change in bird abundance or distribution should be tested rather than accepted uncritically.

Of course, human development itself is no more a unitary phenomenon than is fragmentation. Different forms of anthropogenic disturbance differ in their effects on habitat loss, fragmentation, and the structure of the landscape as a whole. Some human activities, such as the low-density housing development that occurs when people build cabins in the woods or isolated ranchettes in the prairie, may do little more than dissect or perforate the existing mosaic (J.M. Fraterrigo & J.A. Wiens, unpublished data). At the opposite extreme, urban development typically relegates vestiges of 'natural' habitat to parks or greenways immersed in a matrix of buildings, streets, parking lots and housing developments with tiny manicured yards. Between these extremes lie a variety of land uses, such as forestry, agriculture or grazing (Fig. 10.1), each of which imposes a characteristic imprint on the landscape and produces differing patterns and probabilities of habitat loss and fragmentation.

The degree to which habitat loss and fragmentation are current or future threats to biodiversity, or have long since passed the point at which a return to natural conditions is possible through effective management, depends on where a location is on the gradients of development and habitat alteration depicted in Fig. 10.1. These conditions vary among ecosystem types and among regions of the world that differ in culture, history and economies. Thus, the impacts of land use on the form and pattern of landscapes may be less in arid and semi-arid ecosystems, where productivity is low and options for development are limited, than in ecosystems with greater productivity, such as forests or tallgrass prairie. Many parts of the world have already lost most of their 'natural' habitats, either over the last century (e.g. the Australian wheatbelt), the past several centuries (e.g. The Netherlands), or millennia (e.g. the Mediterranean region). Here the fragmentation threshold has long since been passed and conservation efforts are generally focused on managing and preserving the remnants of native vegetation (Hobbs & Saunders 1993). Other areas, such as portions of Amazonia, some boreal regions, or the tropical savannas of northern Australia, still retain large areas of relatively natural vegetation. It is in these regions that the rate of habitat loss and probability of fragmentation are greatest and the threats to overall biodiversity most acute. It is also in these regions, or in the relatively unaltered landscapes to the left side of the gradient shown in Fig. 10.1, that landscape management to attain conservation goals can still be proactive rather than reactive. Here efforts can be focused on managing landscapes to reduce the changes of complete degradation and loss of biodiversity, rather than the much more difficult (and expensive) task of attempting to restore severely altered ecosystems.

The landscape context

Clearly, areas of habitat do *not* exist in isolation from their surroundings, and the surroundings are *not* a uniformly unsuitable matrix. 'Habitat' is part of a landscape mosaic, whose properties may affect ecological processes within patches or fragments of habitat. Four attributes of landscapes are particularly important. First, the elements of a landscape mosaic differ in the costs and benefits (e.g. predation risk, food availability, mating opportunities) that organisms occupying them experience. Not all places contain equally suitable habitat – *patch quality* varies. One way to ameliorate the effects of habitat loss, then, might be to manage a larger area of poorer quality habitat. Second, the patches in a landscape mosaic have *edges*. The effects of edges have received considerable attention in studies of fragmentation, as the ratio of fragment edge to interior increases with reductions in fragment size and predation risk is often greater close to a habitat edge (Paton 1993). The magnitude of these effects, however, may vary depending on the nature of the edge – its sharpness, form, width, or permeability to movement by individuals. Third, *patch context* is a key determinant of what happens at the edges of patches or fragments and of the ease or difficulty of movement of individuals into and out of a patch. Whether individuals nesting in a forest fragment, for example, suffer increased predation losses with a reduction in fragment size may depend on the composition of the adjacent landscape and whether or not those landscape elements harbour predator populations (Andrén 1992). Finally, these three features of landscape structure combine to determine the overall *connectivity* of a landscape. Although conservation biologists and managers tend to think of connectivity in terms of corridors – linear strips of habitat connecting patches of similar habitat – how individuals actually move through a landscape depends on how different kinds of habitats of different quality are arrayed in a landscape and the relative permeabilities of the boundaries between them.

INDIVIDUAL AND POPULATION RESPONSES TO LANDSCAPE STRUCTURE

To predict how landscape changes will affect birds, one must consider how individuals and populations respond to landscape structure. Much has been written about these mechanisms, but little of it is placed within a landscape context and the concepts and theories that have been developed generally deal with 'landscapes' only in terms of habitat patches immersed in a featureless background matrix (see e.g. Shorrocks & Swingland 1990; Wiens 1995c; Tilman & Kareiva 1997). We will not attempt to review this large body of literature, but instead focus on how these mechanisms can interact with landscape composition and structure to affect the dynamics of populations and communities, and thus the maintenance of avian biodiversity.

Individual mechanisms

Individuals respond to habitat conditions by moving and deciding to stop. *Movement* occurs over a range of time scales and distances, from short-term movements of individuals during foraging bouts to seasonal migrations to annual or lifetime dispersal, and these different forms of movement relate to landscape structure in different ways. How individuals move within their home ranges or within stopover sites during migration, or their movement pathways during short-distance, non-volant dispersal (as in Bewick's wren, *Thryomannes bewickii*; Kroodsma 1974), are likely to be affected by the particulars of landscape structure – the size and distribution of habitat patches, the shape and sharpness of patch boundaries, and the characteristics and quality of intervening components of the landscape. Some tropical species, for example, are reluctant to cross even small breaks in forest cover (Bierregaard *et al.* 1992; see also Grubb & Doherty 1999). In Western Australia, western yellow robins (*Eopsaltria griseogularis*) are restricted to patches of remnant woodlands and move between them only along well-vegetated corridors (Saunders 1989). In contrast, singing honey-eaters (*Lichenostomus virescens*) readily cross open agricultural areas to reach woodland patches (Merriam & Saunders 1993). The composition of a landscape, combined with the mobility and behaviour of individuals (which vary substantially among species), determine the probability that an individual will move from one point to another within a landscape and, therefore, its sensitivity to habitat loss and fragmentation.

Patch choice (or habitat selection) also affects how organisms respond to landscape structure. According to theory (e.g. Fretwell & Lucas 1969; Wiens 1997), individuals select the habitat or territory in which their individual fitness will be maximised or the ratio of costs to benefits of occupying a habitat is minimised. This implies that as birds have to invest more time or energy in monitoring potential habitats and dispersing between them (as is probably the case in discontinuous habitat), the distribution of individuals over habitat-quality classes will diverge from the theoretical ideal. For nuthatches, Matthysen & Currie (1996) found that territories in continuous forest were taken up in order of decreasing quality, whereas in isolated fragments there was no pattern at all. Of course, how species respond to dissection, perforation, or fragmentation of their primary habitat may depend on the relative suitability and spatial configuration of other elements in the landscape. Because patterns of habitat occupancy may depend on local population density (Fretwell & Lucas 1969), the effects of landscape change will vary not only among species but among different phases of the dynamics of a population. To understand how fragmentation affects populations it is necessary to understand how individuals respond to landscape change.

Population consequences

Individual behavioural responses to landscape structure and change ultimately translate into the spatial structure of a population. There is considerable theoretical support for the conclusion that such structure may affect population dynamics (Tilman & Kareiva 1997). The theoretical foundation for considering spatially structured populations is perhaps best developed with reference to metapopulations (Hanski 1999) and source–sink dynamics (Pulliam 1988). Both of these theoretical models apply most clearly to situations in which isolated fragments of habitat are scattered through a uniformly unsuitable background matrix. It is therefore instructive to consider them, even though most real-world populations adhere strictly to neither but contain elements of both.

Metapopulations occur in intermediate stages of habitat loss and fragmentation. According to theory, the probability of persistence of the metapopulation is determined by the dynamics of spatially separated subpopulations that vary asynchronously from one another and that are linked by low levels of dispersal. Local populations, especially those in small and relatively isolated habitat patches, suffer extinction due to increased susceptibility to environmental or demographic stochasticity (Lande 1993). Dispersal from other habitat patches may result in recolonisations (as found in nuthatches by Verboom *et al.* 1991) or even prevent the extinction of local populations (Brown & Kodric-Brown 1977). Metapopulation structure may be expressed when fragmentation has reached an extent sufficient to reduce dispersal and patch colonisation to a low level, but has not gone so far as to preclude any patch recolonisation (Fig. 10.3). The thresholds that bound

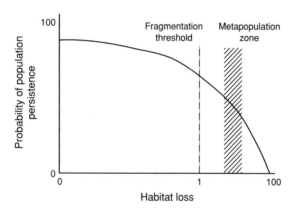

Fig. 10.3. The probability of long-term persistence of a population as a function of the degree of loss of suitable habitat from the landscape. At some point (the fragmentation threshold), habitat connectivity is broken. This creates conditions conducive to the development of metapopulation dynamics, but where the 'metapopulation zone' is located relative to the fragmentation threshold and the degree of habitat loss depends on landscape permeability and the dispersal stream (how many individuals leave the habitat patches and cross the landscape). Thus, the boundary of the metapopulation zone need not correspond with the fragmentation threshold. The metapopulation zone ends when habitat loss and fragmentation are sufficient to reduce among-patch dispersal to a level insufficient to reoccupy empty patches before additional local-patch extinctions occur.

this 'metapopulation zone' are determined by the density of habitat and the degree of habitat connectivity, which depend on the area sensitivity and dispersal characteristics of the species in relation to the composition and configuration of the overall landscape mosaic (Fahrig & Merriam 1994; Andrén 1996; Hanski & Ovaskainen 2000; Vos *et al.* 2001; Wiens 2001b; P. Opdam *et al.*, unpublished data). As more habitat is lost from the network, or dispersal through the matrix becomes more difficult, the spatial cohesion of network may pass the threshold below which the local extinction rate exceeds the recolonisation rate, leading to deterministic extinction of the metapopulation. With increasing variation in habitat amount, habitat quality, and large-scale fluctuations in environmental conditions, metapopulations may shift between the domains of deterministic extinction and dynamic equilibrium.

Source–sink population models explicitly recognise that habitat patches may differ in quality, and therefore in their capacity to support a stable or growing population (source patches) or in their dependence on dispersal from elsewhere to maintain patch occupancy (sink patches) (Wiens 1981; Pulliam 1988; but see Watkinson & Sutherland 1995). If a population has a source–sink structure, some areas of unsuitable habitat (in terms of demography) will be occupied, perhaps even at greater density than occurs in source habitats. Attempts to infer habitat preferences by correlating occupancy with environmental measures will be confounded (see e.g. Van Horne 1983; Bernstein *et al.* 1991; Garshelis 2000). Such approaches are further complicated if patch quality varies through time, so that what are now source patches are later sinks and vice versa, or if a population exhibits a combination of metapopulation structure and source–sink dynamics. Because both source and sink habitat patches at any time are part of a larger landscape mosaic that may present varying barriers to or opportunities for movement, evaluating source–sink dynamics apart from the landscape context is likely to produce incomplete and possibly misleading conclusions. Of course, as landscape structure changes in any of the ways shown in Fig. 10.1, the relative 'sourceness' or 'sinkness' of habitat patches is also likely to change. For example, human disturbances, such as traffic noise along highways, heavy recreation, or urban development, may turn habitat patches into sinks (Reijnen & Foppen 1994; Forman & Deblinger 2000).

The importance of scale

When the spatial pattern of a landscape is changed, as a result of either natural processes or human activities, the effects differ at different scales.

The magnitude of habitat loss or fragmentation is therefore not the same at all scales. For example, the maps that have been used to illustrate habitat loss and fragmentation (e.g. Cadiz township, Wisconsin: Curtis 1956; the Kellerberrin region of Western Australia: Arnold & Weeldenberg 1991; or São Paulo Province, Brazil: Oedekoven 1980) represent vastly different scales, and their ecological consequences are therefore likely to be quite different. Statements and measurements of habitat loss, perforation, fragmentation, etc. must be referenced to particular spatial scales to be useful.

Bird species also differ in the scales on which they perceive and respond to habitat distribution and landscape structure. This 'scaling window' is defined by *grain*, the finest scale on which an individual responds to spatial pattern, and *extent*, the broadest scale on which it experiences landscape heterogeneity. Because species differ in their scaling properties, a landscape that is fragmented to one species may be connected to another species that operates at a finer or broader scale (Wiens *et al.* 1993; Haila 1999; McIntyre & Hobbs 1999; Fig. 10.4). Because bird species that differ in body size generally differ in area requirements, movement rates and dispersal distances as well (Peters 1983; Calder 1984), larger species may often respond to landscape structure at broader scales of grain and extent than smaller species. Body size may therefore provide a useful first approximation to derive the scale range relevant to a species of interest.

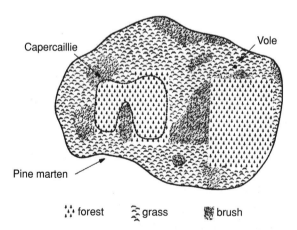

Fig. 10.4. A typical forest-clearcut mosaic in Scandinavia, showing the relative home-range scales of a vole (*Microtus oeconomus*; *c.* 0.05 ha), a capercaillie cock (*Tetrao urogallus*; *c.* 50 ha), and a pine marten (*Martes martes*; *c.* 500 ha). (From Wiens *et al.* 1993, © 1993 Munksgaard International Publishers Ltd. Copenhagen, Denmark.)

HABITAT LOSS AND FRAGMENTATION: WHEN AND WHERE IS IT A PROBLEM?

How can we implement our knowledge about the relationship between bird biodiversity and landscape pattern in conservation planning? In most areas of the world, conservation of natural values is only part of a larger, complex planning process in which solutions are sought for the ever changing needs for space and resources of many concurrent land uses. Ideally, this planning process starts by defining problems. Subsequently, options are chosen to solve the problems and then, in an iterative process, these options are implemented in a landscape design that (again ideally) allows a sustainable partnership of functions. The final phase of planning is evaluation: to what extent are the problems solved (Opdam *et al.* 1995)? A problem, then, is defined here as a situation where the conditions of the landscape (quantity or quality of the resources) do not meet the requirements for landscape functions that are given priority by the authorities or land users. In many landscapes where humans are the dominant force, a few habitat types are highlighted for conservation aims. As a result, the landscape consists of a fragmented pattern of habitats of conservation priority embedded in a matrix with diverse, but lower, natural values. A problem arises whenever that configuration of habitat patches does not offer the conditions for sustaining the defined conservation target (e.g. a group of species, overall biodiversity).

Fragmentation in natural and man-made landscapes

Fragmentation can be seen both as a pattern, a discontinuous distribution of habitat across space, and as a process, the decrease of continuity and connectivity of target habitat due to land-use changes. As stated above, a discontinuous distribution of habitat is a natural phenomenon in untouched landscapes at many spatial scales. Because species in natural systems have adapted to the spatial configuration and disturbance regime of their habitats, fragmentation due to natural disturbance is generally not a conservation problem.

Fragmentation does become a problem under human land use, particularly when mature ecosystems are turned into early successional ecosystem types. Under the assumption that species of young, dynamic systems have better dispersal capacities than species of stable, mature ecosystems, such a change of land pattern will increase the continuity of the habitat for species with the better dispersal capacities, whereas to poor dispersers the habitat becomes increasingly fragmented. With increasing land-use pressure, the

proportion of very small focal habitat patches will grow and the distances between patches will increase, while the inter-patch matrix becomes less per-
meable due to barriers and inhospitable habitat. All of these factors cause
the dispersal stream between patches to become weaker, which results in a
growing number of species for which the habitat configuration falls below
a functional fragmentation threshold.

Habitat coverage or habitat fragmentation: what should be the focus?

There is some debate about whether habitat fragmentation or habitat coverage should be a focus of landscape management (Fahrig 1997). Trzcinski
et al. (1999) argue that percentage cover has a greater impact on the distribution of birds than degree of fragmentation. However, Trzcinski *et al.*
based their conclusion on presence/absence in 10 × 10 km squares over
a 5-year sampling period, neglecting the details of habitat configuration
and matrix characteristics as well as spatial population dynamics within the
5-year period. We argue that, by this method, the role of habitat configuration is easily underestimated (cf. McGarigal & McComb 1995). In a more
detailed study, Villard *et al.* (1999) concluded that forest cover and configuration are equally good predictors of the presence of woodland bird species.
It is important to know the threshold level of habitat loss below which spatial configuration of the landscape becomes a critical factor to birds, but
studies focusing on the independent effects of coverage and configuration
are scarce (Trzcinski *et al.* 1999). We join Andrén (1996) in concluding that
this threshold will differ between species, so a search for general thresholds,
while theoretically interesting, has little practical value. Because many empirical studies have found correlations between bird distribution and habitat
configuration (e.g. Van Dorp & Opdam 1987; Opdam 1991; Dunning *et al.*
1995a, b; Hinsley *et al.* 1995; Villard *et al.* 1999), we conclude that configuration is important to consider in the management of most anthropogenic
landscapes. Such a focus offers more opportunities to find management solutions that can be combined with other land-use demands than does simply
increasing the amount of habitat.

Diagnosing a fragmentation problem

Habitat fragmentation is a problem when the emphasis of conservation is
on habitat types that are disappearing due to land use, or when habitat loss
has gone so far that the distribution of individuals across the remaining
habitat is inhibited by spatial factors rather than habitat quality alone. In
systems that are naturally spatially continuous, species are less adapted to

cope with spatial discontinuity and dynamics than in ecosystems that are naturally heterogeneous. A fragmentation problem, however, cannot be inferred from a landscape pattern alone. Species differ in spatial scaling with respect to dispersal capacity and area requirements. This implies that descriptors of landscape pattern should be ecologically scaled (Vos *et al.* 2001). The challenge of landscape ecology is therefore not the development of more GIS-based landscape indices (e.g. Jager 2000), but the ecological calibration of simple indices. This development is only beginning (Vos *et al.* 2001; P. Opdam *et al.* unpublished data).

Box 10.1. An example for Marshlands.

In The Netherlands, marshlands are of high importance to nature conservation. To safeguard marshland biodiversity, marshland areas are planned to function as a habitat network, which includes marshland restoration and new corridor zones. The government wants to know whether the plan is adequate to reach the goal, and where enlargement of existing areas, development of stepping stones and corridor zones is most effective.

Studies on the distribution of bird species in the marshland network shared that marshland birds were often absent in suitable habitat and their presence was related to the amount and spatial configuration of habitat (Foppen *et al.* 1999b; Foppen 2001). Bitterns (*Botaurus stellaris*) showed these effects on a national scale, sedge warblers (*Acrocephalus schoenbaenus*), reed warblers (*Acrocephalus scirpaceus*) and bluethroat (*Lusciana svecica*) on a regional scale. Dispersal data derived from ringing schemes and literature showed that even in relatively mobile species like the great reed warbler (*Acrocephalus arundinaceus*) dispersal is very limited (Foppen 2001). Two typical species profiles were distinguished, based on variation in dispersal distance and area requirements: the small marshland songbirds, and the marshland herons, like the bittern (Foppen 2001). These species profiles were the basis of the development of minimal area rules for key patches. A key patch is defined as a habitat patch in a network with a very small probablity of going extinct (<5% in 100 years). Empirical data on presence/absence, formalised in regression models, were used to estimate the size of key patches for the two species profiles (Table 10.1). A metapopulation model METAPHOR, parameterised and calibrated for marshland birds, was used as an independent tool to check these estimates and to generalise them as planning rules (Verboom *et al.* 2001).

These rules were built into a GIS-based system for landscape cohesion assessment (Opdam *et al.* 2001). The system, LARCH, determines the potentials of a landscape for a set of target species with the help of the standards of the key patch. It was used to predict the added value of the National Ecological Network Plan for marshland bird populations.

Table 10.1. *Population sizes (in pairs at carrying capacity) in two landscape configurations as a result of METAPHOR simulations for a 'marsh heron' and a 'marsh songbird' (see Box 10.1 for details). Indicated are the average size and the range for a network with and without a key population (KP).*

Species	KP	Network with KP	Network without KP
Marsh heron profile	20	83 (62-190)	122 (97-1009)
Marsh warbler profile	100	130 (120-175)	150 (132-160)

Because the fragmentation effects of importance ultimately involve population processes, distribution patterns may provide some insight into a potential fragmentation. With ongoing fragmentation, the increasing role of stochastic processes becomes expressed in the distribution pattern of a species within the habitat network. If calibrated stochastic models are available, such a pattern can be extrapolated in terms of persistence probability (Verboom *et al.* 2001). Because the percentage of occupied patches (which can be inferred from a distribution map) is related to persistence probability, a promising approach is to find critical values of average patch occupation rate. Vos *et al.* (2001) showed that a patch occupancy of 50% can be regarded as a critical threshold for persistence, independent of the type of species. If distribution data are available, the percentage occupied patches is useful to indicate a potential fragmentation problem.

It would be useful if we could couple landscape indices to this 50% threshold. Villard *et al.* (1999) showed that the 50% probability of presence occurs at a forest coverage ranging between 1% (ovenbird, *Seiurus aurocapillus*) and 40% (hairy woodpecker, *Picoides villosus*). For spotted owls, Lamberson *et al.* (1992) found the 50% level between 10% and 35% of habitat coverage, depending on different assumptions regarding juvenile habitat-search abilities. Andrén (1996) showed that model species differing in area sensitivity and dispersal capacity reached a 50% occupation rate at habitat coverage levels varying between 3% and 25%. In a study combining empirical and modelling data, Vos *et al.* (2001) found that nuthatch (in a landscape with 1.5% mature forest coverage) and reed warbler (*Acrocephalus scirpaceus*; 0.2% habitat coverage) are close to the critical threshold of metapopulation persistence. Given the variability among these figures, the best way to proceed is to look for similarities between species, classify species into functional groups, and then determine critical threshold levels for these groups (see Andrén 1996; Vos *et al.* 2001).

FINDING SOLUTIONS

There are always several options for solving a fragmentation problem (Fig. 10.5). For example, one can either enlarge key patches or improve the matrix permeability by corridors or mosaic management. We distinguish

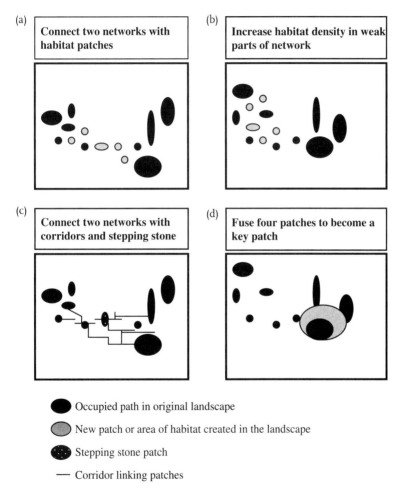

(a) **Connect two networks with habitat patches**

(b) **Increase habitat density in weak parts of network**

(c) **Connect two networks with corridors and stepping stone**

(d) **Fuse four patches to become a key patch**

● Occupied path in original landscape

◯ New patch or area of habitat created in the landscape

⬤ Stepping stone patch

— Corridor linking patches

Fig. 10.5. Several options for improving the spatial cohesion of habitat networks. For simplicity, networks are shown as patches in a featureless (i.e. unsuitable) matrix. In a heterogeneous landscape, the 'matrix' could contain a variety of landscape elements of differing permeability and suitability, and the composition of the overall matrix would therefore influence how one might select among these options.

three strategies. Choosing between options could be done with the help of rule-based models based on ecologically scaled landscape indices (see Box 10.1).

Increasing the number of patches of the network

Some options are adding patches either at the margins or in between other patches, or connecting two networks by a strategically situated additional patch. These measures result in a higher carrying capacity of the landscape for the particular habitat, and consequently in an enhanced dispersal stream. The development of general rules for minimal sizes of sustainable networks is in its infancy (see Box 10.1 for an example).

Enlarging a patch to the size of a key population capacity

Large patches are key patches for conservation. For spotted owls, Lamberson *et al.* (1994) showed by model simulations that, with a fixed habitat coverage, greater clustering of habitat increases the probability of occupation. Verboom *et al.* (2001) introduced the concept of *key patch*, which supports a local population that has at most a 5% chance of local extinction, under the condition of one immigrant per generation. In other words, a key patch in a network almost always contains a fairly large local population, which still is not big enough to persist independently of other local populations. The model simulations showed that networks with a key patch need 30% less habitat area compared to networks with only small patches, making the key patch approach an efficient strategy.

Adding stepping stones and corridors to the network

Landscape patches too small or not suitable for breeding may, none the less, enhance inter-patch movement of birds and diminish losses due to dispersal mortality. This is evident from direct observations of preferred movement patterns (Saunders & Hobbs 1991; Haas 1995; Machtans *et al.* 1996), most of which entail daily or seasonal movements between parts of the home range (review in Bennett 1999). Indirect evidence comes from spatial analysis of distribution patterns that allow for matrix variation (e.g. Van Dorp & Opdam 1987) or experimental treatment of landscapes (Schmiegelow *et al.* 1997).

Choosing between options

There is not a single best solution to a fragmentation problem. If one can add only a limited amount of habitat to a landscape, the best approach is to compare various potential scenarios of the future landscape, encompassing a range of solutions and strategies. Solutions for different species may often conflict (Liu *et al.* 1995). Metapopulation models and rule-based GIS models (e.g. Opdam *et al.* 1995; Dunning *et al.* 1995b; Reijnen *et al.* 1995; Foppen *et al.* 1999b) can help to explore which of the options offers the highest conservation value. They can also be used to decide whether or not, and where, additional habitat should be added. These models need to be developed into tools that can generate the best locations for additional habitat. Van Langevelde *et al.* (2000) published a first attempt for one type of solution (adding habitat patches) and a single species (nuthatch), which deserves to be developed into a more general conservation planning tool.

PREDICTING BIRD BIODIVERSITY AT THE LANDSCAPE LEVEL

Defining a problem and choosing a cost-effective solution require that we can predict, at the landscape level, what will or might happen to populations under a given combination of present or future habitat and spatial conditions. Is such a prediction reliable? In terms of exactly predicting the future, the answer is clearly 'no'. Even if we could know everything about nature, the stochastic processes inherent to natural populations make predictions uncertain. Consequently, a prediction about the fate of a metapopulation should always be in terms of probabilities. An even greater source of uncertainty is the overriding effect of human societal processes on landscapes: economic development, population growth and, most importantly, shifts in ethical values and the general sense of the quality of life. Therefore, predictions at the landscape level should be in terms of 'What happens if . . . , all other things being equal?' Because of the uncertainty in our predictions, we should focus on comparing different conservation options or different land-use scenarios (Verboom *et al.* 2001). We can then predict which of the scenarios comes closest to the various goals of land use, and can support decision-making about the best road to the future.

Tools for prediction

What should be in our predictive toolbox, given the different needs in the various stages of the planning process (Opdam *et al.* 2002)? We argue that tools based on extrapolation of the present state of a population in an actual landscape are based on at least three major oversimplifications. First, it is assumed that the actual population is in equilibrium with the actual landscape (thus neglecting time lags in population responses to landscape change). Second, one assumes that the spatial distribution of the species is linearly related to the changing landscape components (but see above). Third, one does not account for spatial relationships between different parts of the habitat network, like that between source and sink patches. Habitat suitability (HSI) models extrapolate from the present into the future, and often neglect spatial relationships (Van Horne & Wiens 1991). GAP analysis extends HSI with a GIS basis (Scott *et al.* 1993; Stine *et al.* 1996; Jennings 2000), but it is still not based on the spatial dynamics of populations in discontinuous habitat networks. Consequently, patches in the network that happen to be unoccupied in the year of inventory are erroneously disregarded as part of the necessary habitat area. We agree with Bolger *et al.* (1997) that landscape factors should be included in predictive habitat models, especially in heterogeneous areas (as all areas ultimately are).

Some statistical models (e.g. Van Dorp & Opdam 1987; Bolger *et al.* 1997; Swetnam *et al.* 1998) do account for spatial correlations between occurrence probability and landscape characteristics. Nevertheless, they should be used with care in predictions, because of potential time lags between landscape change and the metapopulation response (Opdam 1991). Of course, as with any statistical model, extrapolation outside the measured range of landscape variation is unwarranted.

Provided that they are spatially explicit, metapopulation models follow a mechanistic approach, include non-linearity and stochasticity and, therefore, can account for the problems mentioned above. In addition, they can predict the impact of landscape change in terms of population viability (Day & Possingham 1995; Hanski & Ovaskainen 2000). Only models with enough realism are useful for quantitative predictions of viability for a target species, but they need a lot of data to be developed and calibrated. Such models have been used for scanning management options for threatened species (i.e. the effectiveness of translocations of helmeted honeyeater (*Lichenostomus melanops cassidix*) individuals as a conservation strategy; Akçakaya *et al.* 1995). If single species are used as indicators for conservation value in landscape planning, such models can be useful as well. For example, Reijnen *et al.* (1995) used metapopulation models for discriminating between river management options in terms of the expected increase in number and abundance of target species. Most applications in landscape planning, however, require predictions on the multispecies level. Metapopulation models are too time consuming to be used effectively in a planning process where many species and many options are involved.

Predictive tools for planning purposes

Except for the metapopulation model, these tools can only be used if species distribution data are available. All too often, this is not the case, and usually time or money to produce them is restricted (e.g. White *et al.* 1997). Therefore, a practical tool should only require data on the habitat pattern within the landscape, and should yield predictions in terms of the conservation potential of the landscape (Opdam 2001). The challenge is to develop generally applicable predictive tools that can handle multispecies planning assignments. The only available methods at present are landscape indices. The power of these indices is their simplicity, but the weakness of most of the published indices is that we do not know what they mean ecologically (Opdam 2001). Such indices should be ecologically scaled with the help of spatially explicit population models for groups of ecologically similar species ('species profiles'; Vos *et al.* 2001). Such indices can be built into rule-based GIS systems. An example is LARCH (Foppen *et al.* 1999b), an extension of Landscape Cohesion Assessment (Opdam 2001), which is used to assess the conservation potential of a network of nature areas. The model evaluates at the species level which areas form a cohesive network and, subsequently, which of those include the minimal spatial requirements for long-term population persistence. Such GIS models can also be used to detect bottlenecks in the network.

To develop such rule-based models, it is essential to consider several complicating factors.

1 Time lags in the response of populations should be included. Opdam *et al.* (1993) presented evidence that forest bird species needed several decades to spread over habitat networks that became available after the maturation of large-scale forest plantations in The Netherlands. Another example of a time lag is the recovery time of reed warbler populations after heavy mortality due to drought in the African wintering range (Foppen *et al.* 1999a). During recovery, the percentage of occupied patches fell far below the critical threshold level of 50%, especially in landscapes with heavily fragmented marshland. The risk that such environmental disasters add to fragmentation must be built into critical thresholds of landscape variables.

2 Habitat-quality differences, such as source–sink relations, must be considered.

3 The response within the planning area may be mitigated by influx of individuals from the surrounding areas. Consider, for example, the same planning area with a particular habitat network in two situations: in one

case, the habitat network continues into the surroundings of the planning area, and in another the network stops at the border and is isolated from other, similar networks. In the latter case, the minimal required connectivity of the network is much greater, since there is no support from outside.

4 Obviously, scale is important. The same change of land-use pattern may affect one species in the quality of the individual home range (cf. Redpath 1995), another in the structure of the habitat patch of a local population, and a third species in the spatial cohesion of the overall habitat network. In developing general rule-based systems, one must deal with the different mechanisms underlying these responses.

5 A landscape change may affect individuals without any measurable response at the population level. For instance, willow warblers (*Phylloscopus trochilus*) are not reproductive in a 500 m zone next to a heavily used highway but, due to influx from yearlings from adjacent zones, the density may be similar to that in undisturbed areas (Reijnen & Foppen 1994).

6 Only a few species can be studied in detail to build our predictive toolbox. So, instead of arguing that no two species are alike, we must search for similarities in ecology and life history among species and use them to construct species profiles, based on spatial requirements, dispersal abilities and operational scale (Vos *et al.* 2001; Wiens in 2001c).

7 Mönkkönen & Reunanen (1999) have argued that life histories of species may differ substantially among geographical locations. If this is so, then extrapolation across geographical regions is not possible, and models will have to be differentiated for defined geographical regions.

CONCLUSIONS

Although it has received the most attention, fragmentation is only one of several ways in which human activities can affect the distribution and availability of habitat to individuals. We suggest that it is important to focus our attention on land use as the driving force, and to move away from a typological, 'habitat' versus 'non-habitat' view of the world to one that recognises the compositional and structural heterogeneity of entire landscapes. Because the responses of organisms to landscape composition and structure differ among species and exhibit complex scale dependencies, time lags and thresholds, it is difficult to derive general models that can be used indiscriminately in any management situation. Instead, it will be necessary to consider carefully how the points enumerated above apply to the particular situations of interest.

Clearly, these considerations all add complexity to our efforts to evaluate how changes in land use and landscape patterns are likely to affect bird populations and communities. It is our view, however, that more simplistic approaches have led us astray, and that developing a capacity to make reasonable predictions of the consequences of these human actions requires a consideration of the spatial texture of habitats, of thresholds in landscape structure, and of the ecological and behavioural characteristics of the species of interest.

11

The interface between research, education and training

LEON BENNUN

INTRODUCTION

There are many controversial issues in bird conservation. On some topics, however, a degree of unanimity can be expected. Most would agree that, especially in the tropics, our knowledge of many bird species and communities – their ecology and natural history, response to habitat change, even their population sizes – is extremely limited. For example, 79% of the world's 1,186 threatened bird species, mainly tropical, require baseline surveys to map their distributions, estimate population size or identify protected areas (BirdLife International 2000). It is often pointed out that this lack of knowledge, of birds or other biodiversity, should not be an excuse for a similar lack of action (WRI/IUCN/UNEP 1992; Gadgil 1996). Nevertheless, additional research would in many cases be helpful for designing more effective conservation approaches: at least we might have a better idea what we are talking about (Jenkins 1988; Stork & Samways 1995; Stuart 1995).

At the same time, the public's understanding of birds, and related issues to do with biodiversity conservation and sustainable resource use, is often desperately poor (WRI/IUCN/UNEP 1992; Miller *et al.* 1995; Orr 2000). Decision-makers are not immune, unfortunately, to this lack of awareness, and this in itself is a serious conservation problem. To carry out the research needed to underpin conservation, to educate the public and create awareness among those who make important decisions, and to enthuse and inspire younger scientists and conservation workers, we need well-trained personnel. This technical capacity is lacking in most tropical countries, which of course hold the bulk of the world's biodiversity, birds included (Raven 1988; Wilson 1988, 1994; Rosenzweig 1995; Stattersfield *et al.* 1998).

This chapter considers how research, education and training fit together to support bird conservation – or can, without excessive application of force, be made to do so. This topic is relevant to very many people and institutions, but is perhaps not often looked at explicitly. Ecologists from the 'developed' world, for instance, still often visit other countries to do their research but include no training or education component in their work. It is easy to see this as someone else's job, of course, or simply as a distraction from one's important and (no doubt) cutting-edge research. Yet linking up with local institutions and initiatives can add enormous conservation value to research. It often also improves the quality (and, for applied projects, the relevance) of the data being collected. I hope this chapter may stimulate some thought about how these mutually beneficial linkages can in practice be made.

Two caveats are in order before we get to grips with this subject. First, the chapter draws very largely from my own experience at the National Museums of Kenya, a quasi-Government research institution in a developing country. It is thus much more of a case study than a global conspectus. Nevertheless, the framework we have developed, and the lessons more or less painfully learned, seem likely to be broadly applicable elsewhere.

Second, almost any topic has nowadays turned into a respectable field of academic study. Thus there probably should be a journal called something like *Conservation Capacity-building*, but (so far as I know) there isn't. Instead this kind of work is documented, if anywhere, in ephemera such as grant proposals, scholarship applications, reports to donors and the like. It is not generally useful to cite such documents, so I have not done so. Readers accustomed to paragraphs foliaged luxuriantly with names and dates should therefore brace themselves for the bibliographic equivalent of semi-desert.

EDUCATION AND TRAINING NEEDS FOR BIRD CONSERVATION

Effective bird conservation needs to be underpinned by training and education at many different levels.

(1) Obviously, skilled ornithologists are required to plan and carry out research, interpret and synthesise information and advise decision-makers. Some of the necessary skills include sampling design and statistical analysis, field survey techniques (including mist-netting, ringing, assessment of biometrics, behavioural observation, blood-sampling and perhaps radio-tracking), species identification, making field descriptions and report

writing. Other, more administrative, skills are also becoming increasingly relevant: writing proposals for funding, budgeting and accounting, handling logistics and managing field teams are all things that researchers find themselves needing to become good at.

The work these individuals would be involved in might include, for example, ecological studies of threatened species, investigating how birds respond to habitat fragmentation and degradation, and designing and implementing practical monitoring schemes. The wide range of studies needing to be undertaken argues against narrow specialisation – to be useful, ornithologists will have to turn their hands to many different techniques, species and habitats.

Professional ornithologists will usually have at least a first, and probably a further, degree. Highly skilled amateur birders may or may not have a formal scientific training. The latter group may lack the interest or background to contribute to research design. However, they can be extremely useful in other ways, such as keeping track of national or regional species lists, vetting records and helping to compile status reports. They may also contribute a great deal to ringing and survey schemes.

Skilled technicians are also important to support research work. These are individuals who may lack sophisticated scientific training but who have excellent skills in identifying, censusing and handling birds.

(2) Different, though partially overlapping, sets of skills are needed for managing bird conservation projects, particularly where these combine development with conservation; running research or conservation organisations (such as a BirdLife International Partner); and conservation advocacy.

Relevant skills might be in the areas of development and gender issues, economics and micro-enterprise, natural resource management, appropriate technologies, project management, monitoring and evaluation, personnel management, training, environmental education, budgeting, accounting and financial management, proposal writing, fund-raising, strategic planning, and institutional development.

(3) Bird tourism initiatives require trained guides. Guides must be able to identify species accurately. They should also be able to show birds to visitors, to interpret what they see and give some background information, and to adjust their approach to the preferences and requirements of their clients.

Other 'sustainable use' ventures, like managed gamebird wing-shooting, also need trained scouts or assistants. Their work will be a little more specialised, but they will need broadly similar skills to the bird guides (Simiyu & Bennun 2000).

(4) Local conservation groups are becoming increasingly involved in conservation work, especially monitoring, at particular sites. Especially notable is the development of 'site support groups' (SSGs) at individual Important Bird Areas (IBAs) (Bennun & Njoroge 1999; Ngari *et al.* 2001). These groups require a broad range of skills, from species identification and monitoring techniques to organisational and financial management.

(5) Interested amateur birdwatchers need to be able to develop their identification and (to a lesser extent) counting skills to a level where they can contribute meaningful data to large-scale schemes – such as bird atlases, nest records and waterbird monitoring (e.g. Nasirwa & Bennun 2000). In developed countries, coordinated data collection by volunteers makes an enormous contribution to biological survey and monitoring efforts. Examples include the various schemes (constant effort and other ringing, nest records, common birds census and waterways bird survey) that contribute to the British Trust for Ornithology's integrated population monitoring (Baillie 1990; Greenwood *et al.* 1993), or the long-established Breeding Birds Survey in North America (Bystrak 1981; DeSante & Rosenberg 1998). In tropical countries, such valuable schemes are usually only in the fledgling stage, a major constraint being the lack of capable and motivated birders to take part.

Many of these skill requirements may seem remote from the concerns of researchers. However, applied research projects (including environmental monitoring) can, if carefully designed, make substantial contributions to meeting them.

BUILDING CAPACITY THROUGH RESEARCH

What projects are relevant?

Focusing on priorities

Any well-planned field research is arguably useful for capacity building. Research to answer questions in community or behavioural ecology will develop skills in framing hypotheses, sampling and experimental design, careful observation and field techniques. Indeed, for developing these particular skills this kind of research might sometimes be more effective than applied studies. There should of course be no difference in the level of scientific rigour, but some applied studies may be largely descriptive or focus more on socio-economic than biological aspects.

This is fine in so far as the main purpose is to train someone to do research, and assuming the project is scientifically worthwhile. Opportunities provided by visiting researchers – who may need local assistants, or can sponsor local students – should certainly be used, whether or not their research questions are directly relevant to conservation.

All else being equal, however, it is most useful to focus research on recognised conservation priorities. As well as giving scientific training, such a project will provide information that may be directly useful for conservation. It is also likely to give much better scope for linkages with ongoing conservation projects, local conservation groups, conservation NGOs (non-governmental organisations) and Government departments. Practically speaking, such work is often easier to fund, to obtain permission for (where this is necessary), and to follow up with appropriate additional work.

National bird conservation strategies

There are so many conservation issues needing attention, and so many potential research topics, that it is essential to set priorities. These should ideally form part of a national bird conservation strategy. The strategy provides a framework that shows how both research and conservation action fit in. It also outlines clearly which species, sites, habitats and issues need most urgent research and monitoring attention (Box 11.1). Globally threatened species (BirdLife International 2000) are obvious priorities for research, especially where their status and biology are poorly known. At the site level, Important Bird Areas, now identified for Europe (Grimmet & Jones 1989), the Middle East (Evans 1994) and Africa (Bennun & Fishpool 2000) and being assessed for Asia and the Americas, are global priorities too.

Box 11.1. Setting bird research and conservation priorities for Kenya.

Producing a comprehensive national bird conservation strategy is easier said than done. In Kenya, a step in this direction was taken some years ago (Fanshawe & Bennun 1991). The resulting document has had considerable influence on research undertaken since. Further priority-setting has happened more recently. The revised world list of threatened birds, *Birds to watch 2* (Collar *et al.* 1994) was used to set priorities for Kenyan research. This focus has allowed a good deal to be accomplished: between 1994 and 2000, more-or-less detailed work on conservation biology was carried out for two-thirds (16) of the 24 globally threatened species that have significant populations in Kenya (references are cited in the latest account of threatened birds (BirdLife International 2000)).

A regional Red List for East African birds was compiled to complement the global version (Bennun & Njoroge 1996; Bennun *et al.* 2000). This permitted more fine-scaled assessment of conservation value, and pinpointed a number of species that were in severe regional decline. By bringing to light new information that was not available to Collar *et al.* (1994), it also prompted reassessment of the global conservation status of several species. As a result, for example, Aberdare cisticola (*Cisticola aberdare*) and Sharpe's longclaw (*Macronyx sharpei*) were listed as globally threatened in the revised global Red List (BirdLife International 2000).

The Important Bird Areas programme, begun in 1995, involved collecting data on sites of international importance for bird conservation (Bennun & Njoroge 2000). These were assessed using global criteria, based on the presence of birds under threat, with narrow ranges, representative of a particular biome, or forming large congregations (Bennun & Fishpool 2000). The 60 IBAs identified in Kenya are all global priorities for conservation. However, some are in more urgent need of attention than others. Priorities for conservation action within the set of IBAs were assessed based on biological importance and degree of threat (Bennun & Njoroge 1999). To a large extent, this analysis confirmed priorities that had already been set informally, and had been used to direct site- and habitat-based research. Research projects have already examined a number of the Critical sites, including Kakamega Forest, Mt Kenya, Taita Hills Forests, several south coast forests, and the central Kenyan river valleys (e.g. Brooks *et al.* 1998a, b; Oyugi *et al.* 1998; Njoroge & Bennun 2000; Waiyaki & Bennun 2000).

From species and sites, the third strand in a conservation strategy is habitats. In Kenya, priority habitats emerged from the IBA analysis: forests of all types, highland and mid-level grasslands, and wetlands. Semi-arid habitats are, by and large, of less immediate conservation concern. Studies on the priority habitats have mainly concentrated on understanding the effects of degradation and fragmentation (e.g. Bennun & Fanshawe 1997; Brooks *et al.* 1999; Githiru *et al.* 2002; Harper *et al.* 1998; Lens *et al.* 1999a, b, 2000, 2001; Nasirwa *et al.* 2002).

How useful has it been to identify priorities for research? We now have a much better understanding of a suite of threatened sites, species and habitats. This information has fed into the IBA process and into the revised global Red List. In some cases (such as Sharpe's longclaw in the Kinangop Grasslands) the results of ecological research are being used to direct conservation campaigns by local site support groups. All Kenyan students and most (but not all) overseas researchers have indeed worked on priority topics. Because they have also involved trainees and local assistants, a substantial number of people now have direct field experience with the priority species, sites and issues.

Being a priority for conservation action does not necessarily imply that research on that site, species or habitat is urgently needed. The issues may already be well understood, or so obvious that the next step is action on the ground rather than further study. Identifying research needs is a second and subsidiary step once conservation priorities have been listed. Research is in effect an action designed to address a specific conservation problem – the lack of enough information to allow effective conservation intervention.

Coordination

How can these priorities be put to use? One needs a list of potential projects that will address the priority needs that have been identified. This list must then be to be 'sold' to potential researchers.

In Kenya, this has been relatively straightforward because almost all bird conservation research is coordinated by one institution – the National Museums of Kenya (NMK). Those wishing to study Kenya's birds approach the Museums for affiliation. This provides an opportunity for priorities to be made clear. It also means that we could exert considerable leverage to encourage these priorities to be taken up. In practice, this is rarely necessary: most researchers are interested in doing work that is likely to be of significant conservation value.

In other countries the situation may be more complex. Ornithologists are often scattered, and there may be no central body that pulls them together. However, one organisation still needs to take the lead, if sensible priorities are to emerge and be used. This could involve setting up a committee of interested people, with a designated focal point. Whichever organisation represents the BirdLife International[1] network might often be a good candidate for this. (At present, the BirdLife network in Africa has been rather reticent in putting forward priority lists of research topics – perhaps because national NGOs feel that their technical expertise in ornithology is not sufficiently strong. Whether or not this is so, they are an obvious focal point for bringing that expertise together.)

Priority-setting should in any case be a collaborative process. It will be most effective to involve as many as possible of those who can contribute – academic ornithologists, skilled amateurs, Government officers, and so on. In East Africa the regional Red List and national IBA lists were developed through such a participatory process, bringing in all those who had data or ideas to contribute. There will soon be substantial information to support the process, with a new global list of threatened species published (BirdLife International 2000), and IBA directories for Africa, Asia and the Americas soon to appear.

---

[1] BirdLife International (www.birdlife.net) is a Partnership of NGOs with a special focus on birds. The BirdLife Partnership works together on shared priorities, policies and programmes of conservation action, exchanging skills, achievements and information and so growing in ability, authority and influence. The BirdLife International Partnership strives to conserve birds, their habitats and global biodiversity, working with people towards sustainability in the use of natural resources.

Coordination, whether by a single institution or a joint technical committee, is also important to ensure a coherent approach to capacity building. Institutional rivalries and jealousies, among other factors, might make this difficult at first. However, a great deal more can be achieved by bringing the available expertise together than by allowing it to remain disjointed.

Supervision and training

Research students can do priority research

Many priority projects (such as investigations of the ecology of particular threatened species) are very well suited for postgraduate students working for their master's or doctoral degrees. Kenya is not atypical of many African countries in the long-term decline of its universities. These continue to grow in number (we now have around six public ones, and several private institutions), but not in facilities and resources. Talented academics are difficult to retain (though many committed individuals do stick it out, against heavy odds) and administrative systems are often haphazard and unsatisfactory. Despite a proliferation of departments with a biological focus, none has strong expertise in ornithology.

For these reasons, Kenyan students working on birds tend to affiliate to the National Museums of Kenya. By first-world standards NMK is hardly well endowed, but it can provide the basic minimum in equipment and reference material. In return for scientific supervision and help in finding funds for fieldwork, we expect that students will work on our priority projects. In this situation, everyone benefits. Priority research, that the staff has no time to tackle, is done. The student is properly trained and supervised, and (usually!) carries out a solid piece of useful science. Finally, some burden is taken off the university, which is nevertheless there to assess the final product for the award of a degree.

Some students acquire those much sought-after scholarships to go overseas. This is of course a wonderful opportunity to broaden horizons, gain international exposure and make use of facilities that (compared with those available locally) are almost limitless. Even in these cases, an institutional link in the home country is usually very valuable. For research degrees, it makes sense to carry out fieldwork on a priority problem relevant to one's own country, rather than to the USA, Australia or Europe. If students are to return and do fieldwork in their home country, local supervision will again be very important. This can usually only be provided effectively if some coordinating mechanism exists. The Wellcome Trust Fellowships in Biodiversity Conservation (now, sadly, suspended) were an excellent example of scholarships that provided for just this – a year abroad doing an MSc, then a year's follow-up, supervised research on a conservation problem at home. This is a model that other funders could usefully follow.

The serious disorientation that studying abroad can induce, especially in relatively young and inexperienced students, should not be underestimated. A formal institutional link to the home country helps provide a psychological anchor and a point of reference when the environment abroad seems too overwhelmingly strange.

How widely should such coordinating mechanisms work? Even within Africa, there are great disparities between countries in the level of institutional support for ornithological research. Perhaps students in a country that has little ornithological base should consider studying (or at least doing their fieldwork) somewhere else on the continent, where they can receive better guidance and assistance. There are many advantages to training in another tropical (or maybe subtropical) country, as opposed to the developed world. Costs are likely to be much lower; the avifauna and conservation issues are much more similar; and it is a step towards forming valuable cross-linkages. In Africa, the BirdLife International network is in a good position to encourage such a process.

If research is genuinely to build scientific capacity, research students need proper supervision. Anyone who has dealt with postgraduate students will know that there is much more to this than meets the eye. Students are demanding. In countries where public universities are in decline, recent graduates often need quite intensive assistance to bring them to the point where they can plan (and find funds for) their own research.

A priority list of research topics makes it easier to get things started. A library of successful proposals and theses from past students also helps. These need not all be from within the country: useful examples can be borrowed from elsewhere.

Interns and trainees

Interns are essentially volunteers who spend time working in an institution or attached to a project to gain experience. They occur in several different varieties. An approximate taxonomy of Kenyan interns would be as follows.

- Students (in universities or technical/vocational colleges) who are gaining experience in the vacations or as part of a formal work attachment. Not all of them will necessarily have a strong interest in birds (though this can develop as a result of their attachment).
- Non-graduates (school or college leavers) who are jobless and who have an interest (anywhere between vague and burning) in becoming research

assistants or bird guides. There is a huge pool of such young people. With very little opportunity for employment, or even voluntary place-ments, it is not surprising that the demand for internship slots is great. This might not have been the case ten years ago. A dramatic rise in environmental awareness, and a parallel spread in enthusiasm for birdwatching, means that ornithology is now seen as a serious career choice – indeed, one that is not only respectable but exciting.

• Graduate biologists, looking for chances for further study, who are on track to become trained ornithologists. In many northern countries stu-dents often continue directly to an MSc or PhD after finishing a first degree. However, in Kenya it is highly desirable for potential students to have some 'hands-on' experience in research or conservation before they go on to further studies – even if this is only for a year or less. The university undergraduate experience gives little grounding in how the 'real world' of research and practical conservation operates. It also is often inadequate in teaching students how to think critically and apply scientific methods to new problems. By exposing them to a range of on-going projects, the internship experience should aim to help students develop in both these areas. It is thus an essential bridging period for orientation and the development of basic field and intellectual skills. It also provides a chance for individuals to prove their ability and dedica-tion, and to develop a CV that is more attractive to potential sponsors (finding a scholarship straight after graduation can be very difficult in-deed). More subtly, this is a period when young conservationists can identify suitable role models, and develop a real commitment to their future work (Orr 1999).

Research projects provide tremendous opportunities for training all these categories of interns – but particularly the latter two, who are in for the long haul and likely to benefit most from the practical experience of re-search work. Interns can be extremely useful project assistants (both in the field and back in the office), making up in enthusiasm and commitment what they might lack in experience and skills.

What happens, though, when the project ends? Are the interns thrown back onto the street, to 'tarmac' for another opportunity? Some safety-net is needed to allow them to continue to train and learn within the system.

Our own internship programme has evolved gradually and almost im-perceptibly over the years. It started simply as a few keen young birdwatchers spending a little time in the department and helping out with routine work. Now six or more full-time, long-term interns are in place at any moment.

They are trained in a number of different areas (including bird ringing and computer literacy) and their progress is formally assessed each quarter. If a vacant place arises it is filled by competitive selection from a large set of hopeful applicants.

Several interlinked features here are worth mentioning. First, that in several respects this seems to be a remarkably effective way of building capacity. The interns are attached long-term, with no definite terminal date, but not permanently. Building on the skills and experience they have gained, individuals go on to obtain scholarships or 'real' salaried jobs. Because the scheme usually contains several relatively skilled people, the intern pool forms a useful group, supplementing the permanent staff, who can help with field work that crops up at short notice. This further builds the interns' experience and helps supplement their incomes.

It has been necessary to invest in this scheme to make it successful. Very few people, however interested, can afford to work on a totally voluntary basis, without any income whatever. This requires a level of family support that is simply lacking for most young Kenyans. They may be lucky enough to find a relative who can house them in Nairobi, and perhaps feed them for some time. They still have to pay their bus fare to commute each day; and they work more effectively if they can take more than 'air burgers' (i.e. nothing) for lunch. The internship scheme pays a minimal stipend to cover these expenses. Simply, this allows the individual concerned to concentrate on the work, without daily anxiety about how their basic costs will be covered. (Anxieties there still are – Nairobi is an expensive and difficult city to live in – but some minimal security is provided.) The stipend is very modest (about US$40 a month), not because we think interns do not deserve to be paid, but because that is what we can afford. At present these funds come not from the Museums' own coffers, which have been empty for a number of years, but through a generous grant from the RSPB. Of all this organisation's invaluable support to ornithology in Kenya and across Africa, I suspect this has probably been one of the most effective, pound for pound, in developing a real human resource for bird conservation.

Investment goes beyond providing a stipend. Interns need supervision, guidance and training, and this requires staff time and energy. Work must be assigned, monitored and assessed; advice must be provided; at some stage there may be testimonials to write, proposals to edit, and career counselling to dispense. The interns learn a variety of things. Work in the collection room and at the taxidermy table teaches about diversity, anatomy, identification and information management. The Nairobi Ringing Group (see Box 11.2), set up specifically for this purpose, trains in the important but

Box 11.2. The Nairobi Ringing Group.

Capturing and ringing birds is a basic field technique for ornithological research. In countries where ringing is popular, such as the UK and parts of Western Europe, it is largely done by amateur enthusiasts in their own free time. High technical and ethical standards are strictly observed, and the data collected provide an invaluable source of information for monitoring bird populations and movements (e.g. Baillie 1990).

The Ringing Scheme of eastern Africa started in 1960, coordinated by the East Africa Natural History Society. Over the ensuing 25 years more than 300,000 birds were ringed, mostly in Kenya. Until recently, virtually all of the ringing in Kenya was done by a handful of devoted expatriate enthusiasts and researchers. Most birds ringed have been Palaearctic migrants, mainly at the important site of Ngulia, in Tsavo West National Park – Afrotropical species have, on the whole, been ignored.

Ringing is a specialised skill and requires intensive training and practice. The Nairobi Ringing Group (NbiRG), a project of the Department of Ornithology, National Museums of Kenya, began work in June 1994. It was started in recognition that very few of the fast-growing number of Kenyan birders and ornithologists had any ringing experience, and almost all lacked the necessary resources and opportunity to train as ringers.

The Group provides ringing training for interested Kenyans. Most Group members are ornithologists, students or interns in the Ornithology Department; others are amateur birders. The Group observes the high training standards set by the British Trust for Ornithology. A Training Record Sheet adapted for East Africa is used to help assess a trainee's progress. This is a first step in developing a nationally recognised certification process.

The Group was started and initially coordinated by a VSO volunteer, Colin Jackson. Since 1998 it has been run by a set of the initial trainees, now fully competent ringers who are in turn training others.

Regular ringing takes place two to three times a week at a training site beside the Nairobi River on the Nairobi Museum grounds. Once every month the Group rings at a constant effort site. Since 1999, this has been the Arboretum in central Nairobi. Whenever possible, excursions are made to other areas to handle additional species. Each year the NbiRG has managed to visit and help in the annual ringing programme at Ngulia, and visited other sites such as Lake Magadi for training in wader ringing and Arabuko-Sokoke Forest to ring forest birds.

The ringing group is now able to handle field projects quite independently. Members have recently undertaken a number of different assignments for visiting researchers. Particular individuals are also applying their skills as research assistants on several longer-term projects. The routine data collected are proving useful for understanding the seasonal cycles of central Kenyan birds. Notes on plumage and moult are allowing ageing and sexing methods to be developed for a number of little-known species.

Financially, the NbiRG's relatively modest costs have been met so far by local donors, notably the Kenya Museum Society.

demanding techniques of safely capturing, handling and measuring birds (Jackson 2000). Miscellaneous fieldwork, and Nature Kenya's Wednesday morning bird walks, give exposure to bird identification by sight and sound, counting, and habitat assessment. All interns are encouraged to improve their computer literacy, and training is given in fundamental skills.

It works – though it is *hard* work. As overall capacity grows, however, the system becomes self-reinforcing. There are more people to do the training and provide support; interns are better prepared when they join and ever more highly motivated; a collegial peer group builds up that is able to learn and share experience internally. A lot can be accomplished for much, much less in direct costs than is needed for a single postgraduate scholarship.

Research assistants

Assisting with a real-life research project, collecting real data to answer a real question, is an invaluable learning experience. Researchers, whether visiting or local, at postgraduate or professorial levels, can make a valuable contribution to capacity building by employing one or more national research assistants. They should build into their grants the resources to do this. Attitudes have improved greatly, but among some overseas researchers one still detects a certain reluctance to do so. Certainly it adds something to the project expense (though usually not much, and this is often amply compensated for by improvements in the data collected). It also complicates the logistics (though having someone who knows how things operate locally can also save a great deal of time and energy) and may mean investing some effort in training. This does not seem much of a sacrifice to make for something that is so obviously helpful to building local capacity for research and conservation.

In many countries, hiring a local assistant is in any case more or less mandatory. Some researchers accept this rather grudgingly, and invest no effort in selecting someone suitable. By taking on the first person who happens to come along, they often turn their misgivings into self-fulfilling prophecies. Obviously, there are good reasons – the success or otherwise of the project, if nothing else – for choosing an assistant with care. Local institutions can advise, or even assemble applications for one to choose from. The Tropical Biology Association (Box 11.3) runs field courses in East Africa and has a pool of highly motivated and qualified alumni from across the continent.

The Earthwatch Institute provides a special case of building capacity through participation in field research. Earthwatch is an international organisation mobilising volunteers to participate in field projects ranging

Box 11.3. Tropical Biology Association.

The Tropical Biology Association is a charitable NGO established in 1993. Its goal is to build capacity in biodiversity conservation and research in the Africa region, and to strengthen co-operation between institutions and individuals working in this field. The TBA's programme uses European and Africa-wide expertise to provide relevant and up-to-date field training to African biologists and conservation practitioners alongside biologists from European countries. Several month-long field courses are held each year, presently in East Africa. Through its courses, and the links subsequently forged, the TBA aims to build the capacity of tropical institutions to carry out their own training and research programmes, and is laying the foundation for future regional collaborative activities.

The TBA Alumni Association is a follow-up support scheme for course participants to help them realise their career and research objectives. Alumni register their interests and requirements and are circulated with appropriate information about opportunities by the TBA.

The TBA can be found on the web at www.zoo.cam.ac.uk/tba and contacted in Africa at: Tropical Biology Association, Nature Kenya, PO Box 44486, Nairobi, Kenya; tel. +254 (0)2 749957 or 746090, fax: +254 (0)2 741049, email: tba2@africaonline.co.ke and in Europe at: Tropical Biology Association, Department of Zoology, University of Cambridge, Downing Street, Cambridge CB2 3EJ, UK; tel./fax: +44 (0)1223 336619; email: TBA@zoo.cam.ac.uk

from archaeological excavation to large carnivore tracking. Volunteers contribute to the projects both through their time and energy (collecting data and helping with nitty-gritty tasks such as camp maintenance), and with funds. A special class of volunteers, so-called Earthwatch Fellows, have their expenses covered through sponsorship. In Africa, Fellows include many young biologists. Although they take part in fieldwork for only a fortnight, this is often their first exposure to a serious scientific project run by an experienced researcher. The experience is always valuable. It can be revelatory.

Creating an enabling environment

Deciding on priorities, mentoring students, supporting and training interns and creating opportunities for research assistants all link education and training – building capacity – with research. They all also link closely together.

These linkages suggest that the individual activities should not be tackled piecemeal. The underlying requirement for them all is an enabling institutional environment. What exactly does this mean? Like most resounding bits of jargon it is a little hard to define. In essence, it involves creating a structure that encourages the right things to happen. This structure could be within a single institution (as in our case at the National Museums of Kenya) or a consortium of co-operating researchers and organisations.

Some of the elements of an enabling environment would include:

- A clear strategy for bird research and conservation against which proposed work can be assessed;
- Sufficient skilled staff to handle aspects of training at various levels – from bird ringing and identification to sample design and data analysis;
- Sufficient field equipment and vehicles to meet basic survey needs (researchers should pay for the use of these, but the facilities need to be available);
- Encouragement, support, supervision and guidance for students, interns and trainees;
- Some official standing and recognition, to facilitate permits and arrangements for research work;
- Encouragement and facilitation of non-national researchers wanting to work in identified priority areas;
- Clear, straightforward and properly documented protocols for handling collaborative projects and research funds;
- Good linkages with other national and international organisations – and especially with supportive 'developed' world institutions;
- A good network among those working in ornithology, at all levels, in-country.

Linkages

An enabling environment demands strong and effective linkages with the outside world – nationally, regionally and internationally (Sodhi & Liow 2000). Linkages can work at many different levels, from sharing information to managing collaborative projects.

Linkages do not necessarily form automatically, and they usually need some work to sustain. Key aspects here include:

- Information flow – others need to be kept informed of what is happening. This is obviously the case for projects where they are involved or providing resources. However, all linked organisations should receive some routine feedback about activities. This might, for instance, be through copies of research reports, newsletter or magazine articles and scientific publications;

- Clear, written, agreements for any collaborative work;
- Prompt attention to (and with luck, resolution of) conflicts or misunderstandings;
- Giving credit where it is due – and not being over-zealous to demand recognition;
- Replying reasonably rapidly to communications (nothing disrupts links more effectively than a Sargasso Sea of becalmed correspondence);
- Being proactive in forging and strengthening links.

All these are fairly obvious. As with other obvious things, though, they soak up time and energy. The amount of effort that links require to service can be minimised by standardising and documenting procedures, and imposing a simple routine on information flow.

What kinds of linkages are important? In bird conservation, the global Partnership of BirdLife International is starting to provide an extraordinarily powerful network across the world. Nationally, each member of the network usually links in to many other institutions, including universities, Government departments, other conservation NGOs, and local conservation groups. For any researcher, this would be a logical place to start.

Sustainability
How many ornithologists do we need?

Everything above grows from the implicit assumption that building more capacity for bird conservation is always a Good Thing. Is this so? How much such capacity is really required, and when should we start applying the brakes?

There are two ways of looking at this. One is to match up the work that needs doing with the people who have the skills and are available to do it. There is a huge gap here in just about every tropical country. The task is immense, the skilled scientists and conservationists few and scattered. It is hard to imagine anyone running out of problems to grapple with in the foreseeable future. So no worries, then – we can bust our guts building capacity without any risk of overdoing it.

There is of course another perspective. Matching up the jobs available against the people being trained, there is also a gap – or an impending one. In some countries there may already be too many ornithologists for the posts that employers in either the public or private sectors can provide. Is it then pointless to train yet more people, if they will merely be thrown onto the employment scrap-heap? And will it be possible to attract the right people to be trained, anyway, if they see no prospect of a career in the field?

Obviously, the real issue is to address the gap between the work that needs doing and the jobs that are being funded. This is a complex problem, just one aspect of the meagreness of global resources being devoted to bio-diversity conservation. Continuing pressure on the world's decision-makers might conceivably turn this drip-feed into a weak trickle. If this happens, we will need the trained people in place right away. That is one argument for continuing to build capacity.

In the short term, there is no choice but to capture more of those slow-dripping resources for bird conservation. In practice, this usually means snagging project funds. Unfortunately, once on the project treadmill there is no easy way to get off it. Time-limited projects are almost by definition un-sustainable (despite the best reality-denying efforts of both applicants and funding agencies). As one project draws to a close, the only way to keep the treadmill moving is to find another to take its place. Institutions readily find themselves hoist on their own petard. To obtain funds they have to guaran-tee that a particular project will achieve sustainability; when it, inevitably, does not, they cannot justify any further funding without deviating into a new and usually unwanted direction.

In the long term, we badly need to jump off the project treadmill. Fund-ing agencies are experimenting cautiously with instruments such as Trust Funds, like the one successfully established for Bwindi Forest in Uganda (Hamilton *et al.* 2000) and National Environment Funds (Miller *et al.* 1995). The idea is to put aside money that can either earn interest or be replenished regularly, in order to fund long-term conservation activities. The Global Environment Facility, funding mechanism for the Convention on Biological Diversity, is drawing up plans to fund capacity-building initiatives (which has not hitherto been possible), and this is a positive step. What is needed though is not just capacity building but capacity *keeping*, and it is unclear whether GEF will allow for this. Altogether, such a mechanism appears much harder to accomplish. Giving away chunks of money to be invested against apparently ill-defined future returns does not greatly appeal to donors of any stripe. Although this would be the most logical and appropriate way actually to solve the problem of support for biodiversity conservation, it does not fit neatly into the current mind-set of development assistance.

Four types of brain drain

Whatever the wider issues, from the practical point of view training must go hand-in-hand with creating opportunities. If they cannot make a living working in bird conservation in their country, trained ornithologists will find other ways of doing so. This 'brain drain' can happen in at least four different ways, some more damaging than others.

(1) **Taking up posts in other countries.** Despite the formidable barriers raised by visas and work permits, trained people are still often lost through emigration. Most commonly, this simply involves a failure to return after finishing a course overseas. This sounds disastrous but can have its positive aspects. It may be very useful to have a sympathetic national, a person who furthermore understands bird conservation concerns, with inside knowledge of an international conservation organisation. When people move to another tropical country, this may help to spread expertise around and build linkages. More usually, and less usefully, individuals end up teaching in a foreign university, or working in a foreign research institute – or leaving birds and biology behind altogether (see below).

(2) **Moving into careers outside conservation.** Birders not infrequently find a new niche in some entirely different sector – banking, accounting, agriculture, corporate management or the like. Again, this is not always negative: it could be useful to have inside contacts in a big multinational, or even a small local company. Unfortunately, many people seem to find it very hard to maintain their interest in conservation once they are sucked in to this new and different world.

(3) **Shifting concerns to a different field.** One's training may be on birds, but the positions are in integrated pest management, or rhino monitoring, or agro-forestry. Bird conservation might lose out, but conservation as a whole does not. Thus, this kind of brain-drain (which is relatively uncommon) should not be a major worry. If the skills learned while working on birds can be usefully applied elsewhere in the environmental sphere, well and good.

(4) **Continuing with irrelevant further study.** If there are no jobs out there, best go back to school. Perhaps no further study really is 'irrelevant', but some scholarships can divert students from a more productive track. How useful is it to do, say, a second MSc in environmental studies to add to your existing one? Or a PhD in behavioural ecology when you really want to manage integrated conservation and development projects? Organisations granting scholarships sometimes do a remarkably poor job of matching awards up to the people who can best benefit from them. This is not quite a brain drain, perhaps, but a diversion through some narrow and circuitous plumbing.

There is another, more direct and distressing form of loss that cannot be completely avoided. Once in a while promising biologists and conservationists suffer psychological breakdowns at foreign universities, are killed in car accidents on their way to the field, are shot by bandits or trampled by rogue elephants, or are struck down by HIV. Fortunately these are far from everyday occurrences, but they are statistical possibilities, and underline the importance of spreading investment across as many people as possible.

RESEARCH AS CONSERVATION ACTION

Maximising direct benefits

Research obviously assists conservation through its results. At least in theory, these provide a better understanding of the problems, allow us to draw up sensible management and action plans, and therefore feed directly into conservation work on the ground.

How often these ideals are really achieved is somewhat moot, since translating research into practical management depends on much more than doing good scientific work – above all the results must be made relevant and accessible (Kochert & Collopy 1998; Flashpohler *et al.* 2000; Hejl & Granillo 2000; Latta 2000). Nevertheless, the process of carrying out research can itself make a direct contribution to conservation in several different ways.

Reduction of illegal or inappropriate activity

Researchers often work where there are serious conservation problems caused by illegal or inappropriate activities – hunting of threatened species, conversion of forests into logs and charcoal, industrial pollution of wetlands, etc. Researchers are not policemen and are not empowered to act as such. Their mere presence, however, can help to improve the situation. This is both because wrongdoers feel that they are being observed (and perhaps reported to the authorities) and because someone is showing an interest in, and demonstrating the importance of, a particular place or bird. Researchers must act circumspectly, but they can often help to publicise the issues, and bring them to the attention of those responsible (e.g. Oyugi 1997).

Local involvement, and building awareness and skills

By employing local assistants, or just buying produce or hiring accommodation locally, researchers make a contribution to local economies. This gives the resource that they are studying some additional value, and may help in awakening local enthusiasm for its conservation. Local assistants often gain valuable skills by working for research projects, skills that they can use in future to work with other projects, or for guiding visitors. They are also likely to acquire a much better understanding of the importance and vulnerability of the natural resources around them, an awareness that can be passed on to others in due course. Often, individuals who have worked on research projects can form nuclei for the establishment of Important Bird Area Site Support Groups (see below).

Increasingly, researchers recognise that their responsibilities go beyond just data collection, and make efforts to do something directly for conservation. This might involve talking to wildlife clubs in local schools, or raising funds to build an education centre (to take two recent Kenyan examples). Researchers often have the knowhow and the contacts to do good things for conservation; more should be trying to do so.

Large-scale coordinated projects

Large-scale coordinated projects, such as bird atlas schemes and waterbird censuses (Box 11.4), have great potential for building a constituency for conservation. Usually, such projects involve volunteers, who give their time and energy for collecting data. Those involved gain in awareness, skills and commitment, as well as helping to provide essential information for conservation.

Box 11.4. Waterbird counts in Kenya (from Bennun 2001).

Waterbirds have been counted every January since 1991 at five major Rift Valley lakes in Kenya (Bennun 1996; Nasirwa & Bennun 2000). The count has been expanded gradually to include sites around Lake Victoria, around Nairobi and at the Kenya coast. The counts are co-ordinated by the Ornithology Department of the National Museums of Kenya, working with the Kenya Wildlife Service (the Ramsar management authority in Kenya) and Nature Kenya (the BirdLife International Partner in Kenya).

About 150 volunteer counters are involved in the counts each year. Coordination and data analysis are the responsibility of two staff members in the Ornithology Department, and occupy an estimated 18 person-months each year. The counts have been funded primarily by grants from the Ramsar Bureau Wetlands Conservation Fund, by the KWS–Netherlands Wetland Programme, by local support from, among others, the Elsa Trust, and by provision of fuel, vehicles, boats and time by many volunteers.

The counts have provided baseline data on bird populations and their fluctuations at key sites, and permitted the identification of species or groups that are in long-term decline (Bennun & Nasirwa 2000). Some of the observed patterns can be related to ecological changes at particular Rift Valley lakes. Analysis of variation also demonstrates that the individual Rift lakes can be monitored independently, as few patterns are correlated across sites (Owino *et al.* 2001). More generally, the 'monitoring' programme has involved and trained a large number of volunteer counters, and interested many young Kenyans in birds and in wetland conservation.

The total cost of the counts is hard to calculate, as many contributions are made in kind and not quantified. However, around US$4,000 is required each year to cover direct costs. In 1999, the funding from both the Ramsar Bureau and KWS–Netherlands programme came to an end, and raising resources to keep the programme running is proving to be a challenge. The counts are a major organisational task: they could not take place without staff whose time is dedicated primarily to this work.

Such projects are usually carried out at a national scale. They require substantial attention to coordination, data compilation and analysis, and information feedback. Volunteers will also have to be trained, often more or less continuously. All these aspects need, once again, time and money, but the costs and effort involved are not insuperable.

To be most useful, such projects should involve people across a wide geographic area, not just those living in the capital. This is an especially good way of involving and enthusing local groups, especially if they see feedback from the data they are contributing.

Site support groups

Conservation approaches have shifted over recent years to recognise the importance of local communities in protecting and managing sites and species (Thomas *et al.* 1997; Aumeeruddy-Thomas *et al.* 1999; Bennun 1999; Gichuki 2000). The exact way in which local communities should be involved remains intensely controversial, in part because circumstances differ hugely from site to site, but that they have a significant role is now widely recognised (for a flavour of the debate see e.g. Spinage 1998, 1999; Hackel 1999; Martin 1999; McLarney 1999; Oates 1999; Schwartzman *et al.* 2000; Redford & Sanderson 2000).

The Important Bird Areas programme (Bennun & Fishpool 2000; Tilaye & Yilma 2000) uses birds as the focus for developing local conservation groups. These 'site support groups' normally evolve from existing, usually somewhat unfocused, environmental groups, or coalesce around one or two interested and committed individuals (Ngari *et al.* 2001). The groups are helped to focus and develop their objectives, to formalise their structures, and to plan and carry out some initial activities. Once properly established, groups will need some basic assistance with infrastructure, equipment and running costs, technical advice on running their conservation programme, training in a variety of skills, and help in securing funding for projects to support their development.

The experience so far has shown that IBA SSGs are an effective means for creating awareness, taking conservation action and also carrying out site monitoring. Monitoring schemes to be carried out by SSGs need to be robust, simple and inexpensive, while still providing meaningful data (Bennun 2001; Bennun & Matiku 2001). If such monitoring can be designed, it is likely to be both useful and sustainable.

Involving SSGs in research and monitoring, and in implementing the recommendations arising from such work, looks likely to be a powerful mechanism for conservation in the future.

CONCLUSIONS: THINKING STRATEGICALLY

Research can be a powerful force for conservation. It can also be a sterile academic exercise that merely charts the disappearance of species and habitats. For research to achieve more than this, researchers need to think strategically about the research *process* itself, as well as the expected findings. Research can be used to help build institutions, build networks, build constituencies for conservation, build committed and skilled groups of people, and build the opportunities for them to function effectively. It may even help, in a small way, to refine and improve funding mechanisms so that they serve biodiversity conservation more effectively.

This may all seem rather too much for the ordinary researcher, who simply wants to go to the field to collect her data. Why should she be bothered with these additional responsibilities? The answer is that she need not be – so long as she links up with some co-ordinating organisation. Ensuring that your own research helps to build capacity may just take a few simple steps. Build in funds to the grant proposal for local involvement; make contact with appropriate national institutions, such as the BirdLife Partner or representative; and take on and train local assistants. These steps are likely to improve the quality of the research itself. They will certainly make its overall impact for conservation much greater. Researchers, donors and tropical-country institutions all have important roles to play in making research work more effectively for conservation. With a little effort and lateral thinking, we can make the minuscule funds available go considerably further – and help prevent the species, sites, habitats and processes that we like to study from disappearing forever.

12

Conservation policies and programmes affecting birds

GERARD C. BOERE & CLAYTON D.A. RUBEC

INTRODUCTION

For millennia, ducks, geese and swans have migrated across our landscapes in an annual ritual that evokes a sense of wonder at the forces, mysterious yet consistent, that send millions of birds the length of continents and back again. Yet, among conservationists, the mystery of bird migration is accompanied by the certain knowledge that these species are dependent upon a complex and increasingly vulnerable chain of habitats extending across international borders. Underlying the spectacle of migration is a challenge of unprecedented proportions – the conservation of a migratory resource at national, multinational and intercontinental scales.

The conservation of these migratory birds is dependent on a wide range of initiatives, ones that transcend international borders, sectors of the economy, academic disciplines, environmental funding traditions and management of landscapes.

Birds have historically fascinated people not only as a food source, which has sometimes been easy to harvest (e.g. in the case of flightless or colonial birds) but also for cultural, religious and decorative reasons. However, during recent decades there has been a significant shift in the relationships between people and wildlife, and birds in particular.

In this chapter, we look at some national and many international conservation programmes and policies that reflect a global concern for the sustainable use or protection of bird biodiversity.

THE NEED FOR A CONSERVATION FOCUS

Conservation policies concerning birds have, in the past, been characterised by a focus on protection of a single species or use with little regard to the systematic conservation of birds and their habitat.

Historically, regulations existed for falconry or private hunting by the élite in society, and various cultures kept and protected waterbirds. Egyptian wall paintings, for example, feature several bird species, some of which are now extinct. Conservation policy tended to be *ad hoc*, aimed at regulating the taking of birds (including their young and eggs) to maintain sustainability (e.g. 1876 Act for the Preservation of Wildfowl in the UK), or limiting their use to privileged groups or individuals (e.g. royalty or tribal leaders).

Over-exploitation in the absence of regulations resulted in many extinctions, classic examples including the dodo (*Raphus calcullatus*), great auk (*Alca impennis*), passenger pigeon (*Ectopistes migratorius*) and eskimo curlew (*Numenius borealis*).

THE EVOLUTION OF POLICY

Many European bird conservation movements in Western Europe, such as 'Vogelbescherming' in The Netherlands and the Royal Society for the Protection of Birds (RSPB) in the United Kingdom, developed in the late nineteenth and early twentieth centuries, triggered by protest against the use of bird feathers. For example, in 1889 the Fur and Feather Group was formed in the UK by a group of women pledging to refrain from wearing feathers from birds of paradise, egrets and other species used by milliners and dressmakers. In 1891, this group became the RSPB (Lemon 1943; Samstag 1988). These organisations are among the oldest nature conservation organisations worldwide, and are today actively facing the challenges and threats that modern society places on birds and the environment.

With the development of these non-governmental organisations (NGOs) and their actions, bird conservation policies moved up the political agendas of many governments. The early twentieth century saw the development of bird conservation policies and regulations such as the Convention for the Protection of Birds Useful to Agriculture (Paris, 1902) and its successor treaty, the International Convention for the Protection of Birds (Paris, 1950). While both of these treaties are technically still in force, they have now been superseded.

During the 1960s and 1970s, with conservation and environment issues firmly on many national political agendas, several international treaties affecting birds were developed. The development of the Convention on Wetlands of International Importance especially as Habitat for Waterfowl (Ramsar Convention, 1971) originally used birds as the main criterion for site designation. The First United Nations Conference on Human Health and Environment (Stockholm, 1972) strongly stimulated the development of a number of these international agreements. This includes the

Convention on the Conservation of Migratory Species of Wild Animals (CMS) (Bonn, 1979) that affects the global conservation of the many migratory bird species.

The institutional framework for international co-operation in conserving North America's migratory birds was established early in the twentieth century. In 1916, Canada and the United States signed a bilateral Convention on the Conservation of Migratory Birds, and in 1936, the United States and Mexico signed a similar convention. By the 1980s, a long tradition of international co-operation in waterfowl population surveys and harvest management was in place across the continent. Population data confirmed that accelerated habitat loss and degradation resulting from human activities, and an extended period of low precipitation on mid-continent prairie landscapes, had led to a series of record low populations of most duck species. The need was clear – international cooperation in harvest management had to be extended to include habitat conservation. This need was answered by the Canada–USA–North American Waterfowl Management Plan signed in 1986, its updates in 1994 and 1998 and inclusion of Mexico as a Party in 1994 (Governments of Canada, the USA and Mexico, 1998).

PRESENT POLICIES AND LEGISLATION

Today, many international legal instruments assist in setting priorities for direct conservation actions for birds. These fall into the following categories: (i) legally binding accords, mainly between governments, and often of a multilateral nature; (ii) bilateral accords; and (iii) a wide variety of co-operative arrangements between countries, between countries and NGOs, or between NGOs. The numerous policy documents can be grouped as follows, all with specific uses and implementation.

1 Global, regional and subregional conventions and treaties. These are mainly intergovernmental legally binding instruments, but also include less binding instruments such as a Statements of Cooperation or Memoranda of Understanding.

2 Global, regional, subregional and national overviews. These are reports on threatened species or species at risk; often presented as Red Data Lists, and generally based on standard criteria developed by The World Conservation Union (IUCN) or a specialised related organisation. Some larger countries with a federal structure (e.g. the USA, Canada, Germany, Russia), have adopted national regulations to develop Red Lists at a national or subnational (province, state) scale.

3 Overviews of birds of particular conservation concern. These are focused on species not currently threatened, but that may become so without attention.

4 Overviews and action plans for regions, flyways, groupings of protected areas. These have a geographic focus.

5 Action plans for single species or species groups. These are either based on taxonomic groups or on a shared conservation problem.

6 Inventories of important habitats and areas. These can be for birds at all stages of their lifecycle (e.g. the Important Bird Areas [IBA] Program of BirdLife International).

BASIC REQUIREMENTS FOR CONSERVATION POLICY

Conservation policy requires good data and a clear objective. Bird biodiversity conservation partners worldwide have recognised the need to know what species are where, in what numbers, at what times of the year, and why they are there (see Chapter 3). Key questions must be tackled to develop species-specific conservation policy: what is the distribution and population size; how is the annual cycle of breeding, migration and wintering organised; what ecological requirements determine distribution, population size and movements; which external factors pose the greatest threats?

Justification of strong conservation policy requires adequate species monitoring and sound scientific research. The collection of such data requires substantial human and financial resources; consequently, few countries are able to develop integrated monitoring and research programmes adequate to answer the questions above. The need for such data is recognised in all international treaties and its collection often compulsory for Contracting Parties (WCMC 1992).

Integrated monitoring of breeding birds

Integrated bird monitoring programmes exist mainly in Western European and North American countries, Australia and some Southern African countries. Even in these countries, many data are only available because of the large number of dedicated and experienced volunteers undertaking fieldwork. It takes time to develop reliable and standardised systems to survey breeding birds that can be reliably used by volunteers. The European Bird Census Council (EBCC), with participation from Canada and the USA, has for more than 25 years played a crucial role in developing these standards for monitoring. Nationally, the results are often published as Breeding or

Wintering Bird Atlases (e.g. Gibbons *et al.* 1993); international atlases include the Breeding Birds of Europe (Hagemeijer & Blair 1997).

Species monitoring programmes exist in North America mainly for those migratory waterfowl covered by the two bilateral conventions (Canada–USA; USA–Mexico) and the North American Waterfowl Management Plan (NAWMP). New initiatives for other migratory birds (shorebirds, songbirds, forest species) are being developed through the North American Bird Conservation Initiative (NABCI). Such biological data underpin the recommendations of the NAWMP, including long- and short-term population goals for species identified in the plan.

Large information gaps remain in most African countries, except for Southern Africa, with the recent publication of the Atlas of Breeding Birds of Southern Africa (Harrison *et al.* 1997). Few monitoring schemes exist in regions such as Central America, South America and Asia, although on a regional or local level, scientists and groups of volunteers are active in collecting data of many kinds, often supported with funds from international organisations. Important here is the role of BirdLife and its IBA programme (see below). The recent publication of a number of field guides for birds in Asian countries (e.g. Kazmierczak & van Perlo 2000; Robson 2000) and, for example, the Russian Federation (Flint *et al.* 1987), can help in stimulating public interest and volunteer assistance in data collection and monitoring programmes.

Important Bird Areas (IBA)

Worldwide, the IBA Programme of BirdLife International and the BirdLife Partnership[1] provides an extremely important input to bird conservation policies. The Project is aimed at describing all important bird areas of the world following a clear and standardised methodology focused on species and habitat types.[2] The first inventory for Europe became available in 1989 (Grimmett & Jones 1989) and became an important policy tool for NGOs. Clearly identified IBAs with no protected status became the focus of conservation actions. The European Union (EU) has used the IBA inventory as a so-called 'shadow list' to monitor the designation by EU member states of Special Protection Areas (SPAs are areas classified under Article 4 of

---

[1] BirdLife International is a global alliance of national conservation organisations (BirdLife Partner organisations) working in more than 100 countries worldwide.

[2] Details of the criteria used to select IBAs can be found in any of the national, regional or continental directories, or on www.wing-wbsj.or.jp/birdlife/importan.htm

Directive 79/409/EEC).[3] An updated European IBA inventory was published in 2000 (Heath & Evans 2000). This massive two-volume inventory
describes more than 3,500 IBAs in Europe. In particular, the addition of
information from Central and Eastern European countries (often not possible for the first inventory), has contributed greatly to a better knowledge of
bird habitats at a pan-European level. In several countries, national (native
language) IBA volumes have been published, e.g. European Part Russian
Federation, Ukraine, Czech Republic, Lithuania, The Netherlands, UK.

IBA programmes are under way in other parts of the world and the
results will greatly contribute to bird conservation. The African IBA inventory will be published in 2001; in Canada, a national report has just
been published (Commission for Environmental Cooperation 1999) and
IBA overviews of many other countries have recently or will soon be published. *Endemic Bird Areas of the World* (Stattersfield *et al.* 1998) is another
important overview that identifies the 'hotspots' of bird biodiversity in the
world. Research has shown that these areas are also of world importance
for many other fauna and flora groups.

List of Globally Threatened Species

The List of Globally Threatened Bird Species (BirdLife International 2000),
developed by BirdLife International, is an example of a well-organised, well-
defined and standardised evaluation of the status of the world birds; the list
is often used in developing and implementing conservation policies of all
kinds. Areas where bird species on this list occur, receive special attention
in conservation policies and are leading to the development of protected areas networks. The list also assists in setting of priorities for species-related
action plans and has a major influence on guiding agencies' project funding in priority countries and areas. *Birds in Europe: their conservation status*
(Tucker & Heath 1994) is an example of a regional list of 195 bird species
with an unfavourable conservation status (of which 24 are globally threatened and the remainder of regional concern).

International Waterbird Census

In the 1950s and 1960s, activity to determine important areas for birds was
directed to the development of standards for wetlands of international importance for waterbirds. Coordinated waterbird monitoring was one of the

---

[3] The EC Directive on the Conservation of Wild Birds (79/409/EEC) requires member
states to safeguard the habitats of migratory birds and certain particularly threatened
birds.

first schemes to take place on an international scale and has evolved into the International Waterbird Census(IWC) organised by Wetlands International (previously known as the International Waterfowl and Wetlands Research Bureau, IWRB). The IWC in Europe and SE Asia takes place in mid-January, when waterbirds are concentrated in their wintering areas; timing of the IWC is different in other parts of the world. The results have lead to the famous 1% criterion to determine a wetland of international importance in the framework of the Ramsar Convention[4] (Ramsar Convention, 2000). It means that a wetland is of international importance if it holds at a given time of the year at least 1% of the global population of a species or subspecies of a flyway. This 1% criterion has become the basis for designation of Wetlands of International Importance under the Ramsar Convention. Currently, every 3-4 years Wetlands International publishes an overview, *Waterbird population estimates*, of the population size of more than 2,000 waterbirds (species, subspecies and flyway populations of species), and presents an update for the 1% criterion level (Rose & Scott 1997). Wetlands International regularly publishes the results of the IWC, by means of reports for various regions of the world (Delany *et al.* 1999).

Migration

Long-term systematic monitoring of migration, through population census and ringing (bird banding) activities, takes place at many specific points with mass migration. World famous ringing locations include Ottenby and Falsterbö in Sweden, Eilat in Israel, Long Point and Point Pelee in Canada, and Manomet in the USA. Bird ringing provides data on migration routes and mortality, and can give information on the origins and population sizes.

Ringing is well developed in Europe and the many national schemes are co-ordinated by EURING[5] with its standardised programs of data storage and data handling. North American countries have well-developed ringing schemes and standardised methods, as do countries like Australia and New Zealand. SAFRING coordinates the ringing of birds in Southern Africa and it is likely that 'AFRING' will be initiated, as the pan-African

---

[4] The Convention on Wetlands - 'Ramsar Convention' - was signed in Ramsar, Iran, in 1971. It is an intergovernmental treaty providing the framework for national action and international cooperation for the conservation and wise use of wetlands and their resources. There are presently (December 2001) 130 Contracting Parties to the Convention, with 1,109 wetland sites, totalling 87.2 million hectares, designated for inclusion in the Ramsar List of Wetlands of International Importance (see www.ramsar.org/).

[5] For links and details of ringing sites and schemes see www.geocities.com/ RainForest/6549/bbsch.htmetail . The EURING databank is held at the NIOO Centre for Terrestrial Ecology, PO Box 40, NL-6666 ZG Heteren, The Netherlands.

counterpart of EURING. Bird ringing schemes in South America, large parts of Africa and in Asia, are scattered and often coordinated and supported by the existing schemes in Europe, North America, Australia and Japan.

A major knowledge gap concerns the migratory behaviour of many tropical forest birds. This creates problems with implementation of the Bonn Convention on the Conservation of Migratory Species (see later in this chapter). Annex 2 of the Convention lists families for which coordinated action is important to maintain populations, and this includes *Muscicapidae* – a group of about 1,500 passerine species, many of which are long-distance migrants for which little information is available. Taxonomic issues also present a problem with implementation of the convention. A global directory (GROMS) of all migratory species, including birds, has been developed in support of the Bonn Convention (Riede 2000).

Clearly, endemic species require different conservation strategies from rare long-distance migrants which many traverse many countries. However, the conservation of all species requires good legislative or strategic programmes. In many countries, international treaties with well-defined and prioritised species annexes are the major conservation tools for achieving conservation objectives.

Hunting statistics and sustainable use

The sustainable use of wildlife populations plays a small but important part in discussions within the United Nations Commission on Sustainable Development. Stimulated by the further development, interpretation and implementation of the Convention on Biological Diversity[6] sustainable use of wildlife populations is considered part of an integrated global environmental conservation strategy. However, this requires good knowledge of both level and timing of 'use' and of the population dynamics of each species, and this often is not available.

Hunting and trade in live specimens are the main direct uses of bird populations. Hunting statistics are collated by a number of countries in Europe, in North America and in Australia, but little information is available elsewhere. Trade in birds is monitored by the intergovernmental Convention on International Trade in Endangered Species (CITES – see

---

[6] The Convention on Biological Diversity was signed by over 150 governments at the Rio 'Earth Summit' in 1992. It came into force on 29 December 1993 and is now the centrepiece of international efforts to conserve the planet's biological diversity, ensure the sustainable use of its components, and promote the fair and equitable sharing of the benefits arising out of the utilisation of genetic resources – see www.unep.ch/bio/biodiv.html

p. 256) and also by TRAFFIC, the wildlife trade monitoring programme of the World Wide Fund for Nature (WWF) and IUCN, The World Conservation Union.

CONVENTIONS, TREATIES AND REGIONAL AGREEMENTS

Besides the availability of the data described above, to be successful, conservation policies require conventions, treaties, agreements and action plans supported by a functional system of institutions. By 'functional', we imply that institutions (whether governmental or otherwise) have a secretariat, staff and resources, and are clearly responsible for the convention, treaty, etc. In the case of intergovernmental conventions or treaties, it is essential that the parties (usually called 'contracting party' countries or nation states) regularly meet (every 2–3 years) to discuss progress and policies on the basis of a system of National Reports.

A strategy with medium- and long-term targets, which contribute to the development of the convention or treaty, is also helpful. Such strategies, which are often rather general, form concrete conservation instruments. Many existing international conventions and treaties are supported by a scientific body (Council, Panel or Committee), which provides the fundamental information necessary for policy development under the convention (see below).

Several international conservation treaties have become silent due to a lack of commitment by their parties to even the most basic infrastructure. An example is the Convention of Algiers (1968), dealing with nature conservation in Africa. This treaty stimulated the development of the fine system of National Parks in many African countries. However, there was no infrastructure support for a central secretariat, there were no regular meetings of the Parties, and no obligatory national financial contributions. Although the Organization of African States (OAS) initially provided the secretariat, there was no long-term support. Thus, the convention was not viable, although it had, and theoretically still has, great potential for African wildlife conservation. It has the potential to act as an African regional implementation tool of the Convention on Biological Diversity, as the well functioning Bern Convention, administered by the Council of Europe, does for Europe.

In the following sections, we highlight the most important current international conventions, treaties, action plans and organisations relevant to the implementation of bird conservation policies. We pay special attention to how research, monitoring, and recent developments influence the functioning of these conventions and treaties. Those that underpin and measure conservation policies and actions will be discussed. Globally, the

Bonn and Ramsar Conventions are by far the most important with respect to direct bird species and habitat conservation policies.

Global conventions

Below we describe 11 global conventions of importance for nature conservation. All are important for bird conservation policy, although only a few are directly applicable. Both formal and working names of conventions are given, along with the year/location where they were concluded, and for some of them a short summary of their main aims (Heijnsbergen 1997; Lyster 1985).

Convention on the Conservation of Migratory Species of Wild Animals (CMS; Bonn, 1979): The Bonn Convention came into force in 1983. It requires the conservation and sustainable use of all migratory species, and so is an important instrument for bird conservation. Annex 1 of the Convention requires strict protection for a number of highly endangered bird species such as the slender-billed curlew (*Numenius tenuirostris*) and Siberian crane (*Grus leucogeranus*), for both of which separate 'soft legal instruments', such as Memoranda of Understanding, have been concluded between the Range States involved.

Annex 2 of the Bonn Convention lists a large group of species and families for which coordinated action is important to maintain populations. This is mainly achieved through agreements between the Range States in which species occur. A good example is the African Eurasian Migratory Waterbird Agreement (AEWA; The Hague, 1995), which covers almost 170 species and 120 countries. It is the largest flyway agreement in the world and entered into force on 1 November 1999. Recently (early 2001) an Agreement was concluded on the conservation of albatross and petrel species (ACAP; Cape Town, January 2001).

The CMS has high potential as a bird conservation treaty and there are many new initiatives under way to develop agreements for flyways and threatened groups or species such as the great bustard (*Otis tarda*) and Andean flamingo (*Phoenicopterus andinus*). Notably, however, the CMS has not been acceded to by some governments as it also covers marine species such as whales that are felt by some to be better governed by other mechanisms.

Some countries have concluded bilateral agreements on migratory species. Examples include agreements for flyways in North America and Central and Southern America, and among Arctic Circumpolar nations (Scott 1998). This is frequently viewed as insufficient for the integrated management of a whole flyway (all species and several continents), but has been shown to be effective regardless.

Convention on Wetlands of International Importance Especially as Waterfowl Habitat (Ramsar Convention; Ramsar, 1971): One of the very first international conservation treaties, the Ramsar Convention is very important for bird conservation. It is a successful convention because of its relatively simple obligations, with over 130 Contracting Parties and major NGO partners. A country can become a Contracting Party by subscribing to the general terms of the convention to conserve and sustainably use the resources associated with all wetlands (not only those of international importance) and by designating at least one wetland of international importance. The results of the International Waterbird Census, along with other criteria, are important in selection of internationally important sites.

The Ramsar Convention is a good example of a convention that has been continuously modernised. It has evolved from a bird-related convention to one dealing with the integrated conservation, management and sustainable use of wetlands, freshwater resources and catchment areas. Many standardised handbooks on management, legislation, sustainable use, and criteria for designating wetlands have resulted. Of particular note are the guidelines for developing legislative initiatives and national wetland policies (Glowka & Shine 2000; Rubec *et al.* 2000). The convention has provided a leading example of how other conventions might develop.

Convention on International Trade in Endangered Species of Wild Fauna and Flora (CITES; Washington, 1973): CITES is particularly important for the protection and regulation of trade in many endangered bird species. More than 150 countries are Contracting Parties to CITES and its provisions are implemented in their national legislation. International trade in an agreed list of endangered species is banned, and trade in less endangered species is regulated and monitored through a system of permits and border checks. Within the 25 years of CITES' existence, clear criteria for listing on annexes and sustainable use have been developed.

Convention Concerning the Protection of the World Cultural and Natural Heritage (World Heritage Convention; Paris, 1972): This Convention results in designation, and protection in some nations, of large areas of heritage value that may indirectly contribute to bird conservation. In practice, many of these sites are protected under other treaties that also focus on bird conservation.

Convention on Biological Diversity (CBD; Rio de Janeiro, 1992): This convention is becoming a global framework convention guiding the activities of other conventions. Many biodiversity conservation components of the CBD are implemented by other conventions by way of mutual Memoranda of Understanding (with work plans). A good example is the recently updated agreement between the CBD and the Ramsar Convention, or the CBD and the Bonn Convention. Several of the CBD's priority programmes are very important for bird conservation, including those being developed on marine and coastal environments, and agriculture and biodiversity. It is also extremely important to acknowledge the strong influence of the fact that almost all countries of the world have ratified the Convention on Biological Diversity. In the framework of that convention, large numbers of countries have developed National Biodiversity Policies where species and habitat conservation are addressed in the framework of national priorities and needs; this includes bird conservation. This whole process at the same time has stimulated the amendment of existing legislation, or the development of new legislation, in many countries.

United Nations Framework Convention on Climate Change (UNFCC, 1992): Climate change is an extremely important issue affecting bird populations (see Chapter 8), and can influence birds, their habitats and food sources at all stages of their life cycles.

The following conventions often regulate activities that can have an indirect impact on birds, although violation of these conventions can have serious impacts; here they are mentioned only by name:

- Framework Convention to Combat Desertification (1995)
- International Tropical Timber Agreement (Geneva, 1983)
- Convention for the Prevention of Marine Pollution by Dumping of Wastes and Other Matter (London, 1972)
- International Convention for the Prevention of Pollution from Ships (MARPOL; London, 1973)
- Convention for the Protection of the Ozone Layer (Vienna, 1985)

Many of these conventions are administered directly by the United Nations (FCCC and FCCD) or by a United Nations organisation, such as the United Nations Environment Program (UNEP, in Nairobi) or the United Nations Science and Education Organization (UNESCO, in Paris).

Regional and bilateral treaties

There are a large number of regional treaties and bilateral agreements of relevance to bird conservation, and they work quite well. Their small-scale projects can often be administered by one country using existing staff and resources, with no need for an international secretariat with its own administration, financed by the participating states. Below are examples of some of the most important treaties, by geographic region.

Europe

Before the EU developed the Birds Directive, the Benelux countries had the Convention on Hunting and Protection of Birds (Brussels, 1970) and the Protocol of 1977 (Brussels, 1977). These treaties have been superseded by the Bern Convention (1979) and the EU Birds Directive (79/409 EEC, 1979).

Directive and Resolution of the Council of the European Community on the Conservation of Wild Birds (Brussels, 1979): The Birds Directive is a powerful instrument imposing strict legal obligations on EU Member States to maintain populations of all naturally occurring wild birds at levels corresponding to the ecological requirements of individual species. It regulates hunting and trade and requires Member States to designate Special Protected Areas of sufficient numbers and size to meet the obligations of the Directive and its annexes, in particular Annex 1 on species in need of special protection. The Directive has become a powerful instrument as the European Commission can bring a Member State to the European Court of Justice if it does not meet the obligations of the Birds Directive. A condemnation by the European Court can lead to substantial penalties and the reduction of structural funding. Several countries have court cases in place.

The European Community Directive on the Conservation of Natural Habitats and of Wild Fauna and Flora (Brussels, 1992): This instrument adds broader conservation policy to the Birds Directive and is a major instrument to protect large areas of remaining natural habitats in Western Europe via the Natura 2000 network of protected areas. The present negotiations with the 15 EU candidate members also include these two directives. Their application will be of great value in Central and Eastern Europe, where most of Europe's remaining unspoiled nature is situated.

Convention on the Conservation of European Wildlife and Habitats (Bern, 1979): The Council of Europe administers this convention, which came into force in 1982. Most bird species are protected under the Bern Convention, with special attention to migratory species. For this reason, some African States (Senegal, Mali, Tunisia and Morocco) are also Parties to this European convention. However, the Bonn Convention, developed simultaneously, has taken over the protection of migratory species. Thus, the Bern Convention now concentrates mainly on European fauna and flora. The implementation of the convention by the Parties is well monitored through a system of species and habitat 'case files'. Rather unusually, NGOs have a strong involvement by bringing substantial case files to the attention of the Standing Committee (the decision-making body of the convention), often with positive results.

Protocol to the Barcelona Convention (Convention for the Protection of the Mediterranean Sea Against Pollution; Barcelona, 1976) Concerning Mediterranean Specially Protected Areas (Geneva, 1982): Besides the general nature conservation aspects of the Barcelona Convention, this protocol helps in particular to protect coastal areas and small islands, and is therefore of great importance for the conservation of many seabird breeding sites.

Within the European region, there are also a number of conventions and treaties dealing with pollution – particularly marine pollution. In most cases, elements of the texts, and their annexes or protocols, can be important for bird conservation policies. Good examples are: the *Oslo and Paris Convention for the Protection of the Marine Environment of the North-east Atlantic* (Paris, 1992); *OSPAR*, which has a special Protocol on habitat protection; the *Convention on the Protection of the Marine Environment of the Baltic Sea Area* (Helsinki, 1974); HELCOM; and the *Barcelona Convention*, mentioned above.

Africa

Few regional treaties exist in Africa, certainly not specifically for birds. However, a most important one is:

The African Convention on the Conservation of Nature and Natural Resources (Algiers, 1968), which is not functional owing to lack of infrastructure (see above). Clearly, the African continent has numerous socio-economic and civil problems, and nature conservation is not easy to achieve. Whilst many African nations consider nature conservation important, many countries lack the basic resources and infrastructure to implement conservation policies. There are notable exceptions, such as the Wetlands Strategy of Uganda, and countries where wildlife observation has become an important tourist industry.

The Protocol Concerning Protected Areas and Wild Fauna and Flora in the Eastern African Region (Nairobi, 1985): This is part of the Convention for the Protection, Management and Development of the Marine and Coastal Environment of the Eastern African Region (Nairobi, 1985). The protocol contains a paragraph that requests countries to take into account the importance of these areas as migration routes, wintering, staging, feeding or moulting sites for migratory species. This applies mainly to birds but also includes species like marine turtles (note: for Marine Turtles Regional Bonn Convention MoUs – Memoranda of Understanding – are also in place).

Many bilateral arrangements exist between European (including EU) and African countries, relating to aid for development and nature conservation initiatives, including coastal and marine areas, wetlands and tropical forests. In some cases, bird conservation is specifically mentioned in bilateral cooperation agreements, as in the *Developing Aid Treaty* between The Netherlands, Benin, Costa Rica and Bhutan.

Other EU instruments affecting Africa concern agriculture and structural funds.

Asian–Pacific Region

Notable bilateral treaties and agreements are those between the Russian Federation and Japan, the Russian Federation and India, Australia and Japan (JAMBA), Australia and China [People's Republic] (CAMBA), the Russian Federation and the Republic of Korea, and Japan and China. Most of these are treated like a convention, with basic implementation and monitoring infrastructure. Many concentrate on joint research projects and the protection of site networks important for migrating and wintering birds, particularly endangered species.

All Asia-Pacific bilateral agreements concentrate on shared migratory species, but several thousand agreements would be necessary for full coverage of all species and Range States. Whilst the development of a multilateral treaty like the African Eurasian Migratory Waterbird Agreement could be a solution, current political problems prevent this.

Within the *Convention on Conservation of Nature in the South Pacific* (Apia, 1976) the focus is on endangered and migratory species, and much attention is paid to sustainable use (e.g. the taking of birds, eggs, nests and shells). *The Convention for the Protection of the Natural Resources and Environment of the South Pacific Region* (Noumea, 1986), also pays attention to habitat protection and the establishment of special protected areas, including those for birds.

Conventions have also been concluded for restricted areas, mainly dealing with pollution and the marine environment. Examples are those for the Gulf Area (Kuwait, 1972) and the Red Sea and Gulf of Aden (Jeddah, 1982).

The Americas

In North America, many birds breed and migrate only between Canada, the United States and Mexico. Bilateral agreements include early Conventions such as the *Convention between the United States of America and Great Britain (acting for Canada) for the Protection of Migratory Species* (Washington, 1916).

In 1999, the conclusion of a Protocol brought the bilateral *Canada–USA Convention* in line with aspects of subsistence hunting by indigenous peoples in Canada and Alaska. Although the treaty between Canada and the USA protected the interests of many migratory species, many other birds migrate to areas south of the USA. This led to the development of the *Convention Between the United States of America and the United Mexican States for the Protection of Migratory Birds and Game Animals* (Mexico City, 1936, as amended in 1972). So far, no other 'whole-flyway' general treaties have been developed to protect migratory species in the Americas.

The Convention on Nature Protection and Wildlife Preservation in the Western Hemisphere (Washington, 1940) is generally not used but remains a tool for USA support for various programmes in Latin America.

Canada, the United States and Mexico also participate in other conservation and trade alliances that directly affect waterfowl, including the *1992 North American Free Trade Agreement*, the parallel *North American Agreement on Environmental Cooperation*, and the *Trilateral Committee for the Conservation and Management of Wildlife and Ecosystems*. Whilst each initiative reflects an increasing awareness of the economic and environmental benefits of international cooperation, together they form an increasingly complex and diverse institutional context within which the North American Waterfowl Management Plan (NAWMP) has been implemented since 1986 (Governments of Canada, the United States and Mexico 1998 – see above for details of NAWMP).

In 1986, waterfowl conservation on an international level was largely synonymous with migratory bird conservation since formal international partnerships aimed at non-game migratory birds were only beginning to emerge. The Western Hemisphere Shorebird Reserve Network was less than one year old, and it would be almost five years before Partners in Flight[7] would begin to address more than 700 other species of non-game

---

[7] The 'Partners in Flight' initiative by the US National Fish and Wildlife Foundation (NFWF) focuses on all migratory species.

migratory birds. More recently, a coalition of interested partners has begun to consider a conservation plan for colonial waterbirds.

Inspired by the success of the NAWMP, North American international efforts are now engaged in conservation planning on a continental scale, thus broadening the scope and vitality of migratory bird conservation in North America. In addition, a broad coalition of government, NGOs, and academia is considering how best to coordinate and integrate these bird conservation plans. The Commission on Environmental Cooperation is facilitating this effort through the North American Bird Conservation Initiative (NABCI).

The US government provided an incentive for Canada, the United States, and Mexico to accelerate cooperative migratory bird conservation efforts with the passage of the *North American Wetlands Conservation Act* in 1989. The Act has a regulated grant programme that encourages and supports partnerships to conserve wetland ecosystems and waterfowl, other migratory birds, fish and wildlife that depend upon these habitats in the three countries.

Further to the south, Central and South America and Caribbean nations have established various bilateral agreements, mainly on general aspects of nature conservation; tropical forests (particularly in the Amazon and Pantanal areas) and transborder protected areas. Such agreements exist between Argentina and Bolivia (La Paz, 1976); Colombia and Brazil (Bogota, 1973); Peru and Brazil (Lima, 1975); and Colombia and Peru (1979). Through such mechanisms, considerable work on the conservation of breeding, endemic and migratory birds is being achieved. It has to be noted that many tropical forest birds are strictly sedentary and rely completely on the conservation and strictly sustainable use of parts of the remaining tropical forest area.

There are in this region two other important agreements, mainly dealing with the conservation of migratory bird species. These are the agreements between the USA and Japan (*Convention Between the Government of the United States of America and the Government of Japan for the Protection of Migratory Birds and Birds in Danger of Extinction, and Their Environment*; Tokyo, 1972) and between the USA and the former USSR (*Convention between the United States of America and the Union of Soviet Socialist Republics Concerning the Conservation of Migratory Birds and Their Environment*; Moscow, 1976). Both agreements are still in force and functioning, with regular meetings of experts and joint research projects. An example is the long-lasting cooperation on the conservation of the Snow Goose populations of Wrangel Island (Russia), which winter mainly in California (USA).

Canada also has a number of bilateral bird agreements: with the Russian Federation, Great Britain and Ireland; with Iceland for geese populations; with nations such as Suriname, Cuba and others for general cooperation on migratory species.

Several conventions dealing with pollution and the marine environment include provisions for habitats and wildlife protection that could be used to develop bird conservation policies and actions. Examples are conventions for the South-East Pacific (Lima, 1981) and the Wider Caribbean Region (Cartagena, 1983).

Other regions and themes

The Antarctic Treaty (Washington, 1959) and its related Protocols and treaties such as one on environmental protection (Madrid, 1991) and Arctic Flora and Fauna (Brussels, 1964) are important for bird conservation. In particular, CCAMLR (Convention on the Conservation of Antarctic Marine Living Resources; Canberra, 1980) can play an important role in the protection of seabirds, albatrosses in particular together with the recently concluded ACAP (see above).

The Antarctic Treaty is exceptional as it deals with a large area not divided into territories under national jurisdiction. In the Arctic, the eight Arctic Countries have launched a series of initiatives and institutions to coordinate their conservation activities on a circumpolar basis. This includes bird conservation policies discussed within the Working Group on the Conservation of Arctic Flora and Fauna (CAFF) and the Working Group on Seabirds, as part of CAFF's activities (Scott 1998).

There are numerous other international agreements, legally binding, on fisheries and other marine resources. They almost all deal with regulations concerning sustainable use of populations, particularly shared populations. The United Nations Food and Agriculture Organization (FAO) plays an important role concerning these treaties. However, the role of the EU may be even more important as fishing by EU member states takes place over the whole world. Many of these treaties could be of great importance for bird conservation policies if applied effectively with an open eye on conservation aspects.

POLICIES AND PROGRAMMES OTHER THAN CONVENTIONS AND TREATIES OF IMPORTANCE FOR CONSERVATION

There are a large variety of initiatives, programmes, project declarations, strategies, etc., sometimes very specifically related to birds, but often of a more general nature and not legally binding. It is impossible to mention them all but a number are reviewed below that are particularly valuable for birds.

Global initiatives

On a global level, there are several major intergovernmental programmes, such as *UNEP's Regional Seas Program*, which started in 1974 and now covers 24 different agreements, dozens of countries and many action plans. The programme is still in full action and successful on the regional level. For protected areas, *UNESCO's Man and Biosphere Program* (1970) is still active. In this category is also the *FAO Action Plan on Tropical Forestry* that is of importance regarding sustainable management of tropical forests worldwide. Many long-distance migratory passerine birds winter in tropical forest areas in South America, Africa and Southeast Asia. The FAO could play a more active role in their work in aspects of their agriculture, fisheries and tropical timber policies and action plans.

Other major global initiatives already mentioned in other sections of this chapter are:

- Important Bird Areas Programme, organised by BirdLife International
- International Waterbird Census, organised by Wetlands International
- Inventories of Wetlands of International Importance, often organised by joint ventures of Wetlands International, BirdLife International, Ramsar Convention, IUCN and WWF
- Flyway conservation activities related to waterbirds in general, as co-ordinated on the global level by Wetlands International

Clearly, most of these programmes are biased towards waterbirds and to wetlands-related birds. There is of course much more to protect and only the Important Bird Areas (IBA) Programme, together with *Endemic Bird Areas of the World* (Stattersfield *et al.* 1998), is currently focusing on the wider spectrum of species and species groups. In addition, a recent BirdLife publication, *Raptor Watch* (Zalles & Bildstein 2000), a global directory of raptor migration sites, fills an important gap in this respect.

Regional initiatives

Europe

Much of the work in Europe is organised within the conventions, and EU directives and their institutions (including working groups on bird conservation), dealing with Europe. This includes the Ramsar Convention's MedWet Initiative. This is a wetland conservation initiative for the whole Mediterranean Region, including North Africa, and contains strong bird conservation elements. It is an initiative by governments and NGOs together and is strongly funded by the European Commission.

The Council of Europe's Network of Genetic Reserves is effectively dormant, but taken over by the Natura 2000 Protected Areas Network under the EU and a related Emerald Network for non-EU states under the Bern Convention. Together with the national systems, they constitute the Pan European Ecological Network (PEEN).

In the European context, and given the great importance of agricultural areas in Europe for bird populations (Pain & Pienkowski 1997; Tucker & Evans 1997), the Common Agricultural Policy (CAP) of the European Union (and future new members) is of the greatest importance for bird conservation and has had a long-term negative effect. However, since the MacSharry (EU Commissioner on Agriculture) reforms in 1992, the character of the CAP has shifted to some extent towards better integration of environmental interests into the agricultural policy by partially breaking the link between subsidies to farmers and production. Policy instruments, such as set-aside schemes, have produced conservation benefits. The Agenda 2000 reforms have stimulated reforms to progress in this direction by introducing cross-compliance. This means that direct payments to farmers should be conditional on following environmentally sound agricultural practices.

Indeed, since 1985, the CAP has provided special support to environmentally sound agricultural production methods and countryside maintenance (Regulation 2078/92 which superseded Article 19 of Regulation 97/85 and Article 21 of Regulation 2328/91). This instrument (Cammarata 1997) has great potential for bird conservation in the wider countryside, particularly if implemented early in the low-input agricultural areas still existing in large parts of future EU Members States in Central and Eastern Europe.

The Agenda 2000[8] discussions within the EU incorporate these measures into the new Rural Development Regulation, where funds can be provided for integrated rural development plans, for example in 'Less Favoured Areas'[9] where agricultural conditions are marginal, and also to maintain ecologically valuable forests.

These regulations benefit both bird and wider biodiversity conservation in the European countryside. In addition, the Community Biodiversity Strategy[10] and Action Plans will have great influence, once published (2001).

---

[8] Agenda 2000 is a programme aimed at strengthening Community policies and giving the EU a new financial framework for the period 2000–06, with a view to EU enlargement.

[9] Less Favoured Areas are areas that are marginal in terms of agricultural productivity but may be very biologically rich.

[10] On 4 February 1998, the European Commission adopted a Communication on a European Biodiversity Strategy, which aims to anticipate, prevent and attack the causes of significant loss or reduction of biodiversity. With this strategy, the EU reinforces its

Asian–Pacific

A number of initiatives on wetlands conservation have evolved, based on the outcome of a series of conferences initiated by Wetlands International and the governments of a few countries (Karachi, 1991, Bogor, 1994 and Beidaihe, 1997).

Existing bilateral agreements on the conservation of migratory birds (between the governments of Australia, Japan and China [People's Republic] in particular), coordinated through Wetlands International with other countries of the region, have led to the development of a number of site-related flyway initiatives such as:

- *Shorebird Action Plan and East Asian–Australasian Shorebird Reserve Network* (Brisbane, 1996)
- *Asia–Pacific Migratory Crane Action Plan and North East Asian Crane Site Network* (Beidaihe, 1997)
- *Action Plan for the Conservation of Anatidae in the East Asian Flyway* (Costa Rica, 1999)

These activities are taking place under the umbrella of the Asian–Pacific Migratory Waterbird Conservation Strategy; updated in October 2000 at a conference in Okinawa, Japan. Recently, the Central Asian Indian Flyway Programme was initiated (early 2001). This aims to develop an Action Plan and, in the long term, a conservation strategy and formal flyway Agreement under the Bonn Convention. This long-awaited programme is bridging the geographical gap between the flyway conservation activities co-ordinated under the African Eurasian Migratory Waterbird Agreement and the new Asian–Pacific Migratory Waterbird Conservation Strategy.

The Americas

The Western Hemisphere Shorebird Reserve Network (WHSRN) (1985) is one of the Americas' earliest initiatives concerning the conservation of long-distance migrants. This has a strong component in South America but also in sites scattered across North America. Another inspiring example for flyway initiatives is the regularly updated and expanded North American Waterfowl Management Plan between Canada and the USA (1986; and Mexico in 1994). The Partners in Flight (PIF) initiative, a coalition of government agencies, conservation groups, academic institutions, private businesses and everyday citizens, focuses on all migratory species. PIF is strongly involved in conservation projects in the wintering areas of

role in the efforts to find solutions for biodiversity within the framework of the United Nations' Convention on Biological Diversity (CBD).

North American breeding birds in Central and South America and the Caribbean.

At a national level, there are many valuable actions supporting bird conservation, including specific habitat protection policies and statements of commitment by governments and partners. Examples include Canada's *Federal Policy on Wetland Conservation* (Government of Canada 1991), the first of its kind globally and since used as a reference in many other nations (Rubec *et al.* 2000). Canada's development of a Vision for Wetland Conservation for Canada (North American Wetlands Conservation Council 1998) also inspired the global Ramsar Convention to adopt a Vision for the Ramsar List of Wetlands of International Importance in 1999. The Neotropical Migratory Bird Conservation Act, passed by the American Government in July 2000, also has promising potential. This opens a possibility to become more active in Central and South America, beyond the present jurisdiction of the Migratory Birds Act of 1923, which encompasses only Canada, the USA and Mexico.

This would strongly stimulate the activities of, for example, PIF in Central and South America, where the conservation of tropical forests is of utmost importance for the conservation of both endemic and North American migratory bird species. Economic developments such as mining, tropical timber harvest, cattle grazing, etc., have had severe impacts on birds and biodiversity.

Initiatives are also under way to establish coordinated conservation actions in the framework of the American–Pacific Flyway Programme.

Finally, there are several regional economic and political integration initiatives. Well-known examples include the EU, ASEAN, NAFTA, OAS[11] etc. They often have a special Committee on Environmental and Nature Conservation issues with the potential to influence regional and national policies.

FUNDING OF CONSERVATION POLICIES

Developing conservation policies is one thing, implementation with necessary resources quite another. Bird conservation should be based on national policies, legislation and funding instruments. As many countries have no, or insufficient resources, international funding instruments have also been developed.

Many of the conventions, treaties and initiatives discussed here are also permanently under-resourced. Finding resources to implement projects is

[11] Association of Southeast Asian Nations (ASEAN); North American Free Trade Agreement (NAFTA); Organization of American States (OAS).

time consuming, with variable success, and larger conventions and organisations have dedicated fund-raising staff. Governmental funding is multilateral or bilateral. Multilateral funds support the conservation programmes and initiatives of international organisations, bilateral for bird conservation initiatives included within MoUs between two countries. Besides support from country agencies for environment and conservation, large funds are increasingly made available via development aid agencies. Countries like Canada (CIDA), The Netherlands (DGIS) and the Scandinavian countries have very active agencies in this respect. Within the NGO sector, there are numerous private organisations and foundations.

Small-scale, restricted multilateral funding is available from UNEP and UNESCO. Globally, the Global Environment Facility (GEF) is the most important source for bird conservation programmes. It is the funding mechanism related to the CBD and UNFCC. For instance, over US\$250 million have been invested in migratory species conservation; however, this included large amounts for tropical forests in Central and South America. GEF also recently started to fund flyway initiatives, such as the African Eurasian Migratory Waterbird Agreement and Siberian Crane Memorandum of Understanding. Many of the integrated biodiversity policies and programmes in developing countries are funded with GEF money, often with matching funds provided on a bilateral basis by the development aid agencies of a relatively small number of countries.

Applying for GEF funding is a long three-step process with various (funded) Project Development stages (Project Development Funds, A and B, etc.). The total procedure can take 2–3 years, but a successful programme may receive upto US\$20 million.

Within Europe, various budget lines within the EU are very important for funding bird conservation. An important instrument is the LIFE Fund for conservation projects, based on the Birds Directive and Habitats Directive. Various other funding possibilities exist (e.g. via the Rural Development Regulation, The Lome Treaty, etc.).

RESEARCH

Whilst the need for information for the various conventions, treaties, policy documents etc. is enormous, resources for applied research are even scarcer than for conservation actions. Much of the basic information needed for effective conservation and management is lacking, whereas fundamental research questions are relatively well addressed via research programmes in science institutions.

Many of the international conventions have technical and scientific institutions, which advise on research and data collection priorities, and translate scientific information into policy proposals. Examples of such bodies are:

- Scientific and Technical Review Panel (STRP) of the Ramsar Convention (a relatively small team of experts); meetings are open to observers on invitation.
- Scientific Council of the Bonn Convention with a representative of each Party (over 70) and a large number of experts. Council meetings are open for observer countries and a number of NGOs.
- Subsidiary Body on Scientific, Technical and Technological Advice (SBSTTA) of the Convention on Biodiversity. This is a large body with representatives of all Parties and meetings include hundreds of people, including many NGOs.
- Subsidiary Body for Scientific and Technical Advice (SBSTA) for the Framework Convention on Climate Change; however, the independent International Panel on Climate Change (IPCC) is effectively the scientific body.

The level of information available is extremely biased towards developed countries, notably Western Europe and North America, despite the exchange of experts and training facilities available for developing countries.

Below we outline some priorities for data collection and research to help answer conservation and management questions in relation to the policies described in this chapter.

- A global overview of all Important Bird Areas.
- More and detailed information on migration routes and the importance of staging posts.
- Long-term influences of climate change (Sahel and the Arctic) on bird populations; including an analysis of existing databases containing long-term monitoring data.
- Long-term influences of large-scale logging of tropical forests.
- Impacts of ecological changes in the wintering areas of migratory birds.
- Impact of coastal and shallow-water fisheries (for flatfish) on wintering birds.
- Population effects of harvesting birds for food (i.e. not sports hunting).
- More work on the value of birds as bio-indicators.

CONCLUSIONS

There are numerous well-developed international instruments of all types, and with wide geographical coverage, available for bird conservation policy. Whilst some, such as flyway agreements, could usefully be developed further, much can be achieved with existing treaties, conventions and initiatives. It is, however, important that these instruments are seen to be in force, in order that pressure can be applied to governments to deliver on the obligations for which they are signatory. The role of NGOs cannot be underestimated in this respect. The 'Convention's Paradox' is that conventions are concluded by governments, but they function mainly through NGO involvement.

It is also very clear that to function effectively, many treaties require a certain minimal infrastructure, such as a secretariat, regular meetings of the parties, and implementation strategies and plans supported by funding. Increasingly, international instruments develop their own work plans, and the larger ones, such as the CBD, have a fast growing influence on the way that governments and NGOs set their own priorities at the global level. It is essential, therefore, that bird conservation issues continue to be addressed in these fora, not only at a species level, but also and above, in relation to the conservation of their habitats and ecosystems.

References

Abbitt, R.J.F., Scott, J.M. & Wilcove, D.S. (2000). The geography of vulnerability: incorporating species geography and human development patterns into conservation planning. *Biological Conservation*, **96**, 169-175.

Abell, R.A., Olson, D.M., Dinerstein, E., Hurley, P.T., Diggs, J.T., Eichbaum, W., Walters, S., Wettengel, W., Allnutt, T., Loucks, C.J. & Hedao, P. (2000). *Freshwater ecoregions of North America. A conservation assessment.* Washington, DC: Island Press.

Aebischer, N.J. (1999). Multi-way comparisons and generalised linear models of nest success: extensions of the Mayfield method. *Bird Study*, **46**(Suppl.), S22-S31.

Aebischer, N.J., Evans, A.D., Grice, P.V. & Vickery, J.A. (ed.) (2000). *Ecology and conservation of lowland farmland birds.* Tring: British Ornithologists Union.

Aebischer, N.J., Potts, G.R. & Rehfisch, M. (1999). Using ringing data to study the effect of hunting on bird populations. *Ringing & Migration*, **19**, 67-82.

Ainley, D., Wilson, P. & Fraser, W.R. (2001). Effects of climate change on Antarctic sea ice and penguins. In *Impacts of climate change on wildlife*, ed. R.E. Green, M. Harley, M. Spalding & C. Zöckler, pp. 24-25. RSPB/UNEP/WCMC/EN/WWF.

Akçakaya, H.R., Ferson, S., Burgman, M.A., Keith, D.A., Mace, G.M. & Todd, C. (2000). Making consistent IUCN classifications under uncertainty. *Conservation Biology*, **14**, 1001-1013.

Akçakaya, H.R., McCarthy, M.A. & Pearce, J.L. (1995). Linking landscape data with population viability analysis: management options for the helmeted honeyeater *Lichenostomus melanops cassidix*. *Biological Conservation*, **73**, 169-176.

Akçakaya, H.R. & Raphael, M.G. (1998). Assessing human impact despite uncertainty: viability of the northern spotted owl metapopulation in the northwestern USA. *Biodiversity and Conservation*, **7**, 875-894.

Allen-Wardell, G., Bernhardt, P., Bitner, R., Burquez, A., Buchmann, S., Cane, J., Cox, P.A., Dalton, V., Feinsinger, P., Ingram, M., Inouye, D., Jones, C.E., Kennedy, K., Kevan, P., Koopowitz, H., Medellin, R., Medellin-Morales, S., Nabhan, G.P., Pavlik, B., Tepedino, V., Torchio, P. & Walker, S. (1998). The potential consequences of pollinator declines on the conservation of biodiversity and stability of food crop yields. *Conservation Biology*, **12**, 8-17.

Andelman, S.J. & Fagan, W.F. (2000). Umbrellas and flagships: efficient conservation surrogates or expensive mistakes? *Proceedings of the National Academy of Sciences, USA*, **97**, 5954-5959.

Ando, A., Camm, J., Polasky, S. & Solow, A. (1998). Species distributions, land values, and efficient conservation. *Science*, **279**, 2126-2128.

Andrén, H. (1992). Corvid density and nest predation in relation to forest fragmentation: a landscape perspective. *Ecology*, **73**, 794-804.

Andrén, H. (1994) Effects of habitat fragmentation in birds and mammals in landscapes with different proportions of suitable habitat: a review. *Oikos*, **71**, 355-366.

Andrén, H. (1996). Population responses to habitat fragmentation: statistical power and the random sample hypothesis. *Oikos*, **76**, 235-242.

Andrén, H. (1999). Habitat fragmentation, the random sample hypothesis and critical thresholds. *Oikos*, **84**, 306-308.

Anon. (1998). Bali starling. *World Birdwatch*, **20**, 4.

Anon. (1999a). *Quality of life counts. Indicators for a strategy for sustainable development for the United Kingdom: a baseline assessment.* London: Department of the Environment, Transport and the Regions.

Anon. (1999b). Karori predator fence completed. *Forest & Bird*, **293**, 4.

Anon. (2000). *The New Zealand Biodiversity Strategy.* Wellington: Department of Conservation & Ministry for the Environment.

ApSimon, H., Pearce, D. & Özdemiroğlu, E. (1997). *Acid rain in Europe: counting the cost.* London: Earthscan Publications Ltd.

Araújo, M.B. & Williams, P.H. (2000). Selecting areas for species persistence using occurrence data. *Biological Conservation*, **96**, 331-345.

Archibald, G.W. (1978). Winter feeding programs for cranes. In *Endangered birds. Management techniques for preserving threatened species*, ed. S.A. Temple, pp. 141-148. Wisconsin: University of Wisconsin Press.

Ardern, S.L. & Lambert, D.M. (1997). Is the black robin in genetic peril? *Molecular Ecology*, **6**, 21-28.

Arendt, W.J., Gibbons, D.W. & Gray, G. (1999). Status of the volcanically threatened Montserrat Oriole *Icterus oberi* and other forest birds in Montserrat, West Indies. *Bird Conservation International*, **9**, 351-372.

Arnold, G.W. & Weeldenberg, J.R. (1991). *The distribution and characteristics of remnant native vegetation in parts of the Kellerberrin-Tammin-Trayning and Wyalkatchem shires of Western Australia.* Australia: CSIRO Division of Wildlife and Ecology Technical Memo 33.

Askins, R.A., Lynch, J.F. & Greenberg, R. (1990). Population declines of migratory birds of eastern North America. *Current Ornithology*, **7**, 1057.

Atkinson, C.T., Woods, K.L., Dusek, R.J., Sileo, L.S. & Iko, W.M. (1995). Wildlife disease and conservation in Hawaii: pathogenicity of avian malaria (*Plasmodium relictum*) in experimentally infected Iiwi (*Vestiaria coccinea*). *Parasitology*, **111**, S59-S69.

Atkinson, I.A.E. (1990). Ecological restoration on islands: prerequisites for success. In *Ecological restoration of New Zealand islands*, ed. D.R. Towns, C.H. Daugherty & I.A.E. Atkinson, Conservation Sciences Publication, **2**, 73-90. Wellington: Department of Conservation.

Atkinson, I.A.E. (1999). Managing New Zealand's Biodiversity: identifying the priorities and widening the options. In *Biodiversity now!* Joint societies conference, Wellington, 29 June-3 July 1997, selected papers, ed.

P.M. Blaschke & K. Green, pp. 1–12. Wellington: Department of Conservation.

Atkinson, I.A.E. & Millener, P.R. (1991). An ornithological glimpse into New Zealand's prehuman past. *Acta XX Congressus Internationalis Ornithologici*, **2**, 127–192.

Aumeeruddy-Thomas, Y., Saigal, S., Kapoor, N. & Cunningham, A. (1999). Joint management in the making: reflections and experiences. *People and Plants Working Paper* 7. Paris: UNESCO.

Avery, M.I., Gibbons, D.W., Porter, R., Tew, T., Tucker, G. & Williams, G. (1995). Revising the British Red Data List for birds: the biological basis of U.K. conservation priorities. *Ibis*, **137**, S232–S239.

Avise, J.C. (2000). Cladists in wonderland. *Evolution*, **54**, 1828–1832.

Avise, J.C. & Ball, R.M. (1990). Principles of genealogical concordance in species concepts and biological taxonomy. *Oxford Surveys in Evolutionary Biology*, **7**, 45–68.

Avise, J.C. & Walker, D. (1998). Pleistocene phylogeographic effects on avian populations and the speciation process. *Proceedings of the Royal Society of London B*, **265**, 457–463.

Avise, J.C. & Walker, D. (2000). Abandon all species concepts? *Conservation Genetics*, **1**, 77–80.

Bacon, P.J. & Andersen-Harald, P. (1989). Mute swan. In *Lifetime Reproduction in Birds*, ed. I. Newton, pp. 363–386. London: Academic Press.

Bailey, A.M. (1956). *Birds of Midway and Laysan Islands*. Museum Pictorial, 12. Denver, CO: Denver Museum of Natural History.

Baillie, J. (1996). Analysis. In *1996 IUCN Red List of Threatened Animals*, ed. J. Baillie & B. Groombridge, pp. 24–43. Gland, Switzerland: IUCN.

Baillie, S.R. (1990). Integrated population monitoring of breeding birds in Britain and Ireland. *Ibis*, **132**, 151–166.

Baillie, S.R., Sutherland, W.J., Freeman, S.N., Gregory, R.D. & Paradis, E. (2000). Consequences of large-scale processes for the conservation of bird populations. *Journal of Applied Ecology*, **37**(Suppl. 1), 88–102.

Baker, C.S., Medrano-Gonzalez, L., Calambokidis, J., Perry, A., Pichler, F., Rosenbaum, H., Straley, J.M., Urban-Ramirez, J., Yamaguchi, M. & Von Zeigesar, O. (1998). Population structure of nuclear and mitochondrial DNA variation among humpback whales in the North Pacific. *Molecular Ecology*, **7**, 695–707.

Baker, N. & Baker, E. (2001). *Important Bird Areas in Tanzania*. Dar es Salaam: Wildlife Conservation Society of Tanzania (in press).

Ball, R.M. Jr & Avise, J.C. (1992). Mitochondrial DNA phylogeographic differentiation among avian populations and the evolution of subspecies. *Auk*, **109**, 626–636.

Ballou, J. (1995). An overview of small population biology. In *VORTEX A Stochastic Simulation of the Extinction Process, Version 7 User's Manual*, ed. R.C. Lacy, K.A. Hughes & P.S. Miller, pp. 53–62. USA: Chicago Zoological Society and IUCN/SSC Conservation Breeding Specialist Group.

Balmford, A. (1998). On hotspots and the use of indicators for reserve selection. *Trends in Ecology and Evolution*, **13**, 409.

Balmford, A. & Gaston, K.J. (1999). Why biodiversity surveys are good value. *Nature*, **398**, 204-205.

Balmford, A., Gaston, K.J., Rodrigues, A.S.L. & James, A. (2000). Integrating costs of conservation into international priority setting. *Conservation Biology*, **14**, 597-605.

Balmford, A. & Long, A. (1994). Avian endemism and forest loss. *Nature*, **372**, 623-624.

Balmford, A. & Long, A. (1995). Across-country analyses of biodiversity congruence and current conservation effort in the tropics. *Conservation Biology*, **9**, 1539-1547.

Balmford, A., Mace, G.M. & Ginsberg, J.R. (1998). The challenges to conservation in a changing world: putting processes on the map. In *Conservation in a changing world*, ed. G.M. Mace, A. Balmford & J.R. Ginsberg, pp. 1-28. Cambridge: Cambridge University Press.

Balmford, A., Moore, J.L., Brooks, T., Burgess, N., Hansen, L.A., Williams, P. & Rahbek, C. (2001). Conservation conflicts across Africa. *Science*, **291**, 2616-2619.

Baptista, L.F. & Martinez-Gomez, J.E. (1996). El programma de reproduccion de la Paloma de la Isla Socorro, *Zenaida graysoni*. *Ciencia y Desarrollo*, **22**, 30-35.

Barclay, J.H. & Cade, T.J. (1983). Restoration of the peregrine falcon in the eastern United States. *Bird Conservation*, **1**, 3-40.

Barnes, K.N. (1998). *The important bird areas of Southern Africa*. Pretoria: BirdLife South Africa.

Barratt, E.M., Gurnell, J., Malarky, G., Deaville, R. & Bruford, M.W. (1999). Genetic Structure of fragmented populations of red squirrel (*Sciurus vulgaris*) in Britain. *Molecular Ecology*, **S12**, 55-65.

Beiback, H. (1992). Flight-range estimates for small trans-Sahara migrants. *Ibis*, **134**(Suppl.), 47-54.

Beissinger, S.R. (1995). Modelling extinction in periodic environments: Everglades water levels and snail kite population viability. *Ecological Applications*, **5**, 618-631.

Beissinger, S.R., Reed, J.M., Wunderle, J.M. Jr, Robinson, S.K. & Finch, D.M. (2000). Report of the AOU conservation committee on the Partners in Flight species prioritisation plan. *Auk*, **117**, 549-561.

Beissinger, S.R. & Westphal, M.I. (1998). On the use of demographic models of population viability in endangered species management. *Journal of Wildlife Management*, **62**, 821-841.

Bell, B.D. (1975). The rare and endangered species of the New Zealand region and the policies that exist for their management. *Bulletin of the International Council for Bird Preservation*, **12**, 165-172.

Bell, B.D. (1978). The Big South Cape rat irruption. In *The ecology and control of rodents in New Zealand nature reserves*, ed. P.R. Dingwall, I.A.E. Atkinson & C. Hay. Department of Lands & Survey Information series, **4**, 33-40. Wellington.

Bell, B.D. (1991). Recent avifaunal changes and the history of ornithology in New Zealand. *Acta XX Congressus Internationalis Ornithologici*, **2**, 193-230.

Bennett, A.F. (1999). *Linkages in the landscape. The role of corridors and connectivity in wildlife conservation*. Gland, Switzerland: IUCN.

Bennun, L.A. (1996). Training water bird counters to monitor wetlands in Kenya: progress and prospects. In *Proceedings of the 1993 African Crane and Wetland Training Workshop*, ed. R.D. Beilfuss, W.R. Tarboton & N.N. Gichuki, pp. 183-189. Baraboo, Wisconsin: International Crane Foundation.

Bennun, L.A. (1999). Threatened birds and rural communities: balancing the equation. In *Proceedings of the 22nd International Ornithological Congress, Durban*, ed. N.J. Adams & R.H. Slotow, pp. 1546-1555. Johannesburg: BirdLife South Africa.

Bennun, L.A. (2001). Long-term monitoring and conservation: high ideals and harsh realities. *Hydrobiologia* (in press).

Bennun, L. & Fanshawe, J. (1997). Using forest birds to evaluate forest management: an East African perspective. In *African rainforests and the conservation of biodiversity*, ed. S. Doolan, pp. 10-22. Oxford: Earthwatch Europe.

Bennun, L.A. & Fishpool, L.D.C. (2000). The Important Bird Areas Programme in Africa: an outline. *Ostrich*, **71**, 150-153.

Bennun, L. & Matiku, P. (2001). Guidelines for monitoring Kenya's Important Bird Areas. *Nature Kenya Conservation Working Papers* (in press).

Bennun, L.A. & Nasirwa, O. (2000). Trends in waterbird numbers in the southern Rift Valley of Kenya. *Ostrich*, **71**, 220-226.

Bennun, L. & Njoroge, P. (eds) (1996). *Birds to watch in East Africa: A preliminary Red Data list*. Research Reports of the Centre for Biodiversity. Nairobi: National Museums of Kenya, Ornithology 23.

Bennun, L. & Njoroge, P. (1999). *Important Bird Areas in Kenya*. Nairobi: Nature Kenya.

Bennun, L.A. & Njoroge, P. (2000). Important Bird Areas in Kenya. *Ostrich*, **71**, 164-167.

Bennun, L., Njoroge, P. & Pomeroy, D.E. (2000). Birds to watch: a Red Data List for East Africa. *Ostrich*, **71**, 310-314.

Berg, A. & Tjernberg, M. (1996). Common and rare Swedish vertebrates - distribution and habitat preferences. *Biodiversity and Conservation*, **5**, 101-128.

Bernstein, C., Krebs, J.R. & Kacelnik, A. (1991). Distribution of birds amongst habitats: theory and relevance to conservation. In *Bird Population Studies*, ed. C.M. Perrins, J-D. Lebreton & G.J.M. Hirons, pp. 317-345. Oxford: Oxford University Press.

Berruti, A., Underhill, L.G., Shelton, P.A., Moloney, C. & Crawford, R.J.M. (1993). Seasonal and interannual variation in the diet of 2 colonies of the Cape gannet (*Morus capensis*) between 1977/78 and 1989. *Colonial Waterbirds*, **16**, 158-175.

Berthold, P. (1999). Patterns of avian migration in light of current global "greenhouse" effects: a central European perspective. *Proceedings of the XX International Ornithological Congress*, 780-786.

Berthold, P., Fliege, G., Querner, U. & Winkler, H. (1986). The development of songbird populations in central Europe: analysis of trapping data. *Journal für Ornithologie*, **127**, 397-437.

Bibby, C.J. (1998). Selecting areas for conservation. In *Conservation science and action*, ed. W.J. Sutherland, pp. 176-201. Oxford: Blackwell Science.

Bibby, C.J. (1999). Making the most of birds as environmental indicators. *Ostrich*, **70**, 81-88.

Bibby, C.J., Burgess, N.D., Hill, D.A. & Mustoe, S. (2000). *Bird census techniques*, 2nd edn. London: Academic Press.

Bibby, C.J., Collar, N.J., Crosby, N.J., Heath, M.F., Imboden, C., Johnson, T.H., Long, A.J., Stattersfield, A.J. & Thirgood, S.J. (1992). *Putting biodiversity on the map: priority areas for global conservation*. Cambridge: International Council for Bird Preservation.

Bierregaard, R.O., Lovejoy, T.E., Kapos, V., dos Santos, A.A. & Hutchings, R.W. (1992). The biological dynamics of tropical rainforest fragments. *BioScience*, **42**, 859-866.

BirdLife International (2000). *Threatened birds of the world*. Barcelona and Cambridge, UK: Lynx Edicions and BirdLife International.

BirdLife International (2001). The extinction of Spix's Macaw in the wild. *World Birdwatch* **23**(1), 9-11.

Blondel, J., Pradel, R. & Lebreton, J-D. (1992). Low fecundity insular Blue Tits do not survive better as adults than high fecundity mainland ones. *Journal of Animal Ecology*, **61**, 205-213.

Blus, L.J. (1996). DDT, DDD, and DDE in Birds. In *Environmental contaminants in wildlife: interpreting tissue concentrations*, ed. W.N. Beyer, G.H. Heinz & A.W. Redmon, Chapter 2. Boca Raton: SETAC CRC Lewis Publishers.

Boitani, L., Corsi, F., De Biase, A., D'Inzillo Carranza, I., Ravagli, M., Reggiani, G., Sinibaldi, I. & Trapanese, P. (1999). *A databank for the conservation of the African mammals*. Rome: Istituto di Ecologia Applicata.

Bolger, D.T., Scott, T.A. & Rotenberry, J.R. (1997). Breeding bird abundance in an urbanizing landscape in coastal southern California. *Conservation Biology*, **11**, 406-421.

Boon, W.M., Kearvell, J.C., Daugherty, C.H. & Chambers, G.C. (2000). Molecular systematics of New Zealand *Cyanoramphus* parakeets: conservation of orange-fronted and Forbes parakeets. *Bird Conservation International*, **10**, 211-239.

Both, C. & Visser, M.E. (2001). Adjustment to climate change is constrained by arrival date in a long-distance migrant bird. *Nature*, **411**, 296-298.

Bowden, C. (1998). Last chance for the northern bald ibis. *World Birdwatch*, **20**, 12-16.

Bowerman, W.W., Best, D.A., Grubb, T.G., Sikarskie, J.G. & Giesy, J.P. (2000). Assessment of environmental endocrine disruptors in bald eagles of the Great Lakes. *Chemosphere*, **41**, 1569-1574.

Branch, W.R., Benn, G.A. & Lombard, A.T. (1995). The tortoises (Testunidae) and terrapins (Pelomedusidae) of southern Africa: their diversity, distribution and conservation. *South African Journal of Zoology*, **30**, 91-102.

Brandon, K., Redford, K.H. & Sanderson, S.E. (eds.) (1998). *Parks in peril. People, politics, and protected areas*. Washington, DC: Island Press.

Briggs, K.T. & Chu, E.W. (1986). Sooty Shearwaters off California: distribution, abundance and habitat use. *Condor*, **88**, 355-364.

Britten, H.B., Riddle, B.R., Brussard, P.F., Marlow, R. & Lee, T.E. (1997). Genetic delineation of management units for the desert tortoise, *Gopherus agassizii*, in Northeastern Mojave Desert. *Copeia*, **12**, 523-530.

Brock, M.K. & White, B.N. (1992). Application of DNA fingerprinting to the recovery program of the endangered Puerto Rican parrot. *Proceedings of the National Academy of Sciences, USA*, **89**, 11121-11125.

Bromham, L., Rambaut, A. & Harvey, P.H. (1996). Determinants of rate variation in mammalian DNA sequence evolution. *Journal of Molecular Evolution*, **43**, 610-621.

Brook, B.W. & Kikkawa, J. (1998). Examining threats faced by island birds: a population viability analysis on the Capricorn silvereye using long-term data. *Journal of Applied Ecology*, **35**, 491-503.

Brook, B.W., Lim, L., Harden, R. & Frankham, R. (1997). Does population viability analysis software predict the behaviour of real populations? A retrospective study on the Lord Howe Island woodhen *Tricholimnas sylvestris* (Sclater). *Biological Conservation*, **82**, 119-128.

Brook, B.W., O'Grady, J.J., Chapman, A.P., Burgman, M.A., Akçakaya, H.R. & Frankham, R. (2000). Predictive accuracy of population viability analysis in conservation biology. *Nature*, **404**, 385-387.

Brooks, D.R., Mayden, R.L. & McLennan, D.A. (1992). Phylogeny and biodiversity: conserving our evolutionary legacy. *Trends in Ecology and Evolution*, **7**, 55-59.

Brooks, T., Balmford, A., Burgess, N., Hansen, L.A., Moore, J., Pilgrim, J., Rahbek, C. & Williams, P.H. (2002). Continental conservation priorities for Ethiopian terrestrial vertebrates. *Ethiopian Journal of Biological Sciences* (in press).

Brooks, T., Balmford, A., Burgess, N., Hansen, L.A., Moore, J., Rahbek, C., Williams, P., Baker, N., Baker, E., Bennun, L., Byaruhanga, A., Kasoma, P., Njoroge, P., Pomeroy, D. & Wondafrash, M. (2001). Conservation priorities for birds and biodiversity: do East African Important Bird Areas represent species diversity in other terrestrial vertebrate groups? *Ostrich* **515**, 3-12.

Brooks, T., Lens, L., Barnes, J., Barnes, R., Kihuria, J.K. & Wilder, C. (1998a). The conservation status of the forest birds of the Taita Hills, Kenya. *Bird Conservation International*, **8**, 119-139.

Brooks, T., Lens, L., de Meyer, M., Waiyaki, E. & Wilder, C. (1998b). Avian biogeography of the Taita Hills, Kenya. *Journal of East African Natural History*, **87**, 189-194.

Brooks, T.M., Pimm, S.L. & Oyugi, J.O. (1999). Time lag between deforestation and bird extinction in tropical forest fragments. *Conservation Biology*, **13**, 1140-1150.

Brothers, N. (1991). Albatross mortality and associated bait loss in the Japanese longline fishery in the Southern Ocean. *Biological Conservation*, **55**, 255-268.

Brown, A.F., Stillman, R.A. & Gibbons, D.W. (1995). Use of breeding bird atlas data to identify important bird areas: a northern England case study. *Bird Study*, **42**, 132-143.

Brown, J.H. & Kodric-Brown, A. (1977). Turnover rates in insular biogeography: effect of immigration on extinction. *Ecology*, **58**, 445-449.

Bryant, D., Nielsen, D. & Tangley, L. (1997). *The Last Frontier Forests: ecosystems and economics on the edge*. Washington, DC: World Resources Institute.

Buckland, S.T., Anderson, D.R., Burnham, K.P. & Laake, J.L. (1993). *Distance sampling: estimating abundance of biological populations*. London: Chapman & Hall.

Buckland, S.T., Bell, M.V. & Picozzi, N. (1990). *The birds of north-east Scotland*. Aberdeen: North-East Scotland Bird Club.

Buckland, S.T. & Elston, D.A. (1993). Empirical models for the spatial distribution of wildlife. *Journal of Applied Ecology*, **30**, 478-495.

Burton, J.A. (1984). A bibliography of red data books. *Oryx*, **18**, 61–64.

Bustamante, J. (1996). Population viability analysis of captive and released bearded vulture populations. *Conservation Biology*, **10**, 822–831.

Butler, D. (1989). *Quest for the Kakapo*. Auckland: Heinemann Reed.

Butler, D. & Merton, D.V. (1992). *The black robin - saving the world's most endangered bird*. Oxford: Oxford University Press.

Byaruhanga, A., Kasoma, P. & Pomeroy, D. (2001). *Important Bird Areas in Uganda*. Kampala: NatureUganda.

Bystrak, D. (1981). The North American Breeding Bird Survey. In *Estimating numbers of terrestrial birds*, ed. C.J. Ralph & J.M. Scott, pp. 34–41. Studies in Avian Biology no. 6. Lawrence, Kansas: Cooper Ornithological Society.

Cade, T.J. (1978). Manipulating the nesting biology of endangered birds. In *Endangered birds. Management techniques for preserving threatened species*, ed. S.A. Temple, pp. 167–170. Wisconsin: University of Wisconsin Press.

Cade, T.J. & Temple, S.A. (1995). Management of threatened bird species: evaluation of the hands-on approach. *Ibis* (Suppl.), **137**, S161–S172.

Cadman, M.D., Eagles, P.F.J. & Helleiner, F.M. (1987). *The Atlas of breeding birds of Ontario*. Waterloo, Ont: University of Waterloo Press.

Cairncross, F. (1995). *Green Inc. A guide to business and the environment*. London: Earthscan.

Caldecott, J.O., Jenkins, M.D., Johnson, T.H. & Groombridge, B. (1996). Priorities for conserving global species richness and endemism. *Biodiversity and Conservation*, **5**, 699–727.

Calder, W.A. (1984). *Size, function, and life history*. Cambridge, MA: Harvard University Press.

Cammarata, A. (1997). *Agriculture and environment*. Brussels: CAP Working Notes Special Issue, EC.

Campbell, L.H., Avery, M.I., Donald, P.F., Evans, A.D., Green, R.E. & Wilson, J.D. (1997). *A review of the indirect effects of pesticides on birds*. JNCC Report No. 227. Peterborough: Joint Nature Conservation Committee.

Camphuysen, K. (1998). Beached bird surveys indicate decline in chronic oil pollution in the North Sea. *Marine Pollution Bulletin*, **36**, 519–526.

Caro, T.M. & O'Doherty, G. (1999). On the use of surrogate species in conservation biology. *Conservation Biology*, **13**, 805–814.

Carter, M.F., Hunter, W.C., Pashley, D.N. & Rosenberg, K.V. (2000). Setting conservation priorities for landbirds in the United States: the Partners in Flight approach. *Auk*, **117**, 541–548.

Cassidy, K.M., Grue, C.E., Smith, M.R., Johnson, R.E., Dvornich, K.M., McAllister, K.R., Mattocks, P.W., Cassady, J.E. & Aubry, K.B. (2001). Using current protection status to assess conservation priorities. *Biological Conservation*, **97**, 1–20.

Caswell, H. (1978). A general formula for the sensitivity of population growth rate to changes in life history parameters. *Theoretical Population Biology*, **14**, 215–230.

Caswell, H. (1989). *Matrix population models*. Sunderland, MA: Sinauer Associates.

Caswell, H. (2000). Prospective and retrospective perturbation analyses: their roles in conservation biology. *Ecology*, **81**, 619–627.

Caughley, G. (1994). Directions in conservation biology. *Journal of Animal Ecology*, **63**, 215–244.

Caughley, G. & Gunn, A. (1996). *Conservation biology in theory and practice.* Cambridge, MA: Blackwell Science.

Cave, A.J. (1983). Purple heron survival and drought in tropical West Africa. *Ardea,* 71, 217-224.

CCAMLR (1992). *CCAMLR Ecosystem Monitoring Program: standard methods.* Hobart: Commission for the Conservation of Antarctic Marine Living Resources.

Charnov, E.L. (1993). *Life history invariants. Some explorations of symmetry in evolutionary biology.* Oxford: Oxford University Press.

Cincottta, R.P., Wisnewski, J. & Engelman, R. (2000). Human population in the biodiversity hotspots. *Nature,* 404, 990-991.

Clark, C.W. & Butler, R.W. (1999). Fitness components of avian migration: a dynamic model of Western Sandpiper migration. *Evolutionary Ecology Research,* 1, 443-457.

Clark, J.M. & Eyre, J.A. (1993). *Birds of Hampshire.* Hampshire: Hampshire Ornithological Society.

Clobert, H.J., Lebreton, J.D. & Allaine, D. (1987). A general approach to survival rate estimation by recaptures or resightings of marked animals. *Ardea,* 75, 133-142.

Clout, M.N. & Merton, D.V. (1998). Saving the Kakapo: the conservation of the world's most peculiar parrot. *Bird Conservation International,* 8, 281-296.

Collar, N.J. (1996). The reasons for Red Data Books. *Oryx,* 30, 121-130.

Collar, N.J. (1997). Taxonomy and conservation: chicken and egg. *Bulletin of the British Ornithological Club,* 117, 122-136.

Collar, N.J., Crosby, M.J. & Stattersfield, A.J. (1994). *Birds to watch 2: the world list of threatened birds.* Cambridge: Birdlife International.

Collar, N.J., Mallari, N.A.D. & Tabaranza, B.R. (1999). *Threatened birds of the Philippines.* Manila: Bookmark Inc., in conjunction with the Haribon Foundation.

Collar, N.J. & Stuart, S.N. (1985). *Threatened birds of Africa and related islands.* The IUCN/ICBP Red Data Book. Cambridge: IUCN/ICBP.

Collar, N.J. & Stuart, S.N. (1988). *Key forests for threatened birds in Africa.* Cambridge: International Council for Bird Preservation.

Colwell, R.K. & Coddington, J.A. (1994). Estimating terrestrial biodiversity through extrapolation. *Philosophical Transactions of the Royal Society of London B,* 345, 101-108.

Comer, S. (2000). Noisy scrub bird translocated to the Darling Range. *South Coast Threatened Birds,* 4, 1-2.

Commission for Environmental Cooperation. (1999). *North American Important Bird Areas: A directory of 150 Key Conservation Sites.* Montreal, Canada: CEC.

Cooper, A., Atkinson, A.E., Lee, W.G. & Worthy, T.H. (1993). Evolution of the moa and their effect on the New Zealand flora. *Trends in Ecology and Evolution,* 8, 433-437.

Cooper, A., Lalueza-Fox, C., Anderson, S., Rambaut, A., Austin, J. & Ward, R. (2001). Complete mitochondrial genome sequences of two extinct moas clarify ratite evolution. *Nature,* 409, 704-707.

Cooper, A. & Penny, D. (1997). Mass survival of birds across the Cretaceous-Tertiary boundary: molecular evidence. *Science,* 275, 1109-1113.

Coppack, T., Pulido, F. & Berthold, P. (2001). Periodic response to early hatching in a migratory bird species. *Oecologia*, **128**(2), 181-186.

Cordell, H.K., Herbert, N.G. & Pandolfi, F. (1999). The growing popularity of birding in the United States. *Birding*, **31**, 168-176.

Cordell, H.K., McDonald, B.L. & Lewis, B. (1996). United States of America. In *World leisure participation: free time in a global village*, ed. G. Cushman, A.J. Veal & J. Zuzanek, pp. 215-236. Oxford: CAB International.

Cornuet, J.M. & Luikart, G. (1996). Description and power analysis of two tests for detecting recent population bottlenecks from allele frequency data. *Genetics*, **144**, 2001-2014.

Cossons, E. (ed.) (1992). *Mauritian Wildlife Appeal Fund Report 1990-1992*. Tamarin, Mauritius.

Costanza, R., d'Arge, R., de Groot, R., Farber, S., Grasso, M., Hannon, B., Limburg, K., Naeem, S., O'Neill, R.V., Paruelo, J., Raskin, R.G., Sutton, P. & van den Belt, M. (1997). The value of the world's ecosystem services and natural capital. *Nature*, **387**, 253-260.

Costanza, R., Daly, H., Folke, C., Hawken, P, Holling, C.S., McMichael, A.J., Pimental, D., & Rapport, D. (2000). Managing our environmental portfolio. *BioScience*, **50**, 149-155.

Cote, I. & Sutherland, W.J. (1996). The effectiveness of removing predators to protect bird populations. *Conservation Biology*, **11**, 395-405.

Coulson, T., Mace, G.M., Hudson, E. & Possingham, H. (2001). The use and abuse of PVA. *Trends in Ecology and Evolution*, **16**, 219-221.

Cowling, R.M., Pressey, R.L., Lombard, A.T., Desmet, P.G. & Ellis, A.G. (1999). From representation to persistence: requirements for a sustainable system of conservation areas in the species-rich mediterranean-climate desert of southern Africa. *Diversity and Distributions*, **5**, 51-71.

Crabtree, J.R., Leat, P.M.K., Santarossa, J. & Thomson, K.J. (1994). The economic impact of wildlife sites in Scotland. *Journal of Rural Studies*, **10**, 61-72.

Cracraft, J. (1992). The species of the birds-of-paradise (Paradisaeidae): applying the phylogenetic species concept to a complex pattern of diversification. *Cladistics*, **8**, 1-43.

Craig, J.L. (1991). Are small populations viable? *Acta XX Congressus Internationalis Ornithologici*, **4**, 2546-2552.

Cramp, S. & Perrins, C.M. (1994). *Handbook of the birds of Europe, the Middle East and North Africa: the birds of the western Palearctic*. Vol. IX, buntings to new world warblers. Oxford: Oxford University Press.

Cramp, S., Bourne, W.R.P. & Saunders, D. (1974). *The seabirds of Britain and Ireland*. London: Collins.

Crandall, K.A., Bininda-Emonds, O.R.P., Mace, G.M. & Wayne, R.K. (2000). Considering evolutionary processes in conservation biology. *Trends in Ecology and Evolution*, **15**, 290-295.

Crick, H.Q.P. & Baillie, S.R. (1996). *A review of BTO's Nest Record Scheme*. British Trust for Ornithology, Research Report No. 159. Thetford: BTO.

Crick, H.Q.P. & Sparks, T.H. (1999). Climate change related to egg-laying trends. *Nature*, **399**, 423-424.

Crosby, M.J. (1994). Mapping the distributions of restricted-range birds to identify global conservation priorities. In *Mapping the diversity of nature*, ed. R.I. Miller, pp. 145-154. London: Chapman & Hall.

Crouchley, D. (1994). *Takahe Recovery Plan (Porphyrio [Notornis] mantelli)*.
    Threatened Species Recovery Plan Series, 12. Wellington: Department of
    Conservation.

Crowe, T.M., Essop, M.F., Allan, D.G. & Brooke, R.K. (1994). Overlooked units of
    comparative and conservation biology: a case study of a small African bustard,
    the Black Korhaan *Eupodotis afra*. *Ibis*, **136**, 166-175.

Croxall, J.P. & Prince, P.A. (1991). Population regulation of seabirds: Implications
    of their demography for conservation. In *Bird population studies*, ed. C.M.
    Perrins, J-D. Lebreton & G.J.M. Hirons, pp. 272-296. Oxford: Oxford
    University Press.

Croxall, J.P., Prince, P.A., Hunter, I., McInnes, S.J. & Copestake, P.G. (1984). The
    seabirds of the Antarctic Peninsula, islands of the Scotia Sea and Antarctic
    Continent between 80° W and 20° W: their status and conservation. In *Status
    and conservation of the world's seabirds*, ed. J.P. Croxall, P.G.H. Evans & R.W.
    Schreiber, pp. 635-664. Cambridge: ICBP.

Croxall, J.P., Rothery, P., Pickering, S.P.C. & Prince, P.A. (1990). Reproductive
    performance, recruitment and survival of Wandering Albatrosses *Diomedea
    exulans* at Bird Island, South Georgia. *Journal of Animal Ecology*, **59**,
    773-794.

Crozier, R.H. (1992). Genetic diversity and the agony of choice. *Biological
    Conservation*, **61**, 11-15.

Csuti, B., Polasky, S., Williams, P.H., Pressey, R.L., Camm, J.D., Kershaw, M.,
    Kiesler, A.R., Downs, B., Hamilton, R., Huso, M. & Sahr, K. (1997). A
    comparison of reserve selection algorithms using data on terrestrial vertebrates
    in Oregon. *Biological Conservation*, **80**, 83-97.

Cuff, J. & Rayment, M. (eds.) (1997). *Working with nature: economics, employment
    and conservation in Europe*. Brussels: BirdLife International.

Curnutt, J., Lockwood, J., Luh, H-K., Nott, P. & Russell, G. (1994). Hotspots and
    species diversity. *Nature*, **367**, 326-327.

Curry-Lindahl, K. (1981). *Bird migration in Africa, 1*. London: Academic Press.

Curtis, J.T. (1956). The modification of mid-latitude grasslands and forests by man.
    In *Man's role in changing the face of the Earth*, ed. W.L. Thomas, pp. 721-736.
    Chicago: University of Chicago Press.

Czech, B. (2000). Economic growth as the limiting factor for wildlife conservation.
    Wildlife Society Bulletin, **28**, 4-15.

da Fonseca, G.A.B., Balmford, A., Bibby, C., Boitani, L., Corsi, F., Brooks, T.,
    Gascon, C., Olivieri, S., Mittermeier, R.A., Burgess, N., Dinerstein, E., Olson,
    D., Hannah, L., Lovett, J., Moyer, D., Rahbek, C., Stuart, S. & Williams,
    P. (2000). Following Africa's lead in setting priorities. *Nature*, **405**, 393-394.

Daily, G.C. (ed.) (1997). *Nature's services: societal dependence on natural ecosystems*.
    Washington, DC: Island Press.

Dale, V.H. (1997). The relationship between land-use change and climate change.
    Ecological Applications, **7**, 753-769.

Daszak, P., Cunningham, A.A. & Hyatt, A.D. (2000). Emerging infectious diseases
    of wildlife - threats to biodiversity and human health. *Science*, **287**, 443-449.

Davidson, E.A. & Hirsch, A.I. (2001). Fertile forest experiments. *Nature*, **411**,
    431-433.

Davidson, N. & Delany, S. (2000). *Biodiversity impacts of large dams: waterbirds*.
    Funded by UNEP, commission by IUCN from Wetlands International,

Wageningen, The Netherlands. Contributing paper for World Commission on Dams. Thematic Review II.1: Ecosystems (http://www.dams.org).

Day, J.C., Hodgson, M.S. & Rossiter, N. (1995). *The atlas of breeding birds in Northumbria*. Northumberland, UK: Northumberland & Tyneside Bird Club.

Day, J.R. & Possingham, H.P. (1995). A stochastic metapopulation model with variability in patch size and position. *Theoretical Population Biology*, **48**, 333-360.

de Iongh, H. (1983). Is there still hope for the Bali mynah? *Tigerpaper*, **10**, 28-32.

de Kroon, H., van Groenendael, J. & Erlen, J. (2000). Elasticities: a review of methods and model limitations. *Ecology*, **81**, 607-618.

Delaney, S., Reyes, C., Hubert, E., Pihl, S., Rees, E., Haanstra, L. & Van Strien, A. (1999). *Results from the International Waterbird Census in the Western Palearctic and Southwest Asia 1995 and 1996*. Wetlands International Publication No. 54. Wageningen: Wetlands International.

Dennis, M.K. (1996). *Tetrad atlas of the breeding birds of Essex*. Essex, UK: Essex Birdwatching Society.

DeSante, D.F., Burton, K.M. & Williams, O.E. (1993). The Monitoring Avian Productivity and Survivorship (MAPS) program second (1992) annual report. *Bird Populations*, **1**, 1-28.

DeSante, D.F. & Rosenberg, D.K. (1998). What do we need to monitor in order to manage landbirds? In *Avian conservation: research and management*, ed. J.M. Marzluff & R. Sallabanks, pp. 93-110. Washington, DC: Island Press.

Dhondt, A. A. (1989). Blue tit. In *Lifetime Reproduction in Birds*, ed. I. Newton, pp. 15-34. London: Academic Press.

Diamond, A.W. & Filion, F.L. (eds.) (1987). *The value of Birds*. ICBP technical publication no. 6. Cambridge: International Council for Bird Preservation.

Diamond, J.M. (1986). The design of a nature reserve system for Indonesian New Guinea. In *Conservation biology: the science of scarcity and diversity*, ed. M.E. Soulé, pp. 485-503. Sunderland, MA: Sinauer Associates.

Dinerstein, E., Olson, D.M., Graham, D.J., Webster, A.L., Primm, S.A., Bookbinder, M.P. & Ledec, G. (1995). *A conservation assessment of the terrestrial ecoregions of Latin America*. Washington, DC: The World Bank.

Dinerstein, E. & Wikramanayake, E.D. (1993). Beyond hotspots–how to prioritize investments to conserve biodiversity in the Indo-Pacific region. *Conservation Biology*, **7**, 53-65.

Dizon, A.E., Lockyer, C., Perrin, W.F., Demaster, D.P. & Sisson, J. (1992). Rethinking the stock concept: a phylogeographic approach. *Conservation Biology*, **6**, 24-36.

Dobson, A.P., Rodriguez, J.P., Roberts, W.M. & Wilcove, D.S. (1997). Geographic distribution of endangered species in the United States. *Science*, **275**, 550-553.

Donald, P.F. & Fuller, R.F. (1998). Ornithological atlas data: a review of uses and limitations. *Bird Study*, **45**, 129-145.

Donald, P.F., Green, R.E. & Heath, M.F. (2001). Agricultural intensification and the collapse of Europe's farmland bird populations. *Proceedings of the Royal Society of London B*, **268**, 25-29.

Drechsler, M. (2000). A model-based decision aid for species protection under uncertainty. *Biological Conservation*, **94**, 23-30.

Drechsler, M., Burgman, M.A. & Menkhorst, P.W. (1998). Uncertainty in population dynamics and its consequences for the management of the Orange-bellied Parrot *Neophema chrysogaster. Biological Conservation*, **84**, 269–281.

Drennan, S.R. (1996). *Field notes: the ninety-sixth Christmas bird count*. New York: National Audubon Society.

Dudley, N. (1987). *Cause for concern: an analysis of air pollution damage and natural habitats*. London: Friends of the Earth.

Dunning, J.B. Jr, Borgella, R., Clements, K. & Meffe, G.K. (1995a). Patch isolation, corridor effects, and colonization by a resident sparrow in a managed pine woodland. *Conservation Biology*, **9**, 542–550.

Dunning, J.B., Danielson, B.J., Noon, B.R., Root, T.L., Lamberson, R.H. & Stevens, E. (1995b). Spatially explicit population models: current forms and future uses. *Ecological Applications*, **5**, 3–11.

Dvorak, M., Ranner, A. & Berg, H.M. (1993). *Atlas der brutvogel Österreichs*. Vienna: BirdLife Österreich.

Dye, C. & Reiter, P. (2000). Temperatures without fevers? *Science*, **289**, 1697–1698.

Dymond, J.N., Fraser, P.A. & Gantlett, S.J.M. (1989). *Rare birds in Britain and Ireland*. Calton, UK: Poyser.

Edwards, S.V., Arctander, P. & Wilson, A.C. (1991). Mitochondrial resolution of a deep branch in the genealogical tree for perching birds. *Proceedings of the Royal Society of London B*, **243**, 99–107.

Edwards-Jones, G., Davies, B. & Hussain, S. (2000). *Ecological economics*. Oxford: Blackwell.

Eeley, H.A.C., Lawes, M.J. & Reyers, B. (2001). Priority areas for the conservation of subtropical indigenous forest in southern Africa: A case study from KwaZulu-Natal. *Biodiversity and Conservation*, **10**, 1221–1246.

Ehrlich, P.R. (1994). Energy use and biodiversity loss. *Philosophical Transactions of the Royal Society of London B*, **344**, 99–104.

Empson, R.A. & Miskelly, C. (1999). The risks, costs and benefits of using brodifacoum to eradicate rats from Kapiti Island. *Journal of the New Zealand Ecological Society*, **23**, 241–254.

Engbring, J. & Pratt, H.D. (1985). Endangered birds in Micronesia: their history, status and future prospects. *Bird Conservation*, **2**, 71–105.

Erasmus, B.F.N., Freitag, S., Gaston, K.J., Erasmus, B.H. & van Jaarsveld, A.S. (1999). Scale and conservation planning in the real world. *Proceedings of the Royal Society of London B*, **266**, 315–319.

Erwin, T.L. (1991). An evolutionary basis for conservation strategies. *Science*, **253**, 750–752.

Evans, A.D. (1997a). Cirl buntings in Britain. *British Birds*, **90**, 267–282.

Evans, A.D. (1997b). The importance of mixed farming for seed-eating birds in the UK. In *Farming and birds in Europe: the Common Agricultural Policy and its implications for bird conservation*, ed. D.J. Pain & M.W Pienkowski, pp. 331–357. London: Academic Press.

Evans, M.I. (1994). *Important Bird Areas in the Middle East*. Cambridge: BirdLife International.

Evans, P.R. (1997). Migratory birds and climate change. In *Past and future rapid environmental changes: the spatial and evolutionary responses of terrestrial biota*, ed. B. Huntley, C. Cramer, A.V. Morgan, H.C. Prentice & J.R.M. Allen, pp. 227-238. NATO ASI Series. Series I: Global Environmental Change, Vol. 47. Berlin: Springer-Verlag.

EWNHS (1996). *Important Bird Areas of Ethiopia*. Addis Ababa: Ethiopian Wildlife & Natural History Society.

Fahrig, L. (1997). Relative effects of habitat loss and fragmentation on population extinction. *Journal of Wildlife Management*, **61**, 603-610.

Fahrig, L. & Merriam, G. (1994). Conservation of fragmented populations. *Conservation Biology*, **8**, 50-59.

Faith, D.P. (1992). Conservation evaluation and phylogenetic diversity. *Biological Conservation*, **61**, 1-10.

Faith, D.P. (1994). Phylogenetic pattern and the quantification of organismal diversity. *Philosophical Transactions of the Royal Society Series B*, **345**, 45-58.

Faith, D.P. & Norris, R. (1989). Correlation of environmental variables with patterns of distribution and abundance of common and rare freshwater macroinvertebrates. *Biological Conservation*, **50**, 77-89.

Faith, D.P. & Walker, P.A. (1996). How do indicator groups provide information about the relative biodiversity of different sets of areas?: on hotspots, complementarity and pattern-based approaches. *Biodiversity Letters*, **3**, 18-25.

Fanshawe, J.F. & Bennun, L.A. (1991). Bird conservation in Kenya: creating a national strategy. *Bird Conservation International*, **1**, 293-315.

FCCP (1998). *Framework Convention on Climate Change FCCP/CP/1997/7/Add1*. 18 March 1998. Report on the conference of the parties on its third session held at Kyoto from 1-11 December 1997. United Nations.

Ferrier, S., Pressey, R.L. & Barrett, T.W. (2000). A new predictor of the irreplaceability of areas for achieving a conservation goal, its application to real-world planning, and a research agenda for further refinement. *Biological Conservation*, **93**, 303-325.

Fewster, R.M., Buckland, S.T., Siriwardena, G.M., Baillie, S.R. & Wilson, J.D. (2000). Analysis of population trends for farmland birds using generalized additive models. *Ecology*, **81**, 1970-1984.

Finkel, E. (1998). Ecology: software helps Australia manage forest debate. *Science*, **281**, 1789-1791.

Finlayson, M., Hollis, T. & Davis, T. (1992). *Managing Mediterranean Wetlands and their Birds*. Special Publication No. 20. International Waterfowl and Wetlands Research Bureau.

Fishpool, L.D.C. (ed.) (2001). *Important Bird Areas in Africa and associated islands; priority sites for conservation*. Cambridge: Birdlife International.

Fitter, R. & Fitter, M. (ed.) (1987). *The road to extinction*. Gland, Switzerland: IUCN.

Fjeldså, J. (2000). The relevance of systematics in choosing priority areas for global conservation. *Environmental Conservation*, **27**, 67-75.

Fjeldså, J., Burgess, N., de Klerk, H., Hansen, L. & Rahbek, C. (1999). Are Endemic Bird Areas the best targets for conservation? An assessment using all landbird distributions of two continents. In *Proceedings of the 22nd International Ornithological Congress, Durban*, ed. N.J. Adams & R.H. Slotow, pp. 2271-2285. Johannesburg: BirdLife South Africa.

Fjeldså, J. & Rahbek, C. (1998). Continent-wide conservation priorities and diversification processes. In *Conservation in a changing world*, ed. G.M. Mace, A. Balmford & J.R. Ginsberg, pp. 139–160. Cambridge: Cambridge University Press.

Flack, J.A.D. (1978). Interisland transfers of New Zealand Robins. In *Endangered birds. Management techniques for preserving threatened species*, ed. S.A. Temple, pp. 365–372. Wisconsin: University of Wisconsin Press.

Flashpohler, D.J., Bub, B.R. & Kaplin, B.A. (2000). Application of conservation biology research to management. *Conservation Biology*, **14**, 1898–1902.

Flather, C.H., Wilson, K.R., Dean, D.J. & McComb, W.C. (1997). Identifying gaps in conservation networks: of indicators and uncertainty in geographic-based analyses. *Ecological Applications*, **7**, 531–542.

Fleming, C.A. (1962). History of the New Zealand land bird fauna. *Notornis*, **9**, 270–274.

Flint, V.E., Kostin, Y.V., Boehme, R.F. & Kuznetsov, A.A. (1987). *A field guide to birds of Russia and adjacent territories*. Princeton, NJ: Princeton University Press.

Foppen, R., ter Braak, C.J.F., Verboom, J. & Reijnen, R. (1999a). Dutch Sedge warblers *Acrocephalus schoenabaenus* and West African rainfall: empirical data and simulation modelling show population resilience in fragmented landscape. *Ardea*, **87**, 113–127.

Foppen, R., Geilen, N. & van der Sluis, T. (1999b). *Towards a coherent habitat network for the Rhine*. Institute for Forestry and Nature Research report 99/1. The Netherlands: Institute for Forestry and Nature Research.

Foppen, R. (2001). *Bridging gaps in fragmented marshland. Applying landscape ecology for bird conservation*. Thesis, Wageningen University.

Forman, R.T.T. (1995). *Land mosaics*. Cambridge: Cambridge University Press.

Forman, R.T.T., & Deblinger, R.D. (2000). The ecological road-effect zone of a Massachusetts (U.S.A.) suburban highway. *Conservation Biology*, **14**, 36–46.

Frankel, O.H. & Soulé, M.E. (1981). *Conservation and evolution*. Cambridge: Cambridge University Press.

Frankham, R. (1997). Do island populations have less genetic variation than mainland populations? *Heredity*, **78**, 311–327.

Franklin, J.F. (1993). Preserving biodiversity: species, ecosystems or landscapes? *Ecological Applications*, **3**, 202–205.

Fraser, W.R., Trivelpiece, W.Z., Ainley, D.G. & Trivelpiece, S.G. (1992). Increases in Antarctic penguin populations: reduced competition with whales or a loss of sea ice due to environmental warming? *Polar Biology*, **11**, 525–531.

Freitag, S. & van Jaarsveld, A.S. (1997). Relative occupancy, endemism, taxonomic distinctiveness and vulnerability: prioritizing regional conservation actions. *Biodiversity and Conservation*, **6**, 211–232.

Fretwell, S.D. & Lucas, H.L. (1969). On territorial behavior and other factors influencing habitat distribution in birds. I. Theoretical development. *Acta Biotheoretica*, **19**, 16–36.

Frost, P.G.H., Siegfried, W.R. & Cooper, J. (1976). Conservation of the Jackass Penguin (*Spheniscus demersus* L.) *Biological Conservation*, **9**, 79–99.

Fry, A.J. & Zink, R.M. (1998). Geographic analysis of nucleotide diversity and song sparrow (Aves: *Emberizidae*) population history. *Molecular Ecology*, **7**, 1303–1313.

Fuller, E. (1987). *Extinct birds*. London: Viking/Rainbird.

Furness, R.W. & Camphuysen, K. (1997). Seabirds as monitors of the marine environment. *ICES Journal of Marine Science*, **54**, 726-737.

Furness, R.W. & Greenwood, J.J.D. (eds.) (1993). *Birds as monitors of environmental change*. London: Chapman & Hall.

Fyfe, R.W. (1978). Reintroducing endangered birds to the wild - a review. In *Endangered birds. Management techniques for preserving threatened species*, ed. S.A. Temple, pp. 323-329. Wisconsin: University of Wisconsin Press.

Gadgil, M. (1996). Managing biodiversity. In *Biodiversity: a biology of numbers and difference*, ed. K.J. Gaston, pp. 345-366. Oxford: Blackwell Science.

Galbreath, R. (1993). *Working for wildlife - a history of the New Zealand Wildlife Service*. Wellington: Bridget Williams Books Ltd.

Gärdenfors, U., Rodriguez, J.P., Hilton-Taylor, C., Hyslop, C., Mace, G., Molur, S. & Poss, S. (1999). Draft guidelines for the application of IUCN Red List criteria at national and regional levels. *Species*, **31-32**, 58-70.

Gardner, R.H., O'Neill, R.V., Turner, M.G. & Dale, V.H. (1989). Quantifying scale-dependent effects of animal movement with simple percolation models. *Landscape Ecology*, **3**, 217-227.

Garshelis, D.L. (2000). Delusions in habitat evaluation: measuring use, selection, and importance. In *Research techniques in animal ecology: controversies and consequences*, ed. L. Boitani & T.K. Fuller, pp. 111-164. New York: Columbia University Press.

Gaston, K.J. (1994). *Rarity*. London: Chapman & Hall.

Gaston, K.J. (1996a). What is Biodiversity? In *Biodiversity: a biology of numbers and difference*, ed. K.J. Gaston, pp. 1-9. Oxford: Blackwell.

Gaston, K.J. (1996b). Species richness: measure and measurement. In *Biodiversity: a biology of numbers and difference*, ed. K.J. Gaston, pp. 77-113. Oxford: Blackwell.

Gaston, K.J. (1996c). Biodiversity - congruence. *Progress in Physical Geography*, **20**, 105-112.

Gaston, K.J. (1996d). Spatial covariance in the species richness of higher taxa. In *Aspects of the genesis and maintenance of biological diversity*, ed. M.E. Hochberg, J. Clobert & R. Barbault, pp. 221-242. Oxford: Oxford University Press.

Gaston, K.J. & Blackburn, T.M. (1997). Evolutionary age and risk of extinction in the global avifauna. *Evolutionary Ecology*, **11**, 557-565.

Gaston, K.J. & Williams, P.H. (1993). Mapping the world's species - the higher taxon approach. *Biodiversity Letters*, **1**, 2-8.

Gaston, K.J. & Williams, P.H. (1996). Spatial patterns in taxonomic diversity. In *Biodiversity: a biology of numbers and difference*, ed. K.J. Gaston, pp. 202-229. Oxford: Blackwell Science.

Gates, S., Gibbons, D.W. & Marchant, J.H. (1993). Population estimates for breeding birds in Britain and Ireland. In *The new atlas of breeding birds in Britain and Ireland: 1988-1991*, ed. D.W. Gibbons, J.B. Reid & R.A. Chapman. London: T. & A.D. Poyser.

Gibbons, D.W. & Avery, M.I. (2001). Birds. In *The Changing Wildlife of Great Britain and Ireland*, ed. D. Hawksworth, pp. 373-404. London: Taylor & Francis/ Systematics Association.

Gibbons, D.W., Avery, M.I., Baillie, S., Gregory, R., Kirby, J., Porter, R., Tucker, G. & Williams, G. (1996a). Bird species of conservation concern in the United

Kingdom, Channel Islands and Isle of Man: revising the red data list. *RSPB Conservation Review*, **10**, 7-18.

Gibbons, D.W., Bainbridge, I.P., Mudge, G.P., Tharme, A.P. & Ellis, P.M. (1997). The status and distribution of the Red-throated Diver *Gavia stellata* in Britain in 1994. *Bird Study*, **44**, 194-205.

Gibbons, D.W., Gates, S., Green, R.E., Fuller, R.J. & Fuller, R.M. (1995). Buzzards *Buteo buteo* and Ravens *Corvus corax* in the uplands of Britain: limits to distribution and abundance. *Ibis*, **137**, S75-S84.

Gibbons, D.W., Hill, D.A. & Sutherland, W.J. (1996b). Birds. In *Ecological census techniques: a handbook*, ed. W.J. Sutherland, pp. 227-259. Cambridge: Cambridge University Press.

Gibbons, D.W., Reid, J.B. & Chapman, R.A. (eds.) (1993). *The new atlas of breeding birds in Britain and Ireland: 1988-1991*. London: T. & A.D. Poyser.

Gichuki, C.M. (2000). Community participation in the protection of Kenya's wetlands. *Ostrich*, **71**, 122-125.

Gilbert, G., Gibbons, D.W. & Evans, J. (1998). *Bird monitoring methods: a manual of techniques for key UK species*. Sandy, UK: Royal Society for the Protection of Birds.

Gilbert, G., Tyler, G.A. & Smith, K.W. (2001). Local annual survival of booming male Great Bittern *Botaurus stellaris* in Britain, in the period 1990-1999. *Ibis* (in press).

Gill, J.A., Norris, K. & Sutherland, W.J. (2001). Depletion models can predict shorebird distribution at different spatial scales. *Proceedings of the Royal Society of London B*, **268**, 369-378.

Gilpin, M. (1996). Forty-eight parrots and the origins of population viability analysis. *Conservation Biology*, **10**, 1491-1493.

Ginsberg, J.R. (1993). Can we build an Ark? *Trends in Ecology and Evolution*, **8**, 4-6.

Githira, M., Bennun, L.A. & Len, L. (2002). Regeneration among bird-dispersed plants in a fragmented Afro-tropical forest, south-east Kenya. *Journal of Tropical Biology* (in press).

Glowka, L., Burhenne-Guilman, F., Synge, H., McNeely, J.A. & Gundling, L. (1994). *A guide to the convention on biological diversity*. Gland, Switzerland: IUCN.

Glowka, L. & Shine, C. (2000). *Reviewing laws and institutions to promote the conservation and wise use of wetlands*. Handbook No. 3. Gland, Switzerland: Ramsar Convention Secretariat.

Godoy, R., Wilkie, D., Overman, H., Cubas, A., Cubas, G., Demmer, J., McSweeney, K. & Brokaw, N. (2000). Valuation of consumption and sale of forest goods from a Central American rain forest. *Nature*, **406**, 62-63.

Good, S.V., Williams, D.F., Ralls, K. & Fleischer, R.C. (1997). Population structure of *Dipodomys ingens* (Heteromyidae): the role of spatial heterogeneity in maintaining genetic diversity. *Evolution*, **51**, 1296-1310.

Goss-Custard, J.D. (1980). Competition for food and interference among waders. *Ardea*, **68**, 31-52.

Goss-Custard, J.D. (1996). *The oystercatcher: from individuals to populations*. Oxford: Oxford University Press.

Goss-Custard, J.D., Caldow, R.W.G., Clarke, R.T., Durell, S.E.A.le V.dit & Sutherland, W.J. (1995a). Deriving population parameters from individual variations in foraging behaviour: I. Empirical game theory distribution model of oystercatchers *Haematopus ostralegus* feeding on mussels *Mytilus edulis*. *Journal of Animal Ecology*, **64**, 265–276.

Goss-Custard, J.D., Caldow, R.W.G., Clarke, R.T., Durell, S.E.A.le V.dit, Urfi, J. & West, A.D. (1995b). Consequences of habitat loss and change to populations of wintering migratory birds: predicting the local and global effects from studies of individuals. *Ibis*, **137**, S56–S66.

Goss-Custard, J.D., Caldow, R.W.G., Clarke, R.T. & West, A.D. (1995c). Deriving population parameters from individual variations in foraging behaviour: II. Model tests and population parameters. *Journal of Animal Ecology*, **64**, 277–289.

Goss-Custard, J.D., Clarke, R.T., Briggs, K.B., Ens, B.J., Exo, K-M., Smit, C., Beintema, A.J., Caldow, R.W.G., Catt, D.C., Clark, N., Durell, S.E.A.le V.dit, Harris, M.P., Hulscher, J.B., Meininger, P.L., Picozzi, N., Prys-Jones, R., Safriel, U. & West, A.D. (1995d). Population consequences of winter habitat loss in a migratory shorebird. I. Estimating model parameters. *Journal of Applied Ecology*, **32**, 320–336.

Goss-Custard, J.D., Clarke, R.T., Durell, S.E.A.le V.dit, Caldow, R.W.G. & Ens, B.J. (1995e). Population consequences of winter habitat loss in a migratory shorebird. II. Model predictions. *Journal of Applied Ecology*, **32**, 337–351.

Goss-Custard, J.D., Stillman, R.A., West, A.D., McGrorty, S., Durell, S.E.A.le V.dit & Caldow, R.W.C. (2000). Role of behavioural models in predicting the impact of harvesting on populations. In *Behaviour and conservation*, ed. M. Gosling & W.J. Sutherland, pp. 65–82. Cambridge: Cambridge University Press.

Goss-Custard, J.D. & Sutherland, W.J. (1997). Individual behaviour, populations and conservation. In *Behavioural ecology: an evolutionary approach*, 4th edn, ed. J.R. Krebs & N.B. Davies, pp. 373–395. Oxford: Blackwell Science.

Goss-Custard, J.D. & West, A.D. (1997). The concept of carrying capacity and shorebirds. In *Effect of habitat loss and change on waterbirds*, ed. J.D. Goss-Custard, R. Rufino & A. Luis, pp. 52–62. London: The Stationary Office.

Government of Canada (1991). *The federal policy on wetland conservation*, 1991. Ottawa: Environment Canada.

Grant, A. & Benton, T.G. (2000). Elasticity analysis for density-dependent populations in stochastic environments. *Ecology*, **81**, 680–693.

Green, R.E. (1995). Diagnosing causes of bird population declines. *Ibis*, **137**(Suppl.), S47–S55.

Green, R.E., Harley, M., Spalding, M. & Zöckler, C. (eds.) (2001). *Impacts of climate change on wildlife*. Sandy: RSPB.

Green, R.E. & Hirons, G.J.M. (1991). The relevance of population studies to the conservation of threatened birds. In *Bird population studies: relevance to conservation and management*, ed. C.M. Perrins, J-D. Lebreton & G.J.M. Hirons, pp. 594–636. Oxford: Oxford University Press.

Green, R.E., Pienkowski, M.W. & Love, J.A. (1996). Long-term viability of the re-introduced population of the white-tailed sea eagle *Haliaeetus albicilla* in Scotland. *Journal of Applied Ecology*, **33**, 357–368.

Greenaway, J.C. Jr (1967). *Extinct and vanishing birds of the world*, 2nd edn. New York: Dover Publications Inc.

Greenberg, R., Bichier, P., Cruz Angon, A. & Reitsma, R. (1997). Bird populations in shade and sun coffee plantations in central Guatemala. *Conservation Biology*, **11**, 448–459.

Greenwood, A.G. (1996). The echo responds – a partnership between conservation biology, aviculture and veterinary science. *Proceedings of the International Aviculturists Society*, January 1996, pp. 6–7. Orlando, Florida.

Greenwood, J.J.D. (1996). Basic techniques. In *Ecological census techniques: a handbook*, ed. W.J. Sutherland, pp. 11–110. Cambridge: Cambridge University Press.

Greenwood, J.J.D., Baillie, S.R., Crick, H.Q.P., Marchant, J.H. & Peach, W.J. (1993). Integrated population monitoring: detecting the effects of diverse changes. In *Birds as monitors of environmental change*, ed. R.W. Furness & J.J.D. Greenwood, pp. 267–342. London: Chapman & Hall.

Greenwood, P.J., Harvey, P.H. & Perrins, C.M. (1978). Inbreeding and dispersal in the great tit. *Nature*, **271**, 52–54.

Gregory, R.D. & Baillie, S.R. (1998). Large-scale habitat use of some declining British birds. *Journal of Applied Ecology*, **35**, 785–799.

Gregory, R.D., Gibbons, D.W., Impey, A. & Marchant, J.H. (1999). *Generation of the headline indicator of wild bird populations*. BTO Research Report no. 221. Thetford: British Trust for Ornithology.

Gretton, A. (1991). *The ecology and conservation of the Slender-billed Curlew* (Numenius tenuirostris). Cambridge: International Council for Bird Preservation.

Grier, J.W., Gramlich, F.J., Mattsson, J., Mathisen, J.E., Kussman, J.V., Elder, J.B. & Green, N.F. (1983). The bald eagle in the northern United States. *Bird Conservation*, **1**, 41–66.

Griffith, B., Scott, J.M., Carpenter, J.W. & Reed, C. (1993). Animal translocations and potential disease transmission. *Journal of Zoo, and Wildlife Medicine*, **24**, 231–236.

Grimmett, R.F.A & Jones, T.A. (eds.) (1989). *Important Bird Areas of Europe*. ICBP Technical Publication No. 9. Cambridge: International Council for Bird Preservation.

Groombridge, J.J., Jones, C.G., Bruford, M.W. & Nichols, R.A. (2000). 'Ghost' alleles of the Mauritius kestrel. *Nature*, **403**, 616.

Grubb, T.C. Jr & Doherty, P.F. Jr. (1999). On home-range gap-crossing. *Auk*, **116**, 618–628.

Haas, C.A. (1995). Dispersal and use of corridors by birds in wooded patches on an agricultural landscape. *Conservation Biology*, **9**, 845–854.

Hackel, J.D. (1999). Community conservation and the future of Africa's wildlife. *Conservation Biology*, **13**, 726–734.

Hagemeijer, W.J.M. & Blair, M.J. (1997). *The EBCC atlas of European breeding birds: their distribution and abundance*. London: T. & A.D. Poyser.

Hagen, D., Vincent, J. & Welles, P. (1992). Benefits of preserving old growth forests and the spotted owl. *Contemporary Policy Issues*, **10**, 13–25.

Haig, S.M., Beltoff, J.R. & Allen, D.H. (1993). Population viability analysis for a small population of red-cockaded woodpeckers and an evaluation of enhancement strategies. *Conservation Biology*, **7**, 289–301.

Haila Y. (1999). Islands and fragments. In *Maintaining biodiversity in forest ecosystems*, ed. M.L. Hunter, Jr, pp. 234–264. Cambridge: Cambridge University Press.

Halliday, T. (1978). *Vanishing birds – their natural history and conservation*. New Zealand: Hutchinson.

Halliday, T.R. (1980) The extinction of the passenger pigeon *Ectopistes migratorius* and its relevance to contemporary conservation. *Biological Conservation*, **17**, 157-161.

Hamilton, A., Cunningham, A., Byarugaba, D. & Kayanja, F. (2000). Conservation in a region of political instability: Bwindi Impenetrable Forest, Uganda. *Conservation Biology*, **14**, 1722-1725.

Hamilton, S. & Moller, H. (1995). Can PVA models using computer packages offer useful conservation advice? Sooty shearwaters *Puffinus griseus* in New Zealand as a case study. *Biological Conservation*, **73**, 107-117.

Hammond, R.L., Mohammed, O.B., Macasero, W., Flores, B., Wacher, T. & Bruford, M.W. (2001). Phylogenetic reanalysis of the Saudi gazelle and its implications for conservation. *Conservation Biology*, (in press).

Hancock, M.H., Baines, D., Gibbons, D.W., Etheridge, B. & Shepherd, M. (1999). The status of male black grouse *Tetrao tetrix* in Britain in 1995-96. *Bird Study*, **46**, 1-15.

Hanski, I. (1999). *Metapopulation ecology*. New York: Oxford University Press.

Hanski, I. & Ovaskainen, O. (2000). The metapopulation capacity of a fragmented landscape. *Nature*, **404**, 755-758.

Hanski, I. & Simberloff, D. (1997). The metapopulation approach, its history, conceptual domain, and application to conservation. In *Metapopulation biology: ecology, genetics and evolution*, ed. I. Hanski & M. Gilpin, pp. 5-26. San Diego: Academic Press.

Härlid, A. & Arnason, U. (1999). Analysis of mitochondrial DNA nest ratite birds within the Neognathae: supporting a neotenous origin of ratite morphological characters. *Proceedings of the Royal Society of London B*, **266**, 305-309.

Harper, D.M., Adatia, R., Virani, M. & Henderson, I. (1998). Avian indicators of habitat change and conservation requirements in tropical wetlands. *Ostrich*, **69**, 430.

Harrison, J.A., Allan, D.G., Underhill, L.G., Herremans, M., Tree, A.J., Parker,V. & Brown, C.J. (eds.) (1997). *The Atlas of Southern African Birds*. Johannesburg: Birdlife South Africa.

Hayman, P., Marchant, J. & Prater, T. (1986). *Shorebirds: an identification guide to waders of the world*. London: Croom Helm.

Hazevoet, C.J., Monteiro, L.R. & Ratcliffe, N. (1999). Rediscovery of the Cape Verde cane warbler *Acrocephalus brevipennis* on São Nicolau in February 1998. *Bull. B.O.C.*, **119**, 68-71.

Heath, M., Borggreve, C., Peet, N. & Hagemeijer, W. (2000a). *European bird populations: estimates and trends*. BirdLife Conservation Series No. 10. Cambridge: BirdLife International.

Heath, M.F. & Evans, M.I. (eds.) (2000). *Important Bird Areas in Europe: priority sites for conservation*. Cambridge: BirdLife International.

Heath, M., Evans, M.I., Hoccom, D.G., Payne, A.J. & Peet, N.B. (2000b). *Important Bird Areas in Europe: priority sites for conservation*. BirdLife Conservation Series No. 8. Cambridge: BirdLife International.

Hedges, S.B., Parker, P.H., Sibley, C.G. & Kumar, S. (1996). Continental breakup and the ordinal diversification of birds and mammals. *Nature*, **381**, 226-229.

Hedrick, P.W., Lacy, R.C., Allendorf, F.W. & Soulé, M.E. (1996). Directions in conservation biology: comments on Caughley. *Conservation Biology*, **10**, 1312-1320.

Hedrick, P.W. & Parker, K.M. (1998). MHC variation in the endangered Gila topminnow. *Evolution*, **52**, 194–199.

Heijnsbergen, P. van (1997). *International legal protection of wild fauna and flora*. Amsterdam: IOS Press.

Heinzel, H., Fitter, R. & Parslow, J. (1998). *Collins pocket guide to the birds of Britain & Europe*. London: HarperCollins.

Hejl, S.J. & Granillo, K.M. (1998). What managers really need from avian researchers. In *Avian conservation: research and management*, ed. J.M. Marzluff & R. Sallabanks, pp. 431–438. Washington, DC: Island Press.

Henderson, I.M. (1994). Population viability analysis of Blue Duck (*Hymenolaimus malacorhynchos*). Conservation Advisory Science Notes, 104. Wellington: Department of Conservation, NZ.

Hendry, A.P., Vamosi, S.M., Latham, S.J., Heilbuth, J.C. & Day, T. (2000). Questioning species realities. *Conservation Genetics*, **1**, 67–76.

Heppell, S.S., Walters, J.R. & Crowder, L.B. (1994). Evaluating management alternatives for Red-cockaded Woodpeckers: a modeling approach. *Journal of Wildlife Management*, **58**, 479–487.

Hill, S. & Hill, J. (1987). *Richard Henry of Resolution Island: a biography*. Dunedin, New Zealand: John McIndoe.

Hinsley, S.A., Bellamy, P.A. & Newton, I. (1995). Bird species turnover and stochastic extinction in woodland fragments. *Ecography*, **18**, 41–50.

Hiraldo, F., Negro, J.J., Donazar, J.A. & Gaona, P. (1996). A demographic model for a population of the endangered lesser kestrel in southern Spain. *Journal of Applied Ecology*, **33**, 1085–1093.

Hobbs, R.J. & Saunders, D.A. (eds.) (1993). *Reintegrating fragmented landscapes: towards sustainable production and nature conservation*. New York: Springer-Verlag.

Hockey, P.A.R., Underhill, L.G., Neatherway, M. & Ryan, P.G. (1980). *Atlas of the birds of the southwestern Cape*. Cape Town: Cape Bird Club.

Holdgate, M. (1996). *From care to action*. London: Earthscan.

Honey, M. (1999). *Ecotourism and sustainable development: who owns Paradise?* Washington, DC: Island Press.

Houghton, J. (1997). *Global warming*. Cambridge: Cambridge University Press.

Houghton, J., Callander, B.A. & Varney, S.K. (1992). *The supplementary report to the IPCC assessment*. Cambridge: Cambridge University Press.

Howard, P.C. (1991). *Nature Conservation in Uganda's Tropical Forest Reserves*. Gland, Switzerland: IUCN.

Howard, P.C., Viskanic, P., Davenport, T.R.B., Kigenyi, F.W., Baltzer, M., Dickinson, C.J., Lwanga, J.S., Matthews, R.A. & Balmford, A. (1998). Complementarity and the use of indicators for reserve selection in Uganda. *Nature*, **394**, 472–475.

Hughes, A.L. (1999). Differential human impact on the survival of genetically distinct avian lineages. *Bird Conservation International*, **9**, 147–154.

Hughes, J.B., Daily, G.C. & Ehrlich, P.R. (1997). Population diversity: its extent and extinction. *Science*, **278**, 689–691.

Hulme, M. & Jenkins, G.J. (1998). *Climate change scenarios for the UK: scientific report*. UKCIP Technical Report No. 1. Norwich: Climate Research Unit.

Hunter, M.L. Jr (1993). Natural disturbance regimes as spatial models for managing boreal forests. *Biological Conservation*, **65**, 115–120.

Hunter, M.L. Jr (1996). *Fundamentals of Conservation Biology*. Oxford: Blackwell Science.

Hunter, M.L. Jr & Hutchinson, A. (1994). The virtues and shortcomings of parochialism: conserving species that are locally rare, but globally common. *Conservation Biology*, **8**, 1163-1165.

Huntley, B. (1995). Plant species' responses to climate change: implications for the conservation of European birds. *Ibis*, **137**, S127-S138.

Huntley, B. (1998). The dynamic response of plants to environmental change and the resulting risks of extinction. In *Conservation in a changing world*, ed. G.M. Mace, A. Balmford & J.R. Ginsberg, pp. 69-85. Cambridge: Cambridge University Press.

ICBP (1992). *Putting biodiversity on the map: priority areas for global conservation*. Cambridge: International Council for Bird Preservation.

ILOG (1999). *CPLEX 6.5*. Gentilly: ILOG.

Imber, M.J., Taylor, G.A., Grant, A.D. & Munn, A. (1994). Chatham Island taiko *Pterodroma magentae* management and research, 1987-1993: predator control, productivity, and breeding biology. *Notornis (Supplement)*, **41**, 61-68.

IPCC (1990). *Climate change: the IPCC scientific assessment*, ed. J.T. Houghton, G.J. Jenkins & J.J. Ephramus Cambridge: Cambridge University Press.

IPCC (2001a). *Climate Change 2001: impacts, adaptation and vulnerability: summary for policymakers*. A Report of Working Group II of the Intergovernmental Panel on Climate Change. Geneva, Switzerland, 13-16 February 2001.

IPCC (2001b). *Climate Change 2001 The Scientific Basis*. A Report of Working Group I of the Intergovernmental Panel on Climate Change. Geneva, Switzerland, 13-16 February 2001.

IUCN (1994). *IUCN Red List Categories*. Cambridge: International Union for the Conservation of Nature and Natural Resources, The World Conservation Union.

IUCN (1995). *IUCN Guidelines for re-introductions*. Gland, Switzerland: IUCN.

IUCN (1996). *IUCN Red List of Threatened Animals*. Gland, Switzerland: IUCN.

IUCN (1997). *1996 IUCN Red List of Threatened Animals*. Gland, Switzerland: IUCN.

IUCN (1998). *1997 United Nations List of Protected Areas*. Cambridge: WCMC/IUCN.

IUCN/UNEP/WWF (1980). *The World Conservation Strategy: Living Resource Conservation for Sustainable Development*. Gland, Switzerland: IUCN.

IUCN/UNEP/WWF (1991). *Caring for the Earth: A Strategy for Sustainable Living*. Gland, Switzerland: IUCN.

Jackson, C. (2000). Training Kenyan bird ringers. *Ostrich*, **71**, 342.

Jackson, J.A. (1978). Alleviating problems of competition, predation, parasitism, and disease in endangered birds. In *Endangered birds. Manangement techniques for preserving threatened species*, ed. S.A. Temple, pp. 75-84. Wisconsin: University of Wisconsin Press.

Jaffre, T., Bouchet, P. & Veillon, J-M. (1998). Threatened plants of New Caledonia: is the system of protected areas adequate? *Biodiversity and Conservation*, **7**, 109-115.

Jager, J.A.G. (2000). Landscape division, splitting index, and effective mesh size: new measures of landscape fragmentation. *Landscape Ecology*, **15**, 115-130.

James, A.N., Gaston, K.J. & Balmford, A. (1999). Balancing the Earth's accounts. *Nature*, **401**, 323-324.

James, A.N., Gaston, K.J. & Balmford, A. (2001). Can we afford biodiversity? *BioScience*, **51**, 43-52.

Janzen, D.H. (1986). The eternal external threat. In *Conservation biology: the science of scarcity and diversity*, ed. M.E. Soulé, pp. 286-303. Sunderland MA: Sinauer Associates.

Jenkins, R.E. Jr (1988). Information management for the conservation of biodiversity. In *Biodiversity*, ed. E.O. Wilson, pp. 231-239. Washington, DC: National Academy Press.

Jennings, M.D. (2000). Gap analysis: concepts, methods, and recent results. *Landscape Ecology*, **15**, 5-20.

Jepson, P. & Canney, S. (2001). Biodiversity hotspots: hot for what? *Global Ecology and Biogeography*, **10**, 225-227.

Jones, C.G. (1987). The larger land-birds of Mauritius. In *Studies of Mascarene Island birds*, ed. A.W. Diamond, pp. 208-300. Cambridge: Cambridge University Press.

Jones, C.G. (1990). Mauritius kestrel comeback. In *Mauritius Wildlife Appeal Fund Annual Report 1988/1989*, pp. 9-11. Mauritius: Mauritius Wildlife Appeal Fund.

Jones, C.G. (1998). Saved. *On the Edge*, **81**, 1-2.

Jones, C.G., Swinnerton, K., Hartley, J. & Mungroo Y. (1999). The restoration of the free-living populations of the Mauritius kestrel, (*Falco punctatus*), Pink pigeon, (*Columba mayeri*) and Echo parakeet, (*Psittacula eques*). Proceedings of The Seventh World Conference on Breeding Endangered Species, Cincinnati, Ohio, 22-26 May 1999, pp. 77-86.

Kanyamibwa, S., Schreider, A., Pradel, R. & Lebreton, J.D. (1990). Changes in adult annual survival rates in a western European population of the white stork *Ciconia ciconia. Ibis*, **132**, 27-35.

Kark, S., Alkon, P.U., Safriel, U.N. & Randi, E. (1999). Conservation priorities for chukar partridge in Israel based on genetic diversity across an ecological gradient. *Conservation Biology*, **13**, 542-552.

Kattan, G.H. (1992). Rarity and vulnerability: the birds of the Cordillera Central of Colombia. *Conservation Biology*, **6**, 64-70.

Kazmierczak, K. & van Perlo, B. (2000). *A field guide to birds of the Indian subcontinent*. Pica Press.

Kear, J. & Berger, A.J. (1980). *The Hawaiian Goose. An experiment in conservation*. Calton, UK: T. & A.D. Poyser.

Keller, L.F., Arcese, P., Smith, J.N.M., Hochachka, W.M. & Stearns, S.C. (1994). Selection against inbred song sparrows during a natural population bottleneck. *Nature*, **372**, 356-357.

Keller, L.F., Jeffery, K.J., Arcese, P., Beaumont, M.A., Hochachka, W.M., Smith, J.N.M. & Bruford, M.W. (2001). The dynamics of a natural population bottleneck: immigration and ephemerality. *Proceedings of the Royal Society of London B* (in press).

Kendall, B.E. (1998). Estimating the magnitude of environmental stochasticity in survivorship data. *Ecological Applications*, **8**, 184-193.

Kenward, R.E. & Marcström, V. (1988). How differential competence could sustain suppressive predation on birds. *Proceedings of the XIX International Ornithological Congress*, pp. 733-742.

Kerlinger, P. & Eubanks, T.L. (1995). Birding, conservation and economics. *Birding*, **27**, 21-23.

Kerr, J.T. (1997). Species richness, endemism, and the choice of areas for conservation. *Conservation Biology*, **11**, 1094-1100.

Khan, M.L., Menon, S. & Bawa, K.S. (1997). Effectiveness of the protected area network in biodiversity conservation: a case-study of Megahalaya State. *Biodiversity and Conservation*, **6**, 853-868.

King, W.B. (1980). Ecological basis of extinctions in birds. *Acta XVII Congressus Internationalis Ornithologici*, pp. 905-911.

Kirchman, J.J., Whittingham, L.A. & Sheldon, F.H. (2000). Relationships among cave swallow populations (*Petrochelidon fulva*) determined by comparisons of microsatellite and cytochome b data. *Molecular Phylogenetics and Evolution*, **14**, 107-121.

Kitching, I.J. (1996). Identifying complementary areas for conservation in Thailand: an example using owls, hawkmoths and tiger beetles. *Biodiversity and Conservation*, **5**, 841-858.

Kochert, M.N. & Collopy, M.W. (1998). Relevance of research to resource managers and policy-makers. In *Avian conservation: research and management*, ed. J.M. Marzluff & R. Sallabanks, pp. 423-430. Washington, DC: Island Press.

Komdeur, J. (1994). Conserving the Seychelles Warbler *Acrocephalus sechellensis* by translocation from Cousin Island to the islands of Aride and Cousine. *Biological Conservation*, **67**, 143-152.

Kraaijeveld, K. (2000). The phylogenetic species concept and its place in modern evolutionary thinking. *Ardea*, **88**, 265-267.

Krebs, C.J. (1991). The experimental paradigm and long-term population studies. *Ibis* (Suppl.), **133**, S3-S8.

Krebs, J.R. & Davis, N.B. (1997). *Behavioural ecology: an evolutionary approach.* Oxford: Blackwell Scientific.

Krebs, J.R., Wilson, J.D., Bradbury, R.B. & Siriwardena, G.M. (1999). The second Silent Spring? *Nature*, **400**, 611-612.

Kremen, C. (1994). Biological inventory using target taxa: a case study of the butterflies of Madagascar. *Ecological Applications*, **4**, 407-422.

Kremen, C., Colwell, R.K., Erwin, T.L., Murphy, D.D., Noss, R.F. & Sanjayan, M.A. (1993). Terrestrial arthropod assemblages: their use in conservation planning. *Conservation Biology*, **7**, 796-808.

Kroodsma, D.E. (1974). Song learning, dialects, and dispersal in the Bewick's Wren. *Zeitschrift für Tierpsychologie*, **35**, 352-380.

Kuyt, E. (1996). Reproductive manipulation in the Whooping Crane *Grus americana*. *Bird Conservation International*, **6**, 3-10.

Lack, P. (1986). *The Atlas of wintering birds in Britain and Ireland.* Calton, UK: T. & A.D. Poyser.

Lacy, R.C. (1993). Vortex: a computer simulation model for population viability analysis. *Wildlife Research*, **20**, 45-65.

Lamberson, R.H., McKelvey, R., Noon, B. & Voss, C. (1992). A dynamic analysis of Northern spotted owl viability in a fragmented forest landscape. *Conservation Biology*, **6**, 505-512.

Lamberson, R.H., Noon, B., Voss, C. & McKelvey, R. (1994). Reserve design for territorial species: the effects of patch size and spacing on the viability of the northern spotted owl. *Conservation Biology*, **8**, 185-195.

Lande, R. (1993). Risks of population extinction from demographic and environmental stochasticity and random catastrophes. *American Naturalist*, **142**, 911–927.

Lande, R. (1988). Demographic models of the northern spotted owl (*Strix occidentalis caurina*). *Oecologia*, **75**, 601–607.

Latta, S.C. (2000). Making the leap from researcher to planner: lessons from avian conservation planning in the Dominican Republic. *Conservation Biology*, **14**, 132–139.

Laurance, W.F. & Bierregaard, R.O. (eds.) (1997). *Tropical forest remnants. Ecology, management, and conservation of fragmented communities*. Chicago: University of Chicago Press.

Lawton, J.H. (1993). Range, population abundance and conservation. *Trends in Ecology and Evolution*, **8**, 409–413.

Lawton, J.H. (1995). Population dynamic principles. In *Extinction rates*, ed. J.H. Lawton & R.M. May. Oxford: Oxford University Press.

Lawton, J.H., Bignell, D.E., Bolton, B., Bloemers, G.F., Eggleton, P., Hammond, P.M., Hodda, M., Holt, R.D., Larsen, T.B., Mawdsley, N.A., Stork, N.E., Srivastava, D.S. & Watt, A.D. (1998). Biodiversity inventories, indicator taxa and effects of habitat modification in tropical forest. *Nature*, **391**, 72–76.

Leader-Williams, N. & Dublin, H.T. (2000). Charismatic megafauna as 'flagship species'. In *Priorities for the conservation of mammalian diversity. Has the panda had its Day?*, ed. A. Entwistle & N. Dunstone, pp. 53–81. Cambridge: Cambridge University Press.

Leader-Williams, N., Harrison, J. & Green, M.J.B. (1990). Designing protected areas to conserve natural resources. *Science Progress, Oxford*, **74**, 189–204.

Leathwick, J.R., Hay, J.R. & Fitzgerald, A.E. (1983). The influence of browsing by introduced mammals on the decline of the North Island kokako. *New Zealand Journal of Ecology*, **6**, 55–70.

Lebreton, J-D., Burnham, K.P., Clobert, J. & Anderson, D.R. (1992). Modeling survival and testing biological hypotheses using marked animals: a unified approach with case studies. *Ecological Monographs*, **62**, 67–118.

Lee, W.G. & Jamieson, I.G. (2001). *The Takahe: Fifty Years of Conservation Management and Research*. University of Otago Press.

Legge, J.T., Roush, R., DeSalle, R., Vogler, A.P. & May, B. (1996). Genetic criteria for establishing evolutionary significant units in Cryan's Buckmoth. *Conservation Biology*, **10**, 85–98.

Lemon, F.E. (1943). The story of the RSPB. *Bird Notes and News*, **XX**(5), 67–68.

Lens, L., Adriaensen, F. & Matthysen, E. (1999a). Dispersal studies in recently and historically fragmented forests - a comparison between Kenya and Belgium. In *Proceedings of the 22nd International Ornithological Congress, Durban*, ed. N.J. Adams & R.H. Slotow, pp. 2480–2491. Johannesburg: BirdLife South Africa.

Lens, L., Bennun, L.A. & Duchateau, L. (2001). Landscape variables affect the density of Sharpe's longclaw *Macronyx sharpei*, a montane grassland specialist. *Ibis* (in press).

Lens, L., Muchai, M., Bennun, L. & Duchateau, L. (2000). How grassland fragmentation and change in land-use affect Sharpe's Longclaw, *Macronyx sharpei*, a Kenya highland endemic. *Ostrich*, **71**, 300–303.

Lens, L., van Dongen, S., Wilder, C.M., Brooks, T.M. & Matthysen, E. (1999b). Fluctuating asymmetry increases with habitat disturbance in seven bird species of a fragmented tropical forest. *Proceedings of the Royal Society of London B*, **266**, 1241-1246.

Lento, G.M., Haddon, M., Chambers, G.K. & Baker, C.S. (1997). Genetic variation of southern hemisphere fur seals (*Arctocephalus* spp.): investigation of population structure and species identity. *Journal of Heredity*, **88**, 202-208.

Lewington, I., Alström, P. & Colston, P. (1991). *A field guide to the rare birds of Britain and Europe*. United Kingdom: HarperCollins.

Lewis, A. & Pomeroy, D. (1989). *A bird atlas of Kenya*. Rotterdam: A.A. Balkema.

Lewis, J.C. (1995). Whooping crane (*Grus americanus*). In *The birds of North America*, ed. A. Poole & F. Gill, pp. 153. Philadelphia and Washington, DC: The Academy of Natural Sciences & the American Ornithologists Union.

Lewis, J.C. (1997). Alerting the birds. *Endangered Species Bulletin*, **22**, 22-23.

Li, W.H., Ellsworth, D.L., Krushkal, J., Chang, B.H.J. & Hewett Emmett, D. (1996). Rates of nucleotide substitution in primates and rodents and the generation time effect hypothesis. *Molecular Phylogenetics and Evolution*, **5**, 182-187.

Li, X. & Li, D. (1998). Current state and the future of the crested ibis (*Nipponia nippon*): a case study by population viability analysis. *Ecological Research*, **13**, 323-333.

Lindenmeyer, D.B., Clark, T.W., Lacy, R.C. & Thomas, V.C. (1993). Population viability analysis as a tool in wildlife conservation policy: with reference to Australia. *Environmental Management*, **17**, 745-758.

Liu, J., Dunning, J.B. Jr & Pulliam, R. (1995). Potential effects of a forest management plan on Bachman's Sparrows (*Aimophila aestivalis*): linking a spatially explicit model with GIS. *Conservation Biology*, **9**, 62-75.

Lloyd, C., Tasker, M.L. & Partridge, K. (1991). *The status of seabirds in Britain and Ireland*. London: T. & A.D. Poyser.

Lombard, A.T. (1995). The problems with multi-species conservation: do hotspots, ideal reserves and existing reserves coincide? *South African Journal of Zoology*, **30**, 145-163.

Lomnicki, A. (1988). *Population ecology of individuals*. Princeton, NJ: Princeton University Press.

Loomis, J.B. & White, D.S. (1996). Economic benefits of rare and endangered species: summary and meta-analysis. *Ecological Economics*, **18**, 197-206.

Lovegrove, T.G. (1996). A comparison of the effects of predation by Norway (*Rattus norvegicus*) and Polynesian rats (*R. exulans*) on the Saddleback (*Philesturnus carunculatus*). *Notornis*, **43**, 91-112.

Lovejoy, T.E. (1978). Genetic aspects of dwindling populations – a review. In *Endangered birds. Management techniques for preserving threatened species*, ed. S.A. Temple, pp. 275-279. Wisconsin: University of Wisconsin Press.

Lovette, I.J., Bermingham, E. & Rickleffs, R.E. (1999). Mitochondrial DNA phylogeography and the conservation of endangered Lesser Antillean Icterus orioles. *Conservation Biology*, **13**, 1088-1096.

Low, R. (1994). *Endangered parrots*, revised edition. London: Blandford Press.

Ludwig, D. (1999). Is it meaningful to estimate a probability of extinction? *Ecology*, **80**, 298-310.

Lutz, W., Sanderson, W. & Scherbo, V. (1997). Doubling of world population unlikely. *Nature*, **387**, 803-805.

Lynch, M., Conery, J. & Bürger, R. (1995). Mutation accumulation and the extinction of small populations. *American Naturalist*, **146**, 489-518.

Lyster, S. (1985). *International wildlife law.* Cambridge: Grotius Publications Limited.

MacArthur, R.H. & Wilson, E.O. (1967). *The theory of island biogeography.* Princeton, NJ: Princeton University Press.

Mace, G.M. (1994). Classifying threatened species: means and ends. *Philosophical Transactions of the Royal Society of London B*, **344**, 91-97.

Mace, G.M. & Hudson, E. J. (1999). Attitudes toward sustainability and extinction. *Conservation Biology*, **13**, 242-246.

Mace, G.M. & Lande, R. (1991). Assessing extinction threats: toward a reevaluation of IUCN threatened species categories. *Conservation Biology*, **5**, 148-157.

Mace, G.M., Balmford, A., Boitani, L., Cowlishaw, G., Dobson, A.P., Faith, D.P., Gaston, K.J., Humphries, C.J., Lawton, J.H., Margules, C.R., May, R.M., Nicholls, A.O., Possingham, H.P., Rahbek, C., van Jaarsveld, A.S., Vane-Wright, R.I. & Williams, P.H. (2000). It's time to work together and stop duplicating conservation efforts. *Nature*, **405**, 393.

Mace, G.M. & Stuart, S.N. (1994). Draft IUCN Red List Categories, Version 2.2. *Species*, **21-22**, 13-24.

Machtans, C.S., Villard, M. & Hannon, S.J. (1996). Use of riparian buffer strips as movement corridors by forest birds. *Conservation Biology*, **10**, 1366-1379.

MacKinnon, K. & MacKinnon, J. (1991). Habitat protection and re-introduction. *Sympotia of the Zoological Society of London*, **62**, 173-198.

Madge, S. & Burn, H. (1988). *Wildfowl: an identification guide to the ducks, geese and swans of the world.* London: Croom Helm.

Madsen, J. (1995). Impacts of disturbance on migratory waterfowl. *Ibis*, **137**, S67-S74.

Madsen, T., Shine, R., Olsson, M. & Wittzell, H. (1999). Conservation biology - Restoration of an inbred adder population. *Nature*, **402**, 34-35.

Maguire, L.A., Wilhere, G.F. & Dong, Q. (1995). Population viability analysis for red-cockaded woodpeckers in the Georgia Piedmont. *Journal of Wildlife Management*, **59**, 533-542.

Manceau, V., Crampe, J-P., Boursot, P. & Taberlet, P. (1999), Identification of evolutionary significant units in the Spanish wild goat, *Capra pyrenaica* (Mammalia, Artiodactyla). *Animal Conservation*, **2**, 33-39.

Mangel, M. & Tier, C. (1994). Four facts every conservation biologist should know about persistence. *Ecology*, **75**, 607-614.

Manne, L.L., Brooks, T.M. & Pimm, S.L. (1999). Relative risk of extinction of passerine birds on continents and islands. *Nature*, **399**, 258-261.

Marchant, J.H. (1992). Trends in breeding populations of some common trans-Saharan migrant birds in northern Europe. *Ibis*, **134**(Suppl.), 113-119.

Marchant, J.H., Hudson, R., Carter, S.P. & Whittington, P. (1990). *Population trends in British breeding birds.* Tring: British Trust for Ornithology.

Mares, M. A. (1992). Neotropical mammals and the myth of Amazonian biodiversity. *Science*, **255**, 976-979.

Margules, C.R. & Pressey, R.L. (2000). Systematic conservation planning. *Nature*, **405**, 243-253.

Marshall, E., Haight, R. & Homans, F.R. (1998). Incorporating environmental uncertainty into species management decisions: Kirtland's warbler habitat management as a case study. *Conservation Biology*, **12**, 975–985.

Marshall, K. & Edwards-Jones, G. (1998). Reintroducing capercaillie (*Tetrao urogallus*) into southern Scotland: identification of minimum viable populations at potential release sites. *Biodiversity and Conservation*, **7**, 275–296.

Martin, R.B. (1999). The rule of law and African game, and social change and conservation misrepresentation-a reply to Spinage. *Oryx*, **33**, 89–94.

Matson, P.A., Parton, W.J., Power, A.G. & Swift, M.J. (1997). Agricultural intensification and ecosystem properties. *Science*, **277**, 504–509.

Matthysen, E. & Currie, D. (1996). Habitat fragmentation reduces disperser success in juvenile nuthatches *Sitta europaea*: evidence from patterns of territory establisment. *Ecography*, **19**, 72–76.

Mauritius Wildlife Appeal Fund (1990). *Annual Report 1988/1989*. Mauritius: Mauritius Wildlife Appeal Fund.

May, R.M. (1990). Taxonomy as destiny. *Nature*, **347**, 129–130.

May, R.M. (1995). Disease and the abundance and distribution of bird populations: a summary. *Ibis*, **137**, S85–S86.

Mayer, A.L. & Pimm, S.L. (1998). Integrating endangered species protection and ecosystem management: the Cape Sable seaside-sparrow as a case study. In *Conservation in a changing world*, ed. G.M. Mace, A. Balmford & J.R. Ginsberg, pp. 53–68. Cambridge: Cambridge University Press.

Mayfield, H. (1961). Nesting success calculated from exposure. *The Wilson Bulletin*, **73**, 255–261.

Mayfield, H. (1975). Suggestions for calculating nest success. *The Wilson Bulletin*, **87**, 456–466.

Maynard Smith, J. (1982). *Evolution and the theory of games*. Cambridge: Cambridge University Press.

Mayr, E. (1940). Speciation phenomena in birds. *American Naturalist*, **74**, 249–278.

Mayr, E. (1942). *Systematics and the origin of species*. New York: Columbia University Press.

McCarthy, M.A. (1996). Extinction dynamics of the helmeted honeyeater: effects of demography, stochasticity, inbreeding and spatial structure. *Ecological Modelling*, **85**, 151–163.

McCarthy, M.A., Bergman, M.A. & Ferson, S. (1995). Sensitivity analysis for models of population viability. *Biological Conservation*, **73**, 93–100.

McCarthy, M.A., Bergman, M.A. & Ferson, S. (1996). Logistic sensitivity and bounds for extinction risks. *Ecological Modelling*, **86**, 297–303.

McCarty, J.P. (2001). Ecological consequences of recent climate change. *Conservation Biology*, **15**, 320–331.

McCleery, R.H. & Perrins, C.M. (1998). Temperature and egg-laying trends. *Nature*, **391**, 30–31.

McCormack, G. & Künzle, J. (1990). *Kakerori – Rarotonga's endangered flycatcher*. Rarotonga: Cook Islands Conservation Service, 24 pp.

McDowall, R.M. (1967). Extinction and endemism in New Zealand land birds. *Tuatara*, **17**, 1–12.

McGarigal, K. & McComb, W.C. (1995). Relationships between landscape structure and breeding birds in the Oregon coast range. *Ecological Monographs*, **65**, 235–260.

McGowan, P. & Gillman, M. (1997). Assessment of the conservation status of partridges and pheasants in South East Asia. *Biodiversity and Conservation*, **6**, 1321-1337.

McIntyre, S. & Hobbs, R. (1999). A framework for conceptualizing human effects on landscapes and its relevance to management and research models. *Conservation Biology*, **13**, 1282-1292.

McLachlan, G.R. & Liversidge, R. (1957). *Roberts Birds of South Africa*. Cape Town: Trustees of the South African Bird Book Fund.

McLarney, W.O. (1999). Sustainable development: A necessary means for effective biological conservation. *Conservation Biology*, **13**, 4.

Meharg, A.A., Osborn, D., Pain, D.J., Sánchez, A. & Naveso, M.A. (1999). Contamination of Doñana food-chains after the Aznalcóllar mine disaster. *Environmental Pollution*, **105**, 387-390.

Menon, S., Pontius, R.G., Rose, J., Khan, M.L. & Bawa, K.S. (2001). Identifying conservation-priority areas in the tropics: a land-use change modelling approach. *Conservation Biology*, **15**, 501-512.

Merila, J., Bjorklund, M. & Baker, A.J. (1997). Historical demography and present day population structure of the Greenfinch, *Carduelis chloris* - An analysis of mtDNA control-region sequences. *Evolution*, **51**, 946-956.

Merriam, G. & Saunders, D.A. (1993). Corridors in restoration of fragmented landscapes. In *Nature conservation 3: reconstruction of fragmented ecosystems*, ed. D.A. Saunders, R.J. Hobbs & P.R. Ehrlich, pp. 71-87. Chipping Norton, NSW, Australia: Surrey Beatty & Sons.

Merton, D.V. (1975a). Success in restoring a threatened species: The Saddleback - its status and conservation. *XII Bulletin of the International Council for Bird Preservation*, **12**, 150-158.

Merton, D.V. (1975b). The Saddleback: its status and conservation. In *Breeding endangered species in captivity*, ed. R.D. Martin, pp. 61-74. London: Academic Press.

Merton, D.V. (1978). Controlling introduced predators and competitors on islands. In *Endangered birds. Management techniques for preserving threatened species*, ed. S.A. Temple, pp. 121-128. Wisconsin: University of Wisconsin Press.

Merton, D.V. (1983). Christmas Island, Indian Ocean. *Wildlife - A review*, **12**, 64-69.

Merton, D.V. (1990). The Chatham Island black robin: how the world's most endangered bird was saved from extinction. *Forest and Bird. Journal of the Royal Forest & Bird Protection Society NZ Inc.*, **21**(3), 14-19.

Merton, D.V. (1992). The legacy of "Old Blue". *New Zealand Journal of Ecology*, **16**, 65-68.

Merton, D.V. (1999). Kakapo. In *Handbook of Australian, New Zealand & Antarctic birds*, Vol. 4, ed. P.J. Higgins, pp. 633-646. Melbourne: Oxford University Press.

Merton, D.V., Morris, R.B. & Atkinson, I.A.E. (1984). Lek behaviour in a parrot: the Kakapo *Stigops habroptilus* of New Zealand. *Ibis*, **126**, 277-283.

Merton, D.V., Reed, C.& Crouchley, D. (1999). Recovery strategies and techniques for three free-living, critically-endangered New Zealand birds: Kakapo (*strigops habroptilus*), Black Stilt (*Himantopus novaezelandiae*) & takahe (*Porphyrio mantelli*) *Proc. The Seventh World Conference on Breeding Endangered Species, Cincinnati, Ohio*, 22-26 May 1999.

Meyer, W.B. & Turner, B.L. II (1994). *Changes in land use and land cover: a global perspective*. Cambridge: Cambridge University Press.

Miles, S. (2000). *The Game Conservancy Trust review of 1999*. Fordingbridge: Game Conservancy Trust.

Miller, K., Allegretti, M.H., Johnson, N. & Jonsson, B. (1995). Measures for conservation of biodiversity and sustainable use of its components. In *Global biodiversity assessment*, ed. V.H. Heywood, pp. 915-1062. Cambridge: UNEP and Cambridge University Press.

Mills, J.A., Lee, W.G. & Lavers, R.B. (1989). Experimental investigations of the effect of takahe and deer grazing on *Chionochloa pallens* grassland, Fiordland, New Zealand. *Journal of Applied Ecology*, **26**, 397-417.

Mills, J.A. & Williams, G.R. (1978). The status of endangered New Zealand birds. In *The status of endangered Australasian wildlife*, pp. 147-168. Australia: The Royal Zoological Society of South Australia.

Mills, S.L., Doak, D.F. & Wisdom, M.J. (1999). Reliability of conservation actions based on elasticity analysis of matrix models. *Conservation Biology*, **13**, 815-829.

Millsap, B.A., Gore, J.A., Runde, D.A. & Cerulean, S.I. (1990). Setting priorities for the conservation of fish and wildlife species in Florida. *Wildlife Monographs*, **111**, 1-57.

Mindell, D.P. (1997). *Avian molecular evolution and systematics*. San Diego: Academic Press.

Mindell, D.P., Sorenson, M.D., Dimcheff, D.E., Hasegawa, M., Ast, J.C. & Yuri, T. (1999). Interordinal relationships of birds and other reptiles based on whole mitochondrial genomes. *Systematic Biology*, **48**, 138-152.

Mittermeier, R.A., Bowles, I.A., Cavalcanti, R.B., Olivieri, S. & da Fonseca, G.A.B. (1995). *A participatory approach to biodiversity conservation: the regional priority Setting Workshop*. Washington, DC: Conservation International.

Mittermeier, R.A., Gil, P.R. & Mittermeier, C.G. (1997). *Megadiversity: Earth's biologically wealthiest nations*. Mexico City: CEMEX.

Mittermeier, R.A., Myers, N., Gil, P.R. & Mittermeier, C.G. (1999). *Hotspots: Earth's biologically richest and most endangered terrestrial ecoregions*. Mexico City: CEMEX.

Mittermeier, R.A., Myers, N., Thomsen, J., da Fonseca, G.A.B. & Olivieri, S. (1998). Biodiversity hotspots and major tropical wilderness areas: approaches to setting conservation priorities. *Conservation Biology*, **12**, 516-520.

Mittermeier, R.A. & Werner, T. (1988). Wealth of plants and animals unites megadiversity countries. *Tropicus*, **4**, 4-5.

Mönkkönen, M. & Reunanen, P. (1999). On critical thresholds in landscape connectivity: a management perspective. *Oikos*, **84**, 302-305.

Montevecci, W.A. & Myers, R.A. (1997). Centurial and decadal oceanographic influences on changes in northern gannet populations and diets in the north-west Atlantic: implications for climate change. *ICES Journal of Marine Science*, **54**, 608-614.

Moore, J.L., Balmford, A., Brooks, T., Burgess, N., Hansen, L.A., Rahbek, C. & Williams, P.H. (2002). The performance of Sub-Saharan African vertebrates as indicator groups for conservation priority setting. *Conservation Biology* (in press).

Morin, M.P., Conant, S. & McClung, A.M. (1998). Population viability analysis of the Nihoa finch using VORTEX. Abstracts, 12th Annual Meeting of the Society for Conservation Biology. Macquarie University, Sydney.

Moritz, C. (1994a). Applications of mitochondrial DNA analysis in conservation – a critical review. *Molecular Ecology*, **3**, 401–411.

Moritz, C. (1994b). Defining evolutionary significant units for conservation. *Trends in Ecology and Evolution*, **9**, 373–375.

Moritz, C. (1999). Conservation units and translocations: strategies for conserving evolutionary processes. *Hereditas*, **130**, 217–228.

Moritz, C., Worthington Miller, J., Pope, L., Sherwin, W.B., Taylor A.C. & Limpus, C.J. (1996). Applications of genetics to the conservation and management of Australian fauna: four case studies from Queensland. In *Molecular genetic approaches in conservation*, ed. T.B. Smith & R.K. Wayne, pp. 442–456. Oxford: Oxford University Press.

Morony, J.J., Bock, W.J. & Farrand, J. (1975). *Reference list of the birds of the world*. New York: Department of Ornithology, American Museum of Natural History.

Mountfort, G. (1988). *Rare birds of the world: A Collins/ICBP Handbook*. London: Collins.

Mundy, N.I., Winchell, C.S. & Woodruff, D.S. (1997). Genetic differences between the endangered San Clemente Island loggerhead shrike *Lanius ludovicianus mearnsi* and two neighbouring subspecies demonstrated by mtDNA control region and cytochrome b sequence variation. *Molecular Ecology*, **6**, 29–37.

Musters, C.J.M., de Graaf, H.J. & ter Keurs, W.J. (2000). Can protected areas be expanded in Africa? *Science*, **287**, 17–18.

Myers, N. (1995). Environmental unknowns. *Science*, **269**, 358–360.

Myers, N., Mittermeier, R.A., Mittermeier, C.G., da Fonseca, G.A.B. & Kent, J. (2000). Biodiversity hotspots for conservation. *Nature*, **403**, 853–858.

Nantel, P., Bouchard, A., Brouillet, L. & Hay, S. (1998). Selection of areas for protecting rare plants with integration of land use conflicts: a case study for the west coast of Newfoundland, Canada. *Biological Conservation*, **84**, 223–234.

Nasirwa, O. & Bennun, L.A. (2000). Coordinated waterbird counts: the Kenyan experience. *Ostrich*, **71**, 99–101.

Nasirwa, O., Musina, J. & Nalianga, N. (2001). Response of papyrus endemic bird species to habitat fragmentation and degradation in Yala Swamp, Western Kenya. *Ostrich Supplement*, **15**, 30.

Naylor, R.L. & Ehrlich, P.R. (1997). Natural pest control services and agriculture. In *Nature's services: societal dependence on natural ecosystems*, ed. G.C. Daily, pp. 151–174. Washington, DC: Island Press.

Nee, S. & May, R.M. (1997). Extinction and the loss of evolutionary history. *Science*, **278**, 692–694.

Nelson, J.B. (1975). Report on the status and prospects of Abbott's Booby (*Sula abbotti*) in relation to phosphate mining on the Australian territory of Christmas Island, August 1974. *12th Bulletin I.C.B.P.*, 131–140.

Newafrica.com (2001). *Seychelles economic information & indicators*. www.newafrica.com/economy/seychelles.asp

Newton, I. (1998). *Population limitation in birds*. San Diego: Academic Press.

Ngari, M.S., Bennun, L. & Matiku, P. (2001). *Establishing and developing IBA Site Support Groups: suggested guidelines*. Nairobi, Kenya: Nature Kenya Conservation Working Papers (in press).

Nicholls, A.O. (1998). Integrating population abundance, dynamics and distribution data into broad scale priority setting. In *Conservation in a changing world*, ed. G.M. Mace, A. Balmford & J.R. Ginsberg, pp. 251–272. Cambridge: Cambridge University Press.

Nicholls, A.O. & Margules, C.R. (1993). An upgraded reserve selection algorithm. *Biological Conservation*, **64**, 165–169.

Nichols, J.D., Johnson, F.A. & Williams, B.K. (1995). Managing North American waterfowl in the face of uncertainty. *Annual Review of Ecology and Systematics*, **26**, 177–199.

Nicholson-Lord, D. (2000). Armed gang steals rare birds: Bali starling's wild future in doubt as raiders take captive-bred stock. *BBC Wildlife Magazine*, March 2000, 53.

Nisbet, I.C.T. (1978). Concluding remarks on the problems of managing endangered birds. In *Endangered birds. Management techniques for preserving threatened species*, ed. S.A. Temple, pp. 447–451. Wisconsin: University of Wisconsin Press.

Nixon, A.J. (1994). Feeding ecology of hybridising parakeets on Mangere Island, Chatham Islands. *Notornis*, **41**(supplement), 5–18.

Njoroge, P. & Bennun, L. (2000). Status and conservation of Hinde's Babbler *Turdoides hindei*, a threatened species in an agricultural landscape. *Ostrich*, **71**, 69–72.

Noble, D.G., Bashford, R.I. & Baillie, S.R. (2000). *The Breeding Bird Survey 1999*. Thetford: British Trust for Ornithology Research Report No. 247.

North American Wetlands Conservation Council (Canada) (1998). *A Wetland Conservation Vision for Canada*. Ottawa.

Norton, D.A. & Lord, J.M. (1990). On the use of 'grain size' in ecology. *Functional Ecology*, **4**, 719.

Noss, R.F. (1991). Landscape connectivity: different functions at different scales. In *Landscape linkages and biodiversity*, ed. W.E. Hudson, pp. 27–39. Washington, DC: Island Press.

Noss, R.F. (2001). Beyond Kyoto: forest management in a time of rapid climate change. *Conservation Biology*, **15**, 578–590.

NRC (1995). *Effects of past global change on life (studies in geophysics)*. Board of Earth Sciences and Resources, Environmental Commission on Geosciences, Panel on the Effects of Global Change on Life. National Research Council. National Academy Press.

Oates, J.F. (1999). *Myth and reality in the rain forest. How conservation strategies are failing in West Africa*. Berkeley: University of California Press.

O'Driscoll, R. & Veltman, C. (1992). *Viability of simulated Black Stilt populations*. Unpublished report to Black Stilt Recovery Group. Wellington: Department of Conservation.

Oedekoven, K. (1980). The vanishing forest. *Environmental Policy and Law*, **6**, 184–185.

Oliver, I., Beattie, A.J. & York, A. (1998). Spatial fidelity of plant, vertebrate and invertebrate assemblages in multiple-use forest in eastern Australia. *Conservation Biology*, **12**, 822–835.

Olson, D.M., & Dinerstein, E. (1998). The Global 200: A representation approach to conserving the Earth's most biologically valuable ecoregons. *Conservation Biology*, **12**, 502–515.

Omland, K.E., Tarr, C.L., Boarma, W.I., Marzluff, J.M. & Fleischer, R.C. (2000). Cryptic genetic variation and paraphyly in ravens. *Proceedings of the Royal Society Series B*, **267**, 2475-2482.

Opdam, P.F.M. (1991). Metapopulation theory and habitat fragmentation: a review of holarctic breeding bird studies. *Landscape Ecology*, **5**, 93-106.

Opdam, P. (2001). Assessing the conservation potential of habitat networks. In *Concepts and application of landscape ecology in biological conservation*, ed. K.J. Gitzwiller. New York: Springer-Verlag (in press).

Opdam, P., Foppen, R., Reijnen, R. & Schotman, A. (1995). The landscape ecological approach in bird conservation: integrating the metapopulation concept into spatial planning. *Ibis*, **137**, 139-146.

Opdam, P., van Apeldoorn, R., Schotman, A. & Kalkhoven, J. (1993). Population responses to landscape fragmentation. In *Landscape ecology of a stressed environment*, ed. C.C. Vos and P. Opdam, pp. 147-171. London: Chapman & Hall.

Opdam, P., Foppen, R. & Vos, C. (2002). Bridging the gap between ecology and spatial planning in landscape ecology. *Landscape Ecology* (in press).

Ormerod, S.J., Bull, K.L., Cummins, C.P., Tyler, S.J. & Vickery, J.A. (1988a). Egg mass and shell thickness in dippers (*Cinclus cinclus*) in relation to stream acidity in Wales and Scotland. *Environmental Pollution*, **55**, 107-121.

Ormerod, S.J., O'Halloran, J., Gribbin, S.D. & Tyler, S.J. (1991). The ecology of dippers (*Cinclus cinclus*) in relation to stream acidity in upland Wales: breeding performance, calcium physiology and nestling growth. *Journal of Applied Ecology*, **28**, 419-433.

Ormerod, S.J. & Tyler, S.J. (1989). Long-term change in the suitability of Welsh streams for dippers (*Cinclus cinclus*) as a result of acidification and recovery: a modelling study. *Environmental Pollution*, **62**, 171-182.

Ormerod, S.J., Weatherley, N.S., Varallo, P.V. & Whitehead, P.G. (1998b). Preliminary empirical models of the historical and future impact of acidification on the ecology of Welsh streams. *Freshwater Biology*, **20**, 127-140.

Orr, D.W. (1999). Education, careers and callings: the practice of conservation biology. *Conservation Biology*, **13**, 1242-1245.

Orr, D.W. (2000). Ideasclerosis: Part one. *Conservation Biology*, 14, 926-928.

O'Ryan, C., Harley, E.H., Beaumont, M.A., Wayne, R.K., Bruford, M.W. & Cherry, M.I. (1998). Microsatellite analysis of genetic diversity in fragmented South African buffalo populations. *Animal Conservation*, **1**, 124-131.

Owens, I.P.F. & Bennett, P.M. (2000a). Ecological basis of extinction risk in birds: habitat loss versus human persecution and introduced predators. *Proceedings of the National Academy of Sciences, USA*, **97**, 12144-12148.

Owens, I.P.F. & Bennett, P.M. (2000b). Quantifying biodiversity: a phenotypic perspective. *Conservation Biology*, **14**, 1014-1022.

Owens, I.P.F., Bennett, P.M. & Harvey, P.H. (1999). Species richness among birds: body size, life history, sexual selection or ecology? *Proceedings of the Royal Society of London B*, **266**, 933-939.

Owino, A., Oyugi, J., Nasirwa, O. & Bennun, L. (2001). Patterns of variation in waterbird numbers on four Rift Valley lakes in Kenya, 1991-1999. *Hydrobiologia* (in press).

Oyugi, J.O. (1997). Kakamega Forest is dying. *Bulletin of the East African Natural History Society*, **26**(3/4), 47-49.

Oyugi, J.O., Bennun, L. & Brooks, T. (1998). Effects of fragmentation on abundance of forest birds in Kakamega Forest, Kenya. *Ostrich*, **69**, 204.

Padian, K. & Chiappe, L.M. (1998). The origin and early evolution of birds. *Biological Reviews*, **73**, 1-42.

Pain, D.J. (1995). Lead in the environment. In *Handbook of ecotoxicology*, ed. D.J. Hoffman, B.A. Rattner, G. Allen Burton Jr & J. Cairns Jr, Chapter 16, pp. 356-391. USA: CRC Press, Lewis Publishers.

Pain, D.J. & Dixon, J. (1997). Why farming and birds in Europe? In *Farming and birds in Europe*, ed. D.J. Pain & M.W. Pienkowski, pp. 1-24. London: Academic Press.

Pain, D.J., Hill, D. & McCracken, D.I. (1997). Impact of agricultural intensification of pastoral systems on bird distributions in Britain 1970-1990. *Agriculture, Ecosystems and Environment*, **64**, 19-32.

Pain, D.J. & Pienkowski, M.W. (eds.) (1997). *Farming and birds in Europe. The Common Agricultural Policy and its implications for bird conservation*. London: Academic Press.

Pain, D.J., Sánchez, A. & Meharg, A.A. (1998). The Doñana Ecological Disaster: contamination of World Heritage estuarine marsh ecosystem with acidified pyrite mine waste. *Science of the Total Environment*, **222**, 45-54.

Parker, K.M., Sheffer, R.J. & Hedrick, P.W. (1999). Molecular variation and evolutionarily significant units in the endangered Gila topmillow. *Conservation Biology*, **13**, 108-116.

Parker, V. (1994). *The atlas of birds of Swaziland*. Mbabane: Websters.

Parker, V. (1999). *The atlas of the birds of Sul do Save, southern Mozambique*. Cape Town and Johannesburg: Avian Demography Unit and Endangered Wildlife Trust.

Partington, C.J., Gardiner, C.H., Fritz, D., Phillips, L.G. & Montali, R.J. (1989). Atoxoplasmosis in Bali mynahs (*Leucopsar rothschildi*). *Journal of Zoo & Wildlife Medicine*, **20**, 328-335.

Pashley, D. (1996). Watch List. *Field Notes*, **50**, 129-134.

Paton, P.W. (1993). The effect of edge on avian nest success: how strong is the evidence? *Conservation Biology*, **8**, 17-26.

Patterson, H.E.H. (1981). The continuing search for the unknown and unknowable - a critique of contemporary ideas on speciation. *South African Journal of Science*, **77**, 113-119.

Peach, W., Baillie, S. & Underhill, L. (1991). Survival of British Sedge Warblers *Acrocephalus schoenobaenus* in relation to West African rainfall. *Ibis*, **133**, 300-305.

Peach, W.J., Buckland, S.T. & Baillie, S.R. (1996). The use of constant effort mist-netting to measure between-year changes in the abundance and productivity of common passerines. *Bird Study*, **43**, 142-156.

Peach, W.J., Lovett, L.J., Wotton, S.R. & Jeffs, C. (2001). Countryside Stewardship delivers Cirl Bunting, *Emberiza cirlus*, in Devon, UK. *Biological Conservation* (in press).

Peach, W.J., Siriwardena, G.M. & Gregory, R.D. (1999). Long-term changes in over-winter survival rates explain the decline of reed buntings *Emberiza schoeniclus* in Britain. *Journal of Applied Ecology*, **36**, 798-811.

Peakall, D.B. (1976). The peregrine falcon (*Falco peregrinus*) and pesticides. *Canadian Field-Naturalist*, **90**, 301-307.

Pearson, D.L. & Carroll, S.S. (1999). The influence of spatial scale on cross-taxon congruence patterns and prediction accuracy of species richness. *Journal of Biogeography*, **26**, 1079-1090.

Pearson, D.L. & Cassola, F. (1992). World-wide species richness patterns of tiger beetles (Coleoptera: Cicindelidae): indicator taxon for biodiversity and conservation studies. *Conservation Biology*, **6**, 376-391.

Pearson, S.M. & Gardner, R.H. (1997). Neutral models: useful tools for understanding landscape patterns. In *Wildlife and landscape ecology: effects of pattern and scale*, ed. J.A. Bissonette, pp. 215-230. New York: Springer-Verlag.

Pearson, S.M., Turner, M.G., Gardner, R.H. & O'Neill, R.V. (1996). An organism-based perspective of habitat fragmentation. In *Biodiversity in managed landscapes: theory and practice*, ed. R.C. Szaro & D.W. Johnston, pp. 77-95. New York: Oxford University Press.

Pennock, D.S. & Dimmick, W.W. (1997). Critique of the evolutionary significant unit as a definition for "distinct population segments" under US Endangered Species Act. *Conservation Biology*, **11**, 611-619.

Percival, S.M., Sutherland, W.J. & Evans, P.R. (1996). A spatial depletion model of the responses of grazing wildfowl to the availability of intertidal vegetation. *Journal of Applied Ecology*, **33**, 979-992.

Percival, S.M., Sutherland, W.J. & Evans, P. R. (1998). Intertidal habitat loss and wildfowl numbers: applications of a spatial depletion model. *Journal of Applied Ecology*, **35**, 57-63.

Peres, C.A. & Terborgh, J.W. (1995). Amazonian nature reserves: analysis of the defensibility status of existing conservation units and design criteria for the future. *Conservation Biology*, **9**, 34-46.

Perrins, C. (1987). *Collins New Generation Guide to the Birds of Britain and Europe*. London: Collins.

Perrins, C.M. (1991). Constraints on the demographic parameters of bird populations. In *Bird population studies: relevance to conservation and management*, ed. C.M. Perrins, J-D. Lebreton & G.J.M. Hirons, pp. 190-206. Oxford: Oxford University Press.

Peters, R.H. (1983). *The ecological implications of body size*. Cambridge: Cambridge University Press.

Peters, R.L. (1991). In *Global climate change and life on Earth*, ed. R.L. Wyman, pp. 99-118. New York: Chapman & Hall.

Peterson, A.T., Egbert, S.L., Sanchez-Cordero, V. & Price, K.P. (2000). Geographic analysis of conservation priority: endemic birds and mammals in Veracruz, Mexico. *Biological Conservation*, **93**, 85-94.

Peterson, A.T. & Navarro-Sigüenza, A.G. (1999). Alternate species concepts as bases for determining priority conservation areas. *Conservation Biology*, **13**, 427-431.

Peterson, R.T., Mountfort, G. & Hollom, P.A.D. (1993). *Birds of Britain and Europe*, new edition. Collins Field Guide Series. London: HarperCollins.

Pettifor, R.A., Caldow, R.W.G., Rowcliffe, J.M., Goss-Custard, J.D., Black, J.M., Hodder, K.H., Houston, A.I., Lang, A. & Webb, J. (2000a). Spatially explicit, individual-based, behavioural models of the annual cycle of two migratory goose populations. *Journal of Applied Ecology*, **137**, 103-135.

Pettifor, R.A., Norris, K. & Rowcliffe, J.M. (2000b). Incorporating behaviour in predictive models for conservation. In *Behaviour and conservation*, ed. L.M. Gosling & W.J. Sutherland, pp. 198-220. Cambridge: Cambridge University Press.

Pianka, E.R. (1970). On r- and K- selection. *American Naturalist*, **104**, 592-597.

Pickett, S.T.A., Parker, V.T. & Fiedler, P. (1992). The new paradigm in ecology: implications for conservation biology above the species level. In *Conservation biology: the theory and practice of nature conservation, preservation, and management*, ed. P. Fiedler & S. Jain, pp. 65-88. New York: Chapman & Hall.

Pierce, R.J. (1984). Plumage, morphology and hybridisation of New Zealand stilts *Himantopus* spp. *Notornis*, **31**, 106-130.

Pimm, S.L. & Raven, P. (2000). Biodiversity: extinction by numbers. *Nature*, **403**, 843-845.

Pimm, S.L., Russell, G.J., Gittleman, J.L. & Brooks, T.M. (1995). The future of biodiversity. *Science*, **269**, 347-350.

Plissner, J.H. & Haig, S.M. (2000). Viability of piping plover *Charadrius melodus* metapopulations. *Biological Conservation*, **92**, 163-173.

Plunkett, R.L. (1978). Integrated management of endangered birds - a review. In *Endangered birds. Management techniques for preserving threatened species*, ed. S.A. Temple, pp. 387-396. Wisconsin: University of Wisconsin Press.

Pollitt, M., Cranswick, P., Musgrove, A., Hall, C., Hearn, R., Robinson, J. & Holloway, S. (2000). *The Wetland Bird Survey 1998-99; Wildfowl and Wader Counts*. Slimbridge, UK: BTO/WWT/RSPB/JNCC.

Pomeroy, D. (1993). Centers of high biodiversity in Africa. *Conservation Biology*, **7**, 901-907.

Pope, L.C., Sharp, A. & Moritz, C. (1996). Population structure of the yellow-footed rock-wallaby *Petrogale xanthopus* (Gray, 1854) inferred from mtDNA sequences and microsatellite loci. *Molecular Ecology*, **5**, 629-640.

Potts, G.R. (1991). The environmental and ecological importance of cereal fields. In *The ecology of temperate cereal fields*, ed. L.G. Firbank, N. Carter, J.F. Darbyshire & G.R. Potts, pp. 3-21. Oxford: Blackwell Scientific.

Potts, G.R. (1997). Cereal farming, pesticides and grey partridges. In *Farming and birds in Europe: the Common Agricultural Policy and its implications for Bird Conservation*, ed. D.J. Pain & M.W. Pienkowski, Chapter 6. London: Academic Press.

Potts, G.R. & Aebischer, N.J. (1995). Population dynamics of the Grey Partridge *Perdix perdix* 1793-1993: monitoring, modelling and management. *Ibis*, **137**(Suppl.), S29-S37.

Poulsen, B.O. & Krabbe, N. (1997). Avian rarity in ten cloud-forest communities in the Andes of Ecuador: implications for conservation. *Biodiversity and Conservation*, **6**, 1365-1375.

Pounds, J.A., Fogden, M.P.L. & Campbell, J.H. (1999). Biological response to climate change on a tropical mountain. *Nature*, **398**, 611-615.

Power, M.E., Tilman, D., Estes, J.A., Menge, B.A., Bond, W.J., Mills, L.S., Daily, G., Castilla, J.C., Lubchenco, J. & Paine, R.T. (1996). Challenges in the quest for keystones. *Bioscience*, **46**, 609-620.

Prakash, V. (1999). Status of vultures in Keoladeo National Park, Bharatpur, Rajasthan, with special reference to population crash in *Gyps* species. *Journal of the Bombay Natural History Society*, **96**, 365-378.

Prakash, V. (2000). *A Progress Report on the status and distribution of* Gyps *vultures in India*. Bombay: Bombay Natural History Society.

Pratt, H.D., Bruner, P.L. & Berrett, D.G. (1987). *A field guide to the birds of Hawaii and the Tropical Pacific*. Princeton, NJ: Princeton University Press.

Prendergast, J.R., Quinn, R.M., Lawton, J.H., Eversham, B.C. & Gibbons, D.W. (1993). Rare species and the coincidence of diversity hotspots and conservation strategies. *Nature*, **365**, 335-337.

Pressey, R.L. (1994). *Ad hoc* reservations: forward or backward steps in developing representative reserve systems? *Conservation Biology*, **8**, 662-668.

Pressey, R.L. (1996). Protected areas: where should they be and why should they be there? In *Conservation biology*, ed. I.F. Spellerberg, pp. 171-185. Harlow: Longman.

Pressey, R.L. (1998). Algorithms, politics and timber: an example of the role of science in a public, political negotiation porcess over new conservation areas in production forests. In *Ecology for everyone: communicating ecology to scientists, the public and the politicians*, ed. R.T. Will & R.J. Hobbs, pp. 73-87. Chipping Norton, NSW, Australia: Surrey Beatty & Sons.

Pressey, R.L., Humphries, C.J., Margules, C.R., Vane-Wright, R.I. & Williams, P.H. (1993). Beyond opportunism: key principles for systematic reserve selection. *Trends in Ecology and Evolution*, **8**, 124-128.

Pressey, R.L. & Nicholls, A.O. (1989). Efficiency in conservation evaluation: scoring versus iterative approaches. *Biological Conservation*, **50**, 199-218.

Pressey, R.L., Possingham, H.P. & Day, J.R. (1997). Effectiveness of alternative heuristic algorithms for identifying indicative minimum requirements for conservation reserves. *Biological Conservation*, **80**, 207-219.

Pressey, R.L., Possingham, H.P. & Margules, C.R. (1996). Optimality in reserve selection algorithms: when does it matter, and how much? *Biological Conservation*, **76**, 259-267.

Pressey, R.L. & Tully, S.L. (1994). The cost of *ad hoc* reservation: a case study in western New South Wales. *Australian Journal of Ecology*, **19**, 375-384.

Pretty, J. (1999). *What price wildlife in the farmed landscape?* Colchester: University of Essex.

Price, J., Droege, S. & Price, A. (1995). *The summer Atlas of North American birds*. London: Academic Press.

Pulliam, H.R. (1988). Sources, sinks, and population regulation. *American Naturalist*, **132**, 652-661.

Purvis, A. & Hector, A. (2000). Getting the measure of biodiversity. *Nature*, **405**, 212-219.

Purvis, A., Agapon, P-M., Gittleman, J.L. & Mace, G.M. (2000). Non-random extinction increases the loss of evolutionary history. *Science*, **288**, 328-330.

Pyle, R.L. (1990). Native breeding birds of Hawaii. *Elepaio*, **50**, 99-100.

Rabinowitz, D., Cairns, S. & Dillon, T. (1986). Seven forms of rarity and their frequency in the flora of the British Isles. In *Conservation biology: the science of scarcity and diversity*, ed. M.E. Soulé, pp. 182-204. Sunderland, Mass.: Sinauer Associates.

Ramsar Convention (2000). Joint Work Plan 2000-2001 Between Ramsar and CBD. Adopted at CBD Meeting of the Conference of the Contracting Parties. Nairobi, Kenya. May 2000.

Ratcliffe, N., Vaughan, D., Whyte, C. & Shepherd, M. (1998). Development of playback census methods for storm petrels *Hydrobates pelagicus*. *Bird Study*, **45**, 302-312.

Raven, P.H. (1988). Our diminishing tropical forests. In *Biodiversity*, ed. E.O. Wilson, pp. 119-122. Washington, DC: National Academy Press.

Rayment, M. (1995). *Nature conservation, employment and local economies: a literature review*. Sandy, UK: Royal Society for the Protection of Birds.

Rayment, M. (ed.) (1997). *Working with nature in Britain: case studies of nature conservation, employment and local economies*. Sandy, UK: Royal Society for the Protection of Birds.

Redford, K.H. & Sanderson, S.E. (2000). Extracting humans from nature. *Conservation Biology*, **14**, 1362-1364.

Redpath, S.M. (1995). Habitat fragmentation and the individual: Tawny owls *Strix aluco* in woodland patches. *Journal of Animal Ecology*, **64**, 652-661.

Reed, C.M. & Merton, D.V. (1991). Behavioural manipulation of endangered New Zealand birds as an aid toward species recovery. *Acta XX Congressus Internationalis Ornithologici*, **4**, 2514-2522.

Reed, C.E.M., Murray, D.P. & Butler, D.J. (1993). Black stilt recovery plan (*Himantopus novaezelandiae*). Threatened Species Recovery Plan Series, **4**. Wellington: Department of Conservation.

Reed, J.M. (1992). A system for ranking conservation priorities for Neotropical migrant birds based on relative susceptibility to extinction. In *Ecology and conservation of Neotropical migrant landbirds*, ed. J.M. Hagan & D.W. Johnston, pp. 524-536. Washington DC: Smithsonian Institution Press.

Reed, J.M., Elphick, C.S. & Oring, L.W. (1996). Life-history and viability analysis of the endangered Hawaiian stilt. *Biological Conservation*, **84**, 35-45.

Reid, W.V. (1998). Biodiversity hotspots. *Trends in Ecology and Evolution*, **13**, 275-280.

Reijnen, R. & Foppen, R. (1994). The effects of car traffic on breeding bird populations in woodland. I. Evidence of a reduced habitat quality for willow warblers *Phylloscopus trochilus* breeding close to a highway. *Journal of Applied Ecology*, **31**, 85-94.

Reijnen, R., Foppen, R. & Meeuwsen, H. (1996). The effects of traffic on the density of breeding birds in Dutch agricultural grasslands. *Biological Conservation*, **75**, 255-260.

Reijnen, R., Harms, W.B., Foppen, R.P.B., de Visser, R. & Wolfert, H.P. (1995). *RHINE-ECONET. Ecological networks in river rehabilitation scenarios: a case study for the Lower Rhine*. Report 58 of the series 'Ecological Rehabilitation of the Rivers Rhine and Meuse'. Lelystad: Rijks Instituut voor de Zuivering van Afvalwater.

Reyers, B., van Jaarsveld, A.S. & Kruger, M. (2000). Complementarity as a biodiversity indicator strategy. *Proceedings of the Royal Society of London B*, **267**, 505-513.

Reynolds, D. & Ormerod, S.J. (1993). A review of the impact of current and future acid deposition in Wales. Institute of Terrestrial Ecology and University of Wales.

Ricketts, T.H., Dinerstein, E., Olson, D.M., Loucks, C.J., Eichbaum, W., DellaSala, D., Kavanagh, K., Hedao, P., Hurley, P.T., Carney, K.M., Abell, R. & Walters, S.

(1999). *Terrestrial ecoregions of North America: a conservation assessment.* Washington, DC: Island Press.

Ricklefs, R.E. (2000). Density-dependence, evolutionary optimization, and the diversification of avian life histories. *Condor*, **102**, 9–22.

Riddle, B.R., Propst, D.L. & Yates, T.L. (1998). Mitochondrial DNA variation in Gila trout, *Oncorhynchus gilae*: implications for management of an endangered species. *Copeia*, 1998(1), 31–39.

Riede, K. (2000). Conservation and modern information technologies: The Global Register of Migratory Species (GROMS). *Journal of International Wildlife Law and Policy*, **3**(2), 152–165.

Robbins, C.S., Bystrak, D. & Geissler, P.H. (1986). The Breeding Bird Survey: its first fifteen years, 1965–1979. *US Department of the Interior, Fish and Wildlife Service, resource publication* **157**, 1–196.

Robertson, C.J.R. & Nunn, G.B. (1997). Towards a new taxonomy for albatrosses. In *Albatross biology and conservation*, ed. G. Robertson & R. Gales, pp. 13–19. Chipping Norton, NSW, Australia: Surrey Beatty & Sons.

Robertson, H. (1999). Back from the brink. *Forest & Bird*, **294**, 28–31.

Robson, C. (2000). *A field guide to the birds of South-East Asia.* UK: New Holland Publishers.

Rodrigues, A.S.L., Gregory, R.D. & Gaston, K.J. (2000). Using presence–absence data to establish reserve selection procedures that are robust to temporal species turnover. *Proceedings of the Royal Society of London B*, **267**, 49–55.

Rodrigues, A.S.L., Tratt, R., Wheeler, B.D. & Gaston, K.J. (1999). The performance of existing networks of conservation areas in representing biodiversity. *Proceedings of the Royal Society of London B*, **266**, 1453–1460.

Roe, D., Leader-Williams, N. & Dalal-Clayton, B. (1997). *Take only photographs, leave only footprints: the environmental impacts of wildlife tourism.* IIED Wildlife and Development Series No. 10. London: International Institute for Environment and Development.

Rogers, D.J. & Randolph, S.E. (2000). The global spread of malaria in a future, warmer world. *Science*, **289**, 1763–1766.

Root, K.V. (1998). Evaluating the effects of habitat quality, connectivity and catastrophes on a threatened species. *Ecological Applications*, **8**, 854–865.

Root, T. (1988). *Atlas of wintering North American birds.* Chicago: University of Chicago Press.

Rose, P.M. & Scott, D.A. (1997). *Waterfowl population estimates – second edition.* Wageningen, The Netherlands: Wetlands International Publ. 44.

Rosenzweig, M.L. (1995). *Species diversity in space and time.* Cambridge: Cambridge University Press.

Round, P. (1996). Jewels of the forest: protecting Gurney's pitta in the lowland forest of Thailand. *World Birdwatch*, **18**, 12–15.

Rubec, C. *et al.* (2000). *Guidelines for Developing and Implementing National Wetland Policies.* Handbook No. 2. Gland, Switzerland: Ramsar Convention Secretariat.

Russell, G.J., Brooks, T.M., McKinney, M.M. & Anderson, C.G. (1999). Present and future taxonomic selectivity in bird and mammal extinctions. *Conservation Biology*, **12**, 1365–1377.

Ryan, J.C. (1992). Conserving biological diversity. In *State of the world 1992*, ed. L. Brown, pp. 9–26. Washington, DC: Worldwatch Institute.

Ryder, O.A. (1986). Species conservation and systematics: the dilemma of subspecies. *Trends in Ecology and Evolution*, 1, 9-10.

Ryti, R.T. (1992). Effect of focal taxon on the selection of nature reserves. *Ecological Applications*, 2, 404-410.

Saccheri, I.J., Kuussaari, M., Kankare, M., Vikman, P., Fortelius, W. & Hanski, I. (1998). Inbreeding and extinction in a butterfly metapopulation. *Nature*, 392, 401-494.

Saccheri, I.J., Wilson, I.J., Nichols, R.A., Bruford, M.W. & Brakefield, P.M. (1999). Inbreeding of bottlenecked butterfly populations: estimation using the likelihood of changes in marker allele frequencies. *Genetics*, 151, 1053-1063.

Saetersdal, M., Line, J.M. & Birks, H.J.B. (1993). How to maximize biological diversity in nature reserve selection: vascular plants and breeding birds in deciduous woodlands, western Norway. *Biological Conservation*, 66, 131-138.

Sæther, B.E., Tufto, J., Engen, S., Jerstad, K., Røstad, O.W. & Skåtan, J.E. (2000). Population dynamical consequences for a small temperate songbird. *Science*, 287, 854-856.

Samstag, T. (1988). *For the love of birds: the story of the RSPB*. Published for the Royal Society for the Protection of Birds, Sandy, UK by Christopher Helm (Publishers) Ltd.

Saunders, D.A. (1989). Changes in the avifauna of a region, district, and remnant as a result of fragmentation of native vegetation: the wheatbelt of Western Australia. A case study. *Biological Conservation*, 50, 99-135.

Saunders, D.A., Arnold, G.W., Burbidge, A.A. & Hopkins, A.J.M. (eds.) (1987). *Nature conservation: the role of remnants of native vegetation*. Chipping Norton, NSW, Australia: Surrey Beatty & Sons.

Saunders, D.A. & R. Hobbs, eds. (1991). *Nature conservation 2: the role of corridors*. Chipping Norton, NSW, Australia: Surrey Beatty & Sons.

Sawkar, K., Noronha, L., Mascarenhas, A., Chauhan, O.S. & Saeed, S. (1998). *Tourism and the environment: case studies on Goa, India, and the Maldives*. Washington, DC: The International Bank for Reconstruction and Development/The World Bank.

Schall, J.J. & Pianka, E.R. (1978). Geographical trends in numbers of species. *Science*, 201, 679-686.

Schell, D.M. & Abromatis, G. (2000). Hindcast carrying capacity of the Bering Sea: An extended record from carbon isotope ratios in sea birds and marine mammals. Applications of Stable Isotopes to Ecological Studies. Abstracts of oral presentations of the second conference, Braunschweig, Germany, 7-11 May 2000.

Schifferli, A., Geroudet, P. & Winkler, R. (1980). *Verbreitungsatlas der Brudvogel der Schweiz*. Sempach: Schweizerische Vogelwarte.

Schmid, H., Luder, R., Naef-Danzer, B., Graf, R. & Zbinden, N. (1998). *Schweizer Brutvogelatlas*. Verbreitung und Brutvogel in der Schweiz und im Furstentum Lichtenstein. Sempach: Schweizerische Vogelwarte.

Schmiegelow, F.K.A., Machtans, C.S. & Hannon, S.J. (1997). Are boreal birds resilient to forest fragmentation? An experimental study of short-term community responses. *Ecology*, 78, 1914-1932.

Schneider, C.J., Smith, T.B., Larison, B. & Moritz, C. (1999). A test of alternative models of diversification in tropical rainforests: ecological gradients vs.

rainforest refugia. *Proceedings of the National Academy of Sciences, USA,* **96**, 13869-13873.

Schulze, E.D., Wirth, C. & Heimann, M. (2000). Managing forests after Kyoto. *Science,* **289**, 2058-2059.

Schwartzman, S., Moreira, A. & Nepstad, D. (2000). Rethinking tropical forest conservation: perils in parks. *Conservation Biology,* **14**, 1351-1357.

Scott, D.A. (1998). *Global overview of the conservation of migratory Arctic breeding birds outside the Arctic.* Wetlands International Publication No 45; CAFF Technical Report No. 4. CAFF Iceland. Wageningen, The Netherlands: Wetlands International.

Scott, J.M., Davis, F., Csuti, B., Noss, R., Butterfield, B., Groves, C., Anderson, H., Caicco, S., D'Erchia, F., Edwards, T.C. Jr., Ulliman, J. & Wright, R.G. (1993). Gap Analysis: a geographic approach to protection of biological diversity. *Wildlife Monographs,* **123**, 1-41.

Scott, P., Burton, J. A. & Fitter, R. (1987). Red Data Books: the historical background. In *The road to extinction,* ed. R. Fitter & M. Fitter. Gland, Switzerland: IUCN.

Shafer, C.L. (1990). *Nature reserves: island theory and conservation practice.* Washington, DC: Smithsonian Institution Press.

Shaffer, M.L. (1987). Minimum viable populations: coping with uncertainty. In *Viable populations for conservation,* ed. M. E. Soulé, pp. 69-86. Cambridge: Cambridge University Press.

Sharrock, J.T.R. (1976). *The atlas of breeding birds in Britain and Ireland.* Calton, UK: T. & A.D. Poyser.

Sheldon, F.H., Whittingham, L.A. & Winkler, D.W. (1999). A comparison of cytochrome b and DNA hybridization data bearing on the phylogeny of swallows (Aves: Hirundinidae). *Molecular Phylogenetics and Evolution,* **11**, 320-331.

Shorrocks, B., & Swingland, I.R. (eds) (1990). *Living in a patchy environment.* Oxford: Oxford University Press.

Sibley, C.G. & Ahlquist, J. (1990). *Phylogeny and classification of birds.* New Haven, Conn.: Yale University Press.

Sibley, C.G., Ahlquist, J. & Monroe, B.L. Jr (1988). A classification of the living birds of the world based on DNA-DNA hybridisation studies. *Auk,* **105**, 409-423.

Sim, I.M.W., Gibbons, D.W., Bainbridge, I.P. & Mattingley, W.A. (2001). Status of the Hen Harrier *Circus cyaneus* in the UK and the Isle of Man in 1998. *Bird Study,* **48**, (in press).

Simiyu, A.M. & Bennun, L.A. (2000). Gamebird hunting in Kenya: developing local management models. *Ostrich,* **71**, 56-60.

Siriwardena, G.M., Baillie, S.R., Buckland, S.T., Fewster, R.M., Marchant, J.H. & Wilson, J.D. (1998). Trends in the abundance of farmland birds: a quantitative comparison of smoothed Common Birds Census indices. *Journal of Applied Ecology,* **35**, 24-43.

Siriwardena, G.M., Baillie, S.R., Crick, H.Q.P. & Wilson, J.D. (2000). The importance of variation in the breeding performance of seed-eating birds in determining their population trends on farmland. *Journal of Applied Ecology,* **37**, 128-148.

Sjögren, P. & Wyöni, P.I. (1994). Conservation genetics and detection of rare alleles in finite populations. *Conservation Biology,* **8**, 267-270.

Small, M.P., Beacham, T.D., Withler, R.E. & Nelson, R.J. (1998). Discriminating coho salmon (*Oncorhynchus kisutch*) populations within the Fraser River, British Columbia, using microsatellite DNA markers. *Molecular Ecology*, 7, 141-155.

Smith, E.F.G., Arctander, P., Fjeldså, J. & Amir, O.G. (1991). A new species of shrike (Laniidae, *Laniarius*) from Somalia verified by DNA-sequence data from the only known individual. *Ibis*, 133, 227-235.

Smith, F.D.M., May, R.M., Pellew, R., Johnson, T.H. & Walter, K.S. (1993). Estimating extinction rates. *Nature*, 364, 494-496.

Smith, K.W., Dee, C.W., Fearnside, J.D., Fletcher, E.W. & Smith, R.N. (1993). *The breeding birds of Hertfordshire*. Hertfordshire Natural History Society.

Smith, T.B., Freed, L.A., Lepson, J.K. & Carothers, J.H. (1995). Evolutionary consequences of extinctions in a Hawaiian honeycreeper. *Conservation Biology*, 9, 107-113.

Smith, T.B., Wayne, R.K. & Bruford, M.W. (1993). The preservation of process: the missing element of conservation programs. *Biodiversity Letters*, 1, 164-167.

Smith, T.B., Wayne, R.K., Girman, D.J. & Bruford, M.W. (1997). A role for ecotones in generating rainforest biodiversity. *Science*, 276, 1855-1857.

Snow, D.W. (1997). Should the biological be replaced by the phylogenetic species concept? *Bulletin of the British Ornithologists' Club*, 117, 110-121.

Snyder, N.F.R. (1983). California condor reproduction, past and present. *Bird Conservation*, 1, 67-86.

Snyder, N. & Snyder, H. (2000). *The California Condor. A saga of natural history and conservation*. San Diego: Academic Press.

Sodhi, N.S. & Liow, L.H. (2000). Improving conservation biology research in south-east Asia. *Conservation Biology*, 14, 1211-1212.

Soltis, P.S. & Gitzendanner, M.A. (1999). Molecular systematics and the conservation of rare species. *Conservation Biology*, 13, 471-483.

Soorae, P.S. (1996). Report of the Reintroductions Specialist Group. *Species*, 26-27, 143-144.

Sorensen, L.G., Goldberg, R., Root, T.L. & Anderson, M.G. (1998). Potential effects of global warming on waterfowl populations breeding in the Northern Great Plains. *Climate Change*, 40, 343-369.

Soulé, M.E. (ed.) (1986). *Conservation biology: the science of scarcity and diversity*. Sunderland Mass.: Sinauer Associates.

Soulé, M.E. (ed.) (1987). *Viable populations for conservation*. Cambridge: Cambridge University Press.

Soulé, M.E. & Sanjayan, M.A. (1998). Conservation targets: do they help? *Science*, 279, 2060-2061.

SOVON (1987). *Atlas van de Nederlandse Vogels*. Arnhem: SOVON.

Sparks, T.H. & Carey, P.D. (1995). The responses of species to climate over two centuries: an analysis of the Marsham phonological record, 1736-1947. *Journal of Ecology*, 83, 321-329.

Spies, T.A. & Turner, M.G. (1999). Dynamic forest mosaics. In *Maintaining biodiversity in forest ecosystems*, ed. M.L. Hunter Jr, pp. 95-160. Cambridge: Cambridge University Press.

Spinage, C.A. (1998). Social change and conservation misrepresentation. *Oryx*, 32, 265-276.

Spinage, C.A. (1999). A reply to Martin. *Oryx*, **33**, 282–284.

Stattersfield, A.J., Crosby, M.J., Long, A.J & Wege, D.C. (1998). *Endemic bird areas of the world. Priorities for biodiversity conservation.* Cambridge: BirdLife International.

Stevens, G.C. (1989). The latitudinal gradient in geographic range: how do so many species coexist in the tropics? *American Naturalist*, **133**, 240–256.

Still, C.J., Foster, P.N. & Schneider, S.H. (1999). Simulating the effects of climate change on tropical montane cloud forests. *Nature*, **398**, 608–610.

Stillman, R.A., Goss-Custard, J.D., West, A.D., Durell, S.E.A.le V.dit, Caldow, R.W.G., McGrorty, S. & Clarke, R.T. (2000). Predicting mortality in novel environments: tests and sensitivity of a behaviour-based model. *Journal of Applied Ecology*, **37**, 564–588.

Stillman, R.A., Goss-Custard, J.D., West, A.D., McGrorty, S., Caldow, R.W.G., Durell, S.E.A.le V.dit, Norris, K.J., Johnstone, I.G., Ens, B.J., van der Meer, J. & Triplet, P. (2001). Predicting oystercatcher mortality and population size under different regimes of shellfishery management. *Journal of Applied Ecology*, **38**, 857–868.

Stine, P.A., Davis, F.W., Csuti, B. & Scott, J.M. (1996). Comparative utility of vegetation maps of different resolutions for conservation planning. In *Biodiversity in managed landscapes: theory and practice*, ed. R.C. Szaro & D.W. Johnston, pp. 210–220. New York: Oxford University Press.

Stone, B.H., Sears, J., Cranswick, P.A., Gregory, R.D., Gibbons, D.W., Rehfisch, M.M., Aebischer, N.J. & Reid, J.B. (1997). Population estimates of birds in Britain and in the United Kingdom. *British Birds*, **90**, 1–22.

Stork, N.E. & Samways, M.J. (eds.) (1995). Inventorying and monitoring of biodiversity. In *Global biodiversity assessment*, ed. V.H. Heywood, pp. 453–544. Cambridge: UNEP and Cambridge University Press.

Stotz, D.F., Fitzpatrick, J.W., Parker, T.A., & Moskovits, D.K. (1996). *Neotropical birds: ecology and conservation.* Chicago: University of Chicago Press.

Stuart, S. (1995). Conservation of biodiversity in sub-Saharan Africa. In *Conservation of biodiversity in Africa: local initiatives and institutional roles*, ed. L.A. Bennun, R.A. Aman & S.A. Crafter, pp. 185–192. Nairobi: National Museums of Kenya.

Sutherland, W.J. (ed.) (1996a). *Ecological census techniques: a handbook.* Cambridge: Cambridge University Press.

Sutherland, W.J. (1996b). *From individual behaviour to population ecology.* Oxford: Oxford University Press.

Sutherland, W.J. (2000). *The conservation handbook: research, management and policy.* Oxford: Blackwell Science.

Sutherland, W.J. & Allport, G.A. (1994). A spatial depletion model of the interaction between bean geese and wigeon with the consequences for habitat management. *Journal of Animal Ecology*, **63**, 51–59.

Sutherland, W.J. & Anderson, G.W. (1993). Predicting the distribution of individuals and the consequences of habitat loss: the role of prey depletion. *Journal of Theoretical Biology*, **160**, 223–230.

Sutherland, W.J. & Dolman, P.M. (1994). Combining behaviour and population dynamics with applications for predicting the consequences of habitat loss. *Proceedings of the Royal Society of London B*, **255**, 133–138.

Svensson, L. & Grant, P.J. (1999). *Collins bird guide*. London: HarperCollins.

Swain, H.M. (1995). Reconciling rarity and representation – a review of listed species in the Indian-river lagoon. *Bulletin of Marine Science*, 57, 252-266.

Swetnam, R.D., Ragou, P., Firbank, L.G., Hinsley, S.A. & Bellamy, P.E. (1998). Applying ecological models to altered landscapes. Scenario testing with GIS. *Landscape and Urban Planning*, 41, 3-18.

Swinnerton, K., de Ravel, F., Lalinde, A., Jenkin, K. & Eason, D. (1998). Captive breeding and management of echo parakeets, 1997/98. In *Echo parakeet* (Psittacula eques) *management report 1998*, ed. K. Swinnerton, pp. 36-66. Port Louis, Mauritius: Mauritian Wildlife Foundation.

Tarr, C.L. & Fleischer, R.C. (1999). Population boundaries and genetic diversity in the endangered Mariana crow (*Corvus kubaryi*). *Molecular Ecology*, 8, 941-949.

Taylor, B.L. (1995). The reliability of using population viability analysis for risk classification of species. *Conservation Biology*, 9, 551-558.

Taylor, B.L., Wade, P.R., Stehn, R.A. & Cochrane, J.F. (1996). A Bayesian approach to classification criteria for spectacled eiders. *Ecological Applications*, 6, 1077-1089.

Taylor, C. (1995). A most peculiar institution. In *World, mind and ethics: essays on the ethical philosophy of Bernard Williams*, ed. T.R. Harrison & J.E.J. Altham. Cambridge: Cambridge University Press.

Temple, S.A. (1978). *Endangered birds. Management techniques for preserving threatened species*. Wisconsin: University of Wisconsin Press.

Temple, S.A. (1986). The problem of avian extinctions. *Current Ornithology*, 3, 453-485.

Temple, S.A. (1985b). Why endemic island birds are so vulnerable to extinction. *Bird Conservation*, 2, 3-6.

Terborgh, J. (1999). *Requiem for nature*. Washington, DC: Island Press.

Terborgh, J. & Winter, B. (1980). Some causes of extinction. In *Conservation biology*, ed. M. E. Soulé & B. Wilcox, pp. 119-133. Sunderland, MA: Sinauer Associates.

The Nature Conservancy (1997). *Priorities for conservation: 1997 Annual Report Card for US plant and animal species*. Arlington, VA: The Nature Conservancy.

Thiollay, J.M. & Probst, J.M. (1999). Ecology and conservation of a small insular bird population, the Réunion cuckoo-shrike *Coracina newtoni*. *Biological Conservation*, 87, 191-200.

Thirgood, S.J. & Heath, M.F. (1994). Global patterns of endemism and the conservation of biodiversity. In *Systematics and conservation evaluation*, ed. P.L. Forey, C.J. Humphries & R.I. Vane-Wright, pp. 207-227. Oxford: Clarendon Press.

Thomas, C.D. & Lennon, J.J. (1999). Birds extend their ranges northwards. *Nature*, 399, 213.

Thomas, D., Anders, S. & Penn, N.J. (1997). Conservation in the community: the Kilum-Ijim Forest Project, Cameroon. *Ostrich*, 71, 157-161.

Thomson, D.L., Green, R.E., Gregory, R.D. & Baillie, S.R. (1998). The widespread declines of songbirds in rural Britain do not correlate with the spread of their avian predators. *Proceedings of the Royal Society of London B*, 265, 2057-2062.

Thomson, D.R. (1996). Mercury in birds and terrestrial mammals. In *Environmental contaminants in wildlife: interpreting tissue concentrations*, ed. W.N. Beyer, G.H. Heinz & A.W. Redmon, Chapter 14. Boca Raton: SETAC CRC Lewis Publishers.

Tilaye, N. & Yilma, D. (2000). Developing National Conservation Programmes through the IBA process. *Ostrich*, **71**, 162-163.

Tilman, D., Fargione, J., Wolff, B., D'Antonio, C., Dobson, A., Howarth, R., Schindler, D., Schlesinger, W.H., Simberloff, D. & Swackhamer, D. (2001). Forecasting agriculturally driven global environment change. *Science*, **292**, 281-284.

Tilman, D. & Kareiva, P. (eds.) (1997). *Spatial ecology: the role of space in population dynamics and interspecific interactions.* Princeton, NJ: Princeton University Press.

Tisdall, D.J. & Merton, D.V. (1988). Disease surveillance in the Chatham Islands black robin. *Surveillance* **15**(2), Journal of MAFQUAL, New Zealand Ministry of Agriculture.

Todd, C.R. & Burgman, M.A. (1998). Assessment of threat and conservation priorities under realistic levels of uncertainty and reliability. *Conservation Biology*, **12**, 966-974.

Townsend, C.R., Harper, J.L. & Begon, M. (1999). *Essentials of ecology.* Oxford: Blackwell Science.

Triggs, S.J. & Daugherty, C.H. (1996). Conservation and genetics of New Zealand parakeets. *Bird Conservation International*, **6**, 89-101.

Trzcinski, M.K., Fahrig, L. & Merriam, G. (1999). Independent effects of forest cover and fragmentation on the distribution of forest breeding birds. *Ecological Applications*, **9**, 586-593.

Tucker, G.M. (1997). Priorities for Bird Conservation in Europe: the importance of the farmed landscape. In *Farming and birds in Europe*, ed. D.J. Pain & M.W. Pienkowski, Chapter 4. London: Academic Press.

Tucker, G.M. & Evans, M.I. (eds.) (1997). *Habitats for birds in Europe. A conservation strategy for the wider environment.* Cambridge: BirdLife International.

Tucker, G.M. & Heath, M.F. (1994). *Birds in Europe: their conservation status.* Cambridge: BirdLife International.

Tucker, G.M., Heath, M.F., Tomialojc, L. & Grimmett, R.F.A. (1994). *Birds in Europe: their conservation status.* Cambridge, UK: BirdLife International.

Turpie, J.K. & Ryan, P.G. (1998). *The Nature and Value of Birding in South Africa.* BirdLife South Africa research series no. 1. Cape Town: Percy FitzPatrick Institute of African Ornithology.

UN (1998). Population Division of the Department of Economic and Social Affairs of the United Nations Secretariat, Long Range World Population: Based on the 1998 Revision (ESA/P/WP.153), 1999.

Underhill, L. (1994). Optimal and suboptimal reserve selection algorithms. *Biological Conservation*, **70**, 85-87.

Upton, A., Pickerell, G. & Heubeck, M. (2000). *Seabird numbers and breeding success in Britain and Ireland, 1999.* UK Nature Conservation No. 24. Peterborough: Joint Nature Conservation Committee.

US Fish and Wildlife Service (1996). *California condor recovery plan.* Portland, OR: US Fish & Wildlife Service.

US Fish and Wildlife Service (1997). *1996 National survey of fishing, hunting, and wildlife-associated recreation.* Washington, DC: US Fish and Wildlife Service.

US Travel Data Center (1992). *Discover America: tourism and the environment: a guide to challenges and opportunities for travel industry businesses.* Washington, DC: Travel Industry Association of America.

van Balen, B. & Gepak, V.H. (1994). The captive breeding and conservation of the Bali starling (*Leucopsar rothschildi*). In *Creative conservation: interactive management of wild and captive animals*, ed. P.J.S. Olney, G.M. Mace & A.T.C. Feistner, pp. 420-430. London: Chapman & Hall.

Van Dorp, D. & Opdam, P.F.M. (1987). Effects of patch size, isolation and regional abundance on forest bird communities. *Landscape Ecology*, 1, 59-73.

Van Horne, B. (1983). Density as a misleading indicator of habitat quality. *Journal of Wildlife Management*, 47, 893-901.

Van Horne, B. & Wiens, J.A. (1991). *Forest bird habitat suitability models and the development of general habitat models.* US Fish and Wildlife Service, Fish and Wildlife Research 8, 31 pp.

Van Jaarsveld, A.S., Freitag, S., Chown, S.L., Muller, C., Koch, S., Hull, H., Bellamy, C., Krüger, M., Endrödy-Younga, S., Mansell, M.W. & Scholtz, C.H. (1997). Biodiversity assessment and conservation strategies. *Science*, 279, 2106-2108.

Van Langevelde, Schotman, F.A., Claassen, F. & Sparenburg, G. (2000). Competing land use in the reserve site selection problem. *Landscape Ecology*, 15, 243-256.

Van Noordwijk, A.J. & Scharloo, W. (1981). Inbreeding in an island population of the great tit. *Evolution*, 35, 674-688.

Van Tuinen, M., Sibley, C.G. & Hedges, S.B. (2000). The early history of modern birds inferred from DNA sequences of nuclear and mitochondrial ribosomal genes. *Molecular Biology and Evolution*, 17, 451-457.

Vane-Wright, R.I., Humphries, C.J. & Williams, P.H. (1991). What to protect - systematics and the agony of choice. *Biological Conservation*, 55, 235-254.

Veit, R.R., McGowan, J.A., Ainley, D.G., Wahls, T.R. & Pyle, P. (1997). Apex marine predator declines ninety percent in association with changing oceanic climate. *Global Change Biology*, 3, 23-28.

Veitch, C.R. & Bell, B.D. (1990). Eradication of introduced animals from the islands of New Zealand. In *Ecological Restoration of New Zealand islands*, ed. D.R. Towns, C.H. Daugherty & I.A.E. Atkinson, pp. 137-146. Conservation Sciences Publication No. 2. Wellington: Department of Conservation.

Verboom, J., Foppen, R., Chardon, P., Opdam, P. & Luttikhuizen, P. (2001). Standards for persistent habitat networks for vertebrate populations: the key patch approach. An example for marshland bird populations. *Biological conservation* (in press).

Verboom, J., Metz, J.A.J. & Meelis, E. (1993). Metapopulation models for impact assessment of fragmentation. In *Landscape ecology of a stressed environment*, ed. C.C. Vos & P. Opdam, pp. 172-188. London: Chapman & Hall.

Verboom, J. Schotman, A., Opdam, P. & Metz, J.A.J. (1991). European nuthatch metapopulations in a fragmented agricultural landscape. *Oikos*, 61, 149-156.

Vermeij, G. J. (1993). Biogeography of recently extinct marine species - implications for conservation. *Conservation Biology*, 7, 391-397.

Villard, M., Trzcinski, M.K. & Merriam, G. (1999). Fragmentation effects on forest birds: relative influence of woodland cover and configuration on landscape occupancy. *Conservation Biology*, **13**, 774–783.

Virolainen, K.M., Ahlroth, P., Hyvärinen, E., Kormeamäki, E., Mattila, J., Päivinen, J., Rintala, T., Suomi, T. & Syhonen, J. (2000). Hot spots, indicator taxa, complementarity and optimal networks of taiga. *Proceedings of the Royal Society of London B*, **267**, 1143–1147.

Visser, M. E., van Noordwijk, A.J., Tinbergen, J.M. & Lessels, C.M. (1998). Warmer springs lead to mistimed reproduction in great tits (*Parus major*). *Proceedings of the Royal Society of London B*, **265**, 1867–1870.

Vogler, A.P. & DeSalle, R. (1994). Diagnosing units of conservation management. *Conservation Biology*, **8**, 354–363.

von Plessen, V. (1926). Verbreitung und Lebensweise von *Leucopsar rothschildi* Stre. *Ornithologisches Monatsberichten*, **34**, 1–73.

Vos, C.C., Verboom, J., Opdam, P.F.M. & ter Braak, C.J. (2001). Towards ecologically scaled landscape indices. *American Naturalist*, **157**, 24–51.

Waits, L.P., Talbot, S.L., Ward, R.H. & Shields, G.F. (1998). Mitochondrial DNA phylogeography of the North American brown bear and implications for conservation. *Conservation Biology*, **12**, 408–417.

Waiyaki, E.M. & Bennun, L.A. (2000). The avifauna of coastal forests in southern Kenya: status and conservation. *Ostrich*, **71**, 247–256.

Walters, J.R. (1991). Application of ecological principles to the management of endangered species: the case of the red-cockaded woodpecker. *Annual Review of Ecology and Systematics*, **22**, 505–523.

Waples, R.S. (1991). Pacific salmon, *Oncorhynchus* spp., and the definition of "species" under the endangered species act. *Marine Fisheries Review*, **53**, 11–22.

Waples, R.S. (1995). Evolutionary significant units and the conservation of biological diversity under the Endangered Species Act. In *Evolution and the aquatic ecosystem: defining unique units in population conservation*, ed. J.I. Nielson, Symposium 17, pp. 8–27. Bethesda Maryland: American Fisheries Society.

Waples, R.S. (1998). Evolutionarily significant units, distinct population segments, and the endangered species act: reply to Pennock and Dimmick. *Conservation Biology*, **12**, 718–721.

Warner, R.E. (1968). The role of introduced diseases in the extinction of the endemic Hawaiian avifauna. *Condor*, **70**, 101–120.

Watkinson, A.R. & Sutherland, W.J. (1995). Sources, sinks and pseudo-sinks. *Journal of Animal Ecology*, **64**, 126–130.

Watson, J., Warman, C., Todd, D. & Laboudallon, V. (1992). The Seychelles magpie robin *Copsychus sechellarum*: ecology and conservation of an endangered species. *Biological Conservation*, **61**, 93–106.

Watson, R.T., Zinyowera, M.C., Moss, R.H. & Dokken, D.J. (1997). *The regional impacts of climate change: an assessment of vulnerability*. A Special report of the Intergovernmental Panel on Climate Change (IPCC) Working Group II. 1997, IPCC. 28p.

WCMC (1994). *Biodiversity Data Sourcebook*. Cambridge: World Conservation Press.

Weaver, J.C. (1995). Indicator species and scale of observation. *Conservation Biology*, **9**, 939–942.

Weeks, P. (2000). Red-billed oxpeckers: vampires or tickbirds? *Behavioral Ecology*, **11**, 154–160.

Wege, D.C. & Long, A.J. (1995). *Key areas for threatened birds in the Neotropics*. Cambridge: BirdLife International.

Weimerskirch, H., Brothers, N. & Jouventin, P. (1997). Population dynamics of Wandering Albatross *Diomedea exulans* and Amsterdam Albatross *Diomedea amsterdamensis* in the Indian Ocean and their relationships with long-line fisheries. *Biological Conservation*, **79**, 257–270.

Wessels, K.J., Reyers, B. & van Jaarsveld, A.S. (2000). Incorporating land cover information into regional biodiversity assessments in South Africa. *Animal Conservation*, **3**, 67–79.

White, D., Minotti, P.G., Barczak, M.J., Sifneos, J.C., Freemark, K.E., Santelmann, M.V., Steinitz, C.F., Kiester, A.R. & Preston, E.M. (1997). Assessing risks to biodiversity from future landscape change. *Conservation Biology*, **11**, 349–360.

Whiting, A.S., Lawler, S.H., Horwitz, P. & Crandall, K.A. (2000). Biogeographic regionalization of Australia: assigning conservation priorities based on endemic freshwater crayfish phylogenetics. *Animal Conservation*, **3**, 155–163.

Whitney, K.D. & Smith, T.B. (1998). Habitat use and resource tracking by African *Ceratogymna* hornbills: implications for seed dispersal and forest conservation. *Animal Conservation*, **1**, 108–118.

Whittington, P.A. (1999). The contribution made by cleaning oiled African Penguins *Spheniscus demersus* to population dynamics and conservation of the species. *Marine Ornithology*, **27**, 177–180.

Wiedner, D. & Kerlinger, P. (1990). Economics of birding: a national survey of active birders. *American Birds*, **44**, 209–213.

Wiemeyer, S.N., Scott, J.M., Andersen, M.P., Bloom, P.H., & Stafford, C.J. (1988). Environmental contaminants in Californian condors. *Journal of Wildlife Management*, **52**(2), 238.

Wiens, J.A. (1977). On competition and variable environments. *American Scientist*, **65**, 590–597.

Wiens, J.A. (1981). Scale problems in avian censusing. *Studies in Avian Biology*, **6**, 513–521.

Wiens, J.A. (1995a) Recovery of Seabirds Following the *Exxon Valdez* Oil Spill. In *Exxon Valdez oil spill: fate and effects in Alaskan waters*, ASTM STP 1219, ed. P.G. Wells, J.N. Butler & J.S. Hughes, pp. 854–893. Philadelphia: American Society for Testing and Materials.

Wiens, J.A. (1995b). Habitat fragmentation: island *v* landscape perspectives on bird conservation. *Ibis*, **137**, S97–S104.

Wiens, J.A. (1995c). Landscape mosaics and ecological theory. In *Mosaic landscapes and ecological processes*, ed. L. Hansson, L. Fahrig & G. Merriam, pp. 1–26. London: Chapman & Hall.

Wiens, J.A. (1997). The emerging role of patchiness in conservation biology. In *Enhancing the Ecological Basis of Conservation: Heterogeneity, Ecosystem Function, and Biodiversity*, ed. S.T.A. Pickett, R.S. Ostfeld, M. Shachak, and G.E. Likens, pp. 93-107. New York: Chapman & Hall.

Wiens, J.A. (2001a). Ecological heterogeneity: an ontogeny of concepts and approaches. In *The ecological consequences of heterogeneity*, ed. M.J. Hutchings, E.A. John & A.J.A. Stewart. Oxford: Blackwell Science (in press).

Wiens, J.A. (2001b). The landscape context of dispersal. In *Dispersal: individual, population, and community*, ed. J. Clobert, E. Danchin, A.A. Dhondt & J.D. Nichols. New York: Oxford University Press (in press).

Wiens, J.A. (2001c). Understanding the problem of scale in experimental ecology. In *Scaling Relationships in Experimental Ecology*, ed. R.H. Gardner, M. Kemp, V. Kennedy & J. Petersen. New York: Columbia University Press (in press).

Wiens, J.A., Stenseth, N.C., Van Horne, B. & Ims, R.A. (1993). Ecological mechanisms and landscape ecology. *Oikos*, **66**, 369-380.

Wilbur, S.R. (1978). Supplemental feeding of California Condors. In *Endangered birds. Management techniques for preserving threatened species*, ed. S.A. Temple, pp. 135-140. Wisconsin: University of Wisconsin Press.

Wilcove, D.S. (1999). *The Condor's Shadow*. New York: Freeman.

Wilcove, D.S., McLellan, C.H. & Dobson, A.P. (1986). Habitat fragmentation in the temperate zone. In *Conservation biology: the science of scarcity and diversity*, ed. M.E. Soulé, pp. 237-256. Sunderland, MA: Sinauer Associates.

Williams, P.H. (1996). *WORLDMAP 4 WINDOWS: Software and Help Document 4.19*. London: distributed privately and from http://www.nhm.ac.uk/science/projects/worldmap/

Williams, P.H. (1998). Key sites for conservation: area-selection methods for biodiversity. In *Conservation in a changing world*, ed. G.M. Mace, A. Balmford & J.R. Ginsberg, pp. 211-249. Cambridge: Cambridge University Press.

Williams, P.H. & Araújo, M. (2001). Using probability of persistence to identify important areas for biodiversity conservation. *Proceedings of the Royal Society of London B*, **267**, 1959-1966.

Williams, P.H. & Gaston, K.J. (1994). Measuring more of biodiversity: can higher-taxon richness predict wholesale species richness? *Biological Conservation*, **67**, 211-217.

Williams, P.H., Gibbons, D., Margules, C., Rebelo, A., Humphries, C. & Pressey, R. (1996). A comparison of richness hotspots, rarity hotspots, and complementary areas for conserving diversity of British birds. *Conservation Biology*, **10**, 155-174.

Williams, T.D. & Croxall, J.P. (1990). Is chick fledging weight a good index of food availability in seabird populations? *Oikos*, **59**, 414-416.

Williams, T.D. & Croxall, J.P. (1991). Annual variation in breeding biology of the Macaroni Penguin at Bird Island, South Georgia. *Journal of Zoology (London)*, **223**, 189-202.

Wilson, E.O. (1988). The current state of biological diversity. In *Biodiversity*, ed. E.O. Wilson, pp. 3-20. Washington, DC: National Academy Press.

Wilson, E.O. (1994). *The diversity of life*. London: Penguin.

Wilson, E.O. (2000). A global biodiversity map. *Science*, **289**, 2279.

Wilson, E.O. & Willis, E.O. (1975). Applied biogeography. In *Ecology and evolution of communities*, ed. M.L. Cody & J.M. Diamond, pp. 522-534. Cambridge, MA: Harvard University Press.

Wilson, M.H., Kepler, C.B., Snyder, N.F.R., Derrickson, S.R., Dein, F.J., Wiley, J.W., Wunderle, J.M., Lugo, A.E., Graham, D.L. & Toone, W.D. (1994). Puerto Rican parrots and potential limitations of the metapopulation approach to species conservation. *Conservation Biology*, **8**, 114-123.

Wingate, D.B. (1978). Excluding competitors from Bermuda petrel nesting burrows. In *Endangered birds. Management techniques for preserving threatened species*, ed. S.A. Temple, pp. 93-102. Wisconsin: University of Wisconsin Press.

Winston, M.R. & Angermeier, P.L. (1995). Assessing conservation value using centers of population density. *Conservation Biology*, **9**, 1518-1527.

Winterbottom, J.M. (1966). Check lists and the South African Avifauna series. *Bokmakierie*, **18**, 10-11.

Wisdom, M.J. & Mills, L.S. (1997). Sensitivity analysis to guide population recovery: prairie chickens as an example. *Journal of Wildlife Management*, **61**, 302-312.

With, K.A. (1999). Is landscape connectivity necessary and sufficient for wildlife management? In *Forest fragmentation: wildlife and management implications*, ed. J.A. Rochelle, L.A. Lehmann & J. Wisniewski, pp. 97-115. Amsterdam: Brill Academic Publishers.

Witting, L., Tomiuk, J. & Loeschcke, V. (2000). Modelling the optimal conservation of interacting species. *Ecological Modelling*, **125**, 123-143.

Woinarski, J.C.Z., Whitehead, P.J., Bowman, D.M.J.S. & Russel-Smith, J. (1992). Conservation of mobile species in a variable environment: the problem of reserve design in the Northern Territory, Australia. *Global Ecology and Biogeography Letters*, **2**, 1-10.

World Commission on Environment and Development (WCED) (1987). *Our Common Future*. Oxford: Oxford University Press.

World Conservation Monitoring Centre (WCMC) (1992). *Global biodiversity: status of the Earth's living resources*. London: Chapman & Hall.

WRI/IUCN/UNEP (1992). *Global biodiversity strategy*. Guidelines for action to save, study and use Earth's biotic wealth sustainably and equitably.

Wright, T.F., Toft, C.A., Enkerlin-Hoeflich, E., Gonzalez-Elizondo, J., Albornoz, M., Rodríguez-Ferraro, A., Rojas-Suárez, F., Sanz, V., Trujillo, A., Beissinger, S.R., Berovides, V., Gálvez, X., Brice, A.T., Joyner, K., Eberhard, J., Gilardi, J., Koenig, S.E., Stoleson, S., Martuscelli, P., Meyers, J.M., Renton, K., Rodríguez, A.M., Sosa-Asanza, A.C., Villela, F.J. & Wiley J.W. (2001). Nest poaching in neotropical parrots. *Conservation Biology*, **15**, 710-720.

WWF & IUCN (1994-1997). *Centres of Plant Diversity: a guide and strategy for their conservation*. 3 volumes. Oxford: WWF and IUCN.

Wynne, G. (1998). Conservation policy and politics. In *Conservation science and action*, ed. W.J. Sutherland, pp. 256-285. Oxford: Blackwell.

Yamashina, Y. (1978). The feeding of Japanese crested ibises. In *Endangered birds. Management techniques for preserving threatened species*, ed. S.A. Temple, pp. 161-164. Wisconsin: University of Wisconsin Press.

Young, C. (1983). Noisy scrub-bird - a success story. *The State Wildlife Authority News Service (SWANS)*, **13**, 3-9. Perth, Western Australia.

Zalles, J.I. & Bildstein, K.L. (ed.) (2000). *Raptor Watch: a global directory of raptor migration sites*. Cambridge: BirdLife International; and Kempton, PA, USA: Hawk Mountain Sanctuary (BirdLife Conservation series No. 9).

Zimmerman, B.L. & Bierregaard, R.O. (1986). Relevance of the equilibrium theory of island biogeography and species–area relations to conservation with a case from Amazonia. *Journal of Biogeography*, **13**, 133-143.

Zink, R. M. (1997). Species concepts. *Bulletin of the British Ornithologists' Club*, **117**, 97-109.

Zink, R.M., Barrowclough, G.F., Atwood, J.L. & Blackwell-Rago, R.C. (2000). Genetics, taxonomy and conservation of the threatened California gnatcatcher. *Conservation Biology*, **14**, 1394-1405.

Zöckler, C. & Lysenko, I. (2001). Potential impacts of global warming on pothole wetlands and waterfowl. In *Impacts of climate change on wildlife*, ed. R.E. Green, M. Harley, M. Spalding & C. Zöckler, pp. 20-23. RSPB/UNEP/WCMC/EN/WWF.

Index